AFRICAN

CIVILIZATION

REVISITED

From Antiquity to Modern Times

D0082188

AFRICAN

CIVILIZATION

REVISITED

From Antiquity to Modern Times

Basil Davidson

Africa World Press, Inc.

P.O. Box 1892
Trenton, New Jersey 08607

also by Basil Davidson

The Lost Cities of Africa (Old Africa Rediscovered)
Black Mother: The African Slave Trade
The African Genius (The Africans)
Let Freedom Come (Africa in Modern History)
The Fortunate Isles

Africa World Press
P.O. Box 1892
Trenton, New Jersey 08607

Copyright © Basil Davidson
First AWP Edition 1991

Cover design by Ife Nii Owoo

Book design and electronic typesetting from author's disk
by Malcolm Litchfield
This book is composed in ITC Cheltenham Book

Library of Congress Catalog Card Number: 88-83120

ISBN: 0-86543-123-X   Cloth
         0-86543-124-8   Paper

.

Africa is no vast island, separated by an immense ocean from other portions of the globe, and cut off through the ages from the men who have made and influenced the destinies of mankind. She has been closely connected, both as source and nourisher, with some of the most potent influences which have affected for good the history of the world.

Edward Wilmot Blyden in 1880

It is a marvellous country. What is its spell? I cannot tell you, nor wherein lies its strange and unfathomable charm. It lays its hand upon you, and, having once felt its compelling touch, you never can forget it.

Princess Marie Louise in 1925

History acquires meaning and objectivity only when it establishes a coherent relation between past and future.

Edward Hallett Carr

Author's Note

THIS BOOK IS CONCERNED WITH the story of Africa from antiquity to modern times, as told in the chronicles and records of chiefs and kings, travellers and merchant-adventurers, poets and pirates and priests, soldiers and persons of learning.

Framed and introduced as a continuous narrative based on what was thought and written at the time, *African Civilization Revisited* is designed to illustrate the drama and variety, challenge and achievement of humankind in Africa's long history.

It is offered as a contribution to the fuller understanding of Africa today, as well as a guide to the Africa of yesterday and of long ago.

Contents

Introduction

Africa in History

WHEN OUR GRANDCHILDREN reflect on the middle and later years of the twentieth century, above all on the years lying between about 1950 and 1980, and think about us writers of African history, of the history of the black peoples, I think that they will see us as emerging from a time of ignorance and misunderstanding. For these were the liberating years when accounts began at last to be squared with the malice and mystification of racism. And by racism I do not mean, of course, that phalanx of old superstitions, fears and fantasies associated with ancient white ideas about blackness, or not less ancient black ideas about whiteness, the ideas of an old world in which distance always induced distortion. By racism I mean the conscious and systematic weapon of domination, of exploitation, which first saw its demonic rise with the onset of the trans-Atlantic trade in African captives sold into slavery, and which, later, led on to the imperialist colonialism of our yesterdays.

This racism was not a "mistake," a "misunderstanding" or a "grievous deviation from the proper norms of behavior." It was not an accident of human error. It was not an unthinking reversion to barbarism. On the contrary, this racism was conceived as the moral justification—the necessary justification, as it was seen by those in the white man's world who were neither thieves nor moral monsters—for doing to black people what church and state no longer thought it permissible to do to white people: the justification for enslaving black people, that is, when it was no longer permissible to enslave white people.

This weapon of exploitation has its own history, developing new uses in new situations, as many of us know or remember or even now may still experience. But this has been a history, nonetheless, which began to come to an end in the middle and later years of the twentieth century. One of the reasons why it began to come to an end has been the emergence of the Africans from their colonialist subjection. And one of the consequences of this liberation has been, again as a liberating force, the study and analysis of Africa's own history of social formation, change and development over very many centuries. That enlightenment has been the means of tearing down the veils and lies of racism, of finally denying (if not yet finally destroying) the racist assertions of a natural and inherent black inferiority on the human scale, and of demonstrating the natural and inherent equality on the human scale of black peoples with all other peoples. It is a notable conquest (if still to be completed); it is the beginning of historiographical wisdom. We may even say, perhaps, that the non-African world has "rediscovered" the black continent. Exploration of Africa has acquired a depth of human meaning that it did not have before.

There are many anthologies of African exploration. Yet with one or two exceptions, which I shall mention in a moment, they are all built to the same pattern. They are anthologies of the European discovery of Africa, conceived as companion books to a study of Africa which has regarded that subject as no more than an extension to the study of Europe or the New World. Keeping to sources which are largely from the nineteenth century, they aim to show why and how it was that Europe "opened up" a continent which was soon to become a European possession. Their attitude is therefore strictly European in standpoint, and their value lies less in any light they may throw on African life than in the movement they reveal of European penetration and conquest.

Thus the best modern anthology of West African exploration begins with the year 1600, and its introduction is entitled *The Opening of West Africa*. Yet much of West Africa had been "opened" to the outside world—or to a significant part of it— many hundreds of years earlier, and these earlier years are not without important records of their own. To make this point is not to belittle the learned editors of that particular selection, for they could certainly have made it for themselves. As it was, they were concerned with producing an anthology which reflected the colonial situation and met its peculiar requirements. One of these requirements was that no serious consideration of Africa could properly start before the beginning of European (but more especially English and French) exploration: to go back earlier would be to plunge into a fruitless mythology. The late Sir Reginald Coupland, writing some sixty years ago of British penetration into the Zambezi valley, put the point quite clearly when he affirmed that up to the middle of the nineteenth century "the main body of the Africans" had had no history, but had "stayed, for untold centuries, sunk in barbarism . . . [so that] the heart of Africa was scarcely beating." African history could be no fit subject for scholarly investigation because no such history existed: hence anthologies would necessarily begin with the arrival of Europe on the scene.

Now this approach has been overtaken by a wider understanding. The last thirty or forty years have promoted an entirely different attitude to the African past. They have displaced what may be called the "colonial stereotype"—that all in Africa was social chaos or stagnation before the time of European conquest—by a view of the subject altogether to the contrary. These years have raised the study of African history from a mere act of eccentricity, perverse, foolish or regrettably harmful, to a scholarly discipline pursued by institutes of learning in many non-African as well as African countries. A great and growing number of scholars of many nations have accepted that the study of Africa's past is not only possible,

There is thus comparatively little from the nineteenth century and almost nothing from the twentieth.   Denham, Stanley and Speke, Burton, Krapf and many other well-known travellers are altogether absent: not because they do not deserve inclusion, but because their writings are widely available in other anthologies or in their own books.   Yet Mungo Park is here, if in attenuated form, because he marked a turning point in European exploration; and so is Heinrich Barth, the greatest of the nineteenth-century travellers though far too little appreciated even today. All choices of this sort are personal, of course, but I have tried not to be eccentric. Everything here centers, or is intended to center, on the concept of African historical growth and change.   Readers who may be moved to look further into the records (an exercise they will certainly enjoy) will find many omissions mentioned at least by title in various editorials throughout the book. Meanwhile it may be useful to begin by setting the scene.

The Stages of the Past

Most historical writing has reflected man's disunity. In spite of the liberal example of Herodotus, whose sympathies and interests far outleaped the borders of the Greek world, historians have generally written (and no doubt it could not be otherwise) from a firmly and even narrowly national standpoint. The good ones made the best of this limitation; the bad ones, becoming xenophobic, made the worst of it: with few exceptions none achieved or desired to achieve, or even thought they could achieve if they had wished, what is now called a world view.   This is why great segments of historical experience have often become lost or undervalued.   The Ancient World failed to remember the Hittites, for example, just as a recent Europe largely forgot the brilliant skills of Islamic civilization in North Africa and Spain: with this last case, indeed, to the point that we still lack full translation and publication of many medieval works in Arabic, whether by Arabs or not.

The world of our own day has begun to see beyond this national limitation. The general reasons are obvious enough. The particular reasons certainly include the achievements of archeology and the wide audience these have won. More and more clearly, as narrow beliefs about the past give way before the startling evidence of spade and trowel, the interdependence of ancient cultures makes this or that exclusive claim ridiculous.

Less than a century ago the well-educated man would think of antiquity in terms of Greece and Rome but little else. There was of course the Old Testament, with its disturbing hint of a wider background; and there were also the old Egyptians. Yet these last were conceived, quite wrongly however, as being so remote from Greece and Rome as not really to belong to the same category of historical truth. Then archaeologists laid bare the great civilizations of the Fertile Crescent, of Sumer and Akkad and Babylon. They displayed the magnificence of Pharaonic Egypt, explained the Phoenicians, explored the ruins of Minos and Mycenae; and with all this the civilizations of Greece and Rome progressively acquired new and splendid depths of meaning: but still, alas, without being allowed (at least since the 1830s) to stem from their undoubtedly Egyptian roots. Other archaeologists went further afield. China and India were drawn into this revitalized picture of the past. Europe dwindled to the mere segment of a worldwide mosaic.

But as Europe ceased to occupy the center of the picture, the passing of the imperial epoch made way for an ever-quickened impulse of inquiry into the character of the non-European lands. This impulse has now carried us far and wide. It has drawn within the frontiers of history—of human history considered increasingly as a single though infinitely varied

So far as Africa is concerned it now seems clear that the origins of food production, in one form or another, are immensely older than was previously thought, and go back indeed some 9,000 years. They go back, in other words, to the gradual evolution of a "New Stone Age," a Neolithic Age, across the vast plains of the Sahara region and its margins long before these began to degrade, in about 2500 B.C., into desert conditions.   Much has still to be firmly understood about that momentous process.   But what increasingly emerges from recent work is that the Neolithic Sahara in its long "green period," before desertification set in, was indeed the "birth arena" of most of the cultures of a later Africa, including those of the Nile Valley and ancient Egypt.

So much for *prehistory*. Most rock paintings and engravings belong to the Neolithic cultures, but others of these are recent and even modern, being the work of still surviving Khoi and other cultures.   Yet *history* in Africa may reasonably be said to start with the general ending of the Neolithic and the beginning of an Age of Metals—an Iron Age, as I shall prefer to call it, since iron was by far the most important of the metals in question—for it is then that the origins of modern Africa begin to emerge and acquire historical identity. This is not, of course, because the Iron Age "revolution" was sudden or universally effective, but because the introduction of ferrous technology set in motion a series of changes that were crucial and cumulative in their effects, and paved the way for the fully historical Africa of medieval times. It is also true, as we shall see, that the earliest written records of Africa (aside from those of Pharaonic Egypt and the Phoenicians of Carthage or the Sabaeans of Ethiopia) belong to the opening years of the Iron Age. Even within a narrow use of the term, we are broadly justified in saying that a usefully perceptible history of Africa, as a continent, begins with the coming of iron.

Knowledge of how to obtain and use iron reached the valley of the Nile at about the same time as it was penetrating northward into non-Mediterranean Europe. Old Egypt had been content with bronze, and awakened to its disadvantages only when iron-shod Assyrian armies appeared in the 660s B.C.. Thereafter iron tools and weapons became less rare in Egypt. The Phoenicians began using them in Carthage at about the same time. So did the Kushites of the Middle Nile, and later their Axumite neighbors in northern Ethiopia. Kush, Carthage and Axum all played some part in passing the knowledge of iron southward into the main body of Africa. But of these three channels of communication, North Africa probably was the most important.

Donkey-drawn and possibly horse-drawn carts and chariots crossed the western and central Sahara, between North Africa and the regions of the Niger River, throughout a long period before the middle of the first millennium B.C.. Another useful route lay between the Middle Nile and the western region around Lake Chad, passing across Africa by way of Kordofan, Darfur and Zaghawa. Just conceivably the peoples of west-central Africa invented iron mining and smelting for themselves, independently of others. But the great likelihood is that these technologies followed iron tools and weapons along the trans-African trails from north and northeast, and were adapted in sub-Saharan regions rather than invented there.

Whatever the exact truth may turn out to be, it is now certain that communities in the sub-Saharan savanna belt or Sahel (a word of Arabic derivation meaning "shore": in this case the southern "shore" of the sand "ocean" of the Sahara), developed their own specific Iron Age civilization from as early as the sixth century B.C.. By late in the 1970s archaeologists were able to show, beyond serious question, that Iron Age cultures were in full evolution along the course of the Middle Niger river (the great "inland bend") by the fifth century B.C., and as far as the confluence of the Niger with the Benue river: at old Djenne (Jenne-Jeno), at Daboya, and at other places in what are now central Mali and northern Ghana, as well as in Nigeria (with the famous Nok culture, and others now being located). Here, already, were the formative origins of the medieval civilizations of the Western and Central Sudan, and of other polities in or along the fringe of the forest belt of West Africa.

The Kushite culture of Meroe is similarly known to have entered its Iron Age period of development during this same sixth century. Thereafter, from these various centers of experiment and new organization, Africa's Iron Age moved with an astonishing speed towards the south. Associated with the spread and diffusion of the communities and cultures of the great Bantu language-family, Iron Age cultures appeared successively in the forests and savannas of the vast basin of the river Congo; in eastern Africa; and in central Africa north and then south of the Zambezi river by the first centuries A.D.: until, by at any rate the fourth century A.D., iron-using cultures had become established almost as far as the southernmost coast of the continent. What is now South Africa, in short, embarked upon Iron Age types of community development some twelve or thirteen centuries before the arrival there of the earliest European settlers and invaders. Iron-making and iron-using technologies, with all that these implied for socio-economic progress, spread with great rapidity across the continent as soon as they had been mastered.

Rapidly: yet among comparatively few people. Humanity was still sparse in Africa. Before the Iron Age got into its stride, the whole great mass of country from the northern limits of the Congo Basin to the Cape of Good Hope was peopled only by scattered groups who lived by hunting game, gathering wild vegetables and also, but not always, practising a little agriculture. Some of them, notably in the East African high-lands, were stock-breeders as well. These groups had suffi-ciently mastered their environment to be able to survive, but not so successfully as to enable any secure increase in population. Their progress was gradual, but it was assured. They had worked out their way of life over countless genera-tions. Without important innovations, they would no doubt have continued to live in that way. Indeed, this is more or less how the Khoi and a few other rare African peoples still live in our own time.

Rather more than two thousand years ago with the onset of the Iron Age, this ancient stability was upset by new factors. Both made life progressively easier. One of them, the knowledge of how to make iron spears and tools, came from a northerly direction through the basin of the Congo river. Another new factor was a wider choice and availability of foodstuffs, a development closely linked to Iron Age advances. Equipped with better tools, people were now beginning to live in semi-permanent or even permanent villages. They could produce more. They could store food. They could also exchange it in trade with neighbors. Beyond all that, they could experiment with new crops and develop these crops by selection or improvement. These factors promoted and then accompanied a steady but persistent expansion in the size of Africa's populations. It was from this period, beginning around 2000 years ago, that African populations developed in all habitable regions of the continent, and grew from a very few millions to many millions.

This increase and spread of population is closely associated with the emergence of the Bantu-speaking family of African peoples who now inhabit the whole central and southern region of the continent. They may be taken to have been the product of indigenous populations of the Neolithic period intermarried with Iron Age migrants from the African regions to the north of them. Here we meet with a constant and baffling process of weaving and interweaving between migrant and local populations, with new influences and perhaps new peoples arriving generally from the north and northwest.

Why did early Iron Age groups in western and eastern Africa begin to move into the vast but unknown lands to the south? There are two central explanations. The first is that the highly fertile regions of the tropical Iron Age now began to experience a certain pressure of population growth on available food supplies. This pressure of land shortage will have tended to push people southward because, thanks to the Sahara, they could not find useable land to the northward. A second explanation is that the iron-pointed spear was a great social and political innovator. Like the musket later on, the iron spear promoted new ideas and needs of government. The old tribal communities had managed with little or no government at all (as a few African peoples still do), but strong and ambitious groups could now impose their will on weaker groups, and could reap, increasingly, an advantage in so doing. With all this, we begin to see the emergence of centralized political organization, of kingship and a rudimentary bureaucracy, of a systemic social differentiation between masters and servants, rulers and ruled. We are out of the Garden of Eden: a process of social fracturing has been set in motion.

This was the process that divided the "ancestral stocks" into a great variety of distinct peoples—"tribes" as they are often though misleadingly called—through the revolt of chiefs' sons against their fathers, of "junior groups" against "senior groups," of migrant rebels against parent clans and loyalties. In this long and complex disintegration of the Neolithic pattern and its reconstruction within an Iron Age framework we can find the origins of modern African societies, showing as these do, in a multitude of ways, a diversity that is none the less rooted in a profound and ancient unity. This large theme of unity-in-diversity runs throughout subsequent African history. Little about the African past (and therefore about the African present) can be understood apart from it. Pan-African unity is a political ambition of modern times, but its roots go far back into the past.

On the whole Neolithic period, perhaps needless to say, the written records are almost entirely silent, for the Egyptian texts tell us disappointingly little. But with the beginning of the Iron Age we begin to get a little documentary light. We might have had a great deal more if only the Phoenicians had worried less about keeping their commercial secrets, and we may still hope for a little more when the cities of Kush are further examined and their written language fully explained. As it is, we have to rely on scattered memoirs and geographies written by Greeks who were mostly working with secondhand information. Yet with every Iron Age century we approach a more historical context. The written documents multiply, notably with the coming to sub-Saharan Africa of Muslim literacy in Arabic after about the ninth century A.D.. So does the archaeological evidence. All the same, the first thousand years of the African Iron Age—which broadly means, as it happens, the first thousand years of the Christian era—often remain teasingly vague and mysterious. They are least so, however, for the West African grasslands.

The Iron Age in West Africa took its rise, as we have seen, nearly two and a half thousand years ago. Working out a new social and political synthesis, important peoples in the grasslands (and somewhat later in the wide tropical forests which border the western coast and the Congo basin) began to evolve new and more complex forms of government. Ghana emerged, earliest of the big West African political systems. Traditionally, this happened as early as about A.D. 300, but the date is little more than guesswork based on semilegendary king lists written down many centuries later. As a coherent and important state—a form of centralized organization probably not known before in this vast region of Africa, or not in a pronounced form—Ghana may be safely dated to about A.D. 500 or somewhat later, with the reservation, of course, that it will already have had behind it a long experience of previous growth.

The product of Iron Age innovation and development in broad regions of the sub-Saharan Sahel, the ancient realm we know as Ghana (not to be confused with the modern republic of the same name) flourished on local trade and grew strong by the conquest of neighbors. Much later, but increasingly after the ninth century A.D., Ghana became a major partner in a continuous expansion of the trans-Saharan trade with northern

Africa, that became possible after the rise of Muslim civilization.

Ghana is known to have emerged from the ambitions of a small but evidently vigorous people called the Soninke, whose descendants now live along the flanks of the Senegal river. For reasons that we do not know and probably shall never know, they made a bid to control their neighbors: according to an eleventh-century Arab source, no doubt drawing on much older information, they were able to succeed because they fought with iron weapons while these neighbors fought with ebony. They needed and acquired a central organization under a god-protected ruler, the *ghana*, whose title became the name of their state otherwise known locally as Aoukar or Wagadu. By the ninth century, if not earlier, they had won control over the westerly part of the Western Sudan in respect of two great items: their ruler and his appointees controlled the import of salt from the desert fringes, as well as the export of gold towards the north.

By the eleventh century, when the first clear record of Ghana becomes available, a large part of the Western Sudanese grassland was enclosed within a single system of imperial tax and tribute. This empire, we may note, was more or less contemporary with that of the Franks in Western Europe, and the essential organization of the first, allowing for many differences of attitude and detail, was evidently not much different from that of the second. Charlemagne and his Ghanaian contemporary, had they ever met each other, could have talked with keen understanding of each other's political and economic arrangements. In Europe's medieval terminology, each was a *regnum*, a realm whose existence was known by the name of its rulers.

The old Ghanaian pattern set the course of Western Sudanese history for more than a thousand years: time after time a strong central authority strove to impose its will on rival authorities and to hold these vassals in obedience, drawing its military strength from conscripted levies and its financial power from the proceeds of intra-regional and export trade in gold and other goods and of import trade in salt, copper, and manufactures from Egypt, North Africa and even Europe. Now and then the pattern was disturbed by invasion, as from the Berbers and from Morocco in the eleventh and sixteenth centuries; but generally the great systems held firm. This is one of the grand periods of African history. It runs from about A.D. 600 to 1600, and with the passing of the years its documentary sources become increasingly copious and full of pith and meaning. To it belong the rise and fall of Ghana, Mali, Kanem-Bornu, Songhay and the Hausa states, and others no less famous and successful in the forest lands to the immediate south, Oyo and Benin, Akwamu, Denkyira and their like.

Another main center of politico-social development, the eastern Rift Valley and its peripheral lands, has a somewhat different story. An Iron Age began here at about the same period as in West Africa, or not much later, but for a long time there was no corresponding evolution of large states and trading systems, or none that we know of at present. The peoples of the East African interior lacked contact with the world beyond the Sahara, cut off from this as they largely were by the swamps and marshes of the Upper Nile. Maritime trade would eventually make good this lack of contact, but not until the ninth century A.D.. Meanwhile the historical interest of these peoples rests also in the achievements of migrants whom they sent off towards the south. These Iron Age pioneers mingled with the folk whom they found, and the resultant mosaic of peoples, using iron and growing rapidly more numerous, became the founders of new centers of political and economic development.

The first of these new centers lay in the region of the modern Katanga, and was based on the smelting and trading of copper; the second was in the lands of the great central plateau south of the Zambezi river, promoted there by the smelting and trading of gold. This, of course, is a simplification. At least two complicating factors should be kept in mind. One was that there is no clear distinction, so far as the central-southern Iron Age is concerned, between the influences that came from West Africa and those that came from East Africa. The other is that there were other stimulants to social development besides an outside demand for copper and gold.

The fact remains that any general survey of the African societies of the last thousand years in east and central-south Africa will show many points of similarity in growth and technique. Much has still to be explained, for the archeology of this area is still imperfectly known. But already one can point to close affiliations of language, thought, belief and social organization, to related methods of using stone, to terrace-building for hillside cultivation and soil conservation, and to many other parallels between nearly all these peoples. From early Iron Age societies in East Africa men developed mature though nonliterate cultures and civilizations which spread southward across the continent as far as the southern-most areas of modern South Africa. All this forms another large segment of African history, that of the Bantu Iron Age; and here too, as in West Africa, there emerged important states and large systems of government and trade.

These seem to have begun in Uganda in about the twelfth century, and a little earlier in the "mining states" of the south. Archaeologists at present divide the mature Iron Age of central-southern Africa into two large periods, one starting in about the eleventh century, when stone building began at Great Zimbabwe and related sites, and the other in the fifteenth century, when the Karanga people under their Rozwi kings set about founding their notable empire of Monomotapa—named after the title of their king, *mwana-mutapa*, just as Ghana had been. These systems were native to the lands where they emerged but owed much, like those of West Africa, to ideas and influences from other African lands. Their technologies in metal and stone, beliefs and customs, notions of god and government, all go back to a common source which became, with time, an infinitely varied fabric of daily life, religion and behavior.

To this process the course of history along the East African seaboard makes an exciting and even unique contribution. This was a coast of ancient trading intercourse, being the western shore of the Indian Ocean and drawn thereby into the whole wide community of Indian Ocean commerce. Traders from Arabia settled here more than two thousand years ago, choosing convenient islands or mainland harbors, intermarrying with the local peoples, and promoting, as time passed, a civilization that was distinctive to the seaboard. As new political organizations took shape and trade grew more important, these small coastal settlements underwent a double and in some ways contradictory change. They accepted Islam and Arabic culture in the ninth century A.D., but they remained emphatically African in their population and their outlook. This was Swahili civilization. It penetrated no more than a few miles from the coast; but along the coast itself there grew up cities and ports whose accumulating wealth was drawn from the export of gold and ivory, and the import of textiles, porcelain or other manufactured goods from Arabia, India and China.

Among these cities Kilwa became the queen of the south, dominating the gold and ivory trade along the whole southern segment of the shoreline. Their contacts with the inland country of East Africa have yet to be fully researched. In this field there have remained some large mysteries. Perhaps the most intriguing of these has been that of Engaruka, a late Iron Age settlement of several thousand stone houses whose ruins, now well explored, lie on a scorching hillside in the Rift Valley not far south of the Kenya-Tanzania border. They are now seen to have been medieval in date.

A larger question consists in the precise relationship which linked the many Iron Age cultures of East Africa, traceable in a long string of ancient settlements from the southern borders of Ethiopia to the head of Lake Nyasa, with their affiliated cultures further south. In general, though, we may safely conclude that these cultures—from the borders of the Congo basin through Angola and the Congo to southern

Africa, and from East Africa through Tanzania and Mozambique to the slopes of the Drakensberg Mountains in South Africa—all belong to the same broad and many-sided community of Iron Age ideas and organization. Often in isolation from the outside world, usually bereft of any fertilizing help from the high civilizations of the Nile and the East, facing a continent of great physical discouragement or poverty in food-giving crops and yet repeatedly solving the problems of their environment,these African pioneers settled and tamed one of the world's most extensive continental region.

Such was the general reality when the history of Africa was thought, conventionally in Europe, to be about to begin. Coming from industrialized societies, European explorers and conquerors of the nineteenth century easily assumed that they were marching into a zone of immemorial stagnation, and among peoples who had not "developed" because "they could not develop." It has taken more than a hundred years to establish the falseness of this European implication of a natural African inferiority. The records easily show why. Here and there, true enough, the incoming expeditions from Europe came upon strong societies and stable governments. Henry Stanley, for example, was deeply impressed by the rule and order that prevailed in Buganda. But generally they found little of that sort. And they explained the internecine warfare and confusion they so often met by Africa's natural inability to govern itself in peace and prosperity.

Today we can assign perfectly clear historical reasons for the social and political confusion which had overcome a large part of Africa by the middle of the nineteenth century.

The great systems of the Western Sudan had passed into history after the time of the Moroccan invasion of the Songhay empire at the end of the sixteenth century, accompanied and followed as this had been by far-reaching commercial decline as the trans-Saharan trade gave way, increasingly, to a seaborne trade between West Africa and Europe. A brave effort was indeed put forth by Western Sudanese leaders during the nineteenth century to rebuild the systems of the past, but this was soon swept away by European invasion.

To the southward the peoples of the forest had built new states and governments, such as those of the Fon in Dahomey, but these, more often than not, were linked fatally to the oversea trade in slaves, a commerce which sowed disorder wherever it touched. In East Africa, meanwhile, those Iron Age cultures which had produced settlements such as Engaruka had suffered a decline that was in large part the consequence of invasion or infiltration by nomadic cattle-raising peoples coming from the north. The Portuguese had wrecked the Indian Ocean trade on which the coastal cities had built their wealth and welfare. Land-hungry Boers were pushing up from the Cape of Good Hope. These set in motion other pressures, notably the northward-moving migrations of the Nguni and Zulu peoples who invaded the Iron Age states of the central plateau and, however unintentionally, opened the way for European conquest. Even in those areas where stable government generally continued to prevail, an Arab-Swahili and then European-dominated slave trade from the East Coast, beginning in the 1830s, had gone far to disrupt traditional security and peace. The Europeans of the nineteenth century, as the records show, understood little or nothing of all this.

It will be obvious, no doubt, that even without European intervention—whether through the slave trade or colonial invasion—the African Iron Age would have produced many upheavals out of its own inner dynamic. The founding of states led directly to the conquest of other states, just as the enthronement of kings made infallibly for dynastic strife. In all these ways the lord-and-vassal organization of many African states brought stresses and strains that were natural to their situation. Yet arguing from what we know of Iron Age development, and from the not incomparable history of other lands, we may reasonably suppose that one phase of centralizing organization in Africa would have continued to give rise to another and more advanced phase. Here the crucial point to bear in mind is that European invasion arrived in the mid-stream of a time of major internal adjustment. It struck Africa at a moment of confusion that was itself the product of new pressures and needs.

Thereafter nothing could ever be the same. Looking back, one may see now that the colonial period was no more than a large episode in the onward movement of African life: in another sense, however, it was an unexampled means of revolutionary change. At huge cost to many peoples, and with a social and human wastefulness that was characteristic of its times, the colonial system shattered the traditional moulds of Iron Age society, opened Africa to all the winds that blow, and left her peoples to the enormous task of building entirely new ways of life. This last is the stuff of history in very recent years, and is here outside our scope. Yet these modern happenings cannot be grasped in their fuller meaning unless the story of the past is understood. And to understand the story of the past we must also look at the records of the past, in all their illuminations and with all their limitations. They remain essential guides.

African and Asian Records

To the early periods of the African odyssey the inscriptions of Egypt and the geographies of the Hellenic world and Byzantium give us few guides, and these of doubtful value. What the Greek writers show is that the whole central mass of Africa was completely unknown to outside observers but for stray travellers' tales and myths. Nothing exact was said about anything south of the Nile until a Greek Egyptian seafarer published a mariner's handbook to the northerly regions of the

Indian Ocean in about A.D. 150, or possibly a little earlier. This is the famous *Periplus of the Erythraean Sea.*

The anonymous and unhappily unique author of the *Periplus* was evidently a Greek sea-captain of Egypt, and probably of one of the Egyptian ports on the Red Sea, perhaps Berenike. In a book of some 7000 words he describes the carrying-trade between his home harbors and those of north-western India with convincing detail that seems to have come from personal observation. But his great value for African historiography lies in his having added a few sections—sparse but of much interest—on the southern extension of the Indian Ocean trade that carried ships down the East African coast as far as Tanzania. He offers a tantalizingly brief guide to the hazards and advantages of this East African run, noting that it should normally take twenty-three days' sailing from Opone (Ras Hafun, just south of Cape Gardafui on the Horn of Africa) as far as Rhapta, "the last market town of the Azanian [East African] mainland."

Where was Rhapta? Possibly near the modern Tanzanian ports of Pangani or Bagamoyo, or further south on Kilwa Island: unless archeology discovers a major settlement of that period, we shall never be sure. But Rhapta was certainly of great local importance, mainly for the export of ivory to India; and Claudius Ptolemy, another Greek Egyptian of the second century, knew of it as "a metropolis of the barbarians." The relevant passage from the *Periplus*, though famous among Africanists, is perhaps worth giving again:

> Two days' sail beyond [the unidentified island of Menouthias] there lies the very last market-town of the continent of Azania, which is called Rhapta, which has its name from the sowed boats already mentioned; and in which there is ivory in great quantity, and tortoise shell.

The men who lived along this coast in the second century A.D. are described as being "of very great stature." They have "separate chiefs for each place." But Rhapta itself is not quite independent, for "the Mapharitic chief [one of the contemporary rulers of southern Arabia] governs it under some ancient right that subjects it to the sovereignty of the state that is become the first in Arabia. And the people of Muza [Mocha?] now hold it under his authority, and send thither many large ships, with Arab captains and agents. These are familiar with the inhabitants, and both dwell and intermarry with them; they know all their villages and speak their language." Here were the humble origins of the Swahili civilization that was to flower so brilliantly ten centuries later.

After the seventh or eighth century the Chinese contribute a few scraps of information from their capacious experience of the Indian Ocean and its trading ways, while their famous fifteenth-century admiral, Ch'ang-lo, led two large expeditions to the coast of East Africa. As will be seen, these Chinese records yield little of value. For the whole of medieval times we should be almost completely lost without the Arabs. By early Islamic times their merchants were firmly established from southern China to eastern Africa; and gradually they built up and published a body of knowledge which is often of decisive value. Until the tenth century, however, their writers worked mostly from hearsay, mingling probable fact with manifest legend. "The land of Zanj [East Africa] is vast," wrote Suleiman the Merchant: "Its plants are all black in colour."

We catch the echo of many unrecorded voyages in writings of this kind, transmuted often into fabulous adventures. It was of this Sea of the Zanj that Sindbad the Sailor recounted his perilous tales in *The Thousand and One Nights*. Thus Sindbad recalls how on his second voyage, "aided by a favorable wind, we voyaged for many days and nights from port to port, and from island to island, selling and bartering our goods, and haggling with merchants and officials wherever we cast anchor"; and how on his fourth voyage "we sped on the foamy highways of the sea, trading from port to port and from island to island." Such was the distant memory of seamen who went down to Kilwa and Sofala a thousand years ago.

From the tenth century the knowledge of the Arabs began to be placed on a less tenuous foundation. Four great names stand out in this work: those of al-Mas'udi, al-Bekri, Idrisi and ibn-Battuta. Unhappily, we are still without complete English translations of the first three of these, and the case with Idrisi is worst of all. He wrote from hearsay, true enough, but his methods were systematic, intelligent and based on determined efforts to learn the truth. Yet much of his work remains inaccessible.

Apart from the major chroniclers of medieval Islam who dealt with Africa there were others—notably ibn-Said and al-Biruni—who have interesting references to our subject, together with a large number of lesser writers who contribute stray bits of information. The only full review of these appears in Yusuf Kamal's extremely rare *Monumenta Cartographica Egyptae et Africae*, but Yusuf Kamal was interested principally in geography and selected his extracts accordingly. An historical survey of these lesser writers remains to be made from the African standpoint, although two Soviet Africanists have contributed a valuable beginning with selections from twenty-three Arab writers of the seventh to tenth centuries who wrote on Africa.* Similar research and publication are also needed for such records of India and Ceylon as may bear on African subjects. For West Africa, meanwhile, we now have an invaluable anthology translated by J. F. P. Hopkins with N. Levtzion: *Corpus of Early Arabic Sources for West African History*, Cambridge 1981.

What of Africans themselves? Here, as I have mentioned, there is much more to be published than anyone had suspected even a few years ago. Indeed, there is already a great deal of

---

*L. E. Kubbel and V. V. Matveev, *Arabski Istochniki, VII-X Vekov* (Leningrad: 1960).

published material that is generally ignored, and I have taken account of some of this in my selections.

Literacy was one of Islam's gifts to Africa, and the gift was used. For East Africa, admittedly, it was not used in an African language, Kiswahili, until fairly late, so that the earliest known manuscript in that language, the *Utendi wa Tambuka*, an epic poem written in an Arabic script, dates only from 1728. Yet a Swahili poem is embedded in the traditional chronicle of the kings of the island of Pate, off the coast of Kenya, that may belong to the fourteenth century. Even if medieval Swahili documents are never discovered—either because Swahili was not yet a written language or, more probably, because they have vanished forever—we still have a large body of Swahili writing for the eighteenth and nineteenth centuries, and some of it has historical value.

Western Sudanese literacy in Arabic—the scholarly language that corresponded to Latin in Western Europe—goes back through nearly nine centuries, a fact which was proved for the first time in 1939 with the discovery of a number of royal tombstones at Sane, near the old trading city of Gao on the Middle Niger. "Here lies the tomb of the king who defended God's religion, and who rests in God, Abu Abdullah Muhammad," runs the inscription on one of these handsome plaques of Spanish marble, offering a statement of somewhat narrow interest were it not for the added date, which is AH 494, or 1100 of the Christian era. The full beauty of North African historical writings is superbly displayed in the well-known works of ibn Khaldun, who also wrote shortly before A.D. 1400. There is every reason to believe that learned men in the empire of Mali, and just possibly in the last phases of the empire of Ghana, wrote about their beliefs and their condition; no such works, unhappily, have come down to us. Among the earliest known documents, there is one that dates from the Muslim year 913 (May 1507-May 1508), but even this (a safe-conduct issued by the Songhay ruler, Askia Muhammad, from which I give an extract below) comes to us at second hand; although I am glad to be able to include, thanks to the generosity and scholarship of J. O. Hunwick, a little of the famous interchange between Askia Muhammad and the North African theologian al-Maghili, who died in 1504 but whose works are still well known in West Africa.* Up to the nineteenth century the only works of West African scholarship to have survived, unless others are yet discovered, are a few of those of the great schools of Timbuktu and Djenne in the sixteenth to eighteenth centuries. But these remain important.

Ahmad Baba, who was born in 1556, became the best known of these writers of Timbuktu. He must have been a man of grand strength of character as well as learning, for he refused to serve the Moroccan invaders of his city and country, and was taken in chains across the Sahara on charges of fomenting rebellion. He is known to have composed some fifty works on the law of the Malikite tradition of Islam, as well as a biographical dictionary which constitutes his principal claim to a place in history. He also collected a library that was held in such esteem by his successors that it has still not been, according to the *Encyclopaedia of Islam*, entirely dispersed. Thirteen of Ahmad Baba's writings, of varying length and value, are at present known; two of these were discovered recently in Northern Nigeria, and there is a fair hope that still others will be found. None has yet been published in English translation. (See J. O. Hunwick, "Ahmad Baba and the Moroccan Invasion of the Sudan," in *Journal of the Historical Society of Nigeria*, 1963; and M. A. Zouber, *Ahmad Baba de Tombouctou: Sa Vie et Son Oeuvre*, Maissonneuve et Larose, Timbuktu and Paris 1977.)

*Professor Hunwick has published al-Maghili in extensive translation: *Sharia in Songhay: The Replies of Al-Maghili*, Oxford 1985, together with a characteristically valuable commentary. His eagerly awaited English translation of the Timbuktu chronicle, *Tarikh al-Sudan*, was far advanced in 1990.

(London, 1951), while Thomas Hodgkin has included several long extracts in his *Nigerian Perspectives* (Oxford, second edition, 1975).

From about the seventeenth century a number of West African peoples of the forest zone also began to feel the need for writing, and some more or less rudimentary scripts were invented, beginning with that of the Vai (Liberia-Sierra Leone). It is possible that the Bini of Benin had used a pictographic form of writing in earlier times, but the evidence remains inconclusive. Interesting though they are, none of these scripts has yielded documentary evidence of any value to the study of history. It remains to add that from about the middle of the eighteenth century, or soon after, Africans who had been enslaved and won their freedom began publishing memoirs in Europe, notably Olaudah Equiano of Iboland in southern Nigeria and Ottobah Cugoano of Fantiland in southern Ghana.

The Western Contribution

This begins in late medieval times with the Portuguese voyages down the western coast, but remains very sparse until the end of the fifteenth century. Writers were not yet interested in history, for the concept of social evolution was entirely foreign to the mental atmosphere in which they lived. When that most valiant mariner of Portugal, Diogo Cão, had carried his little ships to the waters of the Congo estuary in 1483, he set up a stone on this distant shore whose inscription (at least according to a later reproduction) declared that the year was also that of "1681 of the creation of the world." The earliest chronicles and memoirs therefore give us little more than tales of mere discovery, often marvelously vivid and convincing, as with Zurara's chronicle of 1453 about the first voyages beyond the Moroccan coast, but never seeking to assess the back-ground of development that lay behind African peoples who were now brought into communication with Europe.

The situation improves with the end of the fifteenth century. Now the king of Portugal enters into an alliance with the king of Kongo (northern Angola as it became), and informa-tion begins to filter back to Lisbon from envoys and missionar-ies. Diaz and da Gama pass the Cape of Good Hope, and aboard da Gama's flagship of 1497-99 there is a writer who keeps a daily logbook, a *roteiro*, which has most fortunately survived. Some twenty years later a Portuguese priest called Francisco Alvares brings home a detailed description of Ethiopia. Other mariners and travellers add their memoirs and reports of the West and the East Coast. Few of these will become widely known for several hundred years, but these few are valuable for having offered Europe its first real insight into the lands beyond the southern skyline.

Some of these early books were lucky to see the light at all. Often enough they told too many commercial secrets or set the explorers in a bad light. Censorship suppressed them. Between 1552 and 1563 the Portuguese annalist João de Barros, working on official archives in Lisbon, published the first three sections of his *Decadas da Asia*, an epic of Portuguese discov-ery. His work was continued by Diogo de Couto, also an official historian, who brought out four more sections before he died in 1616. One of these, the sixth, found disfavor with those who wished to conceal the course of Portuguese overseas loot and conquest, and was burnt after being printed; later on, permis-sion was given for a somewhat doctored version. The eighth and ninth sections of the *Decadas da Asia* were stolen while still in manuscript, presumably for the same reason as the sixth had been seized and destroyed, and were rewritten in abstract from de Couto's memory. Yet even these versions were not published until much later, the last of them in 1736. The eleventh section was written but has never been found, while five parts of the twelfth section appeared in 1645. The tenth of cannibalism"—a kindliness to neighbors, we may note, in which these peoples were scarcely alone.   Beliefs about neighbors' "deviancy" have always malignantly doubled with distance.

With Winterbottom, moreover, we find the first clear picture of the evils of intensive slaving to which many peoples of the Guinea Coast were now subjected. "Although," he wrote, "Europeans have carried on the trade with the natives of the western coast of Africa for many centuries, the latter have no cause to rejoice in the intercourse. Instead of introducing amongst the Africans what they pride themselves in possessing, the boasted arts of civilized life—to say nothing of the slave trade, the natural effects of which in degrading and brutalizing the human character are sufficiently apparent—Europeans have taught them only the vices of their own countries . . . ."

This note of condemnation grows stronger with the end of the eighteenth century and the success of the critics of the slave trade. "I need not mention," writes Captain Philip Beaver, a naval philanthropist, in 1805, "the various modes which Europeans also take to overreach the Africans in trade, by light weights, short measure and diminished capacity etc., all of which are now so well known to the natives as to us; and therefore, as before observed, they [the Africans] consider us as a compound of treachery and deceit. There is nothing degrading, nothing base, nothing infamous, but what they consider to form part of the white character." Beaver also had something to say on the subject of racial prejudice, and this too sounded a new note. Of some white women on the West Coast he remarks that these "had been very well treated by the Canabacs, for which they were probably indebted to the national prejudice of these people, who look upon white women rather as objects of disgust than desire. Their devil is white . . . ."

The religious travellers and workers, who dealt in souls and not in bodies, were nicer in their language, having less provocation to be otherwise: besides, many of them were traumatically shocked by what they saw and experienced. Even so, the Christianity of this period of Europe had become as firmly fixed in the toils of racial or national discrimination as a great religion well may; and it was widely taken for granted by men and women of good will that an absence of Christianity must mean not only spiritual misfortune but also, and perhaps worse, utter moral darkness. From this notion of a *necessary* heathen or non-Christian immorality there also flowed in later years the central colonial doctrine of a natural human inferiority among Africans: of the notion that was expressed so often by the advocacy of "trusteeship" for Africans who must otherwise remain in misery and chaos.

Even in African national pride, which Europeans of that time might easily have understood from the habits of their own continent, there was thought to be something perverse and ridiculous. Father Cavazzi could not possibly reconcile Congolese self-confidence with a proper attitude to life. These Congolese nations, he was complaining in 1687, "think themselves, with nauseating presumption, the foremost men in the world, and nothing will persuade them to the contrary . . . . They think their country is the largest, happiest, most enjoyable and most beautiful there is." No doubt these attitudes implied an exaggeratedly hopeful view of life in that part of the world. Yet it was one with which a European missionary might have had some sympathy, coming from a continent more arrogant about itself, perhaps, than any other has ever been.

I rather think it is the religious travellers and missionaries who are usually the most disappointing in the records of European reporting on Africa. With a few outstanding exceptions in the nineteenth century, notably Livingstone and Casalis, they were writers who appear to have found it surprisingly difficult to apply the Christian ethic in its teaching about human equality. Time and again their writings are made puny by fits of merely racial prejudice or superstition. Quite frequently, one feels, they are "fathers" who do not really love their "children," yet who cannot bear, notwithstanding this, that these "children" should grow up and face the world on their own. They demonstrate a kind of "paternalism" that has been common enough in Africa, whether in the regions of Roman Catholic or Protestant influence: a poor sort of paternalism where "fatherhood" has imposed on others the obligations of love and respect but rather seldom displayed those qualities itself.

Viewed historically, however, the great weakness of Christianity in Africa, as a force for unity and progress and therefore enlightenment, seems to have been a long failure to emancipate itself from the imperial establishments; and this, too, has diminished the value of missionary records. In this respect its achievements compare unfavorably with those of Islam. Judged by results, Islam promoted the idea of human equality far more effectively than Christianity, and this has been the case not only between different peoples—conquerors and conquered, immigrants and aboriginals—but also within individual societies. If Islam continued to make converts in Africa at the expense of Christian endeavor, this may have been in no small measure because Islam often offered a wider and more practical sense of personal emancipation. Sometimes, as with the Tijaniyya brotherhood of the Western Sudan in the nineteenth century, branches of Islam have had for Africans the same emotive appeal as had Nonconformist Christianity for the dispossessed peasants and proletariat of industrial England. So far as the Christian records are concerned—though we shall see that there have been a good many exceptions to this rule— the historians of the future will draw more nourishment from the documents and manifestos of a specifically African Christianity over the past fifty years of so, for it has been through these African churches that the authentic voice of Africa has repeatedly spoken.

Another valuable source of light emerges from European and American efforts to establish colonies in West Africa where liberated slaves could find their freedom in a new life. Through these doors in Sierra Leone and Liberia there came to Africa not only men and women out of bondage, but ideas as well; and it is already clear, while the study of African history goes deeper, that some of these ideas became part of the political consciousness of the independent Africa that was to emerge a hundred and fifty years afterwards.   Both the French and American revolutions were important in this respect.

Some of the earlier ideas of this kind read strangely now. Consider, for example, the founding ideas of Sierra Leone. Its main promoter, the antislaving champion Granville Sharp, issued a *Short Sketch of Temporary Regulation* which Christopher Fyfe in his *History of Sierra Leone* has summarized as providing "a constitution bound by a social contract rooted in history, in the institutions of the Anglo-Saxon monarchy, and of Israel under the judges . . . .   Every ten householders would form a tithing, every ten tithings a hundred, collectively responsible for preserving order and keeping watch against outside enemies, each householder with a voice in the Common Council." The colonists translated all this into a code of laws which indicated that they took the spirit as well as the letter of Sharp's advice.   They fixed prices, listed fines for criminal offences, provided protection against debt, and much else besides; but they also, in Fyfe's words, "denied the right of Governor and Council to interfere in anything but the Company's affairs."

This, of course, was premature anticolonialism, and harsh words were said against it. For these were years of revolutionary ferment in France (and, though quickly smothered, in England too), and it was seen that the colonists of Sierra Leone had caught the influence of that. "They have made," opined the famous Wilberforce in 1800, "the worst possible subjects, as thorough Jacobins as if they had been trained and educated in Paris." Rather more than a century later, one may add, the same note would be struck by a West Indian of Hausa origin who had made Liberia his adopted home. Combining the traditions of the French and American revolutions in an African synthesis whose fuller workings are visible in our own day, the ages, in different degrees and at various times, of the Negro and Bushman aboriginals by Hamitic blood and culture." Racist declaration such as this are now seen to be the reverse of the truth, so much so that the very existence of any such people as "Hamites" in Africa is denied by all competent authorities. But they were the natural invention of the Europocentrism which accompanied the years of discovery and conquest.

Against this background there is only one sound way of reaching an estimate about the historical value of the greater part of these abundant nineteenth-century writings. This is to place them within the perspective of previous and, when that becomes fully possible, also of subsequent records. New historical anthologies relating to the Africa of a hundred years hence will ignore most of them; as it is, I have given them significant room in this selection without allowing them to occupy their usually dominant place. There is a minority who are indispensable. Heinrich Barth, for example, remains of primary importance for the Western Sudan. Some of the explorers of southern Africa, whether lay or missionary, are of the same kind. Without men like Abbadie in Ethiopia, Krapf and Rebmann in the interior and Burton along the coast of East Africa, and a good many others, we should be hard put to "make the joint" between discovery and later invasion or, as it was generally called, "occupation by treaty." But the work of these explorers must now be laid alongside the purely African record, whether known in writing, in orally remembered tradition, in the finds of archeology or in the reports of ethnographers. For while the Victorians may be excused for their many wrong and curious judgements, no such justification for ignorance and prejudice exists today. With the twentieth century the records enter upon a period of growing enlightenment.

Quite apart from questions of space, my purpose has not been to anthologize the writings of the twentieth century, and I offer only a handful of extracts to whet the appetite of readers, for the books are quickly available in any good library.

Besides, the records of oral tradition, ethnography and archeology make hard reading for all but the specialist. What needs to be remembered is that the study of African history has become a task for workers in many disciplines. Yet the documentary basis for this great advance, for this intellectual joining of Africa to the mainland of human development, lies none the less in the kind of materials which will be found in the pages that follow here.

There is another theme that will bulk large in the anthologies of the future. With the passage of time we shall better understand the subtle and often veiled process of growth and change in African ideas about many things, and not least about liberty and equality. We shall better appreciate the important part played by the African diaspora, the black peoples of the New World, in reassessing not only their own position but also that of their parent stocks in African itself. We shall more clearly see the interaction of African and non-African thought at many points that are now obscure, especially in the nineteenth century. Even then there were discordant voices in the chorus of European self-congratulation.

> Unutterable mysteries of fate
> Involve, O Africa!, thy future state

declaimed the romantic James Montgomery as early as 1841, offering perhaps the earliest sketch of a united Africa in the distant future:

> Dim through the night of these tempestuous years
> A Sabbath dawn o'er Africa appears;
> Then shall her neck from Europe's yoke be freed,
> And healing arts to hideous arms succeed;
> At home fraternal bond her tribes shall bind,
> Commerce abroad espouse them with mankind . . .

THE RECORDS OF ANCIENT AFRICA begin with Egypt, yet the Egyptian contribution has been little studied on its African side. A familiar habit has considered old Egypt merely and strictly in her relationship to the civilizations of Asia and the Mediterranean. We have had, in consequence, a lopsided view of the true position. Egypt's connections with the Middle East have been lit with brilliant clarity; those with the rest of Africa have remained in darkness, rather as though they had never been.

In this aspect, too, a new approach to African history has lately begun to right the balance. The pendulum swings the other way. Egypt's influence on old Africa, and Africa's on old Egypt, are seen to have had a fertile past, even a crucial one: a past, moreover, in which continental Africa's part was certainly the earlier, and Egypt, as part of Africa, the receiver as well as the giver. "Egyptian art," in the words of a famous Egyptologist, "is the product of the soil of Africa, like the rest of Egyptian civilization." If the history of early Africa is unthinkable without Egypt, so too is the history of early Egypt inexplicable without Africa. Ancient Egypt was essentially an African civilization.

It follows that the Ancient Egyptians were Africans even if immigrants also trickled in from Asia and southern Europe. Whether the Ancient Egyptians were as black or as brown in skin color as other Africans may remain an issue of emotive dispute; probably they were both. Their own artistic convention painted them as pink, but pictures on their tombs show that they often married queens shown as entirely black, being from the south (from what a later world knew as Nubia): while the Greek writers reported that they were much like all the other Africans whom the Greeks knew.

None of this rather fruitless argument, as to the skin color of the Ancient Egyptians before the arrival of the Arabs in the seventh century A.D., would have arisen without the eruption of modern European racism during the 1830s. It became important to the racists, then and since, to deny Egypt's African identity, Egypt's black identity, so that they could deny to Africans any capacity to build a great civilization. We should dismiss all that. What one needs to hold in mind is the enormous value and direct relevance of the Pharaonic records to Africa's remote history. At least as a token of that, space lacking for more, I begin with some of the Pharaonic records. In this I follow an eminent Egyptologist, Professor Jean Leclant, in holding that "African studies may draw to their great advantage on the immense documentation comprised in the abundant monuments, texts and graphic descriptions of five thousand years of history; and that perhaps the greatest service Egyptology can offer is to furnish, as no other branch of study can, precious chronological points of departure for the ancient history of Africa."

Four early journeys to the southward are recorded on the tomb of a nobleman of Aswan in the Sixth Dynasty (conjectural opening date: 2340 B.C.); three made under the Pharaoh Mernere and a fourth under Pepi II. "These caravans," writes A. J. Arkell in his *History of the Sudan* "must have left the Nile at Aswan by the Elephantine road, and one route is likely to have been via the oases of Dunqul and Selima, and so by the Derib al Arba'in to Darfur," the Forty Days' Road which a hardy traveller may still use from Asyut on the Middle Nile to El Fasher in the far west of the modern Republic of Sudan. "Harkhuf brought back ebony, ivory and frankincense from Yam. All of these could have been obtained in Darfur; and even if the intervening country was as desert as it is now—and it probably was not—it would be possible to travel today by the Derib al Arba'in [as Harkhuf did] with three hundred good donkeys—one hundred carrying goods, one hundred forage and one hundred water." Breasted placed Harkhuf among "the earliest known explorers of inner Africa," and Harkhuf's bare descriptions may still be read with the excitement that attends a good report of hidden places and legendary peoples.

Having discovered, the Pharaohs conquered. Here one must imagine a process of two thousand years of enterprise and effort, failure and success. Under many Pharaohs, through many years, expeditions pushed stubbornly to the interior. Settlements were made. Commerce became systematic. And after the traders and raiders there came the armies. Castles were raised, some of them as formidable as any the world has seen. Much of the country of the Middle Nile became vassal to the Pharaohs.

It is not until the eighth century B.C. that we begin to hear the voice of those whom the Pharaohs had placed in tribute. Then the tide of conquest turns upon itself for a while, and sweeps up from the southward. The early kings of Kush, a state whose capital was at Napata (towards the region that had once been Irthet or Wawat for the great Imperial Pharaohs of an already distant past), seized and held the land of Egypt for nearly a century. Kashta began this northern enterprise. After his death in about 751, Piankhi continued it. Taharqa completed it. Kush became a world power and Taharqa, by way of the Old Testament, briefly entered the European idea of history. One startling document survives from the Kushite side, though others may yet appear. In the twenty-first year of his reign (conjecturally 731 B.C.), Piankhi put up a granite stela or tablet of stone at Jebel Barkal, not far from his capital, on which the details of his conquest are inscribed.

Some two hundred years later the rulers of Kush moved their capital southward to Meroe, whose ruins lie about a hundred miles to the north of modern Khartoum. Here they presided over a distinctive civilization which flourished for seven hundred years. The Greeks called it Ethiopian. This has confused later understanding of the matter. The Kushites were entirely different from the ancestors of those called Ethiopians today: "Ethiopian," in the Greek texts, simply meant "black," and Ethiopia "the countries of the black peoples."

Not much detail is at present known of this Meroitic civilization. To begin with it used Egyptian hieroglyphics, and later a pictographic form of writing that was partly hieroglyphic; but later still—at the zenith of its power in about 200 B.C.— the Meroites invented an alphabet of their own. Archaeologists have so far collected nearly one thousand fragmentary texts in this Meroitic script, but nobody has yet succeeded in understanding many of its words. As the mystery of Cretan Linear B was to Mediterranean history until Ventris read it, so now is Meroitic to the story of the ancient Nile.

Early in the fifth century B.C., a memorable Greek of Asia Minor travelled to Upper Egypt, and heard news of Meroe. One of the sorrows of African historiography that this Greek, who was Herodotus, never managed to go any further. Even so, he had a little to say on the subject, and this is still worth repeating. He was profoundly interested in Egypt—and by extension in Kush—because he shared the then universal Greek belief that their own civilization owed many of its origins to Egyptian civilization, especially in religion and mathematics. He also thought, striking once again a very modern note, that continental Africa's influence on Egypt was both wide and deep. On circumcision, for example, "as between the Egyptians and the Ethiopians [that is, the Kushites], I should not like to say which learned from the other . . . ." As to the skin color of the Egyptians, he recalls the story of a dove connected with the Egyptian oracle at Dodona. This bird was said to have been black. Why black? "As to the bird being black," says Herodotus, "they merely signify by this that the woman was an Egyptian." Explaining why the Colchians "are of Egyptian descent," he suggests that they may have descended from

Egyptian soldiers who had served under Sesostris, a Pharaoh whose armies had invaded the Near East. But "my own idea on the subject was based first on the fact that they [the Colchians] have black skins and woolly hair (not that that amounts to much, as other nations have the same), and secondly, and more especially, on the fact that the Colchians, the Egyptians, and the Ethiopians [the Kushites] are the only races which from ancient times have practised circumcision." In all this, Herodotus was at one with other ancient Greek historians, of his time and later, who were convinced of the supreme importance of Egyptian civilization.

Meroe and its sister-cities declined in the third century after Christ, and perished in the fourth. A final blow was delivered by their old trading rival, Axum in what is now northern Ethiopia. King Ezana of Axum, then a rising power, invaded Kush in about 325, burned towns of straw and ruined towns of stone. But fortunately left a useful inscription on the subject. Extracts from it will be found below. Though often obscure, this remains a key document.

Lastly in this brief section, the reader will find a description and discussion by a modern writer of another kind of old African document. Rock paintings and engravings are scattered throughout the continent from the far north to the far south, often in abundance and of high artistic value. They bear witness to peoples and cultures that have long since disappeared, but as well to those surviving peoples of the Stone Age who continue, here and there, to pursue their life in remote corners of the land. These pictures also belong, if at second remove, to the records of Africa.

HARKHUF

Four Journeys to the Unknown South

First Journey from Aswan [c. 2300 B.C.]

The majesty of Mernere, my lord, sent me, together with
my father, the sole companion, and ritual priest Iri to Yam, in
order to explore a road to this country [of the south]. I did it
in only seven months and I brought all (kinds of) gifts from it . . .
I was very greatly praised for it.

Second Journey

His majesty sent me a second time alone; I went forth
upon the [Aswan] road, and I descended from Irthet, Mekher,
Tereres, Irtheth, being an affair of eight months. When I
descended I brought gifts from this country in very great
quantity. Never before was the like brought to this land. I
descended from the dwelling of the chief of Sethu and Irthet,
after I had explored these countries. Never had any companion
or caravan-conductor who went forth to Yam before this, done
(it).

Third Journey

His majesty now sent me a third time to Yam; I went forth
from———upon the———road, and I found the chief of Yam
going to the land of Temeh to smite Temeh as far as the
western corner of heaven. I went forth after him to the land of
Temeh, and I pacified him, until he praised all the gods for the
king's sake . . . . Now when I had pacified that chief of Yam . . .
I found the chief of Irthet, Sethu and Wawat . . . I descended
with three hundred asses laden with incense, ebony, heknu,
grain, (panthers), ivory, (throw-sticks), and every good product.
Now when the chief of Irthet, Sethu, and Wawat saw how strong

and numerous was the troop of Yam, which descended with me to the court, and the soldiers who had been sent with me, (then) this (chief) brought and gave to me bulls and small cattle, and conducted me to the roads of the highlands of Irthet, because I was more excellent, vigilant, and————than any count, companion or caravan-conductor who had been sent to Yam before. Now when the servant there [i.e., himself] was descending to the court (of the Pharaoh), one [i.e., the Pharaoh] sent the...master of the bath, Khuni, upstream with a vessel laden with date wine, (cakes), bread and beer . . .

Fourth Journey

This time Harkhuf returned with "a dancing dwarf of the god from the land of the spirits, like the dwarf which the treasurer Burded brought from Punt in the time of Isesi." Informed of this, the Pharaoh writes as follows:

"Come northward to the court immediately; thou shalt bring this dwarf with thee, which thou bringest living, prosperous and healthy from the land of the spirits, for the dances of the god, to rejoice and (gladden) the heart of the king of Upper and Lower Egypt, Neferkere, who lives forever. When he goes down with thee into the vessel, appoint excellent people, who shall be beside him on each side of the vessel; take care lest he fall into the water. When (he) sleeps at night appoint excellent people, who shall sleep beside him in his tent; inspect ten times a night. My majesty desires to see this dwarf more than the gifts of Sinai and of Punt . . ."

From J. H. Breasted, *Ancient Records of Egypt* (Chicago: 1906), vol. 1, pars. 333-336 and 353.

PEPI-NAKT

Early Empire-Building

This nobleman of Aswan on the Middle Nile was sent by Pepi II—late third millennium B.C.—on two imperial expeditions southward into the southern lands of Wawat and Irthet, thus preparing the way for later conquests. His inscriptions survive:

First Expedition to Nubia

The majesty of my lord sent me, to hack up Wawat and Irthet. I did so that my lord praised me. I slew a great number there consisting of chiefs' children and excellent commanders . . . . I brought a great number of them to the court as living prisoners, while I was at the head of many mighty soldiers as a hero. The heart of my lord was satisfied with me in every commission with which he sent me.

Second Expedition

Now, the majesty of my lord sent me to pacify these countries. I did so that my lord praised me exceedingly, above everything. I brought the two chiefs of these countries to the court in safety, bulls and live (goats) . . . together with the chiefs' children, and the two commanders of——who were with them . . . .

From J. H. Breasted, *Ancient Records of Egypt* (Chicago: 1906), vol. 1, pars. 358 ff.

TUTHMOSIS III

Trade and Tribute

From very early times the Egyptians also traded with Punt, which may be placed at the southern extremity of the Red Sea: i.e. today in Eritrea and along the north coast of modern Somalia. One great expedition ordered by Queen Hatshepsut (1490-1468 B.C. by Gardiner's conjectural dating) is carefully recorded in the queen's temple at Deir el-Bahri. Here, together with many inscriptions, are depicted scenes of Punt, a "portrait" of the chief of Punt and another of his wife, who rides upon a donkey: the earliest pictorial records of Africa "south of the Sahara," together with an explicit list of "the loading of the ships very heavily with marvels of the country of Punt." Hatshepsut's coeval, Tuthmosis III, (1490-1436 by conjectural dating) continued this trade.

Marvels brought to his majesty in the land of Punt in this year: dried myrrh, 1685 heket, gold——gold, 155 deben, 2 kidet; 134 slaves, male and female; 114 oxen, and calves; 305 bulls; total 419 cattle; beside vessels laden with ivory, ebony, (skins) of the southern panther; every good thing of (this) country——

(Tribute of conquered Wawat in Nubia): —— 13 male (negro) slaves; total 20; 44 oxen and calves; 60 bulls; total 104; beside vessels laden with every good thing of this country; the harvest of this place likewise.

From J. H. Breasted, *Ancient Records of Egypt* (Chicago: 1906), vol. 2, pars. 486-487.

that point) . . . ." Unfortunately, these "other writers" of Classical Greece have been largely lost to us.

But we have ample means of knowing that Classical Greek philosophers and scientists took care to study in Egypt, often for periods of many years, and well understood that Egyptian philosophy and science had prepared the way for their own. The Classical Greek historians followed the same practice, as their surviving world-histories show. Among these last the most important and the most vivid in its detail is that of Herodotus, who spent time in Egypt around 450 B.C.. Of other sources which have survived, the histories written by Diodorus (the Sicilian) and by Strabo have much to teach.

HERODOTUS

The Gift of the Nile

It is at Heliopolis that the most learned of the Egyptian antiquaries are said to be found . . . . As to practical matters, they all agreed in saying that the Egyptians by their study of astronomy discovered the solar year and were the first to divide it into twelve parts . . . . They also told me that the Egyptians first brought into use the names of the twelve gods, which the Greeks took over from them, and were the first to assign altars and images and temples to the gods, and to carve figures in stone. They proved the truth of most of these assertions, and went on to tell me that the first man to rule Egypt was Min, in whose time the whole country, except the district around Thebes, was marsh, none of the land below Lake Moeris—seven days' voyage upriver from the sea—then showing above water. I have little doubt that they were right in this; for it is clear to any intelligent observer, even if he has no previous information on the subject, that the Egypt to which we sail nowadays is, as it were, the gift of the river and has come only recently into the possession of its inhabitants.

From A. de Selincourt: *Herodotus: The Histories*, Penguin, London and Baltimore, 1954.

DIODORUS SICULUS

"The First of All Men"

Diodorus of Sicily—a member, that is, of the long-established Greek community in that island—wrote his world history about four centuries after Herodotus had written his. His vivid story puts together what the historians of Greece by this time—about 50 B.C.—knew or thought they knew about the world; and he draws accordingly on many Greek sources which have been lost to us.

Now the Ethiopians [i.e., the black peoples], as historians relate, were the first of all men, and the proofs of this statement, they say, are manifest. For that they did not come into their land as immigrants from abroad but were natives of it, and so justly bear the name of "autochthones" is, they maintain, conceded by practically all men . . . .

And they [i.e., the Greek historians relied on by Diodorus] say that they [i.e., the black peoples] were the first to be taught to honor the gods and to hold sacrifices and processions and festivals and other rites by which men honor the deity; and that in consequence their piety has been published abroad among all men, and it is generally held that the sacrifices

Alexandria are already sailing with fleets by way of the Nile and of the Arabian Gulf as far as India, these regions also have become far better known to us of today than to our predecessors. At any rate when Gallus was prefect of Egypt, I accompanied him [in 25 and 24 B.C.] and ascended the Nile as far as Syene and the frontiers of Ethiopia [i.e., Kush], and I learned that as many as one hundred and twenty vessels were sailing from Myos Hormos [a Red Sea port] to India, whereas formerly, under the Ptolemies [who had ruled Egypt before the Roman invasion], only a very few ventured to undertake the voyage and to carry on traffic in Indian merchandise.

From *The Geography of Strabo*: English translation by H. L. Jones: Loeb Classical Library, London and Harvard, 1917, 8 vols., here from vol. 1, p. 455.

HERODOTUS

A City named Meroe

Unlike Europeans of our own time, the great historians and travellers of Classical Greece had no conception of Egypt's not being part of Africa: they would have thought any such idea absurd. For them, Ancient Egypt largely *was* the Africa they knew and respected: a part of Africa, as Diodorus recorded, that was initially populated from the far African interior, from the lands they called "Ethiopia": that is, from the lands of the blacks. Not surprisingly, then, Herodotus was one of those Greeks who tried to visit the lands "beyond Egypt," the "lands of the blameless Ethiopians." In some wonderfully vivid passages Herodotus describes how he managed (in about 450 B.C.) to go as far south, up the Nile, as Elephantine Island beside what is now the tourist

town of Aswan. There he failed to get any further. So he content-
ed himself with information provided by the learned priests of
Elephantine. Part of what they told him referred to the city and
powerful state of Meroe: of the Kushite kingdom which had briefly
conquered most of Egypt two centuries earlier.

[c. 450 B.C.] I went as far as Elephantine [Aswan] to see
what I could with my own eyes, but for the country still further
south I had to be content with what I was told in answer to my
questions. The most I could learn was that beyond Elephantine
the country rises steeply; and in that part of the river boats
have to be hauled along by ropes—one rope on each side—
much as one drags an ox. If the rope parts, the boat is gone in
a moment, carried away by the force of the stream. These
conditions last over a four days' journey, the river all the time
winding greatly, like the Maeander, and the distance to be
covered amounting to twelve *schoeni*. After this one reaches a
level plain, where the river is divided by an island named
Tachompso.
       South of Elephantine the country is inhabited by Ethiopi-
ans [i.e., Nubians, by this time, as well as Kushites] who also
possess half of Tachompso, the other half being occupied by
Egyptians. Beyond the island is a great lake, and round its
shores live nomadic tribes of Ethiopians. After crossing the
lake one comes again to the stream of the Nile, which flows
into it. At this point one must land and travel along the bank
of the river for forty days, because sharp rocks, some showing
above the water and many just awash, make the river impracti-
cable for boats. After the forty days' journey on land one takes
another boat and in twelve days reaches a big city named
Meroe, said to be the capital city of the Ethiopians [i.e., the
black inhabitants of the kingdom of Kush]. The inhabitants
worship Zeus and Dionysus alone of the Gods, holding them in
great honor. There is an oracle of Zeus there, and they make

war according to its pronouncements, taking from it both the occasion and the object of their various expeditions.

Carthage Trades South

The Carthaginians also tell us that they trade with a race of men who live in a part of Libya beyond the Pillars of Heracles [i.e., the Straits of Gibralter of today]. On reaching this country, they unload their goods, arrange them tidily along the beach, and then, returning to their boats, raise a smoke. Seeing the smoke, the natives come down to the beach, place on the ground a certain quantity of gold in exchange for the goods, and go off again to a distance. The Carthaginians then come ashore and take a look at the gold; and if they think it represents a fair price for their wares, they collect it and go away; if, on the other hand, it seems too little, they go back aboard and wait, and the natives come and add to the gold until they are satisfied. There is perfect honesty on both sides; the Carthaginians never touch the gold until it equals in value what they have offered for sale, and the natives never touch the goods until the gold has been taken away.

From A. de Selincourt: *Herodotus: The Histories*, Penguin, London and Baltimore, 1954.

EZANA

The Fall of Meroe

A little patience with this famous text from Axum can win from it a good deal of sense. It really offers a vivid report of King Ezana's war against his neighbors on the Middle Nile in the fourth century. By this time Meroe had lost its old power, and the Meroites—the Kushites of Meroe, the Kasu of this inscription—had clearly passed through many troubles. They were still living in "towns of masonry" that were anything but destitute—'Alwa and Daro in Ezana's report, the former being very possibly Meroe itself—but they had suffered infiltration, and perhaps successful invasion, by the Noba or Nuba. These Noba lived in "towns of straw"—that is, grass-hut settlements—but were evidently at peace with the urban Kasu. However, they were not at peace with Axum, a strong rival for the foreign trade of the region, and they provoked Ezana (or that is what he says) into invading them.

The Noba were of two kinds, the "Red" and the "Black." It was the first of these who most annoyed Ezana. He marched northwest down the Takkaze (the Atbara) and routed them three times, but they were not put down. Then he took the field a fourth time, fought them "on the Takkaze at the ford of Kemalke," and pursued them for twenty-three days. Having got so far, he went further. He "arrived at the Kasu" (the Kushites or Meroites), set up a base at the juncture of the Atbara and the Nile, and pushed raiding parties north and south. Those who went south assaulted the "towns of masonry" of the Kasu—their ruins may still be seen near Shendi on the Nile—while those who went north along the Nile (the Seda in Ezana's language) ravished "the towns of straw" of the Black Noba and two towns of masonry of the Kasu which have not been securely identified, but which L. P. Kirwan, whose interpretation I am largely following here, thinks may have been Kawa and Salam on the Dongola reach of the river.

This is the last sure word we hear of Meroe until the times of rediscovery many centuries later. But the Noba, whether "Red" or "Black," were far from finished. They were the peoples—the Nobatae or the Blemmyes or both of these—who took over much of Meroitic culture, became converted to Christianity in A.D. 543, and built another famous Nubian civilization, Christian and literate, which endured until Islamic conquest many hundreds of years afterwards. Unhappily we have only the scantiest written records of Christian Nubia and its once famous kingdoms.

[c. A.D. 325]

Through the might of the Lord of All I took the field against the
  Noba, when the people of Noba revolted,

When they boasted and "He will not cross over the Takkaze,"
  said the (people of) the Noba,

When they did violence to the peoples Mangurto and Hasa and
  Barya, and the Blacks

Waged war on the Red Peoples and a second and a third time
  broke their oath and without

Consideration (forebearance) slew their neighbors and plundered our envoys and our messengers

Whom I had sent to interrogate them, robbing them of their
  possessions and

Seizing their lances. When I sent again and they did not hear
  me, and reviled me

And made off, I took the field against them. And I armed
  myself (?) with the power of the Lord of the Land

And fought on the Takkaze at the ford of Kemalke. And
  thereupon they fled

And stood not still, and I pursued the fugitives (?) twenty-
  three—23—days

Slaying (some of) them and capturing others and taking booty
  from them, where I came; while prisoners and

Booty were brought back by my people who marched out;
  while I burnt their towns,

Those of masonry and those of straw, and (my people) seized
  their corn and their bronze and the dried meat

And the images in their temples and destroyed the stocks of
  corn and cotton and (the enemy)

Plunged into the river Seda,—and (there were) many who
  perished in the water,

The number I know not—and as their vessels foundered, a
  multitude of people

Men and women, were drowned...

And I arrived at the Kasu, slaying (some of) them and taking
  (others) prisoner

At the junction of the rivers Seda and Takkaze. And on the day
    after my arrival
(I) dispatched into the field the troop of Mahaza and the
    Damaw(a) and Falh(a) and Sera
Up the Seda (against) the towns of masonry and of straw; their
    towns
Of masonry are called 'Alwa, Daro. And they slew and took
    prisoners and threw (them)
Into the water, and they returned safe and sound, after they
    had terrified their enemies and had conquered through
    the power of the Lord of the Land.
And I sent the troop Halen and the troop Laken (?) and
The troop Sabarat and Falh(a) and Sera down the Seda
    (against) the towns of straw
Of the Noba, 4, Negues, 1; the towns of masonry of the Kasu
    which the Noba had taken (were) Tabito (?)
Fertoti; and they arrived at the territory of the Red Noba, and
My people returned safe and sound after they had taken
    (some) prisoner and slain (others) and had seized their
    booty through the power of the Lord of Heaven.
And I erected a throne at the junction of the rivers Seda and
Takkaze, opposite the town of masonry which is on this
    peninsula.

From L. P. Kirwan, "The Decline and Fall of Meroe," *Kush*, 1960.
Kirwan's translation is from the German of that of E. Littmann in
"Äthiopischer Inschriften," *Miscellanea Academica Berolinensia* II/2,
1950, pp. 97 ff.

DESMOND CLARK

Stone Age Art

One of the most remarkable features of the culture of the Later Stone Age peoples, as we have mentioned, was their pictorial art which, particularly south of the Zambezi, reached an extremely high standard of artistic ability in the naturalistic sphere.

In 1797 Barrow visited a cave in the Bamboesberg, a part of the Stormberg Range, in which a Bushman painter had very recently been disturbed. He had been busy making a drawing of a tortoise, the model for which lay close by, on the floor of the cave. Barrow visited other caves which contained paintings made by the hastily departed occupants. In 1869 Stow attempted to gain an interview with one of the last Bushman painters in the mountains near Tylden in the Kei River Area, but he was unsuccessful. This Bushman was named Gou-wa, and he was then an old man. Stow describes him, from hearsay presumably, as the painter of the family and as still carrying two or three of his horn paint-pots on a belt round his waist. He was the artist who painted the representation of the Boer Commando on the wall of his brother's rock shelter and which was said to commemorate the first attack made by the Boers on this particular band. Stow also says that the last survivors of the "painter tribes" took refuge in the Maluti Mountains in Basutoland, and although he gives no specific date it was presumably in the 1860s that the last of the artists there was killed in the Witteberg Native Reserve. He had ten small horn pots hanging from a belt, each of which contained a different colored paint . . . .

One may, very generally speaking, divide the paintings into two main periods, an Earlier Period which is characterized by a "peaceful" and simple, naturalistic art showing no recognizably modern equipment or peoples, and a Later Period which is essentially that of the Bushmen, when the paintings are less carefully or skilfully executed and show a restlessness of approach and an abundance of complicated scenes of fights, raids, and ceremonies, in which Bushman, Bantu, and Hottentot can all be distinguished. This period might again be subdivided into two parts—an earlier half when the different races appear to be more or less at peace with one another, and a later when the struggle for survival has begun. This last group is for the most part confined to South Africa, in particular the southeastern region.

The beginning of rock art in South Africa is believed by some to date back to the later Middle Stone Age of Magosian times, that is to say to about 10,000-8000 B.C. It is by no means improbable that the artistic tradition goes back to those times, but it is most unlikely that any of the art that survives today is as old as that, unless it be some of the earliest engravings. For example, it is interesting to note that a Magosian industry has been found in the Molopo shelter in Basutoland in a deposit containing a serpentine engraving on the lower part of the cave wall. There is reason to suppose that the paintings and a large part of the engravings date to much more recent times, and it is likely that most of this art dates to a time subsequent to the beginning of the Christian era. Some investigators would put it later still and believe that many of the best paintings in the southeastern group are not earlier than the beginning of the eighteenth century.

Two facts clearly emerge from a study of this art. The first is that there is a continuity running through it which, in spite of the differences of style and technique, holds it together and, in view of its indubitable associations, labels it as essentially Later Stone Age in conception. There is too pronounced a stratigraphical break between the Magosian and the Later Stone Age proper, and often too much exfoliation from the rock surface has taken place between the two, for any of the paintings to date back to Magosian times. Secondly, the earliest examples that have come down to us are much too advanced in conception and execution to represent the first expression of this art and it is certain that earlier, more primitive styles must have existed, though the paintings have now disappeared. It is more probable, therefore, that the origins of this parietal art extend back beyond the beginning of the Later Stone Age proper to the time of the microlithic revolution . . . .

A question that is so often asked is, "What was the motive behind this art?" Was it predominantly magical, or was it purely freedom of artistic expression, "art for art's sake," as it were? It would seem that some of the paintings and engravings, in particular the earlier naturalistic ones, were connected with magical beliefs, and especially is this considered to be the case with the geometric art of our Northern Region where the signs and symbols must have had some magical or ceremonial significance. The large animal paintings that constitute some of the earliest art, and the beautifully incised naturalistic engravings, probably followed from the beliefs of many primitive peoples that by drawing an eland, for example, one will be given power to find and kill this animal in the hunt, or that the eland will be drawn towards the hunter so that he may kill it. Or again there is the belief that by depicting a certain beast or by wearing a part of it, the hunter, or perhaps the band, will take on something of its nature. Some of the large and early paintings of elephants in Rhodesia [Zimbabwe since 1980] may perhaps be explained in this way as having been made to endow the band with the strength of the elephant.

Other of the animal paintings may represent the totemic ancestor of the group that occupied the site, and Stow has indicated that there is reason to believe that some of the southern group of paintings may have been done for this purpose.

But the bulk of the paintings which represent hunting scenes and ceremonies, and certainly the later ones showing fights with Bantu, cattle raids, dances, representations of everyday events, must be considered primarily as examples of representational art. These are essentially records of events and provide us with most interesting details of the life and habits of the different peoples depicted, and perhaps some day will be the means of filling some of the still blank pages of our history books.

From J. D. Clark, *The Prehistory of Southern Africa*, 1959. First extract: pp. 255-256; second, p. 265; third, pp. 268-269.

Early West Africa

*M*ODERN ARCHEOLOGY THROWS light upon a distant and otherwise silent past. Extracts from two essays by writers of our own time accordingly open this section. The finding and fixing of the first Iron Age culture to be clearly identified in West Africa—the Nok culture of the Niger-Benue confluence lands—provides a starting point for much African history as well as the likely origins, as will be seen, of the high art of Ife and its neighbors.

Another wide river of information on preliterate Africa flows from the tales and genealogies which African chiefs and others have learned and remembered of their past. But its waves and spates have to be ridden with care, for the dividing line between the hazards of genial invention and the safety of navigable fact is always difficult and sometimes impossible to trace. Yet these remembered traditions must be admitted to the records of history. Even when their details are doubtful or merely fantastic, the general picture they offer can remain of potent value.

Many traditions reach back usefully into the past, and the reconstruction of history that is now going on takes due account of them, not seldom finding them surprisingly reliable. It has seemed right to include a handful of writings drawn from this oral history of Africa. I have chosen these on the simple plan of illustrating the traditional origins of two or three of West Africa's well-known peoples. Among these are the Yoruba of Western Nigeria. Did some of their founding ancestors really come from the Nile, from the neighborhood of Kush, bringing to say, but evidence is now building up indicating that the art style of the Nok Culture must have survived very much longer . . . .

There is now every reason to hope that further finds both in the area of the Nok Culture and in more or less dateable deposits in Yorubaland, Benin and elsewhere on the West Coast will confirm the basic homogeneity of so much of West African sculpture and its derivation from a traditional complex going back at least two thousand years, and at the same time will dispose of the widely held hypothesis that the Ife-Benin complex owes its style and inspiration to origins outside West Africa.

From B. A. B. Fagg, "The Nok Culture in Prehistory," *Journal of the Historical Society of Nigeria*, Dec. 1959, p. 288.

FRANK WILLETT

Two Thousand Years of Sculpture

All the bronzes so far known from Ife (apart from some evidently recent work) are in the naturalistic style, of which far more numerous examples have survived in terra-cotta. A study of the terra-cotta figures reveals stylistic affinities with those of the Nok Culture, already known from a large part of Northern Nigeria, but probably in reality even more widespread. Radio-carbon samples from the type-site suggest that the terra-cotta figures began to be made some time after 900 B.C., probably by a neolithic or early metal-age people; and that the culture may have continued to produce terra-cottas after A.D. 200 . . . . It looks very much as if the art of Ife developed from that of Nok . . . .

In Ife there are examples of terra-cottas which are almost certainly postclassical, and lead on to the modern Yoruba style.

In due time we may hope to find more examples of terra-cottas to illustrate the stages of development from the Nok to the classical Ife style. Some of the sites which have produced Nok terra-cottas may be substantially later than the type-site itself, whilst we know that the apogee of the naturalistic style at Ife was not later than the middle of the fourteenth century. The interval between these two dates represents a crucial phase in the history of most of the major peoples of Nigeria, to judge by traditions. In the case of the Yoruba, it seems likely that a small but influential group of people came into Nigeria during this period and established themselves as rulers over an indigenous iron-using population making Nok terra-cottas . . . .

As yet there is no direct evidence of who these [new-comers] were, where they came from, or when. They seem to have come from the east or the northeast, possibly from Meroe, which collapsed in the early fourth century, or perhaps they came a few centuries later from Zaghawa or from Christian Nubia. The Yoruba migration legends, both those about their origin and those of diffusion within Nigeria, almost certainly refer only to the ruling group.

Yoruba civilization appears therefore to be the result of a small intrusive ruling class, bringing ideas from outside, with a highly artistic indigenous population. The resulting social pattern seems to have borne some resemblance to that of the City States of Ancient Greece, but the unique achievement of the Yoruba was to have possessed such an evolved urban civilization without the knowledge of writing.

From F. Willett, "Ife and Its Archaeology," *Journal of African History*, 2, 1960.

MUHAMMAD BELLO

Where the Yoruba Came From

Sultan Muhammad Bello (1779-1837) was one of a number of distinguished scholars and statesmen of nineteenth-century West Africa (p. 31, p. 375). The English traveller Hugh Clapperton has left an engaging and probably characteristic portrait. "Saw the Sultan this morning," Clapperton wrote (*Journal of Second Expedition into the Interior of Africa from the Bight of Benin to Soccatoo*, London, 1829, p. 198), "who was sitting in the inner apartment of his house, with the Arabic copy of Euclid before him, which I had given to him as a present. He said that his family had a copy of Euclid brought by one of their relations, who had procured it in Mecca; that it was destroyed when part of his house was burnt down last year; and he observed, that he could not but feel very much obliged to the king of England for sending him so valuable a present . . . ."

The country of Yoruba is extensive and has streams and forests and rocks and hills. There are many curious and beautiful things in it. The ships of Christians come there. The people of Yoruba are descended from the Bani Kan'an and the kindred of Nimrud. Now the reason of their having settled in the west according to what we are told is that Ya'rub ibn Qahtan drove them out of 'Iraq to westwards and they travelled between Misr and Habash until they reached Yoruba. It happened that they left a portion of their people in every country they passed. It is said that the Sudanese who live up on the hills are all kindred; so also the people of Yauri are their kindred.

From Muhammad Bello, *Infaq al-maysur*, paraphrased and translated by E. J. Arnett in *The Rise of the Sokoto Fulani* (Kano: 1929), p. 16.

SAMUEL JOHNSON

Yoruba Traditions

The origin of the Yoruba nation is involved in obscurity. Like the early history of most nations the commonly received accounts are for the most part purely legendary. The people being unlettered, and the language unwritten, all that is known is from traditions carefully handed down.

The National Historians are certain families retained by the King at Oyo whose office is hereditary; they also act as the King's bards, drummers, and cymbalists. It is on them we depend as far as possible for any reliable information we now possess; but, as may be expected, their accounts often vary in several important particulars. We can do no more than relate the traditions which have been universally accepted.

The Yorubas are said to have sprung from Lamurudu, one of the Kings of Mecca, whose offspring were: Oduduwa, the ancestor of the Yorubas, the Kings of Gogobiri and of the Kukawa, two tribes in the Hausa country. It is worthy of remark that these two nations, notwithstanding the lapse of time since their separation and in spite of the distance from each other of their respective localities, still have the same distinctive tribal marks on their faces; and Yoruba travellers are free amongst them and vice versa, each recognizing each other as of one blood.

At what period of time Lamurudu reigned is unknown, but, from the accounts given of the revolution among his descendants and their dispersion, it appears to have been a considerable time after Mahomet . . . .

That the Yorubas came originally from the East there cannot be the slightest doubt, as their habits, manners and customs, etc., all go to prove. With them the East is Mecca and Mecca is the East. Having strong affinities with the East, and

Mecca in the East looming so largely in their imagination, everything that comes from the East, with them, comes from Mecca; and hence it is natural to represent themselves as having hailed originally from that city.

From Samuel Johnson, *History of the Yorubas* (London: 1921), pp. 3-5. Completed in 1897 but not published until 1921, Johnson's work has been described by Hodgkin as "the most substantial study of Yoruba history yet undertaken," and is based principally upon the oral traditions of the Yoruba Kingdom of Oyo. Johnson himself was a Yoruba. See also the Benin traditions collected by Chief Egharevba, on p. 118. But Johnson's Yoruba "eastern origin" is certainly mythological.

SABURI BIOBAKU

Yoruba Origins—A Modern View

In our search for the origins of the Yoruba we ought to glance at the Kingdom of Meroe . . . .

The modern Yoruba themselves usually confused the Near East with Arabia and owing to the prestige of Islam locate their origin in Mecca. The probable place is Upper Egypt rather than the Yemen . . . .

It is almost certain . . . that the Yoruba migrations from the Near East occurred between 600 and 1000 A.D. The Yoruba did not emigrate from their original homes in one mass exodus . . . [but] in successive waves which may be grouped into two major waves with an interval of about three hundred years in between . . . .

From S. O. Biobaku in *Lugard Lectures* (Lagos: 1955). Dr. Biobaku is a Nigerian historian who is now in charge of African studies at the University of Ife, and is also the author of *The Egba and Their Neighbours, 1842-1872* (Oxford: 1957).

TAMSIR NIANE AND SURET-CANALE

Foundations of Ghana

From the third century the Sarakolle (Soninke) kingdom of Wagadu was in full development.   The king of Kumbi [its capital] was called *Ghana*, meaning "War Chief," or *Kaya Maghan* meaning "King of the Gold" . . . .

The king of Wagadu early imposed himself on other kings. The kingdoms of Tekrur [in Senegal], Manding [Mali] and Gao recognized his authority; the Berbers of the town of Aouda-ghost did the same. The kingdom of Wagadu became a large empire extending from the Atlantic to the Niger.

From the seventh century the Arabs penetrated Black Africa, passing either by way of Egypt or North Africa. Attracted by the gold of Wagadu, the Arabs and Berbers came with many caravans of camels to trade in the towns of Wagadu.

Some of these traders settled at Kumbi where they formed a big residential quarter apart from the royal palace.   The Arabs were Muslims, but the emperor and people of Wagadu were pagans . . . .

From D. T. Niane and J. Suret-Canale, *Histoire de l'Afrique Occidentale* (Paris: 1961), p. 23. Translated here by B. D.

AL YAKUBI

The King of Ghana

...the king of Ghana [is] a great king. In his territory are mines of gold, and under him a number of kingdoms, among them the kingdom of Sugham and the kingdom of Sama. In all this country there is gold.

From Yakubi, A.D. 891, translation from Houtsmar Text (Brill, Leyden: 1883) by H. R. Palmer (Sir Richmond Palmer) *Sudanese Memoirs* (Lagos: 1928), vol. 2.

AL BEKRI

Ghana in 1067

Ghana is the title of the kings of this people, while the name of their country is Aoukar [Wagadu in surviving traditions, however]. The king who governs them at present . . . is called Tenkaminen; he came to the throne in A.H. 455 . . . . Tenkaminen is the master of a large empire and a formidable power . . . . The king of Ghana can put two hundred thousand warriors in the field, more than forty thousand being armed with bow and arrow . . . .

When he gives audience to his people, to listen to their complaints and set them to rights, he sits in a pavilion around which stand ten pages holding shields and gold-mounted swords: and on his right hand are the sons of the princes of his empire, splendidly clad and with gold plaited into their hair. The governor of the city is seated on the ground in front of the king, and all around him are his viziers in the same position. The gate of the chamber is guarded by dogs of an excellent breed, who never leave the king's seat: they wear collars of gold and silver, ornamented with the same metals. The beginning of a royal audience is announced by the beating of a kind of drum which they call *deba*, made of a long piece of hollowed wood. The people gather when they hear this sound . . . .

Royal Finances

The king [of Ghana] exacts the right of one *dinar* of gold on each donkey-load of salt that enters his country, and two *dinars* of gold on each load of salt that goes out. A load of copper carries a duty of five *mitqals* and a load of merchandise ten *mitqals*. The best gold in the country comes from Ghiaru, a town situated eighteen days' journey from the capital [Kumbi] in a country that is densely populated by Negroes and covered with villages. All pieces of native gold found in the mines of the empire belong to the sovereign, although he lets the public have the gold dust that everybody knows about; without this precaution, gold would become so abundant as practically to lose its value . . . . The Negroes . . . known as Nougharmarta are traders, and carry gold dust from Iresni all over the place . . . .

From Abdullah Abu-Ubayd al Bekri, *Al-Masalik wa 'l-Mamalik* (Cordoba: 1067). Above extracts are from French translation of MacGuckin de Slane (Paris: 1859), 2 vols, but reprinted 1965 by Adrien-Maisonneuve, Paris. Translation here by B. D.

ANONYMOUS

Sundiata's Triumph

In about the year 1240, according to tradition, the Mandingo ruler Sundiata Keita fought a crucial battle against the Sosso (Fulah) King Sumanguru, and won. This is generally accounted as the beginning of the empire of Mali. An anonymous manuscript in Arabic, recovered and translated by the late Maurice Delafosse, tells the story of this battle as popular memory recorded it long afterwards.

As Sundiata advanced with his army to meet Sumanguru, he learned that Sumanguru was also coming against him with an army prepared for battle. They met in a place called Kirina [not far from the modern Koulikoro]. When Sundiata turned his eyes on the army of Sumanguru he believed they were a cloud and said: "What is this cloud on the eastern side?" They told him it was the army of Sumanguru. As for Sumanguru, when he saw the army of Sundiata, he exclaimed: "What is that mountain of stone?" For he thought it was a mountain. And they told him: "It is the army of Sundiata, which lies to the west of us." Then the two columns came together and fought a murderous battle; in the thick of the fight, Sundiata uttered a great shout in the face of the warriors of Sumanguru, and at once these ran to get behind Sumanguru; the latter in his return uttered a great shout in the face of the warriors of Sundiata, all of whom fled to get behind Sundiata. Usually, when Sumanguru shouted, eight heads would rise above his own head.

When they had done this, Sundiata said to Sangaran Danguinia Konnte: "Have you forgotten the taboo?" [A reference to an earlier prophecy of Sumanguru's imminent downfall, and the manner of its bringing about.] As soon as Sangaran Danguinia heard Sundiata's question he came to the front of the army, halted, grasped the arrow (spear?) armed with the spur of a white cock, and threw it at Sumanguru. As soon as it had struck Sumanguru, Sangaran said: "This is the arrow of him who knows the ancient secrets . . . ."   While he was saying this, Sumanguru vanished and was seen no more. Now he had had a gold bracelet on his wrist, and this fell on that spot [i.e., at Kirina]; a baobab tree grew out of it and carries the mark to this day. [Fifty years ago, it is said, the people of Kirina would still show their visitors a baobab tree which they held to be the same one as grew there on the day of Sundiata's famous victory.]

. . .As for Sundiata, he defeated the army of Sumanguru, ravaged the land of the Susu and subjugated its people. Afterwards Sundiata became the ruler of an immense empire [Mali] . . . .

From Delafosse, *Traditions historiques et legendaires du Soudan occidental* (Paris: 1913).   Translated here from version in *Notes Africaines*, Institut Français d'Afrique Noire, Dakar, July 1959: French text and valuable notes.

DJELI MAMOUDOU DOUYATE

The Epic of Old Mali

The above extract was from the only version available when I first compiled this anthology. But African historiography has made progress since the time of Delafosse, not least in its attention to oral or non-written sources. Professor D. T. Niane has thus provided us with a version of the Sundiata epic drawn directly from an oral source who was the Mandingo griot (remembrancer of history, singer of famous songs, counsellor of rulers) Djeli Mamoudou Kouyate, "master in the art of eloquence," available also in translation by G. D. Pickett as *Sundiata: An Epic of Old Mali* his country was very extensive and contiguous with the [Atlantic] ocean . . . .

Ibn Amir Hajib continued: "I asked sultan Musa how the kingdom fell to him, and he said: 'We belong to a house which hands on the kingship by inheritance. The king who was my predecessor did not believe that it was impossible to discover the furthest limit of the Atlantic ocean and wished vehemently to do so. So he equipped 200 ships filled with men and the same number filled with gold, water and provisions enough to last them for years, and said to the man deputed to lead them: "Do not return until you reach the end of it, or your provisions and water give out." They departed and a long time passed before anyone came back. Then one ship returned and we asked the captain what news they brought. He said: "Yes, O Sultan, we travelled for a long time until there appeared in the open sea (as it were) a river with a powerful current. Mine was the last of those ships. The (other) ships went on ahead but when they reached that place they did not return and no more was seen of them and we do not know what became of them. As for me, I went about at once and did not enter that river." But the sultan disbelieved him.

"'Then that sultan got ready 2000 ships, 1000 for himself and the men whom he took with him and 1000 for water and provisions. He left me to deputize for him and embarked on the Atlantic ocean with his men. That was the last we saw of him and all those who were with him, and so I became king in my own right.'"

From Ibn Fadl Allah al Omari, *Masalik al Absar fi Mamalik al Amsar*, in the French version of Gaudefroy-Demombynes (Paris: 1927). Translation by B. D., except the section entitled "Ocean Travels." That section is reproduced from that wonderful mine of new translations: *Corpus of Early Arabic Sources for West African History*, J. F. P. Hopkins, edited and annotated by N. Levtzion and J. F. P. Hopkins, Cambridge, 1981.

IBN BATTUTA

Travels in Mali

The most travelled of all the Muslim writers of the Middle Ages, Muhammad ibn Abdullah ibn Battuta, was born of a Berber family at Tangier in 1304, spent the greater part of his adult life in wandering about the Muslim world from West Africa to India and China, and died in Marrakesh in 1377. Not long before his sixtieth year he dictated his memoirs to Ibn Juzayy, who made a book of them. A complete text of Ibn Jazayy's work was found in Algeria about 145 years ago and translated into French in the middle of the nineteenth century, since when it has become famous for its unique description of West and East Africa in the fourteenth century. I give a few extracts here as bait for the reader who does not yet know Ibn Battuta, a wonderful teller of tales whose cast of character has sting and savour that bring him to life even after six hundred years. With its highly personal mixture of sophistication and simplicity, Ibn Battuta's narrative remains one of the best travel books ever made.

His journey to the Empire of Mali began in 1352. He took the old but still difficult and dangerous caravan route across the western Sahara from Sijilmasa through Teghaza to Walata, crossing, as he says in another famous passage, "a desert haunted by demons" and arriving in Walata two months after leaving Sijilmasa. "[At first] we used to go ahead of the caravan, and when we found a place suitable for pasturage we would graze our beasts. We went on doing this until one of our party was lost in the desert; after than I neither went ahead nor lagged behind."

In Walata our learned friend declared himself shocked by the equality of social status accorded to women there, but he stayed for fifty days, thence continuing by way of the Middle Niger to the capital of Mali, which was probably at Niane on the left bank of the upper reach of the river. He returned north eighteen months later by way of the Middle Saharan route through the Hoggar mountains, thence westward again to Sijilmasa and so to Fez, "the capital of

Security and Justice

Among the admirable qualities of these people, the following are to be noted:

1. The small number of acts of injustice that one finds there; for the Negroes are of all peoples those who most abhor injustice. The sultan pardons no one who is guilty of it.

2. The complete and general safety one enjoys throughout the land. The traveller has no more reason than the man who stays at home to fear brigands, thieves or ravishers.

3. The blacks do not confiscate the goods of white men [that is, of North Africans or Arabs] who die in their country, not even when these consist of big treasures. They deposit them, on the contrary, with a man of confidence among the whites until those who have a right to the goods present themselves and take possession.

4. They make their prayers punctually; they assiduously attend their meetings of the faithful, and punish their children if these should fail in this. On Fridays, anyone who is late at the mosque will find nowhere to pray, the crowd is so great. Their custom is to send their servants to the mosque to spread their prayer-mats in the due and proper place, and to remain there until they, the masters, should arrive. These mats are made of the leaves of a tree resembling a palm, but one without fruit.

5. The Negroes wear fine white garments on Fridays. If by chance a man has no more than one shirt or a soiled tunic, at least he washes it before putting it on to go to public prayer.

6. They zealously learn the Koran by heart. Those children who are neglectful in this are put in chains until they have memorized the Koran. On one festival day I visited the *qadi* and saw children thus enchained and asked him: "Will you not let them free?" He replied: "Only when they know their Koran by heart."

Another day I was passing by a young Negro, a handsome lad and very well dressed, who had a heavy chain on his feet. I said to my companion: "What's happened to the boy? Has he murdered someone?" The young Negro heard what I had said and began laughing. "They have chained him," I was told, "simply to make him memorize the Koran."

But these people have some deplorable customs, as for example:

1.   Women servants, slave women and young girls go about quite naked, not even concealing their sexual parts. I saw many like this during Ramadhan; because it is the custom with the Negroes that commanding officers should break their fast in the sultan's palace, and they are served with food which is brought by women slaves, twenty or more of them who are completely naked.

2.   Women go naked into the sultan's presence, too, without even a veil; his daughters also go about naked. On the twenty-seventh night of Ramadhan I saw about a hundred women slaves coming out of the sultan's palace with food, and they were naked. Two daughters of the sultan were with them, and these had no veil either, although they had big breasts.

3.   The blacks throw dust and cinders on their heads as a sign of good manners and respect.

4.   They have buffoons who appear before the sultan when the poets are reciting their praise songs.

5.   And then a good number of Negroes eat the flesh of dogs and donkeys.

* * * * * * * *

Women and Men

Readers may wonder why writing by women scarcely appears in this anthology. The reasons are partly that the old historical records were written by men, and partly that in literate regions, which in pre-colonial times meant Islamic regions, male prejudice in social and political contexts had often become heavily anti-woman. By the fourteenth century A.D., when Ibn Battuta was travelling in Africa, the mutual gender respect recommended long before by the Prophet had given way to a stiff male supremacism

in the countries north of the Sahara, along the southern shores of
the Mediterranean. But this attitude was not admired or even
admitted by the peoples south of the desert, even when Muslim,
nor was it generally practised among the Berbers of the desert
itself. Visiting the great Berber caravan oasis of Walata (Iwalatan)
in the southern desert regions, Ibn Battuta found what he remembered as a shocking situation.

One day [while at Walata] I visited the house of Abu
Muhammad Yandakin al-Masufi—in whose company we had
come [to Walata]—and found him seated on a carpet. In the
courtyard of his house there was a canopied couch with a
woman sitting on it and talking to a man seated beside her. I
said to Abu Muhammad: "Who is this woman?" He said: "She
is my wife." I said: "What relationship has the man with her?"
He replied: "He is a friend of hers." I said to him: "And you
agree with this, when you have lived in our country [Morocco],
and know the precepts of the *Sharia*?" He replied to me: "The
association of women with men is agreeable to us and a part of
good manners, to which no suspicion attaches. They are not
like the women of your country." I was amazed at his laxity.
I left him, and did not visit him again. He invited me several
times, but I refused.

From Muhammad ibn Abdullah ibn Battuta, *Tuhfat al-Nuzzar fi Ghara'ib
al-Amsar wa 'Adja'ib al-Asfar.* The first two extracts are from the
English of H. A. R. Gibb, *Ibn Battuta, Travels in Asia and Africa* (London:
1929), pp. 324-325, 326-327, 329; the third from the French of C.
Defrémery and B. R. Sanguinetti, *Les Voyages d'ibn Battuta* (Paris: 1854),
vol. IV, translation by B. D.

KANO CHRONICLE

The Hausa States

The Kano Chronicle offers precious evidence of the states of the Hausa people that flourished in what is now Northern Nigeria throughout the Middle Ages and for long afterwards, and which were conquered by the Fulani at the beginning of the nineteenth century.

The manuscript of the Chronicle, Sir Richmond Palmer has commented, "is of no great age, and must on internal evidence have been written during the latter part of the decade 1883-1893; but it probably represents some earlier record which has now perished. It is said, and no doubt with some truth, that the Fulani, in their fanatical zeal, destroyed many old records and books, on the ground that they were the books of 'Kafurai,' for their *casus belli* was that the Hausa *Sarkis* [rulers] were infidels, and as such deserved to be destroyed with all their works. The records on which the Chronicle must be based were apparently an exception. The authorship is unknown, and it is very difficult to make a guess . . . ."

Diplomacy

The eighth *Sarki* was Shekkarau [who reigned A.H. 689-706 or A.D. 1290-1307]. His mother's name was Auta. When he became *Sarki* his men said to him, "*Sarkin* Kano, what do you see in the talk of the people of this city?" He said, "I see nothing between us except things we can settle without fighting." They replied, "If you try to make peace with the people they will say that you are afraid. If they come to you and make smooth talk, turn away from them; then you would not be acting wrongly. If matters do not fall out thus we will fight them, and if we prevail over them we will cut the throats of all their chief men and destroy their god." These counsels prevailed. All the pagans came to the *Sarki* with many presents and said: "*Sarki*, and Lord over us, we come to you to say to you one word: do not take notice of what we have done, we pray you, but put away the slanderous counsel of your advisers. If the domains of a ruler are wide, he should be patient; if they are not so, he will not obtain possession of the whole country by impatience." The *Sarki* said to them, "Your talk is true," and left them their customs and power. They said, "Were it not for fear of what may result we would have told the *Sarki* the secrets of our god." The chief of them, Samagi, said "If we show him the secrets of our god we shall lose all our power, and we and our generation will be forgotten."

So the dispute continued till the *Sarki* died. Shekkarau was *Sarki* seventeen years.

Warfare

The thirty-eighth *Sarki* was Muhammad Kumbari [who reigned A.H. 1143-1156 or A.D. 1731-1743], the son of Sharefa and Luki. He was a liberal *Sarki* but quick to anger. His counsellors liked him, but the common people hated him. In his time there was fierce war between Kano and Gobir.

The name of *Sarkin* Gobir was Soba. If the Gobirawa defeated the Kanawa one day, the Kanawa defeated them the next. This state of affairs continued for a long time. In Kumbari's time *Sarkin* Bornu Mai Ali came to Kano to war. He encamped at Faggi for three nights without a battle being fought, since *Shehu* Tahiru and *Shehu* Bunduu prevented it. He returned to Bornu. Kumbari went to war with Dussi in the time of *Sarkin* Dussi Makuri and very nearly entered the town through the fierceness of his attack, but his advisers prevented him entering the town, saying to him, "*Sarkin* Kano, you have won the day, go home." He listened to their advice and went home. In the Dussi war *Sarkin* Aujera Bugau was killed. Kumbari returned to Kano. In his time shields were first brought from Nupe, which was then ruled over by *Sarkin* Nupe Jibrila. Guns were also brought.

From the translation in H. R. Palmer, *Sudanese Memoirs* (Lagos: 1928), vol. 3.

AL MAGHILI

Social Reform in Songhay

We know what blistering condemnation was evoked from medieval Christian theologians by the morals and manners of feudal Europe. But what did their Muslim contemporaries think about the habits of the countries beyond the Sahara for which they, in their turn, were required to give advice and precept? One might well despair of finding out. As it is, and by great good fortune, a remarkable answer is to hand; or rather a series of answers.

Some one hundred fifty years after Ibn Battuta had reported on the habits of the Western Sudan, the renowned Songhay ruler, Askia Muhammad ben Abi Bakr Ture (Touré) (r. 1493-1528) put a number of questions to the North African theologian, Muhammad ben Abd al-Karim al Maghili (died 1504). Concerned with everyday things, these questions were designed to elicit a programme of social reform. Al Maghili's replies—still well known among the Muslims of West Africa—suggest how strong were the puritanical threads that were early woven into Islam there. Needless to say, this severe puritanism of al Maghali's was not popular, and widely rejected.

course .... *Muwada'a* means that she is placed under the care of a trustworthy man until she menstruates ....

Now, what you mentioned about the free mixing of men and women and leaving the pudenda uncovered is one of the greatest abominations. The commander of the Muslims must exert himself to prevent all these things .... He should appoint trustworthy men to watch over this by day and night, in secret and in the open. This is not to be considered as spying on the Muslims; it is only a way of caring for them and curbing evildoers, especially when corruption becomes widespread in the land as it has done in Timbuktu and Djenne and so on.

The correct and binding thing is that every woman should be taken away from the place where suspicion may arise .... Anyone whom they [the watchers] see talking to a strange woman or entering her house or gazing at her should be seized and brought (to a judge) .... [And if no trustworthy man can be found to act as judge in such matters, nevertheless it will be better to appoint someone than merely neglect the evil ....] However, it is a current practice and State policy in many Muslim countries that, as from the time shortly after the evening prayer, the governor and his helpers patrol the township the whole night long. Anyone they come across in the street is thrown into prison and his case looked into the following day ....

From the translation (1963) by J. O. Hunwick of al Maghili's replies to Askia Muhammad. Mr. Hunwick has established the Arabic text from the two MSS deposited in the Library of the Institut Français de l'Afrique Noire, Dakar, and a manuscript in the Bibliotheque Nationale, Paris. See also Hunwick 1985.

AHMED IBN FARTUA

Kanem and Turkey

Rising obscurely before the tenth century but continuing long into later times, the Kanem-Bornu empire was the political and economic equivalent in the central Sudan of the great systems of Mali and Songhay further to the west. It had links with these but also with the Fezzan in the north, the Nile Valley in the east, and the peoples of the forest country in the south.

Mai (Sultan) Idris Alooma is remembered as one of Kanem's most successful sovereigns, the probable dates of his reign being 1571-1603. He made many expeditions against his eastern rivals, the Bulala kings, and became the most powerful ruler in the west-central Africa of his day. Memoirs of this ruler's life and achievements were written at the time by a man who served and knew him well, the Imam Ahmed ibn Fartua. What follows here is from H. R. Palmer's translation of a copy of Ibn Fartua's *Kanem War of Idris Alooma*. A copy of the latter was obtained by Heinrich Barth nearly 150 years ago, and sent by him to the British Museum.

. . . We travelled on the Saturday to Bari. The Sultan there gave the order that the troops were not to disperse before reaching Ruwaya . . . . On the next day all mounted after arraying themselves and their horses in armour, cuirasses, shields and their best apparel. When we had proceeded a short distance towards the west we met messengers of the king, the Lord of Stambul, the Sultan of Turkey, who had been sent to our Sultan . . . . They were drawn up in order of precedence near the town of Bursalim . . . .

The troops of our Sultan were drawn up on the west in rank after rank, leaving sufficient space between the ranks for the wheeling of a restive horse. Our troops charged towards them and they galloped their horses towards us. This continued for a long time until the infantry were tired with long standing. Then the Sultan went westwards and passed through Bursalim and on to Gatawa and then to the river in the neighborhood of Gambaru. He halted there on Friday. Our army rejoiced . . . .

O my wise friends and companions! Have you ever seen a king equal to our Sultan or like him at the time when the Lord of Stambul, the Sultan of Turkey, sent messengers to him from his country with favorable proposals . . . .

From H. R. Palmer, *Sudanese Memoirs* (Lagos: 1928), vol. 1.

KATI

Bound and Free in 1508

In 1590 a Spanish mercenary led a Moroccan army across the Sahara to the successful invasion in 1591 of the Songhay empire, then centered on the three notable cities of Gao, Timbuktu and Djenne, and brought to a close the grand epoch of medieval Muslim civilization in the Western Sudan. We are fortunate in having some remarkable testimonies of what that closing period was like.

"Here in Timbuktu," Leo Africanus had written eighty years before the Moroccan conquest, "there are great store of doctors, judges, priests and other learned men, bountifully maintained at the king's cost and charges. And hither are brought divers manuscripts or written books out of Barbary, which are sold for more money than any other merchandize." Of these scholars the best remembered was to be Ahmad Baba (page 29). But for the history of the Western Sudan in late and postmedieval times we have books by three other men. These cover the large span of 231 years, from 1519 to 1750, while the first two preserve many of the "founding legends" of Ghana and Mali as well as much material from other chronicles, both oral and written. They are the *Tarikh al-Fettash* of Mahmud Kati and one of his grandsons; the *Tarikh al-Sudan* of Abderrahman es-Sa'di; and the *Tedzkiret en-Nisian* of another but anonymous author of Timbuktu.

The first and perhaps most useful of these works came to European knowledge only in 1911 and 1912, when two somewhat dissimilar manuscript copies of it were obtained by French administrators at Timbuktu and Kayes. These established that the main author was a Soninke scholar, Mahmud Kati, who was born in 1468 and lived to the age of one hundred and twenty-five, an unlikely claim but somewhat sustained by evidence in the book itself. Kati belonged to the personal following of the great Songhay ruler, Askia Muhammad (who reigned from 1493 to 1529). He accompanied the Askia on pilgrimage to Mecca, and evidently began work on his book in 1519. His death came in 1593, three years after the Moroccan invasion, but a grandson later worked on his notes and on the notes of his children (scholars, as he had been) and brought the story down to 1665.

The *Tarikh al-Sudan* offers an eyewitness account of a somewhat shorter period but often in more personal detail, while it also adds to stories of the past that are touched on by the *Tarikh al-Fettash*. Its author, Abderrahman es-Sa'di, was born in Timbuktu in 1596, served in Djenne as a notary, became a *kateb* or government secretary, and embarked on a career of official diplomacy after 1629. His book has potted biographies of many scholars of the period, and carries its narrative down to 1655. A note of sadness runs throughout es-Sa'di's writing, for the whole of his life was overshadowed by the disasters of the Moroccan invasion and its consequences, disasters which he had witnessed as a child.

"I saw the ruin of learning and its utter collapse," he recalls: "and because learning is rich in beauty and fertile in its teaching, since it tells men of their fatherland, their ancestors, their annals, the names of their heroes and what lives these led, I asked divine help and decided to record all that I myself could gather on the subject of the Songhay princes of the Sudan, their adventures, their history, their achievements and their wars. Then I added the history of Timbuktu from the foundation of that city, of the princes who ruled there and the scholars and saints who lived there, and of other things besides . . . ." The great nineteenth-century traveller Heinrich Barth had the first European knowledge of this book.

The identity of the third author, who composed the *Tedzkiret en-Nisian*, remains unknown. He carried on the story of Songhay, but more especially of Timbuktu, from soon after the ending of the *Tarikh al-Sudan* until 1750, but limited himself to giving little more than the names and principal exploits of the postinvasion pashas of Timbuktu, of whom there were 156 in 160 years.

French translations of the Arabic texts were made by Octave Houdas and published in Paris in 1900 (*Tarikh al-Sudan*), 1901 (*Tedzkiret en-Nisian*), and 1913 (*Tarikh al-Fettash*). No complete English translations are available at the time of revising this present anthology, but Professor J. O. Hunwick was far advanced, in 1990, with an English version and annotated edition of the *Tarikh al-Sudan*. I have put these few extracts into this section, rather than a later one, because they seem to fit better here.

The *Tarikh al-Fettash* tells how in A.H. 913 the Songhay emperor, Askia Muhammad, made restitution to three poor scholars who had suffered persecution by Chi Ali, a ruler belonging to a previous and non-Muslim dynasty of whom Mahmud Kati and his fellow-scholars of Timbuktu vigorously disapproved. Having received servants and cattle from the Askia, these men asked for a safe-conduct for all the cities of the empire. Askia Muhammad agreed, "and at once gave order to his secretary to set into writing what he should now dictate." Kati's grandson, who completed this *tarikh*, notes that "I myself have seen this safe-conduct . . . . Worms had eaten several lines, and the paper was mutilated by holes at certain points. But here is what it said . . . ."

After commanding all whom it may concern to respect and protect the three scholars, the document continues with an illuminating picture of the social relations of the time. The "slaves" should be thought of as serfs or servants within the wageless labour context of those times, and not as chattel or plantation slaves.

We exempt them from all State taxes to the point that no person may demand anything of them, not even hospitality. If any accusation or claim be made against or upon them, none may return a judgment save I myself or those who shall succeed me in my functions. If any of my successors should oppress them or extort the least thing from them, may God refuse His blessing during his reign, may He trouble his empire and bring him to a sorry end . . . . I further authorize [these scholars] and their descendants to marry any woman they may wish throughout my empire, from the Kanta to the Sibiridugu [that is, from modern northeastern Nigeria to the region of Segu in modern Mali] where lies the frontier between my states and those of the emperor of Mali: children born of any such marriage shall be free and therefore their mothers also. We except from this the women of the Sorko and the Arbi: the women of these [castes] they may not marry, for these [and therefore their children] are our property. If any of [these scholars] should disobey this order, the child born of such a marriage shall be free by reason of its parentage, but the mother shall not be free; as for the mother, none shall have the right to treat her as a slave so long as she may live within that marriage, but she shall become our property again as soon as her husband should renounce her or should die.

* * * * * * * *

The Duty of Vassals

When Askia Muhammad became emperor of Songhay in 1493, Mahmud Kati explains, he inherited twenty-four tribes or castes of servile or vassal status. This passage is of particular interest to historians because of the light it throws on the social structures of the great states of the medieval Western Sudan. Broadly, who had to work for whom, and why? One answer has been that these structures between masters and servants were, as in Europe at that time or somewhat earlier, feudal in nature: the holder of a fief, granted to the holder by the monarch, came automatically into possession of the peasants inhabiting the fief.

But this comparison is unsatisfactory, for it masks the central difference that existed. European feudal powers rested on the fief-holders' title to ownership of the land in question, a condition which did not generally exist in Africa where land remained the possession of those who worked on it and lived from it. Yet we can see in this passage from Kati's book that a tight network of duties could still bind men and women to the service of powerful rulers. Kingship, here as elsewhere, meant more or less gross forms of exploitation. The medieval kingdoms of the Western Sudan, like their contemporaries in Europe, rested on the accumulation of wealth taken from the many for the profit and advancement of the few.

Three of these [vassal tribes] were from the pagan peoples of the Bambara . . . . Chi Baro [the Askia's predecessor] had inherited them from his father, who had in turn received them by inheritance . . . . These tribes had in fact become vassals of the king of Mali at a time when the latter was of great power, and after having themselves previously enjoyed authority over the king of Mali . . . . They became domestic serfs of the king of Mali . . . .

The fourth of these tribes was called Tyindiketa . . . . Their service . . . was to cut fodder for the horses . . . .

The fifth were that of the Zanj.* Each Zanj from the Kanta to the Sibiridugu owed a duty that was exacted every year at the time of low water on the river. It consisted in ten packets of dried fish for those who could provide it [or less for those who could not] . . . . And every time the prince was

*At that time a common Arabic name for Africans south of the Sahara. It applies here to the riverfolk of Songhay, the fishermen and boatmen of the Middle Niger.

asked for river transport, he provided it from the canoes of this tribe, together with a crew . . . .

The sixth tribe were called Arbi. They were the personal servants and escorts of the prince . . . .

As for the seventh, eighth, ninth, tenth and eleventh tribes, who were blacksmiths, they owed a duty of one hundred spears and one hundred arrows every year for each family of them . . . .

A Dwindling Power

Kankan Musa set forth [upon his pilgrimage to Mecca in 1324] with large forces, carrying large sums with him and being at the head of a numerous army. A *talib* [disciple] tells me that he heard from our master, the very learned *qadi* Abu'l-Abbas . . . that he [the *qadi*] had asked how many people and in what state the pasha Ali ben Abdelkader departed for Tuat on the outset of his [recent] pilgrimage to Mecca. They told him that the pasha had taken with him about eighty men-at-arms. Whereupon the *qadi*, having rendered praise to God, said: "Everything in this world is perishing. When Kankan Musa left here for the pilgrimage to Mecca [in 1324] he had eight thousand men with him. The Askia Muhammad, who made the pilgrimage later [in 1496], had no more than a tenth of that number, or eight hundred. And now Ali ben Abdelkader, who comes after them, has only eighty, the tenth part of eight hundred . . . ."

From Mahmud Kati, *Tarikh al-Fettash*, translated here from the French version of the Arabic text by O. Houdas and M. Delafosse (Paris: 1913).

ES-SA'DI

Djenne

Modern visitors to the Western Sudan, and to the modern republic of Mali, will find Djenne (or Jenne by a simplified and in my opinion more sensible spelling) a remote but charming little town on a branch of the Niger river upstream from Mopti. But Djenne in medieval times was a leading merchant city, linking the forest lands to the south with those of the savannahs and, by way of Timbuktu, with the caravans of the trans-Saharan trade. This was the flourishing Djenne celebrated in the *Tarikh al-Sudan*.

But archaeology in the 1970s was able to prove that this place, historically, has another large importance. Thanks to the work of R. J. and S. K. McIntosh, we can probe back into otherwise unrecorded times, the Early Iron Age in West Africa, when an older but vanished Djenne, or Jenne-Jeno in modern usage, developed as an important center of inter-regional trade, long before there was any great influence by trans-Saharan trade in the West African regions. With startling clarity, the McIntosh excavations portray the emergence of urban forms of civilization, here in sub-Saharan Africa, where no such development had been previously thought to have existed.

These excavations and their analysis "have demonstrated that Jenne-Jeno existed as early as 250 B.C., and was rapidly developing during the early centuries [of the Christian era] into a town measuring a half-kilometer or so along one axis. By A.D. 900 or 1000, it appears likely that Jenne-Jeno and neighboring Hambarketolo formed an urban unit covering more than 40 hectares . . . ." (from R. J. and S. K. McIntosh, "The Inland Niger Delta before the Empire of Mali," in *Journal of African History*, Cambridge University Press, 22 (1981), p. 19).

Meanwhile, for later Muslim times, we are fortunate in having es-Sa'di's graphic historical notes.

This city is large, flourishing and prosperous . . . one of the great markets of the Muslim world.   Here gather the merchants who being salt from the mines of Taghaza and those who bring gold from the mines of Bitou . . . . It is because of this fortunate city that the caravans flock to Timbuktu from all points of the horizon . . . .

Djenne is surrounded by a rampart which used to have eleven gates, but three have since been walled up . . . . The town was founded by pagans in the middle of the second century after the Flight of the Prophet [i.e., about 850] . . . . God has drawn to this fortunate city a certain number of learned and of pious men, strangers to the country, who have come to live here . . . .

From Abderrahman es-Sa'di, *Tarikh al-Sudan*, translated here from the French version of the Arabic text by O. Houdas and Edm. Benoist (Paris: 1900).

LEO AFRICANUS

The Book Trade at Timbuktu

Al-Hasan ben Muhammad al-Wazzan az-Zayyati by his real name, but baptized as Johannes Leo de Medicis (Giovanni Leone, Leo Africanus) after his capture by Christian pirates and conversion to Christianity, was the author of a valuable description of parts of the Western Sudan, notably along the lower reaches of the Middle Niger, drawn from personal travels as a merchant there early in the sixteenth century. Its Italian publication in 1550 (by Ramusio) aroused an interest in Western Europe somewhat comparable with Columbus' news of land beyond the Atlantic, and rapidly became the equivalent in those days of a modern bestseller. No one in Europe hitherto had written so extensively and accessibly of Africa's "mysterious interior."

There are in Timbuktu numerous judges, doctors [of letters] and priests [i.e., learned Muslims]. (The ruler) greatly honors scholarship. Here too they sell many hand-written books that arrive from Barbàry [i.e., North Africa]. More profit is had from their sale than from any other merchandise.

In place of minted money, they use bits of pure gold and, for small purchases, cowrie-shells: shells, that is, imported from Persia which exchange at 400 for a ducat. [Not, in fact, from Persia but from the Maldive Islands in the Indian Ocean; a ducat in Leo's account was the *mitqal* of the North and West African long-distance trade, and weighed four grams 238. B.D.]

From Jean-Léon l'Africain, *Description de l'Afrique*, translated here from the excellent modern French edition by A. Epaulard (Paris: 1956, 2 vols), vol. 2, p. 468.

EGHAREVBA

The Empire of Benin

Like other states in early medieval West Africa, the "forest belt" empire of Benin emerged from the economic and social changes which Iron Age development brought in its train. Benin's earliest beginnings are purely legendary but there is likely to be a core of truth in the legends, for they indicate a probable development as well as a powerful if vague memory of such events. This memory comprises a tradition, an oral history, which goes back more than a thousand years.

Chief Jacob Egharevba, curator of the Benin Museum and a member of the Royal Society of the House of Iwebo, began collecting Benin traditions more than sixty years ago. His *Short History* was published in 1934. Subsequent editions of this indispensable work bear witness to its value. In a foreword to a recent edition, the third (of 1960), Dr. R. E. Bradbury comments on the scholarship and authority of Egharevba's book. "To take one example," Bradbury writes, "it is now extremely difficult to calculate the dates of past *Obas* [rulers of Benin] from sources independent of Chief Egharevba's work, which is relied upon as much in Benin as elsewhere. Nevertheless, his approximate date for the accession of *Oba* Eresoyen has recently been virtually confirmed from Dutch sources which record that an *Oba* died in 1734 or 1735"—the latter being the date which Egharevba gave in 1934. Dr. A. F. C. Ryder is of the same opinion. "Continuing research," he has written,* "will inevitably lead to modifications in any synthesis of oral and documentary material, but this book will retain a permanent value as the major record of Benin traditional history."

Recent scholarship, however, generally rejects the view that Yoruba culture originated outside the limits of the Yoruba homeland in what is modern Nigeria.

Origins

Many, many years ago, the Binis came all the way from Egypt to found a more secure shelter in this part of the world after a short stay in the Sudan and at Ile-Ife, which the Benin people call Uhe. Before coming here, a band of hunters was sent from Ife to inspect this land and the report furnished was very favorable. Tradition says that they met some people who were in the land before their arrival. These people are said to have come from the Sudan originally.

*In the *Journal* of the Historical Society of Nigeria, Dec. 1961, p. 288.

For over a century the management of the affairs of the country was carried out under different leaders. The Empire of the first period or dynasty was founded about A.D. 900. The rulers or kings were commonly known as *Ogiso* before the arrival of Odudua and his party at Ife in Yorubaland, about the twelfth century of the Christian era.

Ultimately, one of the prominent leaders, Igodo, was made *Ogiso* or king. Igodo, the first *Ogiso*, wielded much influence and gained popularity as a good ruler. He died after a long reign and was succeeded by Ere, his eldest son.

Legend and Fact

It is said that thirty-one *Ogisos* reigned but very few of their names are known and they are very hard to trace out. Therefore it is wise to make some research into it because some people doubt the existence of the first period of the Benin Empire [up to about A.D. 1200]. This is partly because many mythical and frightful tales have been attached to the people connected with the *Ogisos*. Whereas, in fact, these people were human beings, ruled by their *Ogisos* in the same way as we have been ruled by our *Obas* from Oranmiyan onwards in the second period of the Benin Empire.

A Ruler from Ife

It was some years after Evian's victory over Osogan [traditionally, sometime before 1170] that Owodo was banished for misrule by the angry people, who then appointed Evian as administrator of the government of the country because of his past services to the people. When Evian was stricken by old age he nominated his eldest son, Ogiamwen, as his successor, but the people refused him. They said he was not the *Ogiso* and they could not accept his son as his successor because, as he himself knew, it had been arranged to set up a republican form of government. This he was now selfishly trying to alter.

While this was still in dispute the people indignantly sent an ambassador to the *Oni* Odudua, the great and wisest ruler of Ife, asking him to send one of his sons to be their ruler. For things were getting from bad to worse and the people saw that there was need for a capable ruler.

In order to test the ability of the Binins to look after his son, Odudua first of all sent seven lice to the Benin chiefs to be cared for and returned after three years. This condition was fulfilled and Odudua was greatly surprised to see the lice in increased sizes when they were sent back to him by the chiefs. He exclaimed that "the people who can take care of such minute pests as lice can undoubtedly take care of my son."

A Discontented Prince

Before he could send his son to Benin, Odudua died, but he left strong orders to his son and successor, Obalufon, that Oranmiyan should be sent there. So Prince Oranmiyan, one of the sons of Odudua of Ife, the father and progenitor of the Yoruba *Obas*, was sent, accompanied by courtiers, including Ogiefa, a native doctor, and he succeeded in reaching the city after much trouble at Ovia River with the ferryman. [The traditional date for the beginning of Oranmiyan's reign, according to Egharevba, is A.D. 1170.]

Ogiamwen, the son and successor of Evian, was much opposed to his coming. He gave it as his reason that it was too difficult to serve a king—"Ogie mianmwen na ga," hence his name Ogiamwen. But as the need for a proper *Oba* was felt to be so great by the inhabitants, no heed was paid to his advice.

Prince Oranmiyan took up his abode in the palace built for him at Usama by the elders (now a coronation shrine). Soon after his arrival he married a beautiful lady, Erinmwinde, daughter of Osanego, the ninth *Onogie* of Ego, by whom he had a son. After some years residence here he called a meeting of the people and renounced his office remarking that the country was a land of vexation, "Ile-Ibinu," (by which name the country was afterwards known) and that only a child born, trained and educated in the arts and mysteries of the land could reign over the people. He caused his son born to him by Erinmwinde to be made *Oba* in his place, and returned to his native land, Ife, leaving Ogiefa, Ihama, Oloton and others at Benin in charge of his son . . . .

On his way back to Ife Oranmiyan halted at Ugha, now Okha, in the northwest of Benin Division where the Binis went to him for decisions in their matters for a period of three years . . . .

Oranmiyan also halted at Obbah and remained there for over two years before leaving for Ife finally. He did this in order to allow some time for the growth of his son, Eweka I, before going to Ife, so that he might not be sent back to Benin by the then *Oni* of Ife, or, as the Bini say, Oghene n'Uhe. After staying about three years in Ife, he left for Oyo where he also left a son behind on leaving the place, and this son ultimately became the first *Alafin* of the present line, while Oranmiyan himself was reigning as the *Oni* of Ife. Therefore, Prince Oranmiyan of Ife, the father of Eweka I, the *Oba* of Benin, was also the father of the first *Alafin* of Oyo.

Brass-Casting

Oba Oguola wished to introduce brass-casting into Benin so as to produce works of art similar to those sent him from Ife. He therefore sent to the *Oni* of Ife for a brass-smith and Iguegha was sent to him. Iguegha was very clever and left many designs to his successors, and was in consequence deified, and is worshipped to this day by brass-smiths. The practice of making brass-castings for the preservation of the records of events was originated during the reign of Oguola. He lived to a very old age.

[The bronzes of Benin are more properly called brasses. While *Oba* Oguola's traditional date is about A.D. 1280 (for the beginning of his reign), there is some reason to believe that the introduction of brass-casting to Benin came from Ife at a later date than Egharevba's account suggests, and perhaps not before about 1400. B.D.]

Ewuare the Great

After the murder of Uwaifiokun, Ogun was crowned the *Oba* of Benin with the title Ewuare (Oworuare) meaning "It is cool" or "The trouble has ceased." [His reign traditionally began in about A.D. 1440.] Prior to his accession he caused a great conflagration in the city which lasted two days and nights as a revenge for his banishment.

Ewuare was a great magician, physician, traveller and warrior. He was also powerful, courageous and sagacious. He fought against and captured 201 towns and villages in Ekiti, Ikare, Kukuruku, Eka and the Ibo country on this side of the river Niger. He took their petty rulers captive and caused the people to pay tribute to him.

He made good roads in Benin City and especially the streets known as Akpakpava and Utantan. In fact the town rose to importance and gained the name "city" during his reign . . . .

Ewuare was the first *Oba* of Benin to come into contact with Europeans, for Ruy de Sigueira visited the Benin area in 1472 . . . .

Guns and Coconuts

A Portuguese explorer named John Affonso d'Aveiro visited Benin City for the first time in 1485-1486. He introduced guns and coconuts into this country.

Missionaries

It is said that John Affonso d'Aveiro came to Benin City for the second time during this reign. [That of *Oba* Esigie, beginning in A.D. 1504.] He advised the *Oba* to become a Christian, and said that Christianity would make his country better. Esigie therefore sent Ohen-okun, the Olokun priest at Ughoton, with him, as an Ambassador to the king of Portugal, asking him to send priests who would teach him and his people the faith. In reply the king of Portugal sent Roman Catholic missionaries and many rich presents, such as a copper stool (*erhe*), coral beads and a big umbrella, with an entreaty that Esigie should embrace the faith. At the same time he also gave presents to the Ambassador and his wife. The king of Portugal also sent some Portuguese traders who established trading factories at Ughoton, the old port of Benin. They traded in ivory, Benin cloths, pepper and other commodities in the king of Portugal's interest. Owing to the unhealthy state of the country their commerce soon ceased.

But John Affonso d'Aveiro with the other missionaries remained in Benin to carry on the mission work, and churches were built at Ogbelaka, Idumwerie and Akpakpava (Ikpoba Road), the last named being the "Holy Cross Cathedral." The residence of the Fathers was situated between the present Roman Catholic School and John Holt's Store. They had another at Idunmwu-Ebo, and the missionary cemetery was where the Government School now stands. The work of the Mission made progress and thousands of people were baptized before the death of the great explorer John Affonso d'Aveiro, who was buried with great lamentations by the *Oba* and the Christians of Benin City.

The missionaries went with Esigie to the Idah war which took place in 1515-1516. [A Portuguese account of life in Benin at this time appears on p. 218.]

From J. V. Egharevba, *A Short History of Benin* (3rd ed., Ibadan: 1960).

Early East Africa

*M*ANY HUNDRED YEARS SEPARATE the *Periplus of the Ery-thraean Sea* (pp. 24-26) from the next eyewitness report on East Africa. With the tenth century these eastern harbors and commercial settlements were growing into wealthy towns, links in the whole great network of Indian Ocean trade, to which they sold ivory and gold. To some of these towns there travelled early in the tenth century an Arab scholar, resident in Cairo, who would be afterwards remembered as one of the outstanding geographers of medieval times. Unfortunately, few of al Mas'udi's works have survived, the best of the these being the early sections of an otherwise vanished historical encyclopedia, *Muruj al-Dhabab*, the "Meadows of Gold," which have a reference to the East African coast, disappointingly short on detail but nonetheless of capital importance. The next long account of East African trade and development is in Idrisi's *Kitab Rujar*, still incompletely published, ill translated into French and little into English, but valuable as a secondary source.

Archeology has made startling finds along the East African seaboard, notably in Tanzania, such as the palace of Husuni Kubwa—Great Husuni—uncovered by Neville Chittick in 1961. But little in this field is more convincing of the breadth and antiquity of this East African coastal civilization of the Swahili than its surviving coins. An extract from Freeman-Grenville's analysis of these will be found below.

China's "discovery of Africa," as Duyvendak called it, merits a little chapter of its own, not because the Chinese records are copious or even very useful—in fact, they are disappointingly meagre—but because they too demonstrate the scope and variety of contacts that were enjoyed by Swahili civilization through a long period of time. China had participated in the Indian Ocean trade since remote antiquity, being generally far ahead of any other country in the development of sailing-ship and navigational technology at least until the fifteenth century. Documentary evidence of this refers back to the Early Han Dynasty (202 B.C. to 8 B.C.), although many of the texts are tantalizingly vague in their identification of the countries which they mention. Thus the *Ch'ien-han-shu*, "an extremely curious notice," in Duyvendak's words, about maritime trade in Early Han times, notes that the country of Tuyuan is five months' sailing beyond Jihnan, which was Upper Annam (modern Vietnam). "Going again by boat about four months, there is the country of Yi-lu-mo. Going by land about ten days, there is the country of Fu-kan-tu-lu." Two months' beyond again, there was Huang-chih; and from Huang-chih the Emperor P'ing (A.D. 1-6) received an envoy who brought a rhinoceros as a present.

How far west were these countries reached by traders and envoys from Peking some two thousand years ago, even if with trans-shipment from one vessel to another? Some scholars think that Han trade reached the Red Sea (just as it certainly went overland to Rome), and certain Meroitic styles of metalware seem to confirm this. But there is apparently no known Chinese document about East Africa until the *Hsin T'ang-shu* of 1060. This contains an extract from a still earlier work, the *Yu-yang-tsa-tsu*, written in 863 (at a time, we may note, when Arab traders were well established at Canton); the full text was published only in the seventeenth century. The *Hsin T'ang-shu* also mentions an East African coastal city called Malin, which has been thought to be Malindi (Kenya coast). Then comes the most instructive of all the old Chinese texts on Africa, being part of the *Chu-fan-chi* of Chao Ju-kua (Zhao Rugua in modern orthography), a foreign-trade commissioner of Ch'uan-chou in Fukien, who completed his book in 1225. Lastly, early in the fifteenth century, there were the voyages of the Ming admiral Zheng He (or Chang Lo in older orthography), some of whose many ships reached Mogadishu and Brava (Somali coastline) in 1418 and 1432; the records of these voyages have survived, however, only in the briefest form.

None of the East African city-states was more successful than Kilwa. With its handsome capital on Kilwa Kisiwani (Kilwa Island on the southern coast of Tanzania), this thrusting commercial polity, a true if much lesser Venice of the South in its political influence, international connections and comfortable wealth, was strongly in control of gold exports from southern Africa between the thirteenth and sixteenth centuries. Two traditional histories have outlived Kilwa's ruin, one in an Arabic text and the other in Kiswahili. According to the first of these (written by a native of Kilwa in about 1520 and surviving in a manuscript copy given to Sir John Kirk by the Sultan of Zanzibar in 1872), the founders of Kilwa were sailors from the Persian Gulf. These Persian or Shirazi ancestors have remained in popular memory, although it is clear enough that the culture of Kilwa, as of its sister ports and cities along the coast, was African (though Muslim) from an early date, and that the Swahili, local Bantu-speaking people, were dominant in them. Indeed, the other traditional history (collected by Velten and published, with four other such chronicles, in *Prosa und Poesie der Suaheli*, Berlin 1907) begins by explaining that the founder of Kilwa, a certain Shirazi (or Persian) called Sultan Ali ben Selimani, married the daughter of the ruling African chief on Kilwa Island, and that the son of this marriage—thus already half-Swahili—was Kilwa's second ruler. The historical truths behind these traditions are still subject to discussion. But the overwhelming balance of modern judgement gives the East African coastland as the place where Swahili culture first took shape; and origins in the Persian Gulf are increasingly rejected.

AL MAS'UDI

The Country of the Zanj

Abdul Hassan ibn Ali al Mas'udi was born of a Hejazi family of Bagdad towards the end of the ninth century and died in Fostat (Old Cairo) in 956 or 957. He wrote many works of erudition of which few have survived; among these, fortunately, is his *Muruj al-Dhabab wa Ma'adin al-Jawhar*, "Meadows of Gold and Mines of Gems," which includes an account of the East African seaboard based at least in part on Mas'udi's own experiences there. Apart from the first short paragraph (which I have taken from Sprenger's English translation of part of the Arabic text, London, 1841), what follows is translated from volume three of the French version entitled *Les Prairies d'Or*, Paris, 1864, nine volumes, by C. Barbier de Meynard and Pavet de Courteille. This work has been reissued in a two-volume edition with new readings by C. Pellat (Paris, 1962 and 1965); but I have allowed the following translations to stand.

When al Mas'udi speaks of the Zanj he means the coastal peoples of East Africa from the Horn to Mozambique. The Island of Kanbalu is sometimes identified with Madagascar, but was more probably one of the smaller and more northerly islands, possibly Pemba. Yet what the report lacks in geographical precision it more than makes up in other detail. Here, most clearly, we find a picture of traditional African society at a period when the central-southern Iron Age was approaching its major period of state-forming maturity.

Various explanations have been given for the title of their kings, *Waklimi*: the most convincing, perhaps, is that of Freeman-Grenville (*Medieval History of the Coast of Tanganyika*, London, 1961, p. 40), who says that this word "appears to be a corruption of the texts for the Swahili *mfalme*, a king, *wafalme*, kings." This would not necessarily mean, of course, that "the Zanj of the Waklimi" were Swahili, although they almost certainly were, but it would in any case mean they were Bantu-speaking people.

The sailors of Oman . . . go on the sea of the Zanj as far as the island of Kanbalu and the Sofalah of the Demdemah, which is on the extremity of the country of the Zanj and the low countries thereabout. The merchants of Siraf are also in the habit of sailing on this sea. I have made a voyage on it from Sohar, which is the capital of Oman, with a crew of Sirafians . . . . And in A.H. 304 [allowing for the shorter Muslim year, this was A.D. 916] I made a voyage from the island of Kanbalu to Oman . . . .

The sea of Zanj reaches down to the country of Sofala and of the Wak-Wak which produces gold in abundance and other marvels; its climate is warm and its soil fertile. It is there that the Zanj built their capital; then they elected a king whom they called *Waklimi*. This name . . . has always been that of their sovereigns. The *Waklimi* has under him all the other Zanj kings, and commands three hundred thousand men. [The Pellat version prints "?" on this number, which is indeed incredible.] The Zanj use the ox as a beast of burden, for their country has no horses or mules or camels and they do not even know these animals. Snow and hail are unknown to them as to all the Abyssinians [black people]. Some of their tribes have sharpened teeth and are cannibals. The territory of the Zanj begins at the canal which flows from the Upper Nile and goes down as far as the country of Sofala and the Wak-Wak. Their settlements extend over an area of about seven hundred parasangs in length and in breadth; this country is divided by valleys, mountains and stony deserts; it abounds in wild elephants but there is not so much as a single tame elephant.

Although constantly employed in hunting elephants and gathering ivory, the Zanj make no use of ivory for their own domestic purposes. They wear iron instead of gold and silver . . . .

To come back to the Zanj and their kings, the name of the kings of the country is *Waklimi* which means supreme lord; they give this title to their sovereign because he had been chosen to govern them with equity. But once he becomes tyrannical and departs from the rules of justice, they cause him to die and exclude his posterity from succession to the throne, for they claim that in thus conducting himself he ceases to be the son of the Master, that is to say of the king of heaven and earth. They call God by the name of Maklandjalu, which means supreme Master . . . .

The Zanj speak elegantly, and they have orators in their own language. Often a devout man of the country, pausing in the midst of a numerous crowd, addresses to his listeners an exhortation in which he invites them to serve God and submit to His orders. He points out the punishments which disobedience must entail, and recalls the example of their ancestors and their ancient kings. These peoples have no code of religion; their kings follow custom, and conform in their government to a few political rules. The Zanj eat bananas, which are as abundant with them as in India, but the basis of their food is *dorrah*, a plant called *kalari* which they take from the ground like a truffle, and the *elecampane* root . . . . They also have honey and meat. Each worships what he pleases, a plant, an animal, a mineral. They possess a great number of islands where the coconut grows, a fruit that is eaten by all the peoples of the Zanj. One of the islands, placed one or two days' journey from the coast, has a Muslim population who provide the royal family; it is the island of Kanbalu . . . .

The Ivory Trade

[Tusks from the country of the Zanj] go generally to Oman, and from there are sent on to China and India. That is the route they follow, and were it otherwise, ivory would be very abundant in Muslim countries. In China the kings and their military and civilian officers use carrying-chairs of ivory; no official or person of rank would dare to visit the king in an iron chair, and ivory alone is used for this purpose . . . . Ivory is much prized in India: there it is made into handles for the daggers known as *harari*, or *harri* in the singular, as well as for the hilts of curved swords . . . . But the biggest use of ivory is in the manufacture of chessmen and other gaming pieces . . . .

FREEMAN-GRENVILLE

The Ivory Trade: A Modern View

As far back as the time of the *Periplus* [*of the Erythraean Sea*, second century] the main export [of the East African coast] was ivory, and this merits some digression. Only the "soft" ivory of East Africa can be used for the making of bangles. These have a special ritual significance in the marriage rites of Hindus, and cannot be made from the tusks of the Indian elephant since they are too narrow in gauge. Once used, no other person may wear these bangles, and they are invariably cremated with the married woman who has employed them. Even today [1960] India imports half of the world's supply of ivory, and of this no less than half is employed in the making of bangles for Hindu brides. To the extent of this trade, even further afield as far as China, not only the *Periplus*, but also al Mas'udi bear witness and there can be no doubt that this was the fundamental reason for the continued Arab interest in East Africa, since the Southern Arabs from time immemorial had dominated the carrying trade of the western and northern parts of the Indian Ocean. There were, of course, other articles of commerce, gold, tortoiseshell and slaves, although of the latter literary references are scarce indeed in the Middle Ages. If there were East African slaves in India in the fifteenth century, it is improbable that there were many elsewhere in the Islamic world, since there were other and ample sources, especially in Caucasia and Western Asia, from which they might be derived.

From G. S. P. Freeman-Grenville, "Islam and Christianity in East Africa Before the Mid-nineteenth Century," in *African Ecclesiastical Review*, July 1960.

IDRISI

The Export of Iron

Abu Abdullah Muhammad al Idrisi (1100-1166) was a Moroccan Muslim scholar who lived at Palermo as a member of the court of a Norman king of Sicily, Roger II. There he devoted himself to collecting information about the whole known world, drawing on other writers and using informants who travelled at his royal patron's expense. His *Kitab Rujar* (Book of Roger), or *Nuzhat al-Mushtaq fi Ikhtiraq al-Afaq*, "the recreation of him who yearns to travel the lands," as Freeman-Grenville has translated this title, was completed in 1154. This long work was accompanied by many maps. One of the omissions of later scholarship is to have failed to produce a full and reliable edition and translation. Four copies of the manuscript are known to exist, two in Paris and two in Oxford, with possibly a fifth in Istanbul; while an Arabic abridgement was published in Rome in 1592 and again in Latin in Paris in 1619. Several translations exist in French, none of them satisfactory; the brief passage I have reproduced here is from the French of P. A. Jaubert, *La Geographie d'Edrisi*, Paris, 1836, 2 vols., p. 65, but no great reliance can be placed on its accuracy of detail. S. Maqbul Ahmad has an important fragment translated reliably into English under the title of *India and the Neighbouring Territories* (Leiden, 1960).

The inhabitants [of the coastal land of Sofala in modern Mozambique] are poor and wretched, and have no other means of livelihood than ironworking. There are, in fact, a great number of iron mines in the mountains of Sofala. The people of the Zanedj Islands and other neighbouring islands [i.e., in Indonesia] come here for iron, which they carry to the continent and islands of India, where they sell it at a good price, for it is a material of great trade and consumption in India . . . .

FREEMAN-GRENVILLE

Money Talks

During the 1950s Freeman-Grenville and others (following in the steps of Walker at the British Museum, who had led the way in 1936) began systematic work on the many coins of various periods which had turned up along the East African seaboard. Much new light has thus been shed on the economy of the Coast. It is now certain that Kilwa and Zanzibar had mints of their own, the former at least from the late thirteenth century, and probable that Mogadishu also had one. About seven thousand coins of the Kilwa sultans were known by the 1950s, about four thousand of the Zanzibar sultans, and about seven thousand from Mogadishu. More have since been found.

Up to April 1959 a total of some 19,600 coins had been examined. They go back in date, as the following analysis (G. S. P. Freeman-Grenville, *Journal of African History*, 1, 1960) clearly shows, to Ptolemaic times in Egypt.

Native East African coins were thought until 1985 to have begun to be issued in the late thirteenth century at Kilwa; they greatly help in fixing of a Kilwa "king list." At the same time they were disappointing in being solely of copper (although Kilwa had much gold available for export), and in bearing neither dates nor values. Another oddity of the known coins is that although they include several hundred Chinese pieces, there are only seven from Portugal and all of copper. The following list refers only to foreign coins of ancient and medieval times, and illustrates the scope and breadth of the old East African connection.

In 1985, however, the archaeologists Mark Horton and Catherine Clark, excavating on the island of Pemba, or more exactly on its neighbouring islet of Mtambwe Mkuu, made the truly sensational find of a hoard of more than 2000 silver coins, "found on the lowland strip close to the beach." Hitherto no more than a handful of East African silver coins were known, having been mostly found on Mafia island further to the south. Horton and Clark were able to establish that their copious find had been minted in East Africa; they identified the names of rulers on the coins; and they were confident that these coins had been minted somewhat before A.D. 1100. Eight gold coins were similarly found, while local villagers volunteered four more; all these gold coins were Arab or Fatimid with dates ranging between A.D. 810 and 1066. It thus appeared that this East African trading civilization had become a coin-using society much earlier than had previously been thought.

	Kilwa	Mafia	Zanzi-bar	Pemba	Kenya	Soma-lia	TOTAL
Hellenistic (3rd to 1st centuries B.C.)	—	1	—	2	—	22	25
Parthian (1st to 2nd centuries after Christ)	—	—	3*	—	—	—	3
Sassanian (3rd century)	—	—	2	—	—	—	2
Roman	—	—	—	2	1	6	9
Byzantine	—	—	—	2	—	46	48
Ummayad	—	—	—	2	—	—	2
'Abbasid	—	—	—	7	—	1	8
Saljuq	—	—	—	1	—	—	1
Mamluk	2	—	—	4	—	6	12
Mongol	2	4	—	1	—	—	7

	Kilwa	Mafia	Zanzi- bar	Pemb a	Kenya	Soma- lia	TOTAL
Other foreign Muslim (un- identified)	—	20	3	15	—	—	38
Chinese:							
T'ang Dyn.	—	—	4	—	—	1	5
Sung Dyn.	—	9	185	—	2	16	212
Ming Dyn.	—	—	—	—	—	6	6
Ching Dyn.	—	—	—	—	—	10	10
Ceylon	—	—	—	—	—	4	4
Annam	—	—	—	—	—	4	4
S. India (13th century)	—	—	—	—	—	1	1
India (Bahmanid)	—	—	—	—	—	1	1

*possibly Dar es-Salaam.

YU-YANG-TSA-TSU

The Blood-Drinkers

(A.D. 863) The country of Po-pa-li [generally agreed to be Berbera in the Horn of Africa] is in the south-western sea. [The people] do not eat any of the five grains but eat only meat. They often stick a needle into the veins of cattle and draw blood, which they drink raw, mixed with milk .... From olden times on they were not subject to any foreign country. In fighting they use elephants' tusks and ribs and the horns of wild buffaloes as lances, and they wear cuirasses and bows and arrows. They have twenty myriads of foot soldiers. The Arabs make frequent raids on them.

From J. J. L. Duyvendak, *China's Discovery of Africa* (London: 1949).

CHAO JU-KUA (ZHAO RUGUA)

Slaves from Madagascar

(A.D. 1225) [In the west] there is an island in the sea on which there are many savages. Their bodies are black as lacquer and they have frizzled hair. They are enticed by [offers of] food and then captured (and sold) as slaves to the Arabic countries, where they fetch a very high price. They are employed as gate-keepers, and it is said that they have no longing for their kinsfolk.

Early Zanzibar

The Tsong-po [Zanj-ba, Zanzibar] country is on an island in the sea south of Hu-cha-la [Gujerat in western India]. To the west it reaches to a great mountain.

The inhabitants are of Ta-shi [Arab] stock and follow the Ta-shi religion. They wrap themselves in blue foreign cotton stuffs and wear red leather shoes. Their daily food consists of meal, baked cakes, and mutton.

There are many villages, and a succession of wooded hills and terraced rocks.

The climate is warm, and there is no cold season.

The products of the country consist of elephants' tusks, native gold, ambergris and yellow sandalwood.

Every year Hu-cha-la and the Ta-shi localities along the seacoast send ships to this country with white cotton cloth, porcelain, copper and red cotton to trade.

From Chao Ju-kua, *Chu-fan-chi*, trans. F. Hirth and W. W. Rockhill (St. Petersburg: 1911). The identification with Madagascar of the island in the first of these two extracts has not, so far as I know, been questioned.

CHANG HSIEH

Advice to Traders

Coming into contact with barbarian peoples, you have nothing more to fear than touching the left horn of a snail. The only things one should be really anxious about are the means of mastery of the waves of the sea—and, worst of all dangers, the minds of those avid for profit and greedy of gain.

From Chang Hsieh, *Tung Hsi Yang Khao* (1618), translated by J. Needham in *Science and Civilisation in China* (Cambridge), vol. 6, 1963.

KILWA CHRONICLE

Emergence of Kilwa

Historians have said, amongst their assertions, that the first man to come to Kilwa came in the following way. There

arrived a ship in which there were people who claimed to
have come from Shiraz in the land of the Persians. It is said
there were seven ships: the first stopped at Mandakha; the
second at Shaugu; the third at a town called Yanbu; the
fourth at Mombasa; the fifth at the Green Island (Pemba);
the sixth at the land of Kilwa; and the seventh at Hanzuan.
They say that all the masters of these (first) six ships were
brothers, and that the one who went to the town of Hanzuan
was their father. God alone knows all the truth!

From the translation by G. S. P. Freeman-Grenville, *East
African Coast, Select Documents* (London: 1962), p. 35.

IBN BATTUTA

Kilwa in 1331

Then I set off by sea from the town of Mogadishu for
the land of the Swahili and the town of Kilwa, which is in the
land of the Zanj. We arrived at Mombasa, a large island two
days' journey from the land of the Swahili. The island is
quite separate from the mainland. It grows bananas, lemons,
and oranges. The people also gather a fruit which they call
jammun (Eugenia jambu) which looks like an olive. It has a
nut like an olive, but its taste is very sweet. The people do
not engage in agriculture, but import grain from the Swahili.
The greater part of their diet is bananas and fish. They
follow the Shafi'i rite, and are devout, chaste, and virtuous.

Their mosques are very strongly constructed of wood.
Beside the door of each mosque are one or two wells, one
or two cubits deep. They draw water from them with a

wooden vessel which is fixed on to the end of a thin stick, a cubit long. The earth round the mosque and the well is stamped flat . . . .

We spent a night on the island [of Mombasa] and then set sail for Kilwa, the principal town on the coast, the greater part of whose inhabitants are Zanj of very black complexion. Their faces are scarred, like the Limiin of Janada. A merchant told me that Sofala is half a month's march from Kilwa, and that between Sofala and Yufi in the country of the Limiin is a month's march. Powdered gold is brought from Yufi to Sofala.

Kilwa is one of the most beautiful and well-constructed towns in the world. The whole of it is elegantly built.* The roofs are built with mangrove poles. There is very much rain. The people are engaged in a holy war, for their country lies beside that of pagan Zanj. The chief qualities are devotion and piety: they follow the Shafi'i rite.

From the translation of the Arabic text by G. S. P. Freeman-Grenville in *East African Coast, Select Documents* (London: 1962), p. 31.

---

*The MS apparently has "built entirely of wood" but this statement, as Freeman-Grenville says, cannot be correct; he accordingly offers an alternative reading. Similarly, two paragraphs earlier, the statement that Kilwa's mosques were made of wood conflicts with the fourteenth century archaeological evidence, which shows beyond doubt that at least the principal mosques were built of stone: that is, of *porites* coral, save for doors and other furniture.

MEDIEVAL ETHIOPIA

A Strong Ruler

The Chronicle of the Emperor Zara Yaqob (1434-1468), from which the following is taken, was written some fifty years after that ruler's death. It offers a glimpse of the vivid pictures of contemporary or almost-contemporary life to be found in these old Ethiopian chronicles.

In the reign of our king Zara Yaqob, there was great terror and great fear in all the people of Ethiopia, on account of the severity of his justice and of his authoritarian rule and above all because of the denunciations of those who, after having confessed that they had worshipped Dasak and the devil, caused to perish many innocent people by accusing them falsely of having worshipped thus together with them . . . .

A certain Zara Seyon, nicknamed Zara Saytan, who by his false accusations had caused the death of a large number of monks, canons and men and women, was, when God revealed his crimes, forced to become a monk and exiled to Hayq.

The office of Aqbe Saat [a court official] was then conferred on Amha Seyon, who was greatly esteemed by our king . . . . The offices of Beit Wiedad of the right and of the left [court officials] were at that time vacant at the palace. The king conferred them on two of his daughters . . . .

The king placed at the head of each province one of his sisters, entrusted with administering the district in his name . . . . Later, the king himself took in hand the government of the whole of Ethiopia . . . . All the peoples trembled before the undaunted might of the king . . . .

When our king Zara Yaqob went into the district of Axum to fulfill the law and the rite of coronation according to the rites followed by his ancestors . . . all of the inhabitants, as well as the priests, went to meet him and welcomed him with a great rejoicing . . . . When he entered within the gates of the town, the king had on his right hand and on his left the governor of Tigre and the administrator of Axum who carried and waved according to custom, olive branches . . . . After arriving within the walls of Axum, the king had brought to him much gold which he scattered as far as the city gate on the carpets which were spread along his route. This amount of gold was more than a hundred ounces; as for more, I do not know whether it was thirty or forty ounces . . . . During his stay at Axum, our king regulated all the institutions of the Church and prescribed to be recited each day, at canonical hours, prayers which up to that time had been neglected . . . .

During the reign of our king Zara Yaqob, there was in the whole land of Ethiopia a great peace and a great tranquility, for the king taught justice and faith . . . .

From the translation in *The Ethiopian Observer*, 2, vol. 5, 1960.

KILWA CHRONICLE

Vasco da Gama

During al-Fudail's reign there came news from the land of Mozambique that men had come from the land of the Franks [in fact, from Portugal]. They had three ships, and the name of their captain was al-Mirate [Admiral Vasco da Gama]. After a few days there came word that the ships had passed Kilwa and had gone on to Mafia [an adjoining island to the northward]. The lord of Mafia rejoiced, for they thought they [the Franks] were good and honest men. But those who knew the truth confirmed that they were corrupt and dishonest persons who had only come to spy out the land in order to seize it. And they determined to cut the anchors of their ships so that they should drift ashore and be wrecked by the Muslims. The Franks learnt of this and went on to Malindi [a trading city on the Kenya coast]. When the people of Malindi saw them, they knew they were bringers of war and corruption, and were troubled with very great fear. They gave them [the Franks] all they asked, water, food, firewood, and everything else. And the Franks asked for a pilot to guide them to India, and after that back to their own land—God curse it!

From the translation of G. S. P. Freeman-Grenville, *The East African Coast, Select Documents* (London: 1962), p. 47.

PATE CHRONICLE

Seafaring

Pate Island occupied much the same position of preeminence along the northern reach of the Swahili coast as Kilwa along the southern. Local tradition preserved in the Swahili Chronicle of Pate asserts, indeed, that Kilwa was subject to it for a time early in the sixteenth century. Having made alliance with Malindi and overawed Mombasa, "the Pate people passed overland and fought the whole of the Mrima coast [as far as Kilwa and beyond]." The original text of this useful work, which begins its story as long ago as 1204, is said to have perished in the bombardment of Witu in 1890; but several versions have survived. A helpful discussion on these texts is in A. H. J. Prins, "On Swahili Historiography," *Journal of the East African Swahili Committee*, July 1958. Readers curious about East African seamanship should consult A. H. J. Prihs, *Sailing from Lamu* (Assen, Netherlands: 1965).

Sultan Muhammad lived in the country of Pate and made it prosper, making plantations and building vessels called *Gharabs* which are now called *Jahazis*.   [Deep-sea dhows, lateen-rigged; even in the 1980s, a few were still in use. The word is from the Hindustani for a ship.]

Now in those days Arab and Indian vessels used to come to Pate harbor.

Sultan Omar had a nephew who was very fond of travelling. On his first journey he set out for India, but was completely lost and his ship sank, and he himself, after meeting with great hardships and difficulties and losing everything, returned home. He remained at home for a year, but the next year he wished to travel abroad again . . . . [His parents now vainly attempted to dissuade him.] As they were unable to stop him they made up a fleet of seven ships for him, and he voyaged away and wrecked all his ships. He returned alone, and he had nothing and no one with him . . . . [But still he persisted in his wish to travel the seas, and again prevailed upon his parents and friends.] When his parents found that they were unable to prevent him, they gave him a fleet according to his wishes.

So he set out and arrived in India where he traded and made much profit. During the return they were lost at sea for many days till from the vessel on board of which he was they saw an island near them.

So they disembarked as they were in need of water, and that youth wished to rest from the discomforts he had suffered. He lay under a tree and told his servants to cook his food and bring it to him here.

They sat down to cook, and when the fire blazed up they saw the sand of that place melt and run away. When it had gone a little from the fire it cooled in separate little pieces . . . . [This the enterprising young man immediately recognized to be silver. He persuaded his crew to jettison most of the cargo they had bought and to load instead with this silver-bearing sand.]

So they took his advice and unloaded all their goods and filled up with sand for three days till the ship could carry no more . . . . [They lost some in a storm but] afterwards they got a safe and favorable wind and arrived home [where he was joyfully received] . . . .

He rested for three days and then at dead of night he brought some of the sand and put it in a store in his house. Then he called skilled workmen and showed them a little, and when they had made an ornament out of it they found that it was very pure silver.

Now it was at this time that the Portuguese arrived in Pate, and first they came in friendship. Afterwards he showed the ore to the Portuguese and they asked him where he got it. He told them the story from first to last because of his joy when he knew that it was real ore.

Those Portuguese wanted him to show them the spot, and they went together with the captain and searched for six months and returned again without finding it . . . .

From the translation in C. H. Stigand, *The Land of Zinj*, 1913.

VASCO DA GAMA'S LOGBOOK

The End of an Epoch

From the European point of view, da Gama performed three great services. He sailed directly from the West Coast of Africa to the neighborhood of the Cape of Good Hope, Diaz before him having followed the long western seaboard by way of the Congo estuary; he discovered the civilization of the Swahili (though he recognized it, as would other Portuguese explorers, merely as Muslim or "Moorish"); and he reached India. From the African point of view, however, his coming was an unrelieved disaster. It brought to an end the long and flourishing epoch of untrammeled trading intercourse with other lands of the Indian Ocean. It signalled the onset of ruin for many of the Swahili cities. Yet da Gama's *Roteiro* can still be useful to African history, if only because it records most graphically the reactions of the Portuguese to an African civilization whose sensitivity and splendor were as impressive as they were unexpected. It will be noticed that Kilwa is missing from the story; on this occasion Kilwa escaped notice, for da Gama's ships—as noted by the Kilwa Chronicle quoted above (pp. 145-46)—were carried past it on the tide. Kilwa's ruin was briefly delayed.

Mossell Bay (South Africa): The "Hottentots"

On Saturday [December 2, 1497] about two hundred negroes came, both young and old. They brought with them about a dozen oxen and cows and four or five sheep. As soon as we saw them we went ashore. They forthwith began to play on four or five flutes, some producing high notes and others low ones, thus making a pretty harmony for negroes who are not expected to be musicians; and they danced in the style of negroes. The captain-major then ordered the trumpets to be sounded, and we, in the boats, danced, and the captain-major did so likewise when he rejoined us. This festivity ended, we landed where we had landed before, and bought a black ox for three bracelets. This ox we dined off on Sunday. We found him very fat, and his meat as toothsome as the beef of Portugal.

On Sunday [December 3] many visitors came, and brought with them their women and little boys, the women remaining on the top of a hill near the sea. They had with them many oxen and cows. Having collected in two spots on the beach, they played and danced as they had done on Saturday. It is the custom of this people for the young men to remain in the bush with their weapons. The (older) men came to converse with

We were told, moreover, that Prester John resided not far from this place; that he held many cities along the coast, and that the inhabitants of those cities were great merchants and owned big ships. The residence of Prester John was said to be far in the interior, and could be reached only on the back of camels. These Moors had also brought hither two Christian captives from India. This information, and many other things which we heard, rendered us so happy that we cried with joy, and prayed God to grant us health, so that we might behold what we so much desired.

In this place and island of Moncobiquy [Mozambique] there resided a chief [*senhor*] who had the title of Sultan, and was like the viceroy. He often came aboard our ships attended by some of his people. The captain-major gave him many good things to eat and made him a present of hats, *marlotas*, corals and many other articles. He was, however, so proud that he treated all we gave him with contempt, and asked for scarlet cloth, of which we had none. We gave him, however, of all the things we had.

One day the captain-major invited him to a repast, when there was an abundance of figs and comfits, and begged him for two pilots to go with us. He at once granted this request, subject to our coming to terms with them. The captain-major gave each of them thirty *mitqals* in gold and two *marlotas*, on condition that from the day on which they received this payment one of them should always remain on board if the other desired to go on land. With these terms they were well satisfied.

On Saturday, March 10 [1498], we set sail and anchored one league out at sea, close to an island, where mass was said on Sunday, when those who wished to do so confessed and joined in the communion.

One of our pilots lived on the island, and when we had anchored we armed two boats to go in search of him. The captain-major went in one boat and Nicolau Coelho in the other. They were met by five or six boats [*barcas*] coming from the island, and crowded with people armed with bows and long arrows and bucklers, who gave them to understand by signs that they were to return to the town. When the captain saw this he secured the pilot whom he had taken with him, and ordered the bombards to fire upon the boats. Paulo da Gama, who had remained with the ships, so as to be prepared to render succor in case of need, no sooner heard the reports of the bombards than he started in the *Berrio*. The Moors, who were already flying, fled still faster, and gained the land before the *Berrio* was able to come up with them. We then returned to our anchorage.

The vessels of this country are of good size and decked. There are no nails, and the planks are held together by cords, as are also those of their boats [*barcas*]. The sails are made of palm-matting. Their mariners have Genoese needles, by which they steer, quadrants, and navigating charts.

The palms of this country yield a fruit as large as a melon, of which the kernel is eaten. It has a nutty flavor. There also grow in abundance melons and cucumbers, which were brought to us for barter.

On the day in which Nicolau Coelho entered the port, the lord of the place came on board with a numerous suite. He was received well, and Coelho presented him with a red hood, in return for which the lord handed him a black rosary, which he made use of when saying his prayers, to be held as a pledge. He then begged Nicolau Coelho for the use of his boat, to take him ashore. This was granted. And after he had landed he invited those who had accompanied him to his house, where he gave them to eat. He then dismissed them, giving them a jar of bruised dates made into a preserve with cloves and cumin, as a present for Nicolau Coelho. Subsequently he sent many things to the captain-major. All this happened at the time when he took us for Turks or for Moors from some foreign land, for in case we came from Turkey he begged to be shown the bows of our country and our books of the Law. But when they learnt that we were Christians they arranged to seize and kill us by treachery. The pilot, whom we took with us, subsequently revealed to us all they intended to do, if they were able.

Malindi (Kenya): An Offer of Pilots

On Easter Sunday [April 15, 1498] the Moors whom we had taken in the boat told us that there were at this city of Malindi four vessels belonging to Christians from India [they were, of course, Hindus], and that if it pleased us to take them there, they would provide us, instead of them, Christian pilots and all we stood in need of, including water, wood and other things.

The captain-major much desired to have pilots from the country, and having discussed the matter with his Moorish prisoners, he cast anchor off the town, at a distance of about half a league from the mainland. The inhabitants of the town did not venture to come aboard our ships, for they had already learnt that we had captured a vessel and made her occupants prisoners . . . .

[Afterwards they went ashore and were formally received by the Sultan of Malindi who] wore a robe of damask trimmed with green satin, and rich *touca*. He was seated on two cushioned chairs of bronze, beneath a round sunshade of crimson satin attached to a pole. An old man, who attended him as page, carried a short sword in a silver sheath. There were many players on *anafils*, and two trumpets of ivory, richly carved, and of the size of a man, which were blown from a hole in the side, and made sweet harmony with the *anafils* . . . .

Journey to India

On the following Sunday, the 22nd of April, the king's *zavra* brought on board one of his confidential servants, and as two days had passed without any visitors, the captain-major had this man seized, and sent word to the king that he required the pilots whom he had promised. The king, when he received this message, sent a Christian pilot, and the captain-major allowed the gentleman, whom he had retained in his vessel, to go away . . . .

We left Malindi on Tuesday, the 24th of the month [of April] for a city called Calecut, with the pilot whom the king had given us . . . .

On Friday, the 18th of May, after having seen no land for twenty-three days, we sighted lofty mountains, and having all this time sailed before the wind we could not have made less than six hundred leagues . . . .

[They anchored off Calecut and were spoken by boats of the port.] On the following day [May 21] these same boats came again alongside, when the captain-major sent one of the convicts to Calecut, and those with whom he went took him to two Moors from Tunis, who could speak Castilian and Genoese. The first greeting that he received was in these words: "May the Devil take thee! What brought you hither?" They asked what he sought so far away from home, and he told them that we came in search of Christians and of spices.

From the translation in *A Journal of the First Voyage of Vasco da Gama*, edited by E. G. Ravenstein, Hakluyt Society, 1898.

DUARTE BARBOSA

Swahili Civilization

The value of Duarte Barbosa's memoirs lies in their picture of the East Coast before the full impact of Portuguese intervention had been felt. They summarize the knowledge of a man who first saw the coast in 1500 or 1501, and last saw it in 1517 or 1518. I have modernized the orthography of the place names.

Sofala

And the manner of their traffic was this: they came in small vessels named *zambucos* from the kingdoms of Kilwa, Mombasa, and Malindi, bringing many cotton cloths, some spotted and others white and blue, also some of silk, and many small beads, gray, red, and yellow, which things come to the said kingdoms from the great kingdom of Cambay [in Northwest India] in other greater ships. And these wares the said Moors who came from Malindi and Mombasa [purchased from others who bring them hither and] paid for in gold at such a price that those merchants departed well pleased; which gold they gave by weight.

The Moors of Sofala kept these wares and sold them afterwards to the heathen of the Kingdom of Benametapa, who came thither laden with gold which they gave in exchange for the said cloths without weighing it. These Moors collect also great store of ivory which they find hard by Sofala, and this also they sell in the [Indian] Kingdom of Cambay at five or six cruzados the quintal. They also sell some ambergris, which is brought to them from the Hucicas, and is exceedingly good. These Moors are black, and some of them tawny; some of them speak Arabic, but the more part use the language of the country. They clothe themselves from the waist down with cotton and silk cloths, and other cloths they wear over their shoulders like capes, and turbans on their heads. Some of them wear small caps dyed in grain in chequers and other woollen clothes in many tints, also camlets and other silks.

Their food is millet, rice, flesh and fish. In this river as far as the sea are many sea horses, which come out on the land to graze, which horses always move in the sea like fishes; they have tusks like those of small elephants, being whiter and harder, and it never loses color. In the country near Sofala are many wild elephants, exceeding great (which the country-folk know not how to tame), ounces, lions, deer and many other wild beasts. It is a land of plains and hills with many streams of sweet water.

In this same Sofala now of late they make great store of cotton and weave it, and from it they make much white cloth, and as they know not how to dye it, or have not the needful dyes, they take the Cambay cloths, blue or otherwise colored, and unravel them and make them up again, so that it becomes a new thing. With this thread and their own white they make much colored cloth, and from it they gain much gold. This they did as a remedy after they had perceived that our people [the Portuguese] were taking from them the trade of the *zambucos*, and that they can only obtain goods through the hands of the factors whom the King our Lord has there in his factories and forts.

The Zambezi Mouths

Journeying from Sofala forty leagues more or less towards Mozambique there is a very great river which they call Cuama, which leads into the inner country over against the kingdom of Benametapa more than a hundred and seventy leagues. In the mouth of the said river is a town whose king they call Mangalo. By this river comes much gold from Benametapa to this Moorish town, and from this river is formed another which goes to a town called Angoya, and it is here that the Moors have many *almadias* [boats] to convey cloth and much other merchandise from Angoya and others to take abundance of gold and ivory thither.

Angoya

Further on, leaving this Cuama, a hundred and forty leagues from it, skirting the coast, is a very great town of Moors called Angoya (which has its own king). In it dwell many merchants who deal in gold, ivory, silk and cotton cloths and Cambay beads as those of Sofala were wont to do. The Moors of Sofala, Mombasa, Malindi and Kilwa convey these wares in very small craft concealed from our ships, and in this wise they carry great store of provender, millet, rice and flesh of divers kinds. The natives thereof are some black and some tawny, they go bare from the waist up, and below it are clad in silk and cotton cloths and they wear other cloths folded like cloaks on their shoulders; some wear turbans on their heads, and other caps made of squares of silk cloth. They speak the native language of the country, that of the heathen, but some speak Arabic. At times these Moors obey the King our Lord, but at other times, being far from our fortresses, they become rebellious.

Mozambique Island

Going forward towards India, and leaving Angoya, there are three islands very near to the mainland, among which is a Moorish town called Mozambique which has a very good haven, formerly the resort of the Moors who traded to Sofala and Cuama to repair their ships—"as they found there good depth of water and wood and provisions." Among the Moors of this isle of Mozambique was a Xarife [sharif] who governed and judged them. These Moors are of the same tongue and have the same customs as those of Angoya.

Here the King our Lord has a fortress, so that the aforesaid Moors are under his rule and governance, and our ships now take in at this port water, wood and provisions which are found in that land, and there they mend the ships that need it, in going as well as in coming, and hence they send supplies to the Portuguese at Sofala, as well as many things which come from Portugal and from India also, as it lies on the way thither. On the mainland appertaining to these islands are many very great elephants and other wild beasts. The land is inhabited by heathen who are like beasts, going naked and smeared with red clay. Their private parts are wrapped in strips of blue cotton cloth with no other clothing. Their lips are bored with three holes, and in each hole three cowries, and in these they place bones with little stones and other little pendants.

Kilwa

Going along the coast from this town of Mozambique, there is an island hard by the mainland which is called Kilwa, in which is a Moorish town with many fair houses of stones and mortar, with many windows after our fashion, very well arranged in streets, with many flat roofs. The doors are of wood, well carved, with excellent joinery. Around it are streams and orchards and fruit-gardens with many channels of sweet water. It has a Moorish king over it. From this place they trade with Sofala, whence they bring back gold, and from here they spread all over *Arabia Felix*, which henceforth we may call by this name (even though it be in Ethiopia) for all the seacoast is well peopled with villages and abodes of Moors.

Before the King our Lord sent out his expedition to discover India the Moors of Sofala, Cuama, Angoya and Mozambique were all subject to the king of Kilwa, who was the most mighty king among them. And in this town was great plenty of gold, as no ships passed towards Sofala without first coming to this island. Of the Moors there are some fair and some black, they are finely clad in many rich garments of gold and silk and cotton, and the women as well; also with much gold and silver in chains and bracelets, which they wear on their legs and arms, and many jewelled earrings in their ears. These Moors speak Arabic and follow the creed of the Alcoran, and have great faith in Mafamede.

This town was taken by force from its king by the Portuguese, as, moved by arrogance, he refused to obey the King our Lord. There they took many prisoners and the king fled from the island, and His Highness ordered that a fort should be built there, and kept it under his rule and governance. Afterwards he ordered that it should be pulled down, as its maintenance was of no value nor profit to him, and it was destroyed by Antonio de Saldanha.

Mombasa

Further on, an advance along the coast towards India, there is an isle hard by the mainland, on which is a town called Mombasa. It is a very fair place, with lofty stone and mortar houses, well aligned in streets after the fashion of Kilwa. The wood is well fitted with excellent joiner's work. It has its own king, himself a Moor. The men are in color either tawny, black or white and also their women go very bravely attired with many fine garments of silk and gold in abundance. This is a place of great traffic, and has a good harbor, in which are always moored craft of many kinds and also great ships, both of those which come from Sofala and those which go thither, and others which come from the great kingdom of Cambay and from Malindi; others which sail to the Isles of Zanzibar, and yet others of which I shall speak anon.

This Mombasa is a land very full of food. Here are found many very fine sheep with round tails, cows and other cattle in great plenty, and many fowls, all of which are exceedingly fat. There is much millet and rice, sweet and bitter oranges, lemons, pomegranates, Indian figs, vegetables of divers kinds, and much sweet water. The men thereof are ofttimes at war but seldom at peace with those of the mainland, and they carry on trade with them, bringing thence great store of honey, wax and ivory.

The king of this city refused to obey the commands of the King our Lord, and through this arrogance he lost it, and our Portuguese took it from him by force. He fled away, and they slew many of his people and also took captive many, both men and women, in such sort that it was left ruined and plundered and burnt. Of gold and silver great booty was taken here, bangles, bracelets, earrings and gold beads, also great store of copper with other rich wares in great quantity, and the town was left in ruins.

Malindi

Leaving Mombasa, and journeying along the coast towards India, there is a fair town on the mainland lying along a strand, which is named Malindi. It pertains to the Moors and has a Moorish king over it; the which place has many fair stone and mortar houses of many stories, with great plenty of windows and flat roofs, after our fashion. The place is well laid out in streets. The folk are both black and white; they go naked, covering only their private parts with cotton and silk cloths. Others of them wear cloths folded like cloaks and waistbands, and turbans of many rich stuffs on their heads.

They are great barterers, and deal in cloth, gold, ivory, and divers other wares with the Moors and heathen of the great kingdom of Cambay; and to their haven come every year many ships with cargoes of merchandise, from which they get great store of gold, ivory and wax. In this traffic the Cambay merchants make great profits, and thus, on one side and the other, they earn much money. There is great plenty of food in this city, rice, millet, and some wheat which they bring from Cambay, and divers sorts of fruit, inasmuch as there is here abundance of fruit-gardens and orchards. Here too are plenty of round-tailed sheep, cows and other cattle and great store of oranges, also of hens.

The king and people of this place ever were and are friends of the King of Portugal, and the Portuguese always find in them great comfort and friendship and perfect peace, and there the ships, when they chance to pass that way, obtain supplies in plenty.

Pemba, Mafia, Zanzibar

Between this island of Sao Lourenco [Madagascar] and the mainland, not very far therefrom, are three islands, one called Mafia, another Pemba, another Zanzibar; which are inhabited by Moors. They have great store of food, for in them are found rice, millet, flesh-meat in great quantity, oranges, limes and citrons, of which the woods are full, and every other kind of fruit. There is great plenty of sugar cane, but they know not how to make the sugar. These islands have Moorish kings. Some of them deal in their stock of flesh and fruit with the mainland in very small, weak, ill-found and undecked boats having but one mast. The planks are bound and sewn together with a cord they call *cairo*, and their sails are palm-leaf mats.

They are a feeble folk and have but few weapons. The kings of these isles live in great luxury; they are clad in very fine silk and cotton garments, which they purchase at Mombasa from the Cambay merchants. The women of these Moors go bravely decked, they wear many jewels of fine Sofala gold, silver too in plenty, earrings, necklaces, bangles and bracelets, and they go clad in good silk garments. They have many mosques, and honor greatly the Alcoran of Mafamede.

Pate and Lamu

And as soon as they pass Malindi, going towards India, they begin to cross the gulf, for the coast doubles back towards the Red Sea.

Going forward along this coast is a town of Moors named Pate and then another named Lamu. These carry on trade with the inland country, and are well walled with stone and mortar, inasmuch as they are often at war with the heathen of the mainland.

Brava

Yet further along the coast, beyond these places, is a great town of Moors, of very fine stone and mortar houses, called Brava. It has no king, but is ruled by elders and ancients of the land, who are the persons held in the highest esteem, and who have the chief dealings in merchandise of divers kinds. And this place was destroyed by the Portuguese, who slew many of its people and carried many into captivity, and took great spoil of gold and silver and goods. Thenceforth many of them fled away towards the inland country, forsaking the town; yet after it had been destroyed the Portuguese again settled and peopled it, so that now it is as prosperous as it was before.

Mogadishu

Proceeding coastwise towards the Red Sea there is a very great Moorish town called Mogadishu; it has a king over it; the place has much trade in divers kinds, by reason whereof many ships come hither from the great kingdom of Cambay, bringing great plenty of cloths of many sorts, and divers other wares, also spices: and in the same way they come from Aden. And they carry away much gold, ivory, wax and many other things, whereby they make exceeding great profits in their dealings.

In this country is found flesh-meat in great plenty, wheat, barley, horses and fruit of divers kinds, so that it is a place of great wealth.

They speak Arabic. The men are for the most part brown and black, but a few are fair. They have but few weapons, yet they use herbs on their arrows to defend themselves against their enemies.

From *The Book of Duarte Barbosa*, translated by Mansel Longworth Dames, Hakluyt Society (2 vols., London: 1918).

HANS MAYR

The Sack of Two Cities

Early Portuguese intentions on the East Coast may be fairly summarized as being, first, to plunder the Indian Ocean trade; secondly, to put the seaboard towns in tribute; thirdly, to accumulate personal loot. In one way or another all three designs were briefly realized. The following eyewitness notes on d'Almeida's behavior at Kilwa and Mombasa in 1505 are thought to have been written by a German called Hans Mayr who travelled in the *Sam Rafael*, d'Almeida's flagship. Another and longer account of d'Almeida's expedition was published by de Barros, *Da Asia*, 1st Decade, translated in G. M. Theal, *Records of South-eastern Africa*, 1900, vol. 6. See also Barbosa's memoirs, p. 155 above.

Kilwa

In Kilwa there are many strong houses several stories high. They are built of stone and mortar and plastered with various designs. As soon as the town had been taken without opposition, the Vicar-General and some of the Franciscan fathers came ashore carrying two crosses in procession and singing the Te Deum. They went to the palace, and there the cross was put down and the Grand-Captain prayed. Then everyone started to plunder the town of all its merchandise and provisions. [Two days later d'Almeida fired the town, destroying, as the account in de Barros explains, "the greater part of this city of abomination."]

Mombasa

The Grand-Captain ordered that the town should be sacked and that each man should carry off to his ship whatever he found: so that at the end there would be a division of the spoil, each man to receive a twentieth of what he found. The same rule was made for gold, silver, and pearls. Then everyone started to plunder the town and to search the houses, forcing open the doors with axes and iron bars. There was a large quantity of cotton cloth for Sofala in the town, for the whole coast gets its cotton cloth from here. So the Grand-Captain got a good share of the trade of Sofala for himself. A large quantity of rich silk and gold embroidered clothes was seized, and carpets also; one of these, which was without equal for beauty, was sent to the King of Portugal together with many other valuables.

From the Portuguese text in E. Axelson, *South-east Africa, 1488-1530,* 1940. This extract is from a translation of the full account in Freeman-Grenville, *The East African Coast, Select Documents* (London: 1962), p. 105.

DIOGO DE ALCANCOVA

Swahili Fiscal Practice

The duties, Sir, which the king of Mombasa receives from the merchants who go to Sofala are the following: any merchant who comes to Mombasa and brings a thousand pieces of cloth pays to the king duties of entrance for each thousand pieces of cloth one *mitqal* of gold; and then they divide the thousand pieces of cloth into two halves; and the king takes one half; and the other half remains with the merchant; and, whether he carries them beyond [Mombasa] or sells them in the city, he has to take this half to the king: and the king sends his to be sold at Sofala or at Kilwa.

And the duties which the king of Kilwa has are: that any merchant who wishes to enter the city pays for each five hundred pieces of cloth he brings, no matter what the quality, one *mitqal* of gold as entrance duty; and, after paying this *mitqal* for the five hundred pieces of cloth, the king takes two-thirds of all the merchandise, and the merchant one-third; and the third which remains to the merchant must not be taken from the city, and the whole merchandise remaining in that third is again valued, and pays for each thousand *mitqals* thirty *mitqals* for the king of Kilwa. And from that place the merchant departs for Sofala; and, on arriving there, he must pay for every seven pieces of cloth one piece for the said king of Kilwa. And when any one returns from Sofala, he is obliged to stop at Kilwa; and he must pay to the king for each thousand *mitqals* of gold he carries with him fifty *mitqals* of gold, and at Mombasa going through costs nothing. And, if he passes Kilwa, and does not enter it, he must however go to Mombasa, and if he does not carry with him a clearance to show that he has paid at Kilwa, there they take these fifty *mitqals* out of every thousand *mitqals*, and send them to the king of Kilwa.

And the duty of ivory which they also pay to the king of Kilwa is: that for each *bahar* he pays twenty *mitqals* of gold in Sofala; and when they come to Kilwa, he pays further for each seven tusks one, and in each *bahar* are twenty *farazulas*, and in each *farazula* there are twenty-three pounds. And since, Sir, this king of Sofala, whom Pedro d'Anaya killed, reigned, no one has ever paid duties to the king of Kilwa out of those collected at Sofala.

From Diogo de Alcançova's letter to the King of Portugal of Nov. 20, 1506, in the translation in G. M. Theal, *Records of South-eastern Africa*, 1898, vol. 1, p. 62. It refers, of course, to Kilwa before the Portuguese sacking and subjection.

An Inland Epic

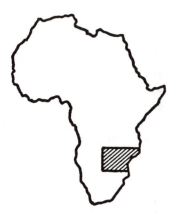

*N*OW THAT AFRICAN HISTORY MAY increasingly be seen from its own standpoint, thanks largely to archeology and the collection of oral tradition, the old European records often deepen in value. They stand exposed, true enough, as markedly partial (though the older records generally come through better, in this respect, than the newer), but much that they have to say acquires a broader meaning. This is notably the case with the Portuguese records of Monomotapa, the inland empire in Central Africa, essentially in Zimbabwe and western Mozambique, with which travellers from Portugal made contact at the beginning of the sixteenth century, and from which, as they rightly believed, much of the gold of the interior was drawn. A later world invested the Monomotapa (*Mwene-Mutapa* is closer to the original Shona)—or, rather, *the* Mono-motapa, for the name, like that of Ghana, was initially the title of a king and not of a kingdom—with a rigamarole of mysteries. Zimbabwe became the land of Ophir. Phoenicians and Ancient Egyptians were named as those who had built the walls and forts of this inland country. Archeology has exorcized these ghosts from the European racist mythology of a century ago.

Great Zimbabwe, like the many other stone structures on the central plateau of Zimbabwe, was the work of Africans. Its last alterations, but for those of Nature, were made less than three centuries ago. They represented, in stone, the climax of a long process of Iron Age growth which began in this region some two thousand years ago (pp. 19-20). Readers who wish mine in (Zimbabwe republic)," comments Roger Summers, "which is not on the site of an 'ancient working'; so it is clear that the 'miners' had a good knowledge of prospecting. It has been deduced that originally the zone from the surface down to about twenty feet was exceptionally rich in gold, and it seems very probable that immense quantities of gold were exported." The Portuguese, by comparison, got very little, for they were trusted neither by the inland people nor by the coastal traders, and they were never able to make the system "work." Yet even the Portuguese gathered no mean quantity. Reporting on trade through Sofala during 1512-1515, a Portuguese royal agent wrote of an annual average export of 12,500 *mitqals* of gold (perhaps 100 lbs.), as well as of a much larger quantity of ivory and copper, some amber, seed pearls, coral, and six slaves. The last entry is interesting as a confirmation of the view that slaving from these eastern ports was of little or no importance until later times.

United under their Rozwi "kings and barons," the Katanga embarked upon imperial conquests. This evidently reached a decisive phase in about 1440, or nearly half a century before the Portuguese raided up round the Cape of Good Hope. Within ten years, according to tradition, the ruling Rozwi king had fastened his suzerainty over the great part of Southern Rhodesia. He now controlled most of the gold mines of the plateau and all the trading routes to and from the coast. He could use his power to impose commercial duties on all incoming goods—textiles and beads, porcelain, brassware and other items from oversea—as well as on the exports of his empire. This Rozwi king, Mutota, died before he could complete the logic of his policy by securing control of the coast as well, but his son and successor Matope, as Mr. Abraham shows in the passage that follows here, valiantly carried on the work. Yet the seeds of decay were already present: characteristically for this political structure, the "barons" began to nourish ambitions of their own. They contested their supreme lord's power, and sought to seize it for themselves.

D. P. ABRAHAM

Conquest and Challenge

Mutota died [c. A.D. 1450] before he could realize his full ambitions, and it fell to his son and successor Matope to fulfill the complete specifications of the blueprint drawn up by his father. Over a period of thirty years Matope moved single-mindedly from area to area with his armies, until finally he succeeded in conquering unopposed right to the shores of the Indian Ocean, south of the Zambezi Estuary—leaving undisturbed, however, the Arab *entrepots** at Sena, Kilimani and Sofala. The southern provinces of Mbire and Guniuswa he entrusted to two Rozwi vassals, Torwa and Changa. The newly won eastern and southeastern provinces—Chidima, Utonga, Barwe, Shiringoma, Manyika, Uteve and Madanda—he placed in the hands of sons and trusted relatives. The northern provinces, adjoining the Zambezi valley, he retained under the immediate control of his brothers and himself, and thus replaced the Katanga homeland in the south as the center of political authority.

Changa Succeeds

Thus came into being the golden—but short-lived—phase of the vast feudal domain created by Matope and his father Mutota Mwanamutapa, after whom the Arabs called this Bantu empire Wilayatu 'lMu'anamutapah, and the Portuguese, following the Arabs, Imperio do Manamutapa. Overextended lines of communication, political intrigue within the ruling circles, and a lack of ethnic and cultural homogeneity in the conquered provinces sufficient to give rise to a sense of

---

*That is, Swahili *entrepots.*

community of interest with the central power, were destined rapidly to disintegrate the new empire into its component parts. Already prior to Matope's death, c. 1480, Changa had taken advantage of the virtual isolation of the southern provinces to transform his position imperceptibly, with the cooperation of his colleague Togwa, into that of independent ruler. On the death of Matope, Changa began openly to flout the authority of his son and successor Nyahuma, and inspired by the title *Amir* flatteringly accorded him by his Arab advisors, adopted the dynastic title *Changamire* to emphasize his separatist policy vis-a-vis the Mwanamutapa paramountcy. This policy led to a head-on collision, resulting in the death of Nyahuma in battle c. 1490 and the usurpation by Changamire of the seat of empire for a period of four years.

Kakuyo Komunyaka, son of Nyahuma, succeeded in staging a military comeback and killed the usurper, thus regaining formal control of the Empire; however Changamire's son and successor was able to retain control of the southern provinces Mbire and Guniuswa, which became *de facto* independent of the Empire. Furthermore, by a strenuous diplomatic campaign the new Changamire was partially able to detach the eastern and southeastern provinces from loyalty to the Mwanamutapa, who was left with effective domain over what would now be the northern half of Southern Rhodesia and a strip of territory varying from one hundred to two hundred miles in depth, running east and then southeast down to the Indian Ocean for a distance of about six hundred miles. This was the political situation which the Portuguese verified after their initial establishment at Sofala in 1505, a situation in which they became progressively involved in pursuit of their policy to supplant the Arab trade monopoly* of the interior.

From D. P. Abraham, "Maramuca: An Exercise in the Combined Use of Portuguese Records and Oral Tradition," *Journal of African History* 2, 1961. Mr. Abraham's work is a pioneering demonstration of the possibility of merging "oral tradition" with available European records, and when written was intended to be crowned by a full-scale history of the kingdom of the Mwanamutapa from about 850 to 1902.

DIOGO DE ALCANÇOVA

"Kings and Barons"

Establishing themselves along the southeast coast during the opening years of the sixteenth century, the Portuguese became at once aware of powers in the inland country upon which they must depend for any hope of gold. They had much trouble in understanding the true situation there, partly because the Swahili merchants whose cities they had seized and subjected were anything but anxious to enlighten them, and partly because they were as yet incapable of going to see for themselves. Alcançova's letter to the king in Lisbon reflects their confusion about the dynastic strife which was then going on between the Monomotapa and his rebellious vassals, notably Changa in the far southwest. Changa having won these wars, in 1513 the Sofala factor duly reports "peace at last."

*That is to say, the monopoly of trade with the interior possessed by the Swahili coastal cities, notably, at this stage, Kilwa by way of its tributary Sofala.

Barbosa told in 1518 what was known or believed about the interior. De Barros, writing somewhat later and basing himself on the royal archives in Lisbon, added a good deal more. But from the middle of the sixteenth century the factors and captains along the coast began to receive information from their own upcountry agents; by the end of the century, when we have the invaluable reports of dos Santos, these agents were well established along the banks of the Middle Zambezi and as far as Masapa, a trading post they were able to maintain near the court of the Monomotapa himself.* In 1573 the ruling Monomotapa had in fact ceded to the Portuguese a large river line area (between Sena and Tete), and much of this area now became settled by Portuguese planters who constantly forwarded their own interests by political and military intervention in the country's affairs. By this time the power of Monomotapa was limited to the northeasterly districts of the modern Zimbabwe republic and perhaps the northwesterly fringe of Mozambique, while the Rozwi-Karanga empire held sway throughout the southerly regions under the heirs of Changa. The kings of Quiteve (Chiteve) continued to rule the upland region along the frontier of the modern republic of Zimbabwe and Mozambique.

This was the period of greatest prosperity for the Rozwi-Karanga state and empire. Never seriously bothered by the Portuguese, much less subjected by them as were the Monomotapas, the Rozwi rulers continued to use Great Zimbabwe as a religious center if no longer as a political capital, rebuilt its walls, and reigned through two centuries, until they in turn suffered defeat at the hands of African invaders from south of the Limpopo river. There appears until then (the 1830s) to have been great security in the land, for none of the large stone structures associated with the Karanga (with the possible exception of the "acropolis" at Great Zimbabwe) shows any sign of serious fortification. The situation was different on the eastern borderlands, where fortified dwellings appeared in the seven-

---

*By this time no longer at Great Zimbabwe but near Mount Darwin (on modern maps) just south of the middle Zambezi river.

teenth and eighteenth centuries, and it was possibly different south of the Limpopo, where the people of the "Mapungubwe Culture" (linked to that of the Zimbabwe Culture) lived in hilltop settlements. This long epic of inner Africa, a title that is surely well deserved, moves on into the eighteenth and nineteenth centuries. Here I have stopped with the illuminating report of Manoel Barreto in 1667. Having fatally intervened in the affairs of the Monomotapa, the Portuguese proved far too weak to impose a new system of law and order in that far country; they merely opened the gate to a new chaos. They made furious if erratic attempts to find gold and silver, but succeeded only in under-mining the dominant social systems which they found. In this they were helped, no doubt, by the point of growth which these inland states had now reached. Crucial fissures repeatedly appeared in the structure of central rule. This fissuring process was of course a common feature of all lord-and-vassal forms of government. Without Portuguese intervention the Monomotapas might have worked out their conflicts to the same stability as the Rozwi kings achieved. As we shall see, they never really had the chance of doing so.

The kingdom, Sir, in which there is the gold that comes to Sofala is called Vealanga, and the kingdom is very large, in which there are many large towns, besides many other villages, and Sofala itself is in this kingdom if not the whole land along the sea. The kings of the interior pay little or no regard to it if the Moors are in possession [of Sofala]; and going along the coast and towards the interior four leagues, because they [the Moors] do not attempt to go farther inland, as the Kaffirs rob and kill them, for they do not believe in anything. And, Sir, a man might go from Sofala to a city which is called Zumubany [Zimbabwe?] which is large, in which the king always resides, in ten or twelve days, if you travel as in Portugal; but because they do not travel except from morning until midday, and eat and sleep until the next morning when they go on again, they cannot go to this city in less than twenty or twenty-four days; and in the whole kingdom of Vealanga gold is extracted; and in this way: they dig out the earth and make a kind of tunnel, through which they go under the ground a long stone's throw, and keep on taking out from the veins with the ground mixed with the gold, and, when collected, they put it in a pot, and cook it much in fire; and after cooking they take it out, and put it to cool, and, when cold, the earth remains, and the gold all fine gold...and no man can take it [the gold] out without leave from the king, under penalty of death.

And this king who now reigns, Sir, in Vealanga, is the son of Mokomba, late king of the said kingdom, and he has the name Kewsarimgo Menomotapam, which is like saying king so and so, because the title of the king is Menomotapam, and the kingdom Vealanga. Your Highness is already aware that for twelve or thirteen years there has been war in the kingdom from which the gold came to Sofala . . . .

* * * * * * * *

Alcançova describes the struggle for power between the reigning Monomotapa and his chief vassal of the south, Changa-mire (cf. D. P. Abraham above, pp. 173-75), in which the Mono-motapa attempts to slay Changamire, but the latter prevails.

. . .and when the ameer [Changamire] saw that the king [wished to kill him], he made up his mind to kill [the king] in the city where he was, which is called Zimhauhy [Zimbabwe]: and he took with him many peoples; and when he arrived near the city, the grandees who were with the king knew that he was coming, they went to receive him, and, when they saw him coming in that way [i.e., with many followers], they would not remain in the city and went out of it [i.e., deserted the Monomotapa]; and the ameer went to the houses of the king, which were of stone and clay very large and of one story, and he entered where the king was with his slaves and some other men; and while speaking to the king the ameer cut his head off; and as he killed him, he made himself king; and all obeyed him; and he reigned peacefully four years; and the king Mokomba [i.e., the Monomotapa] left twenty-two children; and the ameer killed them all, except one, the eldest, who was still young, whose name was Kwekarynugo, who is now the king; and this one fled to another kingdom of his uncle; and when he was twenty years old, he took possession of the kingdom with many people of his father, who came to join him; and he marched against the ameer who had killed his father, in a field close to the town.

And, when the ameer saw that he was coming upon him, he sent many people to fight with him; and the son of the king killed many people of the ameer; and when the ameer saw that they killed so many people, he came out to fight with him; and the son of the king killed the ameer in the field; and the battle lasted three days and a half, in which many people were killed on both sides; and, as the ameer was dead . . . [the Monomotapa] had the kingdom to himself, except that the territories of the ameer would not submit to him; and the ameer left a relative who is named Toloa, who now with a son of the ameer wages war with the king . . . . And in this way, Sir, the war was originated, and is still today. And for this reason, Sir, the gold does not come to Sofala as it used to . . . .

From Alcançova's letter of 1506 in G. M. Theal, *Records of Southeastern Africa*, 1900, vol. 1, p. 62.

PEDRO VAZ SOARES

Peace at Last

. . .At present [1513] the whole country is at peace as far as Monomotapa, who is the chief king and lord of all this country, and to whom all the other kings and lords are subject and obedient, and where there is the greatest quantity of gold in these parts, according to what all say, who, after he had finished some wars in which he was engaged, sent to make peace through all the country which is　obedient to him, in order that all the traders might go and come to carry on traffic wherever they wished in security . . . .

From the translation of a letter to King Manuel of Portugal written in 1513 by his factor at Sofala, Pedro Vaz Soares, in G. M. Theal, *Records of South-eastern Africa*, 1900, vol. 1.

DUARTE BARBOSA

Monomotapa

[What the Portuguese along the Mozambique coast had learned by 1517 was that:] Beyond this country [Sofala, etc.] towards the interior lies the great kingdom of Benametapa [Monomotapa] pertaining to the Heathen whom the Moors [i.e., the Swahili] name Cafres; they are black men and go naked save that they cover their private parts with cotton cloth from the waist down. Some are clad in skins of wild beasts, and some, the most noble, wear capes of these skins with tails which trail on the ground, as a token of state and dignity. They leap as they go, and sway their bodies so as to make these tails fly from one side to the other. They carry swords thrust into wooden scabbards bound with much gold and other metals, worn on the left side, as with us, in cloth girdles which they make for this purpose with four or five knots with hanging tassels to denote men of rank. They also carry assagais in their hands, and others carry bows and arrows of middle size; the arrows not so long as those of the English, and not so short as those of the Turks. The iron arrowheads are long and finely pointed.   They are warlike men, and some too are great traders . . . .

From *The Book of Duarte Barbosa*, translated by M. L. Dames, Hakluyt Society (2 vols., London 1918), vol. 1, par. 5.

JOÃO DE BARROS

Mines and Fortresses

[Summarizing what Lisbon had heard or understood by 1550, this chronicler reports that:] Of the mines of this land from which gold is taken the nearest to Sofala are those which they call Manica, which are in a plain surrounded by mountains having a circumference of about thirty leagues. The place where gold is to be found is generally known from the earth being dry and poor in herbage. The whole of this district is called Matuca, and the people who dig there are called Botongas . . . .

There are other mines in a district called Toroa, which by another name is known as the kingdom of Butua, which is ruled by a prince called Burrom, a vassal of Benametapa, which land adjoins that aforesaid consisting of vast plains, and these mines

There is another habitation of Moores two Caliver shot from the Castle, poore and miserable, which live by serving the Portugals. The women performe there the offices of Tillage and Husbandry; as also doe the Moores. They pay their Tithes to the Dominicans Church. The Fortresse was built An. 1505 by Pero da Nhaya, with consent of the Moorish King Zufe, a man blinde of both his eyes (in both sense, externall and internall, religious and politike) who too late repenting, thought to supplant it with trecherie, which they returned upon himselfe and slew him. In old times they had many such petty Moorish Kings on the Coast, few of which now remaine by reason of the Portugall Captaynes succeeding in their places, and in their amitie and commerce with the Quiteve King of those Countries . . . .

Kingdom of the Quiteve

The King of these parts [inland Mozambique and frontier with Zimbabwe] is of curled haire, a Gentile, which worships nothing, nor hath any knowledge of God; yea, rather hee carries himselfe as God of his Countries, and so is holden and reverenced of his Vassals. Hee is called Quiteve, a title royall and no proper name, which they exchange for this so soone as they become Kings. The Quiteve hath more than one hundred women all within doores, amongst which one or two are as his Queens, the rest as Concubines: many of them are his owne Aunts, Cousins, Sisters and Daughters, which he no less useth, saying, that his sonnes by them are true heires of the Kingdome without mixture of other bloud. When the Quiteve dyeth, his Queenes must die with him to doe him service in the other world, who accordingly at the instant of his death take a poyson (which they call Lucasse) and die therewith. The successor succeedeth as well to the women as to the state. None else but the King may upon paine of death marry his Sister or Daughter. This Successor is commonly one of the eldest Sonnes of the deceased King, and of his great Women or Queenes; and if the eldest be not sufficient, then the next, or if none of them be fit, his Brother of whole bloud. The King commonly whiles hee liveth maketh the choise, and traines up him to affaires of State, to whom he destines the succession. Whiles I lived there . . . the King had above thirtie Sonnes, and yet shewed more respect to his Brother a wise man, then to any of them, all honoring him as apparent heire.

The same day the King dies, he is carried to a Hill where all the Kings are interred, and early the next morning, hee whom the deceased had named his Successor, goeth to the Kings house where the Kings Women abide in expectation, and by their consent hee enters the house, and seates himselfe with the principall of them in a publike Hall, where the King was wont to sit to heare Causes, in a place drawne with curtens or covered with a cloth, that none may see the King nor the Women with him. And thence he sends his Officers, which goe thorow the Citie and proclayme Festivals to the New King, who is now quietly possessed of the Kings House, with the Women of the King decessed, and that all should goe and acknowledge him for their King which is done by all the great Men then in Court, and the Nobles of the Citie, who goe to the Palace now solemnely guarded, and enter into the Hall by licence of the Officers, where the new King abides with his Women; entring some, and some, creeping on the ground till they come to the middle of the Hall, and thence speake to the New King, giving him due obeysance, without seeing him or his Women. The King makes answere from within, and accepts their service: and after that drawes the Curtens, and shewes himselfe to them; whereat all of them clap their hands, and then turne behind the Curtens, and goe forth creeping on the ground as they came in; and when they are gone, others enter and doe in like sort. In this ceremonie the greatest part of the day is spent with feasting, musick and dancing thorow the citie. The next day, the King sends his Officers thorow the Kingdome to declare this his succession, and that all should come to the Court to see him breake the Bowe. Sometimes there are many Competitors, and then Hee succeeds whom the Women admit into the Kings House: for none may enter by Law without their leave, nor can bee King

The second Oath they call, Xoqua, which is made by iron heated red hot in the fire, causing the accused to lick it being so hot with his tongue, saying, that the fire shall not hurt him if hee bee innocent; otherwise it shall burne his tongue and his mouth. This is more common, and is used by the Cafres and the Moores in those parts; yea, (which worse is) some Christians give the same Oath to their slaves suspected of stealth; which one is Sofala caused, on suspicion of a stollen garment, a slave to doe three times without hurt. The third Oath they call, Calano, which is a vessell of water made bitter with certain herbs, which they put into it, whereof they give the accused to drinke, saying, that if he be innocent, he shall drinke it all off at one gulp without any stay, and cast it all up againe at once without any harme: if guilty, he shall not be able to get downe one drop without gargling and choaking...

Far up the Zambezi

The River Cuama is by them called Zambeze; the head whereof is so farre within Land that none of them know it, but by tradition of their Progenitors say it comes from a Lake in the midst of the Continent, which yeelds also other great Rivers, divers wayes visiting the Sea. They call it Zambeze, of a Nation of Cafres dwelling neere that Lake, which are so called. It hath a strong current, and is in divers plaes more than a league broad. Twentie leagues before it enters the Sea, it divides it selfe into two armes, each Daughter as great as the Mother, which thirtie leagues distant pay their Tribute to the Father of waters. The principall of them is called Luabo, which also divides it selfe into two branches, one called Old Luabo, the other Old Cuama. The other lesse principall Arme is named Quilimane.

Luabo is sailed all the yeere laong, but Quilimane only in the Winter. They saile up this River West North-west above two hundred leagues, to the Kingdome of Sacumbe, where it makes a great Fall from Rockes, beyond which they goe up the River twentie leagues to the Kingdome of Chicova, in which are Mines of Silver, which cannot be sailed by reason of the strong current: but from Chicova upwards it is Navigable, but how farre they know not. Luabo hath its name of an Iland so called in the Barre thereof in nineteene degrees, which Iland divides old Luabo on the South from Old Cuama, on the North: and in the East each salutes the other by entercourse of a streame five leagues long, which is the length and breadth of the Iland, peopled with Moores and Cafres. The Pangayos or great Barkes of Mosambique here discharge, being too great to passe higher, and carrie their goods in a Fleet of small Boates to the Fort of Sena, which is sixty leagues . . . .

Sena is a Fort of Lime and Stone, furnished with Artillery; the Captayne is placed by the Captayne of Mosambique. There were in my time eight hundred Christians, of which fiftie Portugalls. Seven or eight leagues from hence on the other side of the River, is the high Hill Chiri, which may be seene twentie leagues off, the Hill and Valleys exceeding fertile. To this Factory of Sena, they come from Tete to buy Merchandize with their Gold.

Tete is a stone Fort sixtie leagues further up the River in the Kingdome of Inhabaze, under the Manamotapa, the Captayne is placed by the Captayne of Mosambique. In this place were in my time sixe hundred Christians, of them fortie Portugalls. There one hundred and twentie leagues the Portugalls goe up the River, and from thence goe by Land with their Merchandize. The Countrey is very fertile, and Portugall wares are here sold at great prizes. From Tete they goe with their wares thorow a great part of Manamotapa to three Marts, Massapa, Luanze, Manzovo, in which the inhabitants of Sena, and Tete have houses and Factories, thence to store all the Countrey.

Massapa is the chiefe, where resides a Portugall Captayne, presented by the Portugalls, and confirmed by the Manamotapa, which cals him his Great Wife, a name of honour, as before is observed. This Captayne holds jurisdiction over all the Cafres without Appeale, as also over the Portugalls in that Kingdome, granted by the Vice-Royes, as all other Captaynes of those parts before, of Quiteve. It is paine of death for any Moore which discovers a Mine to take away any, besides his goods forfeited to the King. And if by chance any find a Mine, he is bound to cry out aloud, that some other Cafar may come to testifie that he takes none: and both are then to cover the Place with Earth, and set a great bough thereon, to give warning to other Cafares to avoyd the place. For if they should come there, it would cost them their lives, although there be no proofe that he tooke any thing. This severitie is used to keep the Mines from the knowledge of the Portugalls, lest covetous desire thereof might cause them to take away their Countrey. It is found in poulder like sand; in graines like beads; in pieces some smooth as they were melted, others branched with snags, others mixed so with Earth, that the Earth being well washed from them, they remayne like Honiecombes; those holes before full of red Earth, seeming as though they were also to be turned into Gold. As for that in stone, we have alreadie spoken . . . .

Although the Manamotapa be greater than those three mentioned, yet hath he not other Kings Vassals or Tributaries to him: only some of his subjects called Encosses or Fumos, are great Lords, and have Tenants subject to them. Botero therefore in his Relations, Gusman, and Osorius, were deceived by false inforamtion, giving to the Manamotapa, so large a Sea-coast with tributary Kings; which, I doubt, whether ever there was any such thing; at lest there is now no memory thereof. Philip Pigafetta also from the Relations of Lopez, hath falsly described these Coasts and Kingdomes, and hath told a long Tale of Amazons in these parts, where neither are such, nor any memoriall of them. They tell also of the Royall Ensignes, a Spade of Gold with an Ivorie head to intimate his Husbandry; and two Arrowes, the notes of his Justice; and that he alwayes is accompanyed with Souldiers; but in all they deceive and are deceived. As for Bows and Arrowes, it is as ordinary with the Cafres as with the Portugalls, to weare a Sword in their Cities; none of them going out of doores without them. And in like manner when the Manamotapa goeth forth, hee carries in his hand his Bow and Arrowes, as likewise doe the Cafres which accompany him, as a custome and not as Warriours. Before him goeth a Cafre beating with his hand on a great Cushion, to give a notice that the King is at hand. When the Manamotapa will not carry his Bow, an Officer called Mascorira (which is as a Page of the Chamber) carries it; and the King carrieth in his hand an Azagay, or Javelin of blacke wood with the point of pure Gold, like the Iron head of a Lance, or three pieces of wood, called Fimbos, of two spannes and a halfe, wrought and slender. And when hee speakes with a Cafre, whom he will have dye, he lets fall one of these Fimbos, and his infices (executioners) take and kill him with an Azagay; and so dye condemned persons.

He hath many women, and the principall, which is most respected, called Mazarira, is his entire sister a great friend of the Portugalls, to whom when they give the King his Curua, they give a Present of Clothes. No man speakes with the King or with his Wife, but hee brings a Present; the Portugalls give Beades, the Cafres Kine, or Goats, or Clothes: and when they are able to give nothing else, they bring a Sacke of Earth to acknowledge subjection, or a bundle of straw to thatch the Kings Houses; for all the Houses in Cafraria are thatched. The Manamotapa which now reignes, is called Mambo, and his subjects use to sweare by his life, saying Xe Mambo; and when they speake with him, they say Xe dico, as we, Please your Majestie. The Kings Children are called Manambo. Hee hath given leave to our Religious men in his Kingdomes, to convert and to build Churches; of which they have built three, to wit, at Massapa, Luanze, Bucutu, where live many Portugals . . . .

From João dos Santos, *Ethiopia Oriental*, in the translation of *Purchas His Pilgrimes* (reprinted Glasgow 1905), vol. 9. Also in J. Pinkerton, *A General Collection of the Best and Most Interesting Voyages and Travels, etc.* (London 1814), vol. 16.

Portuguese, in the name of and as the vassal of their king, and received and guaranteed all the conditions which the Portuguese considered conformable to the honor of the Gospel, and of the Crown of Portugal.

* * * * * * * *

Following this invasion, the same report of 1630 continues, the Monomotapa Manura signed a new treaty with the Portuguese on May 24, 1629.

First that this kingdom is delivered to him [i.e., to Manura] in the name of the king of Portugal, our lord, of whom he shall acknowledge himself to be a vassal . . . .

That he, the said king, shall allow all the religious of whatever order who may be in his *zimbahe* to build churches and in all the other lands in his dominions . . . .

That ambassadors who come to speak to him shall enter his *zimbahe* shod and covered, with their arms in their belts, as they speak to the king of Portugal, and he shall give them a chair on which to seat themselves without clapping their hands; and other Portuguese shall speak to him in the manner of ambassadors, and shall be given a *kaross* to sit upon . . . .

He shall make his lands free to the Portuguese . . . .

Throughout all his kingdom he shall allow as many mines to be sought for and opened as the Portuguese like . . . .

Within a year he shall expel all the Moors [i.e., Swahili and Arab traders from the coastal towns] from his kingdom, and those who shall be found there afterward shall be killed by the Portuguese, and their property shall be seized for the king of Portugal . . . .

From G. M. Theal, *Records of South-eastern Africa*, 1900, vol. 2, p. 249, for the first extract and vol. 5, p. 290, for the second.

KING OF PORTUGAL

Civilities

Two years after the signature of the above treaty of 1629, the King of Portugal writes politely to the Monomotapa Manura.

Most noble and powerful king of Monomotapa, I, Dom Philipe, by the grace of God king of Portugal, of the Algarves, and of the sea on both sides of Africa, lord of Guinea and of the conquest, navigation, and commerce of Ethiopia, Arabia, Persia, and India, etc., greet you well, as one whom I love and esteem as a brother.

I have seen the letter which you wrote to me by the ships of last year, 1630, and having gathered therefrom, as my viceroy of the State of India also wrote to me, how the wars and disturbances in your kingdom had ended, and how my captains gave you the investiture and possession of it . . . . I think fit to inform you that I received great satisfaction from all this . . . .

From G. M. Theal, *Records of South-eastern Africa*, 1900, vol. 4, p. 225.

MANOEL BARRETO

Realities

In a valuable report of 1667 to the viceroy in Goa upon the "State and Conquest of the Rivers of Cuama, Commonly and Truly called the Rivers of Gold," Manoel Barreto explains to the viceroy that he is writing after many years spent in the region. He is speaking mainly of the lands of the Lower Zambezi.

As [the empire of] Maravi is beside us up the river [Zambezi] on the eastern side, so is Mokaranga on the northern side. It commences immediately above Tete, and extends towards the west and north about a hundred and fifty leagues, both in length and breadth . . . .

Mokaranga is very healthy, fertile and verdant . . . . In this kingdom . . . rich in gold, its kings chose for their court, or *zimbaoe*, a site which is dry, sterile and unhealthy, which makes the residence of the chief captain and garrison [i.e., Portuguese] of that court sufficiently difficult. The distance from Tete to Dambarari is about fourteen days' journey, and to the *zimbaoe* twenty.

Dambarari is a noble settlement and good-sized town in the heart of Mokaranga, and has grown to be the center of that conquest, with many rich inhabitants. The Portuguese and even the *mocoques* [chiefs] of Dambarari and of the rest of Mokaranga possess vast lands, or provinces, which they have bought, and buy every day, from the king of Mokaranga. With the people of these lands and their *macamos*, as they call their troops of slaves, they are more powerful than the king of Mokaranga himself. It is a proof of this that while I was there they separated themselves from the poor king, through no fault of his, and declared war against him. Before it came to a battle, when the armies were almost in sight of each other, the *encozes*, who are the lords or chief Kaffirs of that kingdom, killed the poor king (a thing unprecedented among the Kaffirs) for fear of the Portuguese, and came and subjected themselves to them that they might make whom they chose king. They elected a young man of the royal house, but very crafty and cunning, who is now sufficiently feared by them. I fear the punishment of God for the injustice done to the poor dead king, particularly upon Antonio Rois de Lima, who was the head of this unjust rebellion and other great disorders in that conquest.

To keep this new and formidable king in check, Antonio de Mello was obliged to send Antonio Lobo da Silva to Mokaranga as chief captain. . . . Antonio de Mello's motive was that he had been told the gold would fail, because the Kaffirs would not dig for it through fear of the Portuguese.   It is true that the *encozes* do not wish gold to be dug for in their lands, because upon the report of gold being found the Portuguese buy the land from the king, as frequently happened, and they, the *encozes*, being great lords, counts, dukes and marquises, are despoiled of their lands and become poor *caporros*, which signifies laborers. But this objection is not avoided by the Portuguese giving up the lands they have already, as the *encozes* would retain them from the king again, with many more. It would be sufficient, in order to avoid this obstacle, to pass an inviolable law that the king should not give or sell any more lands to the Portuguese, by which the *encozes* who now hold them would be without fear; but who can tie the hands of a king and prevent him from doing what he pleases in his own kingdom? Besides, this would close the door by which the Portuguese become each time more powerful in that kingdom, and which is very conducive to conquest.

This king of Mokaranga is honored by his Majesty with the title of brother-in-arms, but strictly speaking he is his vassal, for in the time of the rebel king Capracina the Portuguese conquered the kingdom by force of arms, and now they elect and depose kings at their pleasure.

If this king should rise in rebellion it would be proper to conquer the whole of the kingdom, and divide the lands among the Portuguese, by which there would be great favours and rich appointments for the deserving. Then the natives would dig as much gold as their masters, the Portuguese, required . . . .

The Gold Fails

There are many reasons to account for the small quantity of gold produced.

First, the repugnance of the *encozes* [chiefs], who will allow no digging in their lands, that the Portuguese may not covet them . . . .

Secondly, the want of population, which is great throughout Kaffraria . . . .

But the principal cause of the want of population is the bad conduct of the Portuguese, from whose violence the Kaffirs flee to other lands . . . .

From the translation of the original (in the Bibliothèque Nationale, Paris) by G. M. Theal, *Records of South-eastern Africa*, 1900, vol. 3, p. 436 for the first extract and p. 490 for the second.

West Africa Meets
Europe

*T*HE MEETING OCCURRED IN THE middle of the fifteenth century, rather more than five hundred years ago. It was brusque and bloody to begin with, an affair of squalid raids and running fights, but soon calmed to a more or less regular trading partnership. In exchange for textiles and metalware, West African gold and ivory and spice began to reach Europe by sea instead of through the hands of middlemen across the Sahara. A new period of history began.

Looking back, we can see that the meeting might well have occurred two or three centuries earlier—Genoese ships had come as far as Sale in Morocco by 1163—but for a major climatic obstacle. Along the Atlantic Coast from Cape Juby to Cape Blanc, a reach of some four hundred miles, the wind is almost always from the northward. Not until the early fifteenth century were the ships of Europe technically capable of sailing into the wind; while their crews, having neither astrolabe nor compass, were understandably reluctant to sail "round the wind" by steering boldly westward out of sight of land. This meant that they could well enough go down the coast beyond Cape Juby, but could hope to get back again only with the use of oars against the wind, a very laborious and perhaps impossible trial of strength. Even so, several attempts are known to have been made, the most famous being that of Jacme Ferrer, who voyaged from Mallorca for the Rio d'Oro (the legendary "river of gold") in 1346, as the Catalan Atlas of thirty-one years later graphically records, but never returned.

Then these nautical problems were solved. Perhaps through the experience of the Crusades, European seamen learned the use of the lateen sail, no doubt from Muslim sailors of the eastern Mediterranean who would have had it from their fellow-seamen of the Indian Ocean. Invented in China, the nautical compass also reached Europe by way of the Arabs. So did the astrolabe, a device for measuring latitude. Cartography enormously improved. The fruits of all this were not long in coming. In 1434 a Portuguese crew sailed beyond Cape Bojador and returned safely against the wind. Others followed. Within little more than half a century these hardy and courageous mariners had pushed their discoveries to the Cape of Good Hope. (An admirable discussion of the technical and political background to all this will be found in Professor Raymond Mauny's *Les Navigations Mediévales sur les Côtes Sahariennes anterieurs à la Découverte portugaise*, Lisbon, 1960.)

The early Portuguese and Spanish material is fairly copious but of greatly varying value. After Azurara's (or Zurara's) picturesque *Discovery of Guinea*, completed in 1453 (English translation by C. R. Beazley and E. Prestage, Hakluyt Society, 2 vols., 1896), there are useful if highly partial memoirs collected by Ruy de Pina, who became chief chronicler of Portugal in 1497, as well as a number of lesser works. An Italian in Portuguese service, Ca'da Mosto, sailed to the Gambia in 1456 and published an interesting account of trade along the coast (English translation by G. R. Crone, Hakluyt Society, 1937). Then comes a work of capital importance, the first detailed and reliable description of the geographical outline of the western reaches of the Guinea seaboard: the curiously named *Esmeraldo de Situ Orbis* of Duarte Pacheco Pereira, written probably between 1505 and 1508. Pereira had sailed to India in one of the three fleets of 1503, returning two years later, and therefore knew the route from his own experience. A systematic picture of the coast now became available in Lisbon.

Other Europeans followed where the Portuguese had led, notably the English and the French and, a little later on, the Dutch. Until the seventeenth century—though rarely even then—their writings are seldom more than laconic tales of adventure or bare recitals of trading profit, laced now and then with more or less fantastic speculations on the nature of African humanity. There are some exceptions to this, as the reader will see, but not many. Yet these ships' logs and seamen's tales throw light on two interesting aspects of this European-African connection of the sixteenth century: they reveal the beginnings of a trade that was profitable to both sides, a trade that was still free of slaving so far as the French and English (though not the Portuguese) were concerned; and they show the relationship of equality and mutual respect that held good between the two sides of a promising commercial partnership. Apart from the slaving voyages of John Hawkins, the English (as the French) were not in the least concerned with buying captives. They wanted gold, pepper and ivory in that order of priority, offering hardware and textiles in exchange. This trade was perilous because of the dangers of the voyage and the enmity of the Portuguese, who claimed a monopoly of access to West Africa, yet it prospered. The voyages of Thomas Windham and John Lok, and William Towerson's three remarkable voyages of 1555-1557, were highly profitable to the merchants of London, and, so far as the records show, no less satisfactory to those of Africa. The story is much the same on the French side.

But the Portuguese were already deeply involved in buying captives for slave labor in the Americas. Like the English and the French, they had begun with other intentions; it was the slave trade on the west coast—as it was their piracy on the east—that dragged their connection with Africa into a morass of bloody violence. On this the records are perfectly clear. They can be followed most easily in relation to the African kingdoms that lay round the estuary of the Congo and southward in western Angola. Here we are fortunate in possessing twenty-four letters written by King Affonso (Mbemba Nzinga) to two successive kings of Portugal, a collection that is of unique value to history in that it offers the earliest African commentary on the European connection.

Reading between the lines of these polite and often puzzled letters we can trace the early hopes of this African monarch and his later disillusionment; the determination with which he tried, time and again, to turn the trade with Portugal to constructive ends; his efforts to circumvent the Portuguese monopoly of contact with Europe; the growing ruin of the slave trade; the steady collapse of trust and confidence, and the multiplying signs of early Portuguese imperialism. A fuller examination of all this may be found in my book about the Atlantic slave trade, *Black Mother*, Boston: 1961 and later editions. Much parallel material from the Roman Catholic missionary side is in *L'Ancien Congo d'après les Archives romaines* (1518-1640), edited by Monsignor J. Cuvelier and Abbé L. Jadin (Brussels: 1954), while the contemporary records and memoirs of Pigafetta (Rome: 1591) and Resende (Lisbon: 1622) are of major importance.

These contemporary writings were composed, one should remember, against a background of grotesque superstition, especially among the Portuguese, and acute religious prejudice. Their authors were quite without a scientific approach. Even the achievements of Muslim science were largely unknown, or, if known at all, filtered at second or third hand through the private libraries of kings and princes. Such libraries were designed to promote national and commercial purposes rather than the pursuit of knowledge, and they were generally barred to public use. No monarch, least of all the king of Portugal, had any interest in sharing what he knew with rivals and competitors; on the contrary, the pioneers and merchants kept their knowledge closely to themselves. It was nearly four centuries before Pereira's book was published, and we have already noted what befell the work of de Barros and de Couto. Not until the end of the imperial epoch was there to be any real chance of seeing "in the round" what Europeans believed or knew of Africa in those early days. But now with fuller knowledge and smaller prejudice it is possible to reassess these memoirs and adventures as a whole, and award them their useful place in the records of the continent. What follows here is a brief but representative selection.

This section also takes in the seventeenth century.

If the sixteenth had been a time of European piracy passing into alliance and regular trading intercourse with maritime chiefs and peoples from the Senegal to the Congo, the seventeenth was one of intensive and developing commercial enterprise. For France and England, this was the period of the early "chartered companies," those stumbling experiments in early forms of banking and capital investment; and, on the Coast itself, of the rise of the Dutch with their emergence as commercial and military leaders of the whole European enterprise. It was likewise the period of Spanish decline, and the strong establishment of the English and the French in the Caribbean. Out of the various factors came the oversea slave trade as a *system*. This system was to dominate European-African relations from the middle of the seventeenth century until the middle of the nineteenth.

For Africa the seventeenth century was similarly a time of large and in some respects crucial change. In the Western Sudan it brought the final collapse of the Songhay Empire of Gao; with declining Muslim prosperity in North Africa, it witnessed a dwindling of the trans-Saharan trade, and the consequent impoverishment of trading cities such as Timbuktu and Djenne. Europe having opened West Africa's back door, the gold and ivory (and now, increasingly, the slaves) went northward or westward by way of the sea. For the same order of reasons there were great organic changes in the forest-belt states between the grasslands and the coast. The ground was laid for the rise of new powers, such as Ashanti and Dahomey, which would soon challenge the old mastery of Oyo and Benin. In central and southern Africa (with the Dutch acquiring a toehold at the Cape of Good Hope in 1652) the seventeenth century brought new constellations of power among some of the leading Bantu-speaking peoples, notably in the lands of the southern Congo basin. Ethiopia triumphed over her Muslim neighbors and rivals. The "black sultans" of the Fung built their powerful state on the Middle Nile where ancient Kush had once held sway.

Some of these inner-African changes were the consequence of indirect pressures from the European connection along the seaboard; most took place, however, beyond the probing reach of European influence. On these the European records are entirely silent, or, if not quite mute, greatly misinformed. Here and there, true enough, envoys and missionaries sent home interesting reports or wrote them after retirement; prominent among these were some of the missionaries in the old Congo kingdoms, Father Giovanni Cavazzi and others, who offer highly impressionist but none the less firsthand views of the situation. Generally, however, the records of the seventeenth century (especially by contrast with those of the eighteenth) are of much greater value to European than to African history, being concerned for the most part with internecine rivalry, largely between the English and the Dutch and between the Dutch and the Portuguese.

Characteristic of their type and temper, for example, is a petition of 1662 by the owners of the *Daniell* to the Privy Council. They had commissioned Henry Oake to sail the *Daniell* "Neere the Gold Coast at Guinny" and there to buy ivory, gold, and captives for the West Indian plantations. "He arrived safely, and did barter away part of his Lading for 83 Negroes, a parcel of Elephants' Teeth, and some Gold. . . ." All seemed well. But "as he was in his lawful employment, one Jasper Vanhuisen, General for the Dutch West India Company residing at Guinny, first seized his Boat and five of his men, going towards Cormantine and carrying them away prisoners; and some days after, a ship of Amsterdam . . . belonging to the Dutch, being mounted with 30 guns, and the ship *Daniell* having but Four, the said ship of Amsterdam . . . took her and all the Goods and Negroes, stripping and plundering the Company . . . ." On this and the immediately following period the magnificent work of Elizabeth Donnan, *Documents Illustrative of the History of the Slave Trade to America* (Carnegie Institution, Washington D.C.: 1930-1935), has put all subsequent writers and readers deeply in her debt.

Encroaching on each other, the Europeans also encroached on their African partners and were frequently rebuffed. Not for a long time would the power of Europe prove capable of carrying things here with a high hand. As late as 1694 an English captain arriving off Accra "bought a five-hand canoe here of the black general [of Akwamu], who had surprised and seized the Danes' fort here [Christiansborg Castle], forced the Danes' general to fly to the Dutch for his life, murdered his second and several of the soldiers and now trades with the Dutch interlopers," an incident that was typical of African impatience with the arrogantly monopolizing habits so often assumed by the European companies. A little further in his *Journal*, published only in 1732, this Captain Phillips describes how the Akwamu authorities allowed the Danes back into their fort on payment of a weighty fee in gold. The colonial threat was still below the skyline. Manners were accordingly polite. "I saw and spoke to the *Oba* of Benin," the Dutchman van Nyendael would record of this time, "in the presence of his three great counsellors. He was seated on an ivory throne under a canopy of Indian silk. He was about forty years old and of lively expression. According to custom I stood about thirty feet away from him. So as to see him better I asked permission to draw closer. He laughingly agreed."

Being commercially and technically more advanced than other Europeans of the seventeenth century, the Dutch were better reporters. In 1668 the efficient and well-informed Amsterdam geographer, Olfert Dapper, published in his immediately famous *Description of Africa* a number of invaluable reports on the condition of Benin and some other African states and cities. For this he drew on compatriots with firsthand experience. He is particularly good on Benin, for which he used eyewitness material by otherwise unknown Dutch merchants who sojourned there. The Empire by that time, according to these witnesses, measured some four hundred fifty miles from west to east and an unknown distance towards the north, having "many towns and an infinity of villages, the capital city itself being enclosed on one side by a wall ten feet high, made of a double palisade of trees" pierced by "several gates eight or nine feet high and five feet wide," each made of a single piece of wood and turning "on a stake."

"The King's palace," these Hollanders reported, "is on the right side of the town . . . [being] a collection of buildings which occupy as much space as the town of Harlem," with numerous apartments and fine galleries "most of which are as big as those on the Exchange in Amsterdam." These galleries "are supported by wooden pillars encased with copper, where their victories are depicted" while the corner of each gallery roof "is adorned with a small pyramidal tower, on the point of which is perched a copper bird spreading its wings." The whole town "is composed of thirty main streets, very straight and 120 feet wide, apart from an infinity of small intersecting streets," the houses being "close to one another, arranged in good order"; and "these people are in no way inferior to the Dutch as regards cleanliness"—no mean tribute from the member of a nation that was probably, in point of cleanliness, the most advanced in Europe of its day. Dapper's informants also brought him much precious detail on the organization and political system of Benin, then still near the height of its power and influence. I have included a few fascinating extracts from the Dutch, but readers who would like to pursue these references further will find them conveniently set forth in Thomas Hodgkin's *Nigerian Perspectives* (Oxford: 1960; reprinted 1975); or, given access to a good library, in Dapper himself.

RUY DE PINA

The Building of Elmina Castle

[1482] The king [of Portugal], considering, as a wise man, the great profit and good health which his subjects would receive in body and soul, and also how his merchandise, and the affairs of his honor, estate, and service would be properly secured, if he were to possess in those parts of Mina [Gold Coast] a fortress of his own, and wishing to know whether such a fortress could or should be built, held a meeting of his council to discuss this matter, and contrary votes and opinions were given there.

While some thought it would be an easy thing to do and very profitable, others believed it would be very dangerous and perilous, and, in fact, impossible, or, even if they allowed it to be built, its upkeep would be very difficult, both on account of the great remoteness of the land and because the climate was very sickening and the Negroes little truthful and less trustworthy. These objections were so considerable, they said, that it ought not to be built. The king, after these arguments had been advanced, nevertheless determined that it should be built.

For this purpose, he ordered that all the timber and freestones, which would be necessary for the gates, the windows, and corner-rafters of the walls, the tower, and other things, should forthwith be cut and shaped in this country, so that without any delay in the work they could be set in place immediately. Moreover, a great quantity of mixed and compounded limes was made ready, together with tiles and bricks, nails and iron tools, and provisions, and all other things pertinent to the work in great abundance. And six hundred men also were ordered and equipped, one hundred masters of masonry and carpentry and five hundred for defence and service. And it was agreed that the whole should be carried, as it was carried, in *urcas* and great ships with the idea that they might not return or sail any more, and, besides these, there went other ships and caravels, strong and sound, with many provisions, medicines, and rich wares, and very honorable men and dependants of the king were appointed captains of these ships.

After certain persons, to whom this work was assigned, had already provided the king with excuses for themselves for fear of the difficulties and perils involved, the first man to accept it freely and to be willing to undertake it was Ferna Lourenco, who was the secretary of his exchequer and had charge of the treasury and factory of these trades, afterwards being officially appointed. But the king, after praising him highly and profusely thanking him for this offer, as his goodwill deserved, refused him, on account of the same charge with which he was entrusted.

Then, being informed of the virtues, loyalty, great courage and good sense of Diego da Azambuja, a knight of his household, who had already been proved in other affairs of considerable importance and great peril, with words about the singular confidence, which he reposed in him, and promising him that he might expect great rewards and preferments, he entrusted him with the work; and da Azambuja, with others of very praiseworthy obedience and sure loyalty, accepted it with a smiling face and a steady heart. And to put this into execution, he then went to make preparations at Lisbon, from where he departed in December on the eve of the day of Santa Luzia in the year one thousand four hundred and eighty-one. . . .

And finally, guided by the Holy Spirit and committing himself to its care, he arrived near the village, which was called das Duas Partes (Village of the Two Parts), where he disembarked on Wednesday, the nineteenth of January, in the year one thousand four hundred and eighty-two, and, examining with great care the lofty situation of the land, which was very suitable for defence and for the health of the people, and having tested and sounded the anchorages of the sea for the ships, he discovered that a better disposition for a fortress could neither be found nor pictured, especially since there was much rock, and a large settlement, which offered hope to the inhabitants of fresh water and other provisions for very long periods.

And on the next day, which was the day of Sam Sebastiam, by the advice of one, Joham Bernaldez, whom he met there bartering, he went on land, clothed in silk and brocade, and with his men in good order. And at the foot of a tree, under its shade, he commanded a mass to be said (which was the first that was said) and he attended; and henceforth that valley was, and shall always be, called the Vale of Sam Sebastiam. Then, after eating, he ordered a richly ornamented platform to be erected; and he sat thereon, accompanied by very honorable men, and with his trumpets, tambourines and drums, and all in an act of peace, in order to receive there, by agreement, the lord of the place, who was called Caramansa, whom the Negroes called king, and to speak with him.

Hither the king came, and before him a great noise of bugles, bells and horns, which are their instruments, and he was accompanied by an endless number of Negroes, some with bows and arrows, and others with assagais and shields; and the principal persons were attended behind by naked page-boys with seats of wood, like stools, to sit upon . . . .

Then the principal persons who came with him, followed him, all first wetting their fingers in their mouths and then wiping them on their breasts, before touching those of the captain, which is a courtesy and a rare grace among them that is specially kept for kings and persons of great estate. When all were again seated and a signal for silence given, the captain began his speech, with the aid of a Negro, familiar with the language, who forthwith interpreted it, and its substance was: that, on account of the good report which the king, his lord, had received about them, and of the good treatment which they above all the men of that land gave to his vassals, who were accustomed to come to trade there, his highness had sent him there to treat with them and for ever to secure peace and friendship. . . . And forasmuch as a house was necessary, because it was reasonable that the merchandise, which they were now bringing, and would in future arrive, might always remain there continuously, fresh and secure, he asked them to give place and licence and even assistance, so that it might be built at the mouth of the river, because from such a house and from the Christians, who would be stationed in it, they would always find and receive protection, profit and favour.

The king, with his principal persons there, then replied to him, saying that the people of the Christians, who up to that time had come there, were few, foul and vile, and that the people, who had now arrived, were very different, particularly he himself, who by his clothes and appearance must be the son or the brother of the king of Portugal. . . . Proceeding in their reply, they said furthermore that, judging by his appearance and by his assurance that he spoke to them in the name of the king, it could not be that he was hiding the truth from them, or that he was intending trickery or malice against them by his requests. Accordingly, they gave him permission then to build the house, as he desired; since, if, when it was built, he kept his promise, it was certain that the king of Portugal, his lord, would be better served, and that the Christians, his subjects, would at all times be treated better; but if he should do the contrary, they would leave him the houses and the land, set their own persons free, and in another land would not want for straws and sticks with which they might soon build other houses. Then the captain responded to them, by a sign, that they might always be sure and certain of everything which he had told them; because Christians were not accustomed to lie; but rather to do and discharge affairs better than they talked of them . . . .

Then the captain, before withdrawing, went at once with the master-craftsman, whom he brought, to put together the base of the fortress, for which they took material from the top of some high rocks, which the Negroes were accustomed to worship and to hold as very sacred. On that day, the captain then divided the work by shifts and captaincies, so that on the next day, which was the twenty-first of January, they might begin it, as they did. Also in like manner, he sent to the king and his men a good present of many lambres, basins, manillas and other cloth, which was to be given to them first before all else to ensure their good will, and he entrusted Joham Bernaldez with this task, who yet went with it not so early but that already the workmen and quarrymen began the work sooner; because at dawn they were busy laying the foundations of the tower and also breaking the stones and then setting them in place.

The Negroes, upon seeing the destruction and utter ruin of their sacred rocks, meanwhile believed that they were looking upon the loss of all hope of their salvation, and all eagerly and in a great rage took up their arms and so struck hard at the workmen, who, not being able to resist them, retreated in flight to the boats. Whereupon, Diego da Azambuja then hurriedly sent help; and because he knew that the present, which he had ordered, had not yet been delivered, he realized that the cause of the tumult proceeded from the negligence of the messenger. Accordingly, he commanded that there was to be no delay in delivering the present, to which he added some more things owing to the greater need of their favour; whereby all the evil of the Negroes was at once turned into good and their direct refusal into a double consent.

As a result of this incident, no other house was marked out or founded and no foundation laid, until the tower was above one story high. When it had been built up to this level, the surround of the castle was forthwith begun, for which it was necessary to demolish some houses of the Negroes, and to this they and their women consented easily and without taking offense in return for large reparations and the gifts which were given to them. Then they began to need water urgently; for they were unable to make use of the supply in the land and near there, on account of the Negroes guarding it continuously and forbidding them to use it, and because they did not wish to attack them and to take it by force. After having considered many remedies, they were obliged by chance and, as it were, miraculously to provide themselves with a supply elsewhere. Though many of the people sickened and some died, the work was pressed on so fast that within twenty days the walls of the fortress were built up to their full height, and so was the tower, and within many houses were finished. Then the fort was assigned the name O Castello de Sam Jorge, as a mark of respect to him who is the patron and protector of Portugal.

Portuguese Reach Benin

[1486] In this year, the land of Beny beyond Myna to the Rios dos Escravos was first discovered by Joham Affom da Aveiro,* who died there; whence there came to these kingdoms the first pepper from Guinee, whereof a great quantity was produced in that land; and presently samples of it were sent to Framdes [Flanders] and to other parts, and soon it fetched a great price and was held in high esteem. The king of Beny [Benin] sent as ambassador to the king a Negro, one of his captains, from a harboring place by the sea, which is called Ugato [Gwato], because he desired to learn more about these lands, the arrival of people from them in his country being regarded as an unusual novelty.

This ambassador was a man of good speech and natural wisdom. Great feasts were held in his honor, and he was shown many of the good things of these kingdoms. He returned to his land in a ship of the king's, who at his departure made him a gift of rich clothes for himself and his wife: and through him he also sent a rich present to the king of such things as he understood he would greatly prize. Moreover, he sent holy and most catholic advisers with praiseworthy admonitions for the faith to administer a stern rebuke about

---

*Other Portuguese had certainly gone as far as the Bight of Benin by 1471-1472.

the heresies and great idolatries and fetishes, which the Negroes practise in that land. Then also there went with him new factors [commercial agents] of the king, who were to remain in that country and to traffic for the said pepper and for other things, which pertained to the trades of the king. But owing to the fact that the land was afterwards found to be very dangerous from sickness and not so profitable as had been hoped, the trade was abandoned.

From the translation of Ruy de Pina's chronicle of John II (*Collecao de livros ineditos de historia portugueza*, 1792) in J. W. Blake, *Europeans in West Africa* (2 vols., Hakluyt Society: 1942), vol. 1, p. 70 for the first extract and p. 78 for the second. In regard to the latter, compare Benin traditions in Egharevba, pp. 123-24.

DUARTE PACHECO PEREIRA

Inland Kingdoms

You find the first Negroes at the Sanagua [Senegal] River, and this where the kingdom of Jolof [Wolof] begins .... The king of Jolof can put ten thousand horsemen and one hundred thousand footmen into the field and all these people go naked save nobles and notables who wear blue cotton shirts and *serouals* (trousers?) of the same stuff .... None of these people nor their neighbors know where the Sanagua River comes from .... We have learned from numerous Ethiopians [that is, Africans], fairly well-informed men who know the country for five hundred leagues upstream, various provinces and countries through which it passes, that its source is unknown; but judging by its course and its point of departure we know that it comes from a big lake of the River Nile which is thirty leagues long and ten broad, in such a way that it [the Sanagua River] seems to be branch that the Nile sends out across lower Ethiopia towards the west. Another branch goes north and reaches the sea through four mouths in Egypt . . . . At the head of this lake there is a kingdom called Tambucutu [Timbuktu] which has a big city of the same name near the lake. There, too, is the city of Jany [Djenne], inhabited by Negroes and surrounded by a wall of baked clay; brass and copper are very expensive there, and so are red and blue stuffs and salt, and everything but the stuffs is sold by weight . . . . The trade of that region is very great . . . .

From Duarte Pacheco Pereira: *Esmeraldo de Situ Orbis*, c. 1505. Translated here from the French of R. Mauny, *Esmeraldo de Situ Orbis* (Bissau: 1956), p. 49. See also G. H. T. Kimble (Hakluyt Society: 1937) for a complete translation in English.

DUARTE PIRES

The King of Benin

[1516] Most high and mighty king and prince, our lord. May God increase your royal estate. Sir, your highness will be pleased to know how Pero Baroso gave me a letter from your highness, which made me rejoice that your highness should be mindful of so humble a man as I; and now I render account to your highness in regard to the letter which you sent me. Sir, with reference to what you say about my being in very great favour with the king of Benin, it is truly so; because the king of Benin is pleased with what I said in favour of your highness, and he desires to be your very good friend and speaks of nothing save what concerns Our Lord and your interest; and so he is very glad, and likewise all his noblemen and his people; and your highness will shortly know about this.

The favour which the king of Benin accords us is due to his love of your highness; and thus he pays us high honor and sets us at table to dine with his son, and no part of his court is hidden from us but all the doors are open. Sir, when these priests arrived in Benin, the delight of the king of Benin was so great that I do not know how to describe it, and likewise that of all his people; and he sent for them at once; and they remained with him for one whole year in war. The priests and we reminded him of the embassy of your highness, and he replied to us that he was very satisfied with it; but since he was at war, that he could do nothing until he returned to Benin, because he needed leisure for such a deep mystery as this; as soon as he was in Benin, he would fulfil his promise to your highness, and he would so behave as to give great pleasure to your highness and to all your kingdom.

So it was that, at the end of one year, in the month of August, the king gave his son and some of his noblemen—the greatest in his kingdom—so that they might become Christians; and also he ordered a church to be built in Benin; and they made them Christians straightway; and also they are teaching them to read, and your highness will be pleased to know that they are very good learners. Moreover, sir, the king of Benin hopes to finish his war this summer, and we shall return to Benin, and I shall give your highness an account of everything that happens. Sir, I Duarte Pires, and Joham Sobrynho, a resident in the island of O Principe, and Grygoryo Lourenco, a black man and formerly the servant of Francysquo Lourenco, all remain in the service of your highness, and we have submitted proposals on your behalf to the king of Benin, and we have described to him how your highness is a great lord and how you can make him a great lord. Done in this war, on 20 October 1516.

To the lord the king.

DUARTE PIRES

From a letter dated Oct. 20, 1516, in Portuguese royal archives of Torre do Tombo. Original text reprinted in J. R. Coelho, *Alguns documentos do Archivo Nacional*, 1892, p. 33. Translation here is that of J. W. Blake, ed., *Europeans in West Africa* (2 vols., Hakluyt Society: 1942), vol. 1, p. 123.

ALONSO DE PALENCIA

A Spanish Raid

In order to set a bound to these insults and cruelties from the Portuguese [who claimed monopoly of access to West Africa by right of Papal Bull], King Don Fernando sent a strong fleet of Andalucians with orders to break their arrogance, and to humble the pride, which the riches of Guinea had inspired in them. The Andalucians joyfully obeyed, and, while a fleet of thirty ships was being prepared in the port of Seville, some fishermen of Palos, already accustomed to warlike expeditions and fortunate against the Portuguese, joined with other mariners of Puerto (de Santa Maria), and arrived in two caravels at the coasts nearest to Guinea. They call that territory "that of the Azanegas [a Berber people of the Mauretanian Coast]," by which name they distinguish those of citrine color from others of a darker color and of customs even darker.

The conditions of these natives, when they feed themselves on fish alone, is very gentle, and as they always walk unarmed by the lagoons, they suffer themselves to be seized without difficulty by warlike and unarmed men. The mariners of the two caravels secured 120 Azenegas and carried them to Andalucia, despising the orders of King Dom Fernando, who absolutely forbade fraudulent trade with the men of Guinea, let alone the making captives of them, and commanded them to attach themselves to the royal fleet and to obey the admiral implicitly. The disturbances of the times emboldened the men of Palos to carry out this exploit, and, provoked moreover by the insolent words of Gonzalo de Estuniga, governor of the fortress of Palos, they fitted out three other caravels and put into the coasts of Guinea with the intention of loading slaves.

The king of that region, through his frequent traffic with the Portuguese, to whom he bartered his prisoners of war for trifles, believed that the ships were Portuguese. After signals of peace had been made by both sides, the king with some of his men entered into the first caravel and inquired who commanded it, and the reply in Portuguese confirmed him in his error. Then, he agreed to the barter of slaves for brass rings, small oval leather shields, clothes of diverse colors, and other objects, which the poverty of the inhabitants caused them to covet greatly. To celebrate the exchanges, the king caused one calf and sheep to be brought for the feast of that day, and he accepted for the following day the hospitality of the patron of the caravels. He appeared on the beach surrounded by a great multitude, and mounted to the ship with his brothers, his close friends, and the most powerful of his people. After the feast was ended, the patron invited him to visit the interior of the ship, and then the treacherous mariners closed the hatch-ways, and, having armed, they secured 140 nobles of splendid physique.

Once on the high seas, the king, complaining of the cruel trick, again inquired who owned the ships. They told him Spaniards. He wished to know whether they obeyed any king, and, when he was told that they obeyed a most noble one, he expressed his confidence that he would free him from such an iniquitous captivity.

On arrival at Palos, the Andalucians wished to force him to walk in the crowd amongst the other slaves. But he resisted, and said that they should take him either dragging by a rope or on horseback, because his misfortune must be either terrible or dignified. Gonzalo de Estuniga, moved by this resolution verily of royal spirit, or perchance spurred on by anxiety about the future ransom, ordered a horse to be brought. The king nimbly mounted upon it, and, going before the slaves, he began to march with a majestic air.

When King Don Fernando learned all this, he commanded that the king be immediately restored to his native land. But as the execution of the order was deferred owing to the disturbances of those days, he ordered us, doctor Antonio Rodriguez de Lillo and myself, to intimate to Gonzalo de Estuniga that he must set the king at liberty. He managed to delay the execution of the order, and it was only at the end of some months of captivity that we succeeded in returning the unhappy monarch to his native land, although we were not able to prevent his brothers and other relatives from being sold in Andalucia as slaves.

That savage maintained a certain regal authority during his captivity, and he displayed dignity in his countenance, gravity in speech, prudence in conduct, and courage in adversity. On reaching his country, he exercised such cunning in order to avenge himself on his treacherous oppressors that, in spite of the distrust with which they travelled, he succeeded in securing some and keeping them as hostages for as many others of his relations.

From Alonso de Palencia, *Cronica de Enrique IV* (ed. Paz y Melia, 1904-1909), decada (volume) III, bk. 25, chap. 4; translated in J. W. Blake, ed., *Europeans in West Africa* (2 vols., Hakluyt Society: 1942), vol. 1, p. 215.

AFFONSO OF CONGO

Evils of the Trade

[1526] Sir, Your Highness [of Portugal] should know how
our Kingdom is being lost in so many ways that it is convenient
to provide for the necessary remedy, since this is caused by
the excessive freedom given by your factors and officials to the
men and merchants who are allowed to come to this Kingdom
to set up shops with goods and many things which have been
prohibited by us, and which they spread throughout our
Kingdoms and Domains in such an abundance that many of our
vassals, whom we had in obedience, do not comply because
they have the things in greater abundance than we ourselves;
and it was with these things that we had them content and
subjected under our vassalage and jurisdiction, so it is doing a
great harm not only to the service of God, but the security and
peace of our Kingdoms and State as well.

And we cannot reckon how great the damage is, since the
mentioned merchants are taking every day our natives, sons of
the land and the sons of our noblemen and vassals and our
relatives, because the thieves and men of bad conscience grab
them wishing to have the things and wares of this Kingdom
which they are ambitious of; they grab them and get them to be
sold; and so great, Sir, is the corruption and licentiousness that
our country is being completely depopulated, and Your
Highness should not agree with this nor accept it as in your
service. And to avoid it we need from those [your] Kingdoms
no more than some priests and a few people to teach in
schools, and no other goods except wine and flour for the holy
sacrament. That is why we beg of Your Highness to help and
assist us in this matter, commanding your factors that they
should not send here either merchants or wares, because it is
our will that in these Kingdoms there should not be any trade of

slaves nor outlet for them.*   Concerning what is referred above, again we beg of Your Highness to agree with it, since otherwise we cannot remedy such an obvious damage.   Pray Our Lord in His mercy to have Your Highness under His guard and let you do for ever the things of His service. I kiss your hands many times.

At our town of Congo, written on the sixth day of July.

Joao Teixeira** did it in 1526.

The King. Dom Affonso.

    [On the back of this letter the following can be read:

    To the most powerful and excellent prince Dom Joao, King our Brother.]

How Slaving Began

    [1526] Moreover, Sir, in our Kingdoms there is another great inconvenience which is of little service to God, and this is that many of our people [*naturaes*], keenly desirous as they are of the wares and things of your Kingdoms, which are brought here by your people, and in order to satisfy their voracious appetite, seize many of our people, freed and exempt men;*** and very often it happens that they kidnap even noblemen and the sons of noblemen, and our relatives, and take them to be sold to the white men who are in our Kingdoms; and for this purpose they have concealed them; and others are brought during the night so that they might not be recognized.

    *Emphasis in the original.

    **Probably, from the evidence, an Angolan secretary educated by Portuguese missionaries at Mbanza Congo (S. Salvador). See J. Cuvelier, *L'Ancien Royaume de Congo* (Brussels: 1946), p. 294.

    ***The corruptions of the slave trade, in short, were already at work.

And as soon as they are taken by the white men they are immediately ironed and branded with fire, and when they are carried to be embarked, if they are caught by our guards' men the whites allege that they have bought them but they cannot say from whom, so that it is our duty to do justice and to restore to the freemen their freedom, but it cannot be done if your subjects feel offended, as they claim to be.

And to avoid such a great evil we passed a law so that any white man living in our Kingdoms and wanting to purchase goods in any way should first inform three of our noblemen and officials of our court whom we rely upon in this matter, and these are Dom Pedro Manipanza and Dom Manuel Manissaba, our chief usher, and Goncala Pires our chief freighter, who should investigate if the mentioned goods are captives or free men, and if cleared by them there will be no further doubt nor embargo for them to be taken and embarked. But if the white men do not comply with it they will lose the aforementioned goods. And if we do them this favour and concession it is for the part Your Highness has in it, since we know that it is in your service too that these goods are taken from our Kingdom, otherwise we should not consent to this . . . .

A Call for Aid (Never Answered)

[1526] Sir, Your Highness has been kind enough to write to us saying that we should ask in our letters for anything we need, and that we shall be provided with everything, and as the peace and the health of our Kingdom depend on us, and as there are among us old folks and people who have lived for many days, it happens that we have continuously many and different diseases which put us very often in such a weakness that we reach almost the last extreme; and the same happens to our children, relatives and natives owing to the lack in this country of physicians and surgeons who might know how to cure properly such diseases. And as we have got neither dispensaries nor drugs which might help us in this forlornness, many of those who had been already confirmed and instructed in the holy faith of Our Lord Jesus Christ perish and die; and the rest of the people in their majority cure themselves with herbs and breads and other ancient methods, so that they put all their faith in the mentioned herbs and ceremonies if they live, and believe that they are saved if they die; and this is not much in the service of God.

And to avoid such a great error and inconvenience, since it is from God in the first place and then from your Kingdoms and from Your Highness that all the good and drugs and medicines have come to save us, we beg of you to be agreeable and kind enough to send us two physicians and two apothecaries and one surgeon, so that they may come with their drugstores and all the necessary things to stay in our kingdoms, because we are in extreme need of them all and each of them. We shall do them all good and shall benefit them by all means, since they are sent by Your Highness, whom we thank for your work in their coming. We beg of Your Highness as a great favour to do this for us, because besides being good in itself it is in the service of God as we have said above.

[Extracts from letter of King Affonso to King of Portugal dated Oct. 18, 1526. By hand of Dom João Teixeira.]

These extracts are translated from the original texts in Visconde de Paiva-Manso, *História do Congo (Documentos)* (Lisbon: 1877), which has 22 of King Affonso's letters, the other two that are known being in A. de A. Felner, *Angola* (Coimbra: 1933) Very strangely, as I continue to find, nobody has yet bothered to produce a full English translation of Affonso's correspondence.

ABREU DE BRITO

Angolan Currency

[1592] And this *zimbo* [cowrie] has such great value in this Kingdom, that, when I was in the village of Loanda, a huge amount of gold coins was sent to Congo for ransoming a number of slaves, but they were rejected by the sellers, who said that the true money and gold was the *zimbo* of Loanda, which made them rich, and the Portuguese should take back that sort of money in gold, which was useless for them; and many other things happen in this matter, for instance, that one *lifuco* [*lufuku*: a numerical measure of value] of *zimbos* is worth two of goods, so that it is clearly seen that the wealth is doubled . . . .

From Visconde de Paiva-Manso, *História do Congo (Documentos)* (Lisbon: 1877), p. 137. Translated from a report by Domingos d'Abreu de Brito on the Kingdom of Angola, dated 1592, offered to King Philip of Spain.

JOHN LANDYE

Guinea Cargoes

Landye's is the second recorded voyage of the English to West Africa, the first being that of William Hawkins ten years earlier.

[February 24, 1540] A ship called the Pawle of Plymouth, whereof John Landye is master, left on the same day.

From William Hawkins, denizen:

for 940 hachettes, 940 comes and 375 sarpes (knives), weighting 30 cwt. of iron———value 75s.	Subsidy 3s. 9d.
for 5 cwt. of copper (100s.) and 5 cwt. of lead (20s.) in manelios———value £6.	Subsidy 6s.
for 3 lengths of woolen cloth without grain———	Customs 3s. 6d.
for 19 dozen night cappes (40s.), 10 cwt. of copper (£10) and 10 cwt. of lead (40s.)———value £14.	Subsidy 14s.

[October 20, 1540] A ship called le Paule of Plymouth, whereof John Landye is master, entered on October 20.

From Wm. Hawkyns, denizen:

for 92 tons of brasyll———value £613. 6s. 8d.	subsidy £30. 13s. 4d.
1 dozen elephants' teeth weighing 1 cwt.———value 30s.	Subsidy 18d.

From Plymouth Customs Accounts, PRO, E122, 116/13. Translation in J. W. Blake, *Europeans in West Africa* (2 vols., Hakluyt Society: 1942), vol. 2, p. 300, from text in J. A. Williamson, *Sir John Hawkins* (1927), p. 13. The *Paul* went to Brazil as well as Guinea.

RICHARD EDEN

English at Benin

[1553] But of force and not of will brought he the ships before the river of Benin, where riding at an Anker, they sent their pinnas up into the river 50 or 60 leagues, from whence certaine of the marchants with captaine Pinteado, Francisco a Portugale, Nicholas Lambart gentleman, and other marchants were conducted to the court where the king remained, ten leagues from the river side, whither when they came, they were brought with a great company to the presence of the king, who being a blacke Moore (although not so blacke as the rest) sate in a great huge hall, long and wide, the wals made of earth without windowes, the roofe of thin boords, open in sundry places, like unto lovers [louvres: ventilators] to let in the aire.

And here to speake of the great reverence they give to their king, it is such, that if we would give as much to our Saviour Christ, we should remoove from our heads many plagues which we daily deserve for our contempt and impietie.

So it is therefore, that when his noble men are in his presence, they never looke him in the face, but sit cowring, as we upon our knees, so they upon their buttocks, with their elbowes upon their knees, and their hands before their faces, not looking up until the king command them. And when they are comming toward the king, as far as they do see him, they do shew such reverance, sitting on the ground with their faces covered as before. Likewise when they depart from him, they turn not their backs toward him, but goe creeping backward with like reverance.

And now to speake somewhat of the communication that was between the king and our men, you shall first understand that he himselfe could speake the Portugall tongue, which he had learned of a child. Therefore after he had commanded our men to stand up, and demanded of them the cause of their comming into that countrey, they answered by Pinteado, that they were marchants traveiling into those partes for the commodities of his countrey, for exchange of wares which they had brought form their countries, being such as should be no lesse commodious for him and his people. The king then having of old lying in a certaine store-house 30 or 40 kintals of Pepper (every kintall being an hundred weight) willed them to looke upon the same, and againe to bring him a sight of such merchandizes as they had brought with them. And thereupon sent with the captaine and the marchants certaine of his men to conduct them to the waters side, with other to bring the ware from the pinnas to the court. Who when they were returned and the ware seen, the king grew to this ende with the marchants to provide in 30 dayes the lading of al their ships with pepper. And in case their merchandizes would not extend to the value of so much pepper, he promised to credite them to their next returne, and thereupon sent the countrey round about to gather pepper, causing the same to be brought to the court: so that within the space of 30 dayes they had gathered fourescore tunne of pepper.

Gold and Ivory

They brought from thence at the last voyage [1554-1555] foure hundred pound weight and odde of gold, of two and twentie carrats and one graine of finenesse; also sixe and thirtie buts of graines, & about two hundred and fifty elephants' teeth of all quantities. Of these I saw & measured some of nine spans in length, as they were crooked. Some of them were as bigge as a man's thigh above the knee, and weyed about foure-score and ten pound weight a peece . . . .

They are very wary people in their bargaining, and will not lose one sparke of golde of any value. They use weights and measures, and are very circumspect in occupying the same. They that shall have to doe with them, must use them gently; for they will not trafique or bring in any wares, if they be evill used. At the first voyage, that our men had into these parties, it so

chanced that, at their departure from the first place where they
did trafick, one of them either stole a muske-cat, or tooke her
away by force, not mistrusting that that should have hindered
their bargaining in another place whither they intended to goe.
But for all the haste they coulde make with full sailes, the fame
of their misusage so prevented them that the people of that
place also, offended thereby, would bring in no wares; insomuch
that they were inforced either to restore the cat, or pay for her
at their price, before they could trafique there.

The first extract is from Richard Eden's memoir of Thomas Windham's
voyage to Guinea and Benin, 1553, in Richard Hakluyt, *The Principal
Navigations, Voyages, Traffiques and Discoveries of the English Nation*
(1598-1600), VI, p. 145. The second is from Richard Eden's memoir of
John Lok's voyage to Guinea in 1554-1555, in Hakluyt, VI, p. 154.

WILLIAM TOWERSON

Metal Goods

All their cloth, cordes, girdles, fishing lines, and all such like
things, which they have, they make of the bark of certaine trees,
and thereof they can worke things very pretily, and yron worke
they can make very fine, and all such things as they doe occupy,
as darts, fishhookes, hooking yrons, yron heads, and great
daggers, some of them as long as a woodknift, which be on both
sides exceeding sharpe, and bended after the maner of Turkie
blades, and the most part of them have hanging at their left side
one of those great daggers.

From the memoir of William Towerson's first voyage to Guinea, 1555-
1556, in Richard Hakluyt, *The Principal Navigations, Voyages, etc.* (1598-
1600), VI, p. 177.

JOHN HAWKINS

Toward the Slave Trade

The following is from a remarkable document, running to about twenty-two thousand words, which provides a detailed and graphic account of Hawkins's slaving voyage of 1562, and was very possibly written in the *Jesus*, Hawkins's ship, during that adventure. Its great interest for African history lies in its illustration of the way in which early European traders and raiders on the Guinea Coast—in this case what is now Sierra Leone—found it possible to make common cause with African potentates who were otherwise far too strong to be challenged; and of how this military partnership led on to the slave trade.

There came two ambassadors with one message (to our general . . . . One) of them from where the King of Serra Lion (had his town, and) the other from Yhoma, King of the Castros, (to ask his aid) against Zacina and Zetecama, two kinges which (fought with them in the w)arres. These two kinges desired oure ge(nerall, as they ha)d besieged the other [kings] in a towne called Conga, . . . that our generall wolde . . . (assault) it by the river and batter it, and for his m(erit they would) help him to negros.

This towne was b(uilt after the) use of that cowntreye verye warlike, and was wal(led round with) mighty trees bownd together with greate wythes (and had) in it soldiers that had come thether 150 leagues. The (kings within) it had in it of principall soldiers negros 6000, bes(ide thereo)f innumberable sight of other menne, women and ch(ildren. Our) generall, thowe it was a harde enterprise, yet by(cawse) he must have departed to the Indias with the negros (above) mencioned, grawnted that he wolde ayde the said kinges, (and) with this awnswere the embassadors, whoe afterward gave oure generall gages for sauf goyng and comyng of oure menne and alsoe took gages of us, and the tyme appoincted that oure generall showlde send his ayde, who showld doe their parte by the river to anoye and enter the towns, and the two kinges oure frendes likewise by londe with their campe . . . .

. . .The (next) daye after oure generall came thether [to the approaches of the town with his troops], somewhat (before) the tyme of assault appoincted, the beseiged (negr)os beganne to treat of peace with the negro kings oure friends by imbassadors, but they were sente awaye withowte doung any thing. In the after noone, as the generall had appoincted, he comaunded to sownde the trompette and, having all thinges readye, beganne to sett menne ashore and put in order, gave assaulte by that parte of the towne which ajoyned to the river. The negros had many engines, as false diches covered with light sticks, leaves and suche trompery, to overthrowe oure menne in, and with theire invenimed arrowes and dartes so defended the walles, having made loopes in everye place to shote owte at for their savetye . . . .

[After a stiff battle the town was taken by setting fire to it.] . . . The kinges Sacina and Setecama escaped, (but there we)re slaine a greate nomber of menne of name (who had come) in soccor of the towne, as the Kinge of Cesta . . . . (Our) menne here saw the negros our frendes eate (the prisoners whom) they slewe everye daye in the camp . . . . And oure generall came downe to his ships and browghte with him abowte 260 negros that he had taken in the towne. When he was come downe he sente to the Castros, where with the negros the kinges sent and them the generall took and others that he had in the rivers by trafique, we had nowe abowt 470 negros in all . . . . (Thus we set our) sayles and directed oure cowrse over with the (West or Spanish) India named America or the Newe Worlde the(re to trade with the sa)id ware . . . .

From Cotton MS, in J. A. Williamson, *Sir John Hawkins*, 1927.

"D. R.": PROBABLY DIERECK RUITERS

Dutch Merchants in Benin

More accustomed to the values of literacy than their Portuguese and other European rivals, the early Dutch traders to and in West Africa have left the best accounts of what they saw and experienced. The first substantial report on Benin was published by Pieter de Marees in Amsterdam in 1602, and republished in English by the chronicler Samuel Purchas: the author we know simply by his initials of "D.R.," thought to be Diereck Ruiters. It is thus a little earlier, and in any case more detailed than the German report which follows here. I have slightly modernized the orthography.

The houses [in Benin] stand in good order, one close and even with the other, as the houses in Holland stand. Such houses as men of quality (who are gentlemen) or others dwell in, have two or three steps to go up; and in front there is as it were a gallery where a man may sit in the dry. This gallery is cleaned every morning by their slaves, and on it a mat is spread for men to sit down. Their rooms are four-square with a roof not closed in its middle so that rain wind and light come in. There they sit and take their meals; but they also have other places such as kitchens . . . .

The king's Court is very great, having within it many four-square yards surrounded by galleries, and where watch is always kept. I was so far within the Court that I passed through four such large yards, and wheresoever I looked, still I saw gate upon gate to go into other yards; and in this way I went in as far as any Netherlander was: which was as far as the stable where his best horses are kept, always passing a great long way.

From the relevant passages translated in *Purchas His Pilgrims* (repr. 1905), p. 354.

ANDREAS JOSUA ULTZHEIMER

Benin in 1603: A German Report

Military surgeon aboard Dutch ships of war and exploration in the years 1596-1610, Ultzheimer's little-known but useful account of "Guinea," but more especially of the kingdom of Benin, dates from a voyage of 1603, at a time when the Dutch were welcomed as allies by the *Oba* of Benin. A native of the German Duchy of Wurttemberg, Ultzheimer had fought on the Protestant side in the German wars of religion, but his anti-Catholic bias was moderated by a sensible tolerance of other people's beliefs. I have translated the following extract from the modern German rendering and notes by Sabine Werg, to whose erudition we owe the revelation of Ultzheimer's long-ignored text of 1616.

This kingdom lies next to Guinea [by which Ultzheimer referred to what became the Gold Coast or Ghana's coast today] towards the sunrise. It is ruled by a powerful king whose residence is in the city of Benin, eight degrees north of the Equator. That is a big city surrounded by a stout fence as though by a wall. Inside it the king has a palace also surrounded by a fence. The palace is about the size of the city of Tubingen [the south German city to which Ultzheimer retired after his many travels], or somewhat bigger. About 700 wives live there, each with her own apartment. The king has not only many servants who wait on him, but also many soldiers who keep strong watch by day and night over the king's house.

This king allows himself to be seen only once a year, and that happens in this way: On his birthday he comes into the city riding on a horse that is ornamented with scarlet cloth and red beads of coral. He rides side-saddle as a woman would, and similarly clad in scarlet cloth, and ornamented not only with red beads but also with other unusual things. A white horsetail hangs over his head and down his back to his heels as though to frighten anyone who sees it. Two men go beside him so as to clear the way, for people crowd in great numbers to see the king, just as people in Rome want to see the Pope in a celebratory year. Six thousand persons gather for the king, and when he comes everyone kneels and claps in greeting. He replies with gestures of his hand, just like the Pope in Rome when he blesses and thanks the people.

Then they lead him out to a house, called the king's house, where all his war commanders are gathered, and together with the king they sacrifice to the devil in this way: they sacrifice two persons, three cows, various goats and dogs, about as many hens and turtles. The goats, dogs and poultry they transfix with spears and leave them to rot in the streets, so that the whole city stinks. They butcher the cows and leave the pieces for the birds to eat. The persons they take to a special small house, called *Obavan*—which means as much the devil's as God's house—and there they sacrifice the persons. They behead them and then hew them in pieces, saying: "And in this way we will hew in pieces the enemies of the king . . . ."

When the sacrifices are over the king sits in a chair outside the house, and the people kneel, including the commanders. Then trumpets blow and bells are struck and the tusks of elephants are sounded: you can hear the noise a quarter of a mile away. That goes on for about two hours after which the people shout *Daberisa oba cada boba oba*, or "Greetings, royal king!" The king replies *Aufiafe*, "I thank you," and rides back into his palace. Then the people eat and drink, dance and leap about, and everyone is happy and content.

From Andreas Josua Ultzheimer, *Warhaffte Beschreibung ettlicher Reisen in Europa, Africa, Asien und America 1596-1610*; transferred to modern German by Sabine Werg; Horst Erdmann, Tubingen 1971; English by B. D.

DAVID VAN NYENDAEL

Manners at Benin: 1700

A century after "D.R." another Dutch merchant, once again after a fairly close acquaintance with the kingdom of Benin and its royal capital, wrote a letter to his fellow-countryman, William Bosman, then the Dutch governor at Elmina (Gold Coast: Ghana). Its interest lies principally in the confirmation of what previous Dutch merchants had reported; as before, this Dutchman found that he fared well in Benin so long as he minded his behavior.

The inhabitants of Great Benin are generally good-natured and very civil, from whom it is easy to obtain whatever we desire by soft means. If we make them liberal presents, they will endeavor to recompense them doubly; and if we want anything and ask it of them, they very seldom deny us, although they have occasion for it themselves.

But they are so far in the right, to expect that their courtesy should be repaid with civility, not with arrogance or rudeness; for to think of forcing anything from them, is to dispute with the moon.

They are very prompt in business, and will not suffer any of their ancient customs to be abolished; in which, if we comply with them, they are very easy to deal with, and will not be wanting in anything on their part requisite to a good agreement.

But worst of all is that they are very tedious in dealing. Many times they have a stock of elephant's teeth by them, which we are generally eight or ten days before we can agree with them for. But this is managed with so many ceremonious civilities that it is impossible to be angry with them.

From William Bosman, *A New and Accurate Description of the Coast of Guinea*, London 1705 in English translation from the original Dutch edition of 1704, reprinted London 1967, p. 433.

RICHARD JOBSON

Mandingo Towns

Written early in the seventeenth century, Jobson's is the first English account of West Africa that goes much beyond personal gossip, and makes a link with the much more solid reports of Dapper (see pp. 209-10) and of the best writers of the eighteenth century. He is writing of the Gambia Coast and neighborhood.

They have likewise Townes of force, according unto the manner of warre they use amongst them, fortified, and trencht in, after a strong and defencible nature; whereof (they say) the countrey within is full, especially where the Kings are seated, and maner whereof wee have seene in some two or three places, whereof I will instance onely one: which is the towne of Cassan, against which (as I sayd before) the shippe which was betrayed did ride, and we in our last voyage, did make it our highest port for our bigger shippe. This Towne is the Kings seate, and by the name of the Towne hee holdes his title, King of Cassan. It is seated upon the Rivers side, and inclosed round, neare to the houses, with hurdles, such as our shepheards use, but they are above ten foot high, and fastened to strong and able poles, the toppes whereof remaine above the hurdle; on the inside in divers places, they have rooms, and buildings, made up like Turrets, from whence they within may shoot their arrowes, and throw their darts over the wall, against their approaching enemies; on the outside likewise, round the wall, they have cast a ditch or trench, of a great breadth, & beyond that againe a pretty distance, the whole Towne is circled with posts and peeces of trees, set close and fast into the ground, some five foot high, so thicke, that except in stiles, or places made of purpose, a single man cannot get through, and in the like manner, a small distance off againe, the like defence, and this is as they do signifie unto us, to keepe off the force of horse, to which purpose, it seemes to be very strong and availeable: considering what armes and Weapons they have in use, which in this place is necessary to be knowne.

Lords and Vassals

I saw and did eate and drinke with sixe of their Kings or Mansas, which have reference to greater Kings living further [inland]; all the South-side of the River as wee went, beeing subject to the King of Cantore, of the North-side halfe subject to the King of Bursale, the rest to the King of Woolley. These wee saw not, and they say, that they shew not themselves abroad but in pompe, hunting with great numbers of Horse, as our men saw the King of Bursall (when they passed to Cape Verde) and there are warres betwixt one side of the River and the other, which were it not, Bursale would soone with his Horse subdue a great part of the Countrey, of if he had meanes of transportation.

Gambia Craftsmanship

There are amongst them three principall Trades, the Smith which of Iron brought to them (for else they have none) makes their Swords, Assegay heads, Darts and Arrow heads barbed; and Instruments of Husbandry, without which they could not live. Hee hath his Bellowes, small Anvill, and Cole of a red wood, which alone will give the true heat to our Iron; who thus cut out Iron for us, eight inches going above as well as twelve inches below, at ten for one gaine. The Smith if he be not looked too, will steale.

The next Trade is the Sepatero, or Gregorie maker, made artificially in all shapes, round and square and triangle, so as Our men would acknowledge Art. They make also Bridles and Saddles, of which I have seene some very neat, hardly to be bettered heere: whereby it seemes they have skill to dress and dye their Deeres skins and Goats skins.

A third Profession is of those which temper the Earth for their wals and pots in which they boyle meats, using for other services the gourd. Their Tabacco Pipes also (without which few or none, either men or women walke, and cannot of all things want) have their bowles and neckes about two inches long of Earth, neatly glased, able commonly to hold halfe an ounce of Tabacco: they put a cane about a yard long into the necke, and so draw the smoake. These are peculiar Trades; other things are common to all, Mats to eate, sit, sleepe on, are their Staple commoditie, as at Mamgegar Market, we saw things bought and sold, without nominating any other price but Mats (How many Mats shall I give you?) for Coyne they have none.

But the generall Trade from which none but the Kings and principall persons are exempted, is Husbandry whereto . . . the people of all sizes after their abilitie are subject: God having not given them wisedome to serve themselves of the beasts to that purpose. They make furrowes as decently as we doe, but with handie labour, having a short sticke about a yard long, on the end of which is a broad Iron like to that of our Paddle-staves; with which Iron set into the ground, one leades the way cutting the Earth before him, others following in the same tract with their severall Irons, so many as will make a sufficient furrow thorow the length of a spacious field: and when they are at the end, they begin againe, many hands making lighter riddance.

From Richard Jobson, *The Golden Trade*, London, 1623.

OLIVEIRA CADORNEGA

A Million Slaves

[1680] And the fabulous amount of people inhabiting these kingdoms can be estimated if we say that the conquest of these kingdoms began about a hundred years ago, and since every second year have been dispatched from this port about eight to ten thousand units of slaves, which sum up almost to a million of souls.

From partial text of Antonio de Oliveira Cadornega, *Descripõam do Reino de Congo, etc.*, 1680-1681, in Visconde de Paiva-Manso, *História do Congo (Documentos)* (Lisbon: 1877), p. 265. "These kingdoms," in what follows, refer chiefly to north-western Angola and the states round the estuary and lower course of the river Congo.

The Eighteenth Century

"**G**OD HAS DRAWN TO THIS fortunate city a certain number of learned and of pious men, strangers to the country, who have come to live here." Thus wrote the author of the *Tarikh al-Sudan* about the city of Djenne on the Middle Niger towards the middle of the seventeenth century. The cities of the Western Sudan were still respected as centers of Muslim learning (indeed, some of them have never ceased to be so), yet their confidence and breadth of contact with the wider world of Islam were sadly cut down. For this their sheikhs and mallams were not responsible. The grand Islamic system of political enterprise and speculative thought was now in far retreat and disarray before the eruptive vigor and violence of Christian Europe. The trans-Saharan routes continued to bear their patient many-camelled caravans. The merchants, now as before, toiled back and forth across the wilderness of sand and polished mountain. But they had lost their monopoly of West African trade with the north. Increasingly, this trade went by ship from the ports of Guinea. Commerce shifted more and more to the southward: commerce, and therefore the means of power.

Along the curving seaboard, now a gateway to livelihood and wealth as never before, new African states crystallized from small clans and scattered peoples. These began to form a girdle of political and economic self-defence—a new monopoly—against the sea-traders on one side and the inland-traders on the other. As time went by, this girdle became impenetrable. From a mere belt of "middlemen" chiefs and groups along the seashore, it broadened to include stronger peoples further into the countryside. By the middle of the eighteenth century, coastal monopoly and "protectionism" became at certain points as wide as two or three hundred miles from south to north. Its dominant powers counted new political and economic systems such as Ashanti and Dahomey.

Along the East Coast, from Zanzibar northwards, there occurred a new and memorable surge of Swahili civilization. Here the Portuguese had never won the suffocating grip by which they ruined the shoreward towns of Tanganyika (mainland Tanzania) and Mozambique. Zanzibar and Pemba, Malindi, Mombasa and other centers of this highly distinctive variant of Islamic African culture, passed into a period of renaissance. Was this a creative reaction to Portuguese assault and battery, or the product of more sheltered buds of intellectual growth? The question remains open. Whatever their causes, the effects were impressive. Swahili literature began in earnest, some of it "as grand in manner and diction," in Freeman-Grenville's enthusiastic view, "as Dante or Milton." Its beginning can be placed in 1728 (see also page 28) with the *Utendi wa Tambuka*, an epic written for the contemporary ruler of Pate (and now in the Library of the Seminar fur Afrikanischen Sprachen at Hamburg)—until or unless, that is, earlier manuscripts should come to light. There was new building and civic growth. Even to the south of Zanzibar, a measure of recovery occurred at Kilwa, where the sultan and richer merchants built new mosques and spacious dwellings, though all in a style and ornamental taste that were much debased and coarsened in comparison with earlier times. A new town appeared at Kua on Juani Island in the Mafia Group: successor to the much older town at Mafia Kisimani, Kua shows in its ruins the same decline of taste but also the same density of new building as eighteenth-century Kilwa.

Far inside the continent, meanwhile, the steady growth of Iron Age state formation within its specifically African framework and appearance continued to buttress old centers of authority and, at the same time, to challenge these by the ambitious hand of "royal heirs and barons." This is the period of supreme Karanga power on the plateau lands west of Mozambique; westward again, in Angola, it is also the period of new dynastic and "national" wars of rivalry for power. In the geographical heart of Africa it is the time of Kuba stability and Lunda expansion, and of a crystallization of new kingdoms in the region of the Great Lakes. In the distant southeast it is likewise the time of a political gestation which was to give birth, less than a century later, to the military initiatives of the Nguni: a prelude to the northward-striking recoil from advancing European settlement, to the rise of the Zulu nation, the destructive migrations of the Matebele (Ndebele), and the founding of Lesotho. The eighteenth century can be regarded as a prolonged phase of Iron Age maturity among those Bantu-speaking peoples who had long commanded central-southern Africa, a culmination that was also the last slow epoch of inner-African isolation from the main currents that moved the world.

But for Europe and North America, if not for Asia, this was a time of tremendous change. Industrialism arrived. Science thrust superstition increasingly aside. The "technology gap" between Europe and Africa widened so far in the eighteenth century that Europe's conquest of Africa in the nineteenth was to seem, for most Europeans, right and even necessary. We can mark the changing temper of European thought in records which increasingly recast the old trading partnership into new terms of "natural master" and "inevitable servant." This was largely the work of the slave trade; slaving must therefore have a place, and even a large and therefore painful place, in any selection of characteristic documents. We can also mark, as I have mentioned earlier, the momentary emergence of a quasi-scientific note of impartial inquiry into the nature of peoples and their institutions. Yet there is little of this until the last years of the century. Ignorance of all but the coastal states remains omnipresent and opaque, anti-black racist prejudice and abuse grow ever worse and more widespread. The maps become sometimes less fantastic; yet even the better European geographers are still inserting "elephants for want of towns."

There is little progress in discovery. The vaguely apprehended presence of a vast continent within the coastline nags continually at the minds of those educated Europeans who are now reaching the shores of Africa in less meagre numbers than before. But there seems no way of penetrating to that inland country, and the few expeditions which make the attempt, and manage to return, fail to solve any of the obvious geographical problems. Bruce reaches the source of the Blue Nile, but everyone still guesses wildly at the source of the White. The Niger is still thought to flow westward, probably into the Senegal, and the springs of the Congo are confounded cartographically with those of the Nile. Only the seaboard of the continent is clearly understood.

Europe's first African colony was enlarged and confirmed in this century. Much earlier, of course, the Portuguese had settled themselves in forts and trading stations along the maritime fringe of Mozambique and Angola as well as far up the Zambezi, and other Europeans had done the same along parts of the Guinea littoral. But these were little more than points of strength from which to promote and monopolize trade with African partners who were generally too strong to be seriously challenged. The Dutch settlement at the Cape of Good Hope was different. Almost from the first it took a colonial shape. "Twenty-five years after the landing of van Riebeeck [in 1652], a cattle and hunting frontier had already come into existence. The sons of the first generation of free burghers became, some of them, genuine frontiersmen .... Their guns gave them self-reliance, their wagons freedom of movement, and their cattle economic independence .... From the beginning of the eighteenth century there was always a fringe of settlement that was not wholly within the official limits of the Colony .... In 1702 a party had wandered far enough afield to brush against some Ama-Xosa tribesmen. It was the first clash between Boer and

Bantu. In 1760 Jacobus Coetzee, an elephant hunter, crossed the Orange River."*

This colony stamped the brand of racial segregation and contempt on all the land it took. The first to suffer were the Khoi (labeled as Hottentots). Van Riebeeck had called them "black stinking dogs." His successors destroyed them. "In the beginning the administration strove desperately to keep whites and Hottentots apart. It even thought at one moment fantastically of digging a canal or growing a hedge across the Cape peninsular .... The Hottentots broke down simply and undramatically .... Before the pressure of the colonists upon them their institutions failed them, and their loose tribal structure collapsed entirely." The colonists took it as a divine gift to their allegedly superior humanity. "According to their belief it was more than their arms that made them prevail over the natives, and their superiority depended upon more than their intelligence or their institutions. Their superiority was born of race and faith, a quality divinely given which could not be transmitted to other races or acquired by them."** The economy of this racism became, by the same token, a slave economy.

The early writings of Boer authors are occasionally useful for the light they throw on the indigenous Khoi peoples, but generally they are little more than studies in a peculiar cast of Christian prejudice. I have accordingly ended this section with some Cape Province memoirs of a Swedish traveller.

*C. W. de Kiewiet, *A History of South Africa* (Oxford: 1950), p. 10.

**C. W. de Kiewiet, *A History of South Africa* (Oxford: 1950), p. 20.

JOHN BARBOT

The Trade in Captives

Although Barbot belongs to the seventeenth century—an agent of the French African companies, he made at least two West African voyages in 1678-1682—he sets the scene better than any other writer for that baleful period of oversea slaving which entirely overwhelmed the whole European-African connection in the eighteenth and early nineteenth centuries. (An inquiry into how this came about, and why and under what conditions some African peoples sold other African peoples, will be found in my *Black Mother: The African Slave Trade*, Boston: 1961 and reissues).

The trade of slaves is in a more peculiar manner the business of kings, rich men, and prime merchants, exclusive of the inferior sort of blacks . . . .

The Gold Coast, in times of war between the inland nations, and those nearer the sea, will furnish great numbers of slaves of all sexes and ages; sometimes at one place, and sometimes at another, as has been already observed, according to the nature of the war, and the situation of the countries between which it is waged. I remember, to this purpose, that in the year 1681, an English interloper at Commendo got three hundred good slaves, almost for nothing besides the trouble of receiving them at the beach in his boats, as the Commendo men brought them from the field of battle, having obtained a victory over a neighboring nation, and taken a great number of prisoners.

At other times slaves are so scarce there, that in 1682 I could get but eight from one end of the coast to the other; not only because we were a great number of trading ships on the coast at the same time, but by reason the natives were everywhere at peace. At another time, I had two hundred slaves at Accra only, in a fortnight or three weeks time; and the upper coast men, understanding I had those slaves aboard, came down to redeem them, giving me two for one, of such as I understood were their near relations, who had been stolen away by inland blacks, brought down to Accra, and sold to us . . . .

As to the different sorts of goods the Europeans generally carry thither for trade; each nation commonly supplies the coast, as much as is convenient, with such as their respective countries afford; and what they want at home for well assorting their cargo, they buy in other parts of Europe.

For instance, the French commonly carry more brandy, wine, iron, paper, firelocks, etc., than the English and Dutch can do, those commodities being cheaper in France; as, on the other hand, they supply the Guinea trade with greater quantities of linen cloth, bugles, copper basons, and kettles, wrought pewter, gunpowder, sayes, perpetuanas, chints, cawris, old sheets, etc., than the French; because they must get those wares from England or Holland.

The French commonly compose their cargo for the Gold Coast trade, to purchase slaves and gold dust; of brandy mostly, white and red wine, ros solis, firelocks, muskets, flints, iron in bars, white and black contecarbe, red frize, looking glasses, fine coral, sarsaparilla, bugles of sundry sorts and colours, and glass beads, powder, sheets, tobacco, taffeties, and many other sorts of silks wrought, as brocardels, velvets, etc., shirts, black-hats, linen, paper, laces of many sorts, beads, shot, lead, musket-balls, flints, callicoes, serges, stuffs, etc., besides the others goods for a true assortment, which they have commonly from Holland.

The Dutch have Coesveld linen, sleysiger lywat, old sheets, Leyden serges, dyed indigo-blue, perpetuanas, green, blue and purple: Konings-Kleederen, ananbas, large and narrow, made at Haerlem, Cyprus and Turkey stuffs, Turkey carpets, red, blue, and yellow cloths, green, red and white Leyden rugs, silk stuffs, blue and white; brass kettles of all sizes; copper basons, Scotch pans, barbers basons, some wrought, others hammered; copper pots, brass locks, brass trumpets, pewter, brass and iron rings, hair trunks, pewter dishes, and plates (of a narrow brim); deep porringers, all sorts and sizes of fishing-hooks, and lines, lead in sheets, and in pipes, three sorts of Dutch knives; Venice bugles, and glass beads, of sundry colours and sizes; Sheepskins, iron bars, brass pins, long and short; brass bells, iron hammers, powder, muskets, cutlasses, cawris, chints, lead balls, and shot, of sundry sorts; brass cups, with handles, cloths of Cabo-Verdo, Quaqua, Ardra, and of Rio-Forcado; blue coral, alias akory, from Benin; strong waters, and abundance of other wares, being near a hundred and fifty sorts, as a Dutchman told me.

The English, besides many of the same goods above-mentioned, have tapseils broad and narrow, micanees fine and coarse; many sorts of chints, or Indian callicoes printed, tallow, red painting colours; Canary wine, sayes, perpetuanas, inferior to the Dutch, and sack'd up in painted tillets, with the English arms: many sorts of white callicoes; blue and white linen, China sattins, Barbadoes rum, or aqua-vitae, made from sugar, other strong waters, and spirits, beads of all sorts, buckshaws, Welsh plain, boysades, romberges, clouts, gingarus taffeties, amber, brandy, flower, Hamburgh brawls, and white, blue and white, and red chequer'd linen, narrow Guinea stuffs chequer'd, ditto broad, old hats, purple beads.

From John Barbot, *A Description of the Coasts of North and South Guinea, etc.*, first published in 1732 in A. and J. Churchill's *Collections of Voyages and Travels*, 5, p. 420.

JOHN CASSENEUVE

Docile Slaves?

The records of the oversea slave trade bear marginally, but at certain points significantly, on African history. It would become part of the white man's "myth of the Negro past," in later years, to consider that Africans were in some way peculiarly fitted for enslavement, since they submitted to it "with docility." Slaving captains like Casseneuve, as the following extracts show, knew otherwise.

[1700] About one in the afternoon, after dinner, we according to custom [on board the *Don Carlos*] caused them, one by one, to go down between decks, to have each his pint of water; most of them were yet above deck, many of them provided with knives, which we had indiscreetly given them two or three days before, as not suspecting the least attempt of this nature from them; others had pieces of iron they had torn off our forecastle door, as having premeditated a revolt, and seeing all the ship's company, at best but weak and many quite sick, they had also broken off the shackles from several of their companions feet, which served them, as well as billets they had provided themselves with, and all other things they could lay hands on, which they imagin'd might be of use for their enterprise.

Thus arm'd, they fell in crouds and parcels on our men, upon the deck unawares, and stabb'd one of the stoutest of us all, who receiv'd fourteen or fifteen wounds of their knives, and so expir'd. Next they assaulted our boatswain, and cut one of his legs so round the bone, that he could not move, the nerves being cut through; others cut our cook's throat to the pipe, and others wounded three of the sailors, and threw one of them overboard in that condition, from the forecastle into the sea;

who, however, by good providence, got hold of the bowlin of the foresail, and sav'd himself, along the lower wale of the quarterdeck, where, [says Casseneuve] we stood in arms, firing on the revolted slaves, of whom we kill'd some, and wounded many: which so terrify'd the rest, that they gave way, dispersing themselves some one way and some another between decks, and under the forecastle; and many of the most mutinous, leapt over board, and drown'd themselves in the ocean with much resolution, shewing no manner of concern for life. Thus we lost twenty-seven or twenty-eight slaves, either kill'd by us, or drown'd; and having master'd them, caused all to go betwixt decks, giving them good words.

From James Barbot and John Casseneuve, *An Abstract of a Voyage to Congo River . . . in the Year 1700*, in A. and J. Churchill, *Collections of Voyages and Travels* (1732), 5, pp. 497-522. This Barbot, a nephew of John, was supercargo of the *Don Carlos*, London, and Casseneuve its first mate.

"BOSTON POST BOY"

Revolt at Sea

By a Vessel lately arrived here from the West-Indies, we have Advice, that a Ship belonging to Liverpool coming from the Coast of Africa, with about 350 Slaves on board, and when in Sight of the Island Guardaloupe, the Slaves, as 'tis supposed, being admitted to come upon Deck to air themselves, took an Opportunity on the 28th of May . . . and kill'd the Master and Mate of the Ship, and threw fifteen of the Men overboard, after which they sent the Boat with two white Lads and three or four others to discover what Land it was, meanwhile the Ship drove to the Leeward, which gave the Lads an Opportunity to discover the Affair to the Commandant of that Quarter of the Island, who immediately raised about 100 Men, and put them on board a Sloop, who went in Pursuit of the Ship, and in a few Hours took her and carried her into Port Louis.

From a report in the *Boston Post Boy*, June 25, 1750, in E. Donnan, *Documents Illustrative of the History of the Slave Trade to America* (Carnegie Institution, Washington DC: 1931), vol. 2, p. 485.

JAMES BARBOT

Slaving Manners

[1700] As it is the usual custom among Europeans that buy slaves in Africa, to examine each limb, to know whether sound or not; the king of Zair [Congo estuary] observing Casseneuve [first mate of the *Don Carlos* slaver of London] thus trying the four slaves he had sold him, burst out a-laughing, as did likewise the great men that were about him. He asked the interpreter what was the occasion of their laughter?, and was answered, it proceeded from his so nicely viewing the poor slaves; but that, however, the king and his attendants were so much asham'd of it, that he requir'd him, for decency sake, to do it in a private place: which shews these Blacks are very modest.

The System in Angola

The chiefest trade of the Portuguese and other whites [in Congo and Angola] consists in slaves.... It is affirm'd that when the Spaniards were masters of Portugal, they transported every year fifteen thousand slaves out of Angola into the new world. And the Portuguese still [1701] transport a very great number.

All those slaves the Portuguese cause to be bought, by their pomberroes [*pombeiros*: Afro-Portuguese subtraders], a hundred and fifty or two hundred leagues up the country, whence they bring them down to the seacoasts . . . .

These slaves, called *Pombeiros*, have other slaves under them, sometimes a hundred, or a hundred and fifty, who carry the commodities on their heads up into the country [to buy captives] . . . .

Sometimes these *Pombeiros* stay out a whole year, and then bring back with them four, five and six hundred new slaves. Some of the faithfullest remain often there, sending what slaves they buy to their masters, who return them other commodities to trade with a-new.

An Angolan "Zimbabwe"

The king of Angola, or [of the country also called] Dongo, resides a little above the city Massingan, on a stony mountain seven leagues in compass, in which are many rich pastures, fields, and meadows, yielding a plentiful provision for all his retinue; into which there is but one single passage, and that according to their method well fortified; so that he needs fear no enemies . . . .

From James Barbot in A. and J. Churchill, *Collections of Voyages and Travels* (1732), 5, pp. 497-522.

WILLIAM BOSMAN

A Report on Gold

Chief factor (or governor) for the Dutch West India Company of what was then their main trading station of Elmina Castle, which the Dutch had lately taken from the Portuguese, William Bosman's description consists of twenty letters to a friend in Holland; the first of them is dated September 1, 1700.

There is no small number of Men in Europe who believe that the Gold Mines are in our Power; that we, like the Spaniards in the West-Indies, have no more to do but to work them by our Slaves: Though you perfectly know we have no manner of access to these Treasures; nor do I believe that any of our People have ever seen one of them: Which you will easily credit, when you are informed that the Negroes esteem them Sacred, and consequently take all possible care to keep us from them. But to come nearer the Subject: This Illustrious Metal is generally found in three sorts of places: First, the best is found in or betwixt particular Hills; and the Negroes apprehending where the Gold is, dig Pits; and separate it from the Earth which comes out with it.

The second place is in, at, and about some Rivers and Waterfalls; whose violence washeth down great Quantities of Earth, which carry the Gold with it.

The third is on the Sea-shore; where (as at Elmina and Axim) there are little Branches or Rivulets into which the Gold is driven from Mountainous Places, as well as to the Rivers; and after violent Showers of Rain in the Night, next Morning these places are sure to be visited by hundreds of Negroe-Women naked, except a Cloth wrapped about them to hide what Modesty obligeth. Each of these Women is furnished with large and small Troughs or Tray, which they first fill full of Earth and

Sand, which they wash with repeated fresh Water, till they have cleansed it from all its Earth; and if there be any Gold, its Ponderosity forces it to the bottom of the Trough; which if they find, it is thrown into the small Tray, and so they go to washing it again: which Operation generally holds them till Noon: Some of them not getting above the value of Sixpence; some of them find pieces of six or seven Shillings, though not frequently; and often they intirely loose their labour. Thus the digging of Pits, the gathering it, at or about the Rivers, and this last mentioned manner, are all the ways they know to come at Gold.

The Guinea Partnership

The first business of one of our Factors when he comes to Fida [Ouidah or Whydah on what was soon to become the Dahomey Coast], is to satisfie the Customs of the King and the great Men, which amount to about 100 Pounds in Guinea value, as the Goods must yield there. After which we have free Licence to Trade, which is published throughout the whole land by the Cryer.

But yet before we can deal with any Person, we are obliged to buy the King's whole stock of Slaves at a set price; which is commonly one third or one fourth higher than ordinary: After which we obtain free leave to deal with all his Subjects of what Rank soever. But if there happen to be no stock of Slaves, the Factor must then resolve to run the Risque of trusting the Inhabitants with Goods to the value of one or two hundred Slaves; which Commodities they send into the In-land Country, in order to buy with them Slaves at all markets, and that sometimes two hundred Miles deep in the Country: For you ought to be informed that Markets of Men are here kept in the same manner as those of Beasts with us.

Not a few in our Country fondly imagine that Parents here sell their Children, Men their Wives, and one Brother the other: But those who think so deceive themselves; for this never happens on any other account but that of Necessity, or some great Crime: But most of the Slaves that are offered to us are Prisoners of War, which are sold by the Victors as their Booty.

When these Slaves come to Fida, they are put in Prison all together, and when we treat concerning buying them, they are all brought out together in a large Plain; where, by our Chirurgeons, whose Province it is, they are throughly examined, even to the smallest Member, and that naked too both Men and Women, without the least Distinction or Modesty. Those which are approved as good are set on one side; and the lame or faulty are set by as Invalides, which are here called Mackrons. These are such as are above five and thirty Years old, or are maimed in the Arms, Legs, Hands or Feet, have lost a Tooth, are grey-haired, or have Films over their Eyes; as well as all those which are affected with any Veneral Distemper, or with several other Diseases.

The Invalides and the Maimed being thrown out, as I have told you, the remainder are numbred, and it is entred who delivered them. In the mean while a burning Iron, with the Arms or Name of the Companies, lyes in the Fire; with which ours are marked on the Breast.

This is done that we may distinguish them from the Slaves of the English, French or others; (which are also marked with their Mark) and to prevent the Negroes exchanging them for worse, at which they have a good Hand.

I doubt not but this Trade seems very barbarous to you, but since it is followed by meer necessity it must go on; but we yet take all possible care that they are not burned too hard, especially the Women, who are more tender than the Men.

We are seldom long detained in the buying of these Slaves, because their price is established, the Women being one fourth or fifth part cheaper than the Men. The Disputes which we generally have with the Owners of these Slaves are, that we will not give them such Goods as they ask for them, especially the

Boesies* (as I have told you, the Money of this Country) of which they are very fond, though we generally make a Division on this Head in order to make one sort of Goods help off another, because those Slaves which are paid for in Boesies cost the Company one half more than those bought with other Goods . . . .

When we have agreed with the Owners of the Slaves, they are returned to their Prison; where from that time forwards they are kept at our charge, cost us two pence a day a Slave; which serves to subsist them, like our Criminals, on Bread and Water: So that to save Charges we send them on Board our Ships with the very first Opportunity; before which their Masters strip them of all they have on their Backs; so that they come Aboard stark-naked as well Women as Men: In which condition they are obliged to continue, if the Master of the Ship is not so Charitable (which he commonly is) as to bestow something on them to cover their Nakedness.

Guns for Africa

The chief of [the coastal Africans' military arms] are Musquets or Carabins, in the management of which they are wonderful dextrous. 'Tis not unpleasant to see them exercise their Army; they handle their Arms so cleverly, discharging them several ways, one sitting, the second creeping, or lying & etc. that 'tis really to be admired they never hurt one another. Perhaps you wonder how the *Negroes* come to be furnished with Fire-Arms, but you will have no Reason when you know we sell them incredible quantities, thereby obliging them with a Knife to cut our own Throats. But we are forced to it; for if we would not, they might be sufficiently stored with that Commodity by the *English, Danes*, and *Brandenburghers*; and could we all agree together not to sell them any, the *English* and *Zeeland* Interlopers [i.e., private traders] would abundantly furnish

*Cowries.

them: And since that and Gunpowder for some time hath been the chief vendible Merchandise here [i.e., on the Gold Coast], we should have found but an indifferent Trade without our share in it. . . .

From William Bosman, *A New and Accurate Description of Guinea, etc.*, translated, London, 1705.

MICHEL ADANSON

A Scientific Traveller

Scientific inquiry appears, however surprisingly amid the horrors of the slave trade, in the eighteenth century. Michel Adanson, a French botanist, is one of its earliest exponents.

[1720] As the island of Senegal is within the dependence of the kingdom of Oualo [Walo], the negroes who live there, especially those who are free, are of that nation. They are, generally speaking, very good-natured, sociable and obliging. Those whom the company entertained in my service were Oualofes, as they call themselves, or by corruption Jallofs.

Immediately after my arrival, I employed some months, not only in studying the manners and character of the inhabitants, but likewise in learning the Oualof language which obtained most generally in that country: for I was sensible that it would be of great service to me, and even indisputably necessary in regard to the researches I purposed to make. With this view I frequented their company, and was among them as much as possible. At length when I looked upon myself as sufficiently acquainted with their usages and manners, and able to judge how to conduct myself in a country which had long been the object of my most ardent wishes, I determined to set out upon a ramble . . . .

After . . . a passage through thorns, rivers and burning sands, where I coursed and herborized all the way, I arrived at the village of Sor.   There I found the governor, whom the negroes distinguished by the name of *Borom-dek*, that is, master of the village.   He was a venerable old man, about fifty . . . whose physiognomy bespoke him a person of gentle manners and great good nature.   His name was Baba-Sec: he was sitting on the sand, under the shade of a jujube planted before his hut, where he was smoking and conversing with a few friends.   As soon as he saw me, he rose up, presented his hand to me thrice, then laid it upon his forehead, and afterwards upon his breast, asking me each time, in his language, how I did.   I performed the same ceremony myself at the same time, because I understood that such was the manner of saluting in this country. . . .   It was near their dinner time, and Baba-Sec counted upon my staying . . . .   He made me sit down by him; then he began to fall to, and thrusting his hand into the dish, he took a handful of couscous, which he rolled about with his fingers, for want of a fork and spoon, a conveniency they have not yet learnt.   He invited me afterwards to do the same.   I did not let him press me hard, but followed his example: for I never departed from this principle, that nothing contributes more to gain the confidence and friendship of strangers among whom you reside, than to conform to their customs and manner of living. . . .

From Michel Adanson, *Voyage au Senegal*: translated in J. Pinkerton, *A General Collection of the Best Voyages, etc.* (London: 1814).

JOHN ATKINS

Ouidah in 1721

Whydah [Ouidah or Fida] is the greatest trading Place on the Coast of Guinea, selling off as many Slaves, I believe, as all the rest together; 40 or 50 Sail (French, English, Portuguese, and Dutch) freighting there every year. The King is absolute as a Boar; making sometimes fair Agreements with his Country Neighbours, it being often the Interest of Traders to be honest (perhaps the only reason that makes them so) but if he cannot obtain a sufficient number of Slaves that way, he marches an Army, and depopulates. He, and the King of Ardra adjoining, commit great Depredations inland.

On the Ships he lays these Impositions, and to prove his Folly, does it mostly for the benefit of those that rule him: First, of having the refusal of all Goods; Secondly, the Value of twenty Slaves from every Ship, small or great, as a Duty; and thirdly, forces his own upon them at an advanced Price. . . .

The French, the Dutch, and English, have each a House, or mud Fort about three miles from the Sea, keeping Tents on the Beach for the convenient receiving and securing their Cargoes as it comes from the Ship, and transmitting the Returns; which, by a dangerous double Barr upon the Coast, is rendred impassable sometimes (by the alteration of the Winds) for a fortnight together; the Negroes only know how to paddle thro' it, and when they think it safe, a Signal is made to the Ships, from those Tents, by hoisting their Flags.

The Chief of either Factory that gets first on board any Ship coming into the Road, has a right to serve her with Boats and Servants, and has a Due of seven Slaves for it.

The Commanders, with their Surgeons, (as skilled in the Choice of Slaves) attend the whole time on shore, where they purchase, in what they call a fair open Market.

The Mates reside on board, receiving from time to time their Master's Directions as to the Goods wanted, and to prepare the Ship for the Reception and Security of the Slaves sent him; where this is a Rule always observed, to keep the Males apart from the Women and Children, to handcuff the former. . . .

From John Atkins, Surgeon in the Royal Navy, *A Voyage to Guinea, etc.* (London: 1735), p. 168. Ouidah (Fida or Whydah) was one of the most important middleman trading-stations of the Slave Coast (Dahomey in later years).

WILLIAM SMITH

The Palace of Benin

The master of the *Bonetta* was on the Coast in 1726-1727. Although the account that follows is mainly at second hand, it is useful in showing how greatly Benin had impressed Europeans, and may be compared with the earlier Dutch accounts.

The King's Court is situated in a very large Plain. The first Place we come into, is, a very long Gallery which is sustained by fifty-eight strong Planks, which are only hack'd out rough. At the End of which we come to the Mudwall with three Gates, at each Corner one, and another in the Middle. At the Top of all is fix'd a large Copper Snake, which is well cast and carved. Entring one of these Gates we next come into a Plain, which is about a Quarter of a Mile Square, and encompass'd with a low Mud-wall; then we come to another Gallery, which has a Gate leading to the third Gallery, which is supported by Human

Figures. Going through a Gate we come to the fourth Gallery, beyond which is the King's House. Here is another Snake. In his Anti-chamber his three Great Lords attend, who acquaint the King with the Desires of his Subjects and report his Answers, for no other Person dare to come nearer to him than the Distance of Thirty Paces.

The King appears publickly but once a Year, and that is at the CORAL-FEAST, as they call it, when he comes to the Plain most magnificently dress'd attended by his Wives, Prime Ministers of State, and all the Gentry, or Viceroys, where His Majesty sacrifices to his Gods in the open Air, which begins the Feast; the Nobles and Gentry follow his Example, and the Day proceeds with all Manner of Drinking, etc. and concludes with great Mirth and Gladness. It is call'd the Coral-Feast, because at this Time the King bestows the Strings of Coral on those, whom he advances to any Preferment, or Post of Honour, which he never does, but on this Festival, unless a particular Urgency of State requires it.

From William Smith, *A New Voyage to Guinea* (London: 1744), p. 236.

RICHARD BREW

A Dearth of Victims

Such was now the demand for slave labor that Europeans were paying in gold for captives—even on the shores of what they had named the Gold Coast.

[1771] . . . there remains only to tell you that gold commands the trade; there is no buying a slave without one ounce of gold at least on it, and the windward Coast has been so ransacked, that there is no such thing as getting gold, even though you sell your goods from forty to fifty per cent. under prime cost . . . .

A most pernicious practice has of late crept into the trade of the Gold Coast, which is the giving gold upon slaves; and it is greatly to be wished that some methods may be fallen upon to put a timely stop to it, otherwise it will be impossible for any man to continue to trade here with any prospect of success; Appolonia, the only place from which the shipping used to be supplied with gold, you are effectively shut out from; that fort, Dixcove, Succondee, and Commenda being factories to the governor of Cape Coast, who is so plentifully supplied with gold from these places, that he carries everything before him; for the truth of which I appeal to all the Liverpool and Bristol captains that have been here this year.

Formerly owners of ships used to send out double cargoes of goods, one for slaves, the other for gold; if slaves happened to be dearer than usual, the cargoe for gold was thrown into the slave cargoe in order to fill the ship; on the other hand, if slaves were reasonable the gold cargoe was disposed of for gold and ivory, at a profit of thirty, forty, or fifty per cent. which went a great way towards paying the portlidge bill in the West Indies; as I have frequently known from five to fifteen hundred pounds sterling in gold and ivory carried off from this coast, over and above a compleat cargoe of slaves. How strangely things are reversed now, you have experienced; we scarce see a ship go off with her complement of slaves, notwithstanding her cargoe is laid in from eighteen to twenty pounds sterling per head on an average, reckoning goods at prime cost, without a shilling charges on them; a great part of which they are obliged to sell where they can for gold, greatly under prime cost, or lie here till their provisions are all expended, and their bottoms eat out with the worms. . . .

There is no buying slaves now [1772] without you give two ounces of gold on each; to procure which, you must sell your goods 20 per cent. under prime cost, and you may think yourself happy to get it even at that rate.

From three letters by Richard Brew in *A Treatise upon the Slave Trade*, written in 1771-1772 from the Gold Coast. In E. Donnan, *Documents Illustrative of the Slave Trade to America* (Carnegie Institution, Washington, DC: 1931), vol. 2, p. 536.

CAPTAIN HEATLEY

The Reverence of Kings

[1789] When a Ship arrives in the River Gambia she comes to an Anchor at Gillofree Port, in the Kingdom of Barra, opposite James Fort on James's Island, Nine or Ten Leagues from the Entrance. You send your Boat on Shore to acquaint the Alkaide or Mayor of the Town of your Arrival; he in common returns with the Boat, and receives from you Anchorage-money, Ten Gallons of Liquor for the King, Value 30 s. and Two Iron Bars for himself, Value 7s. and perhaps Presents, a few Bottles of Wine, Beer, Cyder, etc. He immediately dispatches Messengers with the Liquor as above to the King, informing that such a Vessel is arrived, and only waits to pay his Customs, intending to proceed up the River. The King consults his Councillors for a proper Day to receive the same, and sends Word to the Alkaide accordingly. After a Detention of Four, Five, Six, and Seven Days, he sends his People to receive his Custom, 140 Bars in Merchandize, Amount Sterling on an Average £16. An English Ship seldom or ever meets with Trade here; the French (who have their King's Residence at Albreda, a Town in the Kingdom of Barra, about 17 Miles West of

Gillofree) engross most or all of the Trade of the lower Parts of this River.

From evidence before the 1789 Committee of the Privy Council for Inquiry into the Slave Trade. In E. Donnan, *Documents Illustrative of the History of the Slave Trade to America* (Carnegie Insitution, Washington, DC: 1931), vol. 2, p. 593.

JOHN NEWTON

Some Slave Trade Realities

While merchants and politicians associated with the profits of the Atlantic slave trade rallied in the 1780s, and later, to defend the trade against the arguments of the abolitionists, the latter could rely on the support of men who had taken part in the trade and had turned against it. Among the latter was the Revd. John Newton (1725-1807). As a young man, Newton had been a slaver on the coasts of Sierra Leone, but as an older man he took orders in the Church of England and provided the anti-slaving campaigners with some powerful material evidence.

[1788]   Not an article that is capable of diminution or adulteration is delivered genuine or entire. The spirits [sold for captives on the coast] are lowered by water. False heads are put into the kegs that contain the gunpowder; so that, although the keg appears large, there is no more powder in it than in a much smaller. The linen and cotton cloths are opened, and two or three yards, according to the length of the piece, cut off: not from the end but out of the middle, which is not so readily noticed.

The natives are cheated in the number, weight, measure or quality of what they purchase in every possible way. And by habit and emulation a marvellous dexterity is acquired in these practices. And thus the natives, in their turn, in proportion to their commerce with the Europeans, and (I am sorry to add) particularly with the English, become jealous, insidious and revengeful.

They know with whom they have to deal, and are accordingly prepared: though they can trust some ships and boats, which have treated them with punctuality and may be trusted by them. A quarrel sometimes furnishes a pretext for detaining and carrying away one or more of the natives: which is retaliated, if practicable, upon the next boat that comes to the place from the same port [in Britain]. For so far their vindictive temper is restrained by their ideas of justice that they will not, often, revenge an injury received from a Liverpool ship upon one belonging to Bristol or London.

Retaliation on their part furnishes a plea for reprisal on ours. Thus, in one place or another, trade is often suspended, all intercourse cut off, and things are in a state of war: until necessity, either on the ship's part, or on theirs, produces overtures of peace, and dictates the price which the offending party must pay for it. But it is a warlike peace. We trade under arms; and they are furnished with long knives.

For, with a few exceptions, the English and Africans, reciprocally, consider each other as consummate villains who are always watching opportunities to do mischief. In short we have, I fear too deservedly, a very unfavourable character upon the Coast. When I have charged a black with unfairness and dishonesty, he has answered if able to clear himself, with an air of disdain, "What! Do you think I am a white man?"

From J. Newton, *Thoughts upon the Slave Trade*, published as an appendix to his journals, London 1788, p. 24. His journals are available as *The Journal of a Slave Trader* (ed. B. Martin and M. Spurrell), London 1962.

JAMES PENNY

The Business of Kings

[1789] At Bonny Slaves are purchased of the King, who is the principal Trader, and of other Traders; at New Calabar, of the before-mentioned Amachree, and of other Traders. These Traders go up into the Country to purchase Slaves. They go up the Rivers to the Distance of about Eighty Miles from Bonny, and the same from New Calabar, in large Canoes with Two or Three principal Persons, and about Forty Men in each.   The Canoes go in a Body all together to defend themselves if attacked.   At the Head of these Two Rivers there is a Mart for Trade, where the Black Traders purchase these Slaves of other Black Traders, who bring them from the interior Country.

From evidence before the 1789 Committee of the British Privy Council. In E. Donnan, *Documents Illustrative of the History of the Slave Trade to America* (Carnegie Institution, Washington, DC: 1931), vol. 2, p. 537. Penny was a Liverpool man who had made eleven voyages to West Africa. He told the Privy Council that fourteen thousand slaves were annually exported from the region of Bombay and Calabar in the Niger delta, eleven thousand of these being purchased by the English. His estimate for Congo-Angola annual exports of slaves at this time was thirteen to fourteen thousand, while as many as twenty-five thousand, he thought, were taken every year from the Windward Coast (central and western West African seaboard).

COMPANY DIRECTORS

Abuses of the Trade

[1795] The slave trade is decreasing very much at Sierra Leone, the price of slaves having risen to £25 or £30 sterling each; and not above 1000 are now annually exported from this river. They are chiefly brought down through a chain of factories [warehouses], but not through the company's ground, and a great many are children. The kings and chiefs trade in slaves; but the principal traders are the French and English factors [commercial agents].

It is customary to credit the black factors who either travel themselves, or deal with other factors still farther up, with European goods (chiefly gunpowder and spirits) and, if they fail in bringing the stipulated slaves, they are made slaves themselves; or, if they do not return in a certain time, any one of their families are taken. King Naimbanna, in his letter to Mr. Sharp,* after mentioning "the horrid depredations committed here by all the countries that come here to trade," says, "There are three distant relations of mine now in the West Indies, carried away by one Capt. Cox, captain of a Danish ship. Their names are Corpro, Banna and Morbour. These were taken out of my river Sierra Leone. I know not how to get them back. I never hurt or deprived any person of their right or property, or

---

*Granville Sharp, a leader of the British antislavery movement.

withheld from them what is their due. So I only let you know of these lads, that there will be an account taken of them, one day or another."

King Naimbanna's son relates, that a cousin of his father's, named Jack Rodney, was asked to pilot a slave-ship down from Bance Island. He begged to be put on shore at Robanna; but the captain refused, saying he would land him at the river's mouth, instead of which he carried him to Jamaica. As he spoke good English, he obtained several interviews with the governor of that island, and was recovered by a ship which brought a letter concerning him from Sierra Leone . . . .

An American ship arriving in Sierra Leone river, the supercargo, who seems to have known little of the Company's principles, went hastily to the governor and council and offered them his cargo, for a cargo of slaves, saying he would take no other articles, and hoped they would soon favour him with the slaves he wanted. A counsellor asked him how the American laws stood, respecting this trade. He said that, where he came from, it was prohibited, under forfeiture of the ship and £1000 penalty on the captain. "But," added he, "nobody will inform."

Indeed Sir, replied the counsellor, I myself shall inform, if none else will. I hope, Sir, you will not do so unfriendly a thing. I would rather prevent evil than punish it, (said the counsellor) and I warn you, that if you carry a single slave from this coast, you shall find an information lodged against you in America. The supercargo then said, he was not in earnest, and that he really abhorred the slave trade.

From a report of 1795 by the Directors of the Sierra Leone Company. In E. Donnan, *Documents Illustrative of the History of the Slave Trade to America* (Carnegie Institution, Washington, DC: 1931), vol. 2, p. 618.

———————————

JOHN JOHNSTON

The Price of Slaves

Slave Trade at Quashies Town, August 1789:

	Oz.	Ac.	Oz.	Ac.
Aug. 18th No. 1 a Prime Man slave for				
4 Dane Guns	1	8		
2 Half Barrells powder	2			
2 fine Chintss	1	4		
2 Patna Do	1			
4 Bajudepants	2	8		
2 Necanees	1			
6 Romauls	2	4		
3 Hlf Cottons	12			
3 Two Blues		12		
1 Half Taffaty	10			
4 Lead Barrs		2		
2 Small Brass panns		2	13	14
Aug. 19th No. 2 A Man Slave for				
4 Dane guns 2 1/2 Barrells powder	4			
2 fine Chintz	1	4		
2 Patna Do	1			
2 Nicanees	1			
6 Romauls	2	4		
2 Half Cottons		8		
3 Two Blues		12	10	12
Carried Forward			24	10

	Oz.	Ac.	Oz.	Ac.
Brought Forward			24	10
4 Bajudepants	2	8		
1 Half Taffaty		10		
2 Brass panns		2	3	4

Aug. 21st   No. 3 a Stout Man for Vizt

	Oz.	Ac.	Oz.	Ac.
5 Half Barrells powder	5			
6 Guns	2	4		
2 Bajudepants	1	4		
2 Necanees	1			
2 Green Ells	1			
2 Romauls		12		
1 Two Blue and 1 Half Cotton		8		
1 Patch 3 Kegs Tallow		14		
3 lbs Pewter Basons		2	12	12
			40	10

From a "Manuscript Book kept by one John Johnston, while on a Slaving Expedition in Africa, in 1792, 84 pages, 1792." From *Proceedings* of the American Antiquarian Society, vol. 39, pp. 379-465. In E. Donnan, *Documents Illustrative of the History of the Slave Trade to America* (Carnegie Institution, Washington, DC: 1931), vol. 2, p. 612.

C. B. WADSTRÖM

An Enlightened Ruler

Returning from Africa with his fellow-scientist Sparrman, the Swedish traveller Wadström was in time to give evidence against the slave trade to the British Privy Council Committee of 1789. His account gives a fair picture of the political chaos in which the trade had by now involved large regions of West Africa.

The Wars which the inhabitants of the interior parts of the country, beyond Senegal, Gambia, and Sierra Leona, carry on with each other, are chiefly of a predatory nature, and owe their origin to the yearly number of slaves, which the Mandingoes or the inland traders suppose will be wanted by the vessels that will arrive on the coast. Indeed these predatory incursions depend so much on the demand for slaves, that if in any one year there be a greater concourse of European ships than usual, it is observed that a much greater number of captives from the interior parts of the country is brought to market the next.

The Moors, who inhabit the countries on the north of the River Senegal, are particularly infamous for their predatory Wars. They cross the river, and attacking the negroes, bring many of them off. There are not a few who subsist by means of these unprovoked excursions. The French, to encourage them in it, make annual presents to the Moorish kings. These are given them under certain conditions, first, that their subjects shall not carry any of their gum to the English at Portendic; and, secondly, that they shall be ready on all occasions, to furnish slaves. To enable them to fulfill this last article, they never fail to supply them with ammunition, guns, and other instruments of War.

To confirm what I have now said, I shall put down the following example:

The King of Almammy had, in the year 1787, very much to his honour, enacted a law, that no slave whatever should be marched through his territories. At this time several French vessels lay at anchor in the Senegal, waiting for slaves. The route of the black traders in consequence of this edict of the king, was stopped, and the slaves carried to other parts. The French, unable on this account to complete their cargoes, remonstrated with the king. He was, however, very unpropitious to their representations, for he returned the presents which had been sent him by the Senegal company, of which I myself was a witness; declaring, at the same time, that all the riches of that company should not divert him from his design. In this situation of affairs, the French were obliged to have recourse to their old friends, the Moors. These, who had before shewn themselves so ready on such occasions, were no less ready and active on this. They set off in parties to surprise the unoffending negroes, and to carry among them all the calamities of War. Many unfortunate prisoners were sent, and for some time continued to be sent in. I was once curious enough to wish to see some of those that had just arrived. I applied to the Director of the company, who conducted me to the slave-prisons. I there saw the unfortunate captives, chained two and two together, by the foot.

A second source, from whence the Europeans are supplied with slaves on the coast of Africa, is Pillage, which is of two kinds; publick and private. It is publick, when practised by the direction of the king, private when practised by individuals. I must also make a further distinction, namely, as it is practised by the blacks and the whites. This last I call Robbery, which will be the subject of the next article.

The publick Pillage is, of all others, the most plentiful source, from which the slave trade derives its continuance and support. The kings of Africa (I mean in that part of the country which I have visited) incited by the merchandise shewn them, which consists principally of strong liquors, give orders to their military to attack their own villages in the night. . . .

I have been hitherto describing the Pillage, as it is either publick or private. I have also considered it as practised by the blacks upon one another. I come now to speak of it, as it is practised upon these by the whites; and this I call Robbery . . . .

When I was at Goree,* in the year 1787, accounts came down by some French merchantmen from the Gambia of the following particulars.

The captain of an English ship, which had been some time in that river, had enticed several of the natives on board, and, finding a favourable opportunity, sailed away with them. His vessel however was, by the direction of Providence, driven back to the coast from whence it had set sail, and was obliged to cast anchor on the very spot where this act of treachery had been committed. At this time two other English vessels were lying in the same river. The natives, ever since the transaction, had determined to retaliate. They happened, at this juncture, to be prepared. They accordingly boarded the three vessels, and, having made themselves masters of them, they killed most of their crews. The few who escaped to tell the tale, were obliged to take refuge in a neighbouring French factory. Thus did the innocent suffer the same punishment as the guilty; for it did not appear that the crews of the other two vessels had been at all concerned in this villainous measure.

From C. B. Wadstrom, *Observations on the Slave Trade . . . made in 1787 and 1788 in Company with Dr. A. Sparrman and Captain Arrhenius* (London: 1789).

ARCHIBALD DALZELL

Rise of Dahomey

Forced to defend themselves against slaving raids and eager to break the coastal monopoly on the import of European goods,

---

*An island off Dakar on the Senegal Coast, much used as a slaving base.

notably firearms, the Fon people of Dahomey broke through to the sea in 1724. They became a power with whom the Europeans had to reckon and soon learned to respect.

Dalzell was governor of the English trading station and castle at Cape Coast, and also spent four years at Ouidah where he came into personal contact with the new-risen state of Dahomey.

The Dahomans were formerly called Foys [Fons], and inhabited a small territory, on the northeast part of their present kingdom, whose capital, Dawhee, lay between the towns of Calmina and Abomey, at about 90 miles from the seacoast. . . .

The conquest of Abomey happened about the year 1625; after which, Tacoodonou fixed his residence in that town, assuming the title of King of Dahomy. . . .

It is not till the reign of Guadja Trudo [Agaja], who succeeded Weebaigah in 1708, that any thing is precisely known about this extraordinary people. All before this time stands on the ground of tradition . . . . But when the active spirit of Trudo began to threaten the maritime states [i.e., the coastal city-states of Ardra, Ouidah and the like], his neighbours, it quickly attracted the attention of the Europeans, whom commerce have brought and settled amongst them. . . .

A very little experience must have taught such a mind as that of Trudo, how much more effective in war were the European weapons, than those used by the inland people of Africa; and this must have suggested to him the advantage of a seacoast, where only those weapons were to be obtained. For, as to the supply, that might be procured through the hands of the maritime nations [Ardra and its like], it was at best precarious. Their jealousy might wish to keep from others the means of becoming as formidable as they supposed themselves to be; and so they might either refuse to furnish him at all, or they might set so high a price upon them, as would amount to a prohibition.

This made him determine to possess himself of a part of the coast; but, previous to this undertaking, the event of which was uncertain, he endeavoured to obtain his principal end by negotiation.   He sent ambassadors to Ardra and Ouidah, to whose very borders he had already extended his conquests, requesting an open traffic to the seaside, offering at the same time to pay the customary duties.   This, as he probably expected, was preemptorily refused; which furnished him with a pretence for obtaining his desire by force, when he should find an opportunity. Nor was it long before such an opportunity offered . . . . [Dahomey conquered the coastal city-state of Jacquin in 1724 and of Ouidah—Whydah or Fida—in 1727. Some ten years later Dahomey was in turn invaded by the neighbouring Yoruba empire of Oyo, then very powerful.]

From Archibald Dalzell, *History of Dahomey* (London: 1793), p. 60.

ROBERT NORRIS

Oyo and Dahomey

. . . To the northeast of Dahomy lies a fine, fertile, and extensive country, inhabited by a great and warlike people, called the Eyoes [Oyos]; the scourge and terror of all their neighbours . . . .

The Dahomans, to give an idea of the strength of an Eyoe army, assert, that when they go to war, the general spreads the hide of a buffaloe before the door of his tent, and pitches a spear in the ground, on each side of it; between which the soldiers march, until the multitude, which pass over the hide, have worn an hole through it; as soon as this happens, he presumes that his forces are numerous enough to take the field.

The Dahomans may possibly exaggerate, but the Eyoes are certainly a very populous, warlike and powerful nation.

They invaded Dahomy in 1738 with an irresistible army, and laid the country waste with fire and sword to the gates of Abomey; here, the Foys [Fons, Dahomans] had collected their whole strength, and waited the arrival of the enemy, who were advancing with an incredible multitude.

The Foys though inferior in numbers, were not intimidated; they had seen service under Trudo [King Agaja, 1708-1727], but never was their valour called forth upon a more trying occasion . . . . The enemy attacked them in the morning; they acted wonders on that day; twice they repulsed the Eyoes, and had nearly given them a total defeat; but fresh supplies of the enemy continually pouring in, to replace those who fell, the Foys, worn out with fatigue, were obliged to yield at last and retreated, under cover of the night, into Abomey. . . .

Abomey is a very large town, surrounded with a deep moat, but has no wall nor breastwork to defend the besieged; nor are there any springs of water in it; consequently it could not be tenable. The first care of the Dahomans on the night after the battle, whilst the Eyoes were too much fatigued to interrupt them, was to send away the wounded, and the women and children, to Zassa, a town about twenty-five miles off, where the king then was; who, when he learned the unfortunate issue of the day, was immediately conveyed, with his women and treasures, to an inaccessible retreat. . . .

Agaow, the king's general at Abomey, continued to defend the place, and amuse the enemy, until he learned that the king was safe and Zassa evacuated; he then took advantage of the dark night, conducted the remains of his army safe, passed the enemy, and fled; leaving the town to the mercy of the Eyoes, who afterwards plundered and burnt it, as they also did Calonina and Zassa. . . .

The Eyoes continued for several years to harass Dahomy with an annual visit; the Foys never thought it prudent to engage them afterwards; but when apprized of their coming, used to evacuate their towns, divide into small parties, and shelter themselves as well as they could in their fastnesses and woods. The king used all his efforts to obtain an accommodation, and offered them any reasonable compensation to refrain from hostilities; but it was difficult to satisfy their demands. They claimed, in consequence of an old treaty, an annual tribute; the payment of which had been omitted in the prosperous days of Trudo [King Agaja]. These arrears were considerable; and fresh demands were also added, on account of the conquest of Whydah, which the Eyoes looked upon as an inexhaustible source of wealth to the king.... In the year 1747, however, the Eyoes consented to an accommodation, and compromised the matter for a tribute, which is paid them annually at Calonia, in the month of November. [In the nineteenth century Dahomy in turn invaded Oyo, then in decline.]

From Robert Norris, *Memoirs of the Reign of Bossa Ahadee, King of Dahomey* (London: 1789), p. 11. Norris wrote in 1773. The Bossa Ahadee in question was King Tegbesu, who reigned between about 1727 to 1775.

ABBÉ PROYART

Congo Government

The Abbe Proyart was a French missionary in the states to the immediate north of the Congo estuary. His account refers to the early part of the second half of the eighteenth century, and is useful if read with due allowance for prejudice. It may be compared with the earlier writings on this subject by Father Cavazzi and other missionaries (see pp. 208-9).

Though the kings do not employ the most proper means for promoting the welfare of their subjects, they hold this as a principle, that it is their interest as well as their duty, to occupy themselves with the care of rendering them happy, and maintaining peace and justice among them. Every day they pass several hours in deciding the processes of those who have appealed to them to their tribunals; they hold frequent councils; but it is rare that they have a real friend and a disinterested man among those they invite thither. The ministers stand charged with the execution of whatever has been determined in the king's council; but as this prince blindly defers to them, it frequently happens that while occupied with the details of justice he pacifies the differences of a few families, one of his ministers, in his name though without his knowledge, spreads trouble and desolation over a whole province.

The principal ministers are the *man-ngovo*, the *ma-npontu*, the *ma-kaka*, the *m-fuka*, and the *ma-kimba*. The *ma-ngovo*, whom we call *mangove*, is the minister for foreign affairs, and the introducer of foreigners at court. The *ma-npontu* is associated to the department of the *mangove*, and represents him when absent. The *ma-kaka* is minister of war, and even generalissimo of the armies. It is he who causes the troops to be mustered in time of war, who appoints their officers, reviews them, and also leads them to battle. The *m-fuka*, whom the French call *mfouque*, is minister of commerce. He makes frequent voyages on the sea coasts, where are the warehouses and factories [trade-stations] of the Europeans. He is obliged, by the nature of his office, to make frequent representations of the state of the exchanges which are made between the Europeans and the Africans, and to take care that no frauds are committed on either side. He also presides over the recovery of the taxes which the king exacts from strangers who trade in his states; and he is charged with the general police of the markets. The *ma-kimba* is grand master of the waters and forests. It is he who has the inspection of all the boatmen, fishermen and hunters; and it is to him that the fish and game intended for the king are directed. . . .

These ministers have no offices or houses of business as ours have; they even know not how either to read or write: with the exception of a small number of important affairs, they dispatch all others on the spot and as soon as they present themselves, in order not to run the risk of forgetting them. Their clerks are diligent slaves whom they send into the towns and provinces, to signify to private individuals, as well as persons in place, the king's intentions. In all the provinces and in all the towns, there is a governor for the king. The chiefs of the villages are also king's officers; they administer justice in his name . . . .

The crown among these people is not hereditary, as several authors aver . . . . There is in each kingdom a family, or if you please a class of princes . . . . It is sufficient to be a prince in order to have the right of pretending to the crown; and it must necessarily be so, in order to possess certain noble fiefs which are held more immediately on that tenure.

No nobles are known in these countries, except the princes, and nobility does not descend except by the females, so that all the children of a princess-mother are princes or princesses, though begotten by a plebian father; as, on the other hand, the children of a prince or even those of a king are not nobles, unless their father has married a princess . . . .

On the death of every king, there is always an interregnum, during which are celebrated the obsequies of the defunct, who is commonly interred after the lapse of some years. The kingdom is then governed by a regent who takes the name of *ma-boman*, that is to say, *lord of terror*, because he has the right to make himself feared throughout the whole kingdom . . . . It is during this interregnum that the pretenders to the crown, from their canvass, and by means of presents and promises, try to render the electors favourable to themselves. These electors are the princes, the ministers, and the regent. The present king of Loango [to the north of the Congo estuary] was not elected till after an interregnum of seven years . . . .

When anyone is accused of a crime of which they cannot convict him, they permit him to justify himself by drinking the *kassa*. The *kassa* is prepared by infusing in water a bit of wood so called. This potion is a true poison to weak stomachs, which have not the strength to throw it up immediately. He who stands the proof is declared innocent, and his accuser is condemned as a slanderer. If the fault of which the pretended culprit is accused does not deserve death, as soon as they perceive him ready to expire they make him take an antidote, which excites vomiting, and brings him back to life; but they condemn him as a culprit to the penalty fixed by law.

The inhabitants of the country have the greatest faith in this cordial. The princes and lords sometimes cause *kassa* to be taken in order to clear up their suspicions, but they must first obtain the king's permission to do so, which is not difficult when the suspicions are of weighty concern . . . .

In these countries where the crown is elective, the death of the kings . . . is as it were the signal of a civil war. A prince who, ambitious enough to direct his views to the throne, has no reason to count on the favour of the electors, makes his vassals take up arms to force their suffrages, or to dispute the crown with him whom they may have preferred. If he fears that his party may not be the strongest, he addresses himself to a foreign prince, who, for a few pieces of European stuffs, or vessels of silver, sends him a whole army. . . .

The sovereigns of these countries maintain no regular troops. When a king has determined on war, his *ma-kaka*, minister of war and generalissimo of his armies, transmits orders to the princes and governors of provinces, to levy troops; the latter never fail to lead to the rendezvous the quota demanded of them. . . .

The armies in general do not make long campaigns; a war is sometimes over in less than eight days. When the soldiers have eaten the provisions they brought with them, and find

..one in the hostile country, or when they want powder and lead, nothing can hold them; all, without asking leave, take the road home. . . .

From the Abbe Proyart, *History of Loango, Kakongo, etc.* (Paris: 1776), translated in J. Pinkerton, *A General Collection of the Best and Most Interesting Voyages and Travels, etc.* (London: 1814), vol. 16, p. 568.

OLAUDAH EQUIANO

In Iboland

Olaudah Equiano's memoirs are perhaps the best of all the books written by Africans who were taken into European slavery and won their freedom. Appearing very appropriately in the momentous year of 1789, it argued the case for regarding traditional African society with a new interest, tolerance and understanding; and it did this with a tactful grace which nonetheless contained a powerful note of confidence and determination.

Born in about 1745, Equiano was kidnapped for enslavement in about 1756, sold to Virginia and thence to England. He purchased his freedom in 1777 and made his living as a deep-sea sailor, later became active in the antislavery movement, and married the daughter of James and Ann Cullen of Cambridge, England, in 1792.

This kingdom [of Benin] is divided into many provinces or districts: in one of the most remote and fertile of which I was born. . . . The distance of this province from the capital of Benin and the sea coast must be very considerable, for I had never heard of white men or Europeans, nor of the sea;

and our subjection to the king of Benin was little more than nominal. . . . As our manners [in that country] are simple, our luxuries are few. The dress of both sexes are nearly the same. It generally consists of a long piece of calico, or muslin, wrapped loosely round the body. . . . This is ususally dyed blue, which is our favourite colour. It is extracted from a berry, and is brighter and richer than any I have seen in Europe. . . . Our manner of living is entirely plain . . . bullocks, goats, and poultry supply the greatest part of their food. These constitute likewise the principal wealth of the country, and the chief articles of commerce . . . . In our buildings we study convenience rather than ornament. Each master of a family has a large square piece of ground, surrounded with a moat or fence, or enclosed with a wall made of red earth tempered, which, when dry, is as hard as brick. Within this are his houses to accomodate his family and slaves; which, if numerous, frequently present the appearance of a village. . . . These houses never exceed one story in height; they are always built of wood, of stakes driven into the ground, crossed with wattles, and neatly plastered within and without. The roof is thatched with reeds . . . . Houses so constructed and furnished require but little skill to erect them. Every man is a sufficient architect for the purpose. The whole neigh- bourhood afford their unanimous assistance in building them, and in return receive and expect no other recompense than a feast.

As we live in a country where nature is prodigal of her favours, our wants are few, and easily supplied; of course we have few manufactures. They consist for the most part of calicoes, earthenware, ornaments, and instruments of war and husbandry. . . . We have also markets . . . . These are some- times visited by stout mahogany-coloured men from the southwest of us: we call them *Oye-Eboe*, which term signifies red men living at a distance. They generally bring us fire- arms, gunpowder, hats, beads, and dried fish. . . . They always carry slaves through our land; but the strictest account is exacted of their manner of procuring them before they are suffered to pass. Sometimes indeed we sold slaves to them, but they were only prisoners of war, or such among us as had been convicted of kidnapping, or adultery, and some other crimes, which we esteemed heinous. This practice of kidnapping induces me to think, that, notwithstanding all our strictness, their principal business among us was to trepan our people. . . .

[Equiano then speaks of warfare among the peoples of Iboland.] From what I can recollect of these battles, they appear to have been irruptions of one little state or district on the other, to obtain prisoners or booty. Perhaps they were incited to this by those traders who brought the European goods mentioned amongst us. . . . When a trader wants slaves, he applies to a chief for them, and tempts him with his wares. . . .

[Being kidnapped himself, he was taken with others to the Niger Delta port of sale and embarkation. Seeing "white men with horrible looks, red faces, and long hair," he greatly feared that he was to be eaten—this being, indeed, the common fear of many such captives from the interior.] When I looked round the ship, and saw a large furnace or copper boiling, and a multitude of black people of every description chained together, every one of their countenances expressing dejection and sorrow, I no longer doubted of my fate. . . .

From *The Interesting Narrative of the Life of Olaudah Equiano, or Gustavus Vassa, the African,* written by himself (London: 1789). A much longer extract is in Thomas Hodgkin, *Nigerian Perspectives* (Oxford: 1960, reprinted 1975). The whole work is now reprinted by Longman, UK and USA, 1988, with a valuable introduction by Paul Edwards.

THOMAS WINTERBOTTOM

A Wider Picture

Physician to the colony of Sierra Leone, Thomas Winterbottom was one of the forerunners, perhaps the best, of scientific
reporting on African life and customs. He first visited the Coast in
1796. His admirable book was published in two volumes seven
years later.

The division of labour and separation of trades is almost
unknown, or at least not practised among the people who inhabit the sea coast; the most ingenious man in the village is
usually the blacksmith, joiner, architect, and weaver, the chief
trades which they require or exercise.... Among the Foolas
[Fulani], however, and other nations beyond them, some
progress has been made in forming distinct occupations or
trades. One set of men, called *garrankees* or shoemakers, are
exclusively employed in manufacturing leather, and converting
it into useful articles, as sandals, quivers for arrows, bridles,
saddles & etc.... Another class of men are equally celebrated
as blacksmiths: besides making every kind of necessary utensil,
they inlay the handles and chase the blades of swords & etc.,
with great neatness, and they make a variety of elegant fancy
ornaments for the women out of pieces of gold and silver
dollars. A considerable degree of ingenuity in the arts with
which they are acquainted must be allowed to all these nations,
and is evident in the construction of their houses, and the
formation of a variety of domestic and agricultural utensils with
the rudest instruments. They form canoes, from a single tree,
capable of carrying eight or ten tons. Their mats show much
neatness and ingenuity; they are composed of split bamboo or
grass, and wove into a great variety of patterns, and are stained
with very beautiful and indelible colours....

They have various substitutes for hemp and flax, of which they make fishing lines and nets equal in strength and durability to those of Europeans. . . . Although they are ignorant in the use of the potter's wheel, they make earthen pots fit for every domestic use. . . . Upon the Gold Coast, the accuracy and dexterity of the people called *Goldtakers*, employed by Europeans to detect false gold, is wonderful. They also fuse the gold dust, and work it into buckles, buttons, and a great variety of trinkets. . . . They raise upon most parts of the coast a sufficient quantity of cotton for their own use . . . . They spin the cotton in a very tedious manner, by twirling a spindle, one end of which is loaded with clay, in a large shell or wooden dish, passing the thread between the finger and thumb of one hand. They dye the threads, which are very fine and even, several colours, which are both vivid and permanent, especially blue, of a kind equal or superior to the finest blues of Europe. Upon the Gold Coast, this blue dye is obtained by infusing the leaves of a species of bignonia, and the root of a species of tabernamontana, in a solution of the ashes of the palm nut in water. . . . The looms resemble those used in England to weave shalloons, except in being much narrower . . . . The men are the weavers, and as the cloth is wove so very narrow, not more than six inches in breadth, seven such pieces, between four and five feet in length, must be joined to form a cloth for a woman; but they are so exact in the pattern, that at a small distance the junctures cannot be easily discovered. . . .

Nicotine and Kola

The Mahommedan nations very religiously abstain from the use of spirits and fermented liquors of every kind; but they, as well as the other Africans, are universally enslaved by the charms of tobacco. . . . Tobacco is chiefly used in the form of snuff . . . . The Foolas [Fulani] have no idea of using it in any other way than snuff, and often use it as a dentifrice in this form; but those who live upon the coast frequently smoke this herb, a custom which they have probably copied from the Europeans.

A more innocent luxury in which they indulge, and which ranks in their esteem next to tobacco, is the chewing of kola. This is the fruit of a large and beautiful tree, which grows in abundance upon the coast, and is in as high esteem, and as much used by the natives of this part of Africa, as is the areca nut in the East Indies. The kola, seven or eight kernels of which, of the size and shape of a chestnut, are included in a thick green capsule, is a very pleasant bitter and astringent. It is much esteemed for its stomachic powers, and is generally washed down with a draught of cold water, to which it imparts a remarkably pleasant sweetish taste. . . .

Kola is always presented to the guests, in visits of ceremony or of friendship, and is looked upon as a mark of great politeness. It generally forms a part of every considerable present, and at public meetings, or palavers between different nations, it is a substitute for the olive branch. Two *white* kolas presented by one party to the other betoken peace and a continuance of friendship, while two *red* ones are considered as an indication of war.

From Thomas Winterbottom, *An Account of the Native Africans, etc.* (2 vols., London: 1803).

JAMES BRUCE

Ethiopian Encounters

If his vivid writings were better known or eighteenth-century reports on Abyssinia [Ethiopia] less rare, James Bruce might deserve a lesser place than he here receives. As it is, he seems to merit a large place, not because he was the first European to reach the source of the Blue Nile, although that was much to his credit, but because he offers a personal and political description of Ethiopia that is unique and full of illuminating detail, besides being highly readable. A good deal of what he told on his return was disbelieved in England, and some of the incidents may have been embellished to the man's own advantage; but there is no doubting the veracity of the picture as a whole.

Of considerable education—because of, or perhaps in spite of, Harrow School—Bruce had the dash and courage of a Scottish laird, the physique of a giant (standing six feet four inches tall, and sturdy all the way), and the curiosity of a good journalist. There is no one else quite like him in the annals of European exploration of Africa.

He prepared himself well for his great adventure, serving as British Consul in Algiers, there and elsewhere in North Africa studying antiquities and Arabic, and living for a time in Egypt where his skill in medicine helped to win him influential friends. Some of these gave him valuable letters of introduction to Muslim and Christian leaders further south. More remarkable still, he set himself seriously to learning Amharic before departure on his journey. He reached Gondar, then the Ethiopian capital, in 1770 and stayed until 1772.

In the first passage below we find him in a desperate brush with a swashbuckling nobleman called Guebra Mascal. Later he goes with the emperor's army in its battles against a rebel army, and writes a vigorous description of those internecine wars. He returns by way of the Middle Nile, and guesses rightly that he has seen the ruins of Meroe.

Adventure at Gondar

We went all to Authule's house to supper in violent rage, such anger as is usual with hungry men. We brought with us from the palace three of my brother Baalomaals, and one who had stood to make up the number, though he was not in office;

his name was Guebra Mascal; he was a sister's son of the
Ras,* and commanded one-third of the troops of Tigre, which
carried firearms, that is, about two thousand men. He was
reputed the best officer of that kind that the Ras had, and was
a man about thirty years of age, short, square, and well made,
with a very promising countenance; flat nose, wide mouth, of
a very yellow complexion, and much pitted with the smallpox;
he had a most uncommon presumption upon the merit of past
services, and had the greatest opinion of his own knowledge in
the use of firearms, to which he did not scruple to say Ras
Michael owed all his victories. Indeed it was to the good
opinion that the Ras had of him as a soldier that he owed his
being suffered to continue at Gondar; for he was suspected to
have been familiar with one of his uncle's wives in Tigre, by
whom it was thought he had a child; at least the Ras put away
his wife, and never owned the child to be his.

This man supped with us that night, and thence began one
of the most serious affairs I ever had in Abyssinia. Guebra
Mascal, as usual, vaunted incessantly his skill in firearms, the
wonderful gun that he had, and feats he had done with it.
Petros said, laughing, to him, "You have a genius for shooting,
but you have had no opportunity to learn. Now Yagoube [i.e.,
Bruce] is come, he will teach you something worth talking of."
They had all drank abundantly, and Guebra Mascal had uttered
words that I thought were in contempt of me.   "I believe,"
replied I, peevishly enough, "Guebra Mascal, I should suspect
from your discourse, you neither knew men nor guns; every
gun of mine in the hands of my servants shall kill twice as far
as yours; for my own, it is not worth my while to put a ball in
it. When I compare with you, the end of a tallow-candle in my
gun shall do more execution than an iron ball in the best of
yours, with all the skill and experience you pretend to."

*The redoubtable Ras Michael of Tigre.

He said I was a Frank, and a liar, and, upon my immediately rising up, he gave me a kick with his foot. I was quite blind with passion, seized him by the throat and threw him on the ground, stout as he was. The Abyssinians know nothing either of wrestling or boxing. He drew his knife as he was falling, attempting to cut me in the face; but his arm not being at freedom, all he could do was to give me a very trifling stab, or wound, near the crown of the head, so that the blood trickled down over my face. I had tript him up, but till then had never struck him. I now wrested the knife from him with a full intention to kill him; but Providence directed better. Instead of the point, I struck so violently with the handle upon his face as to leave scars, which would be distinguished even among the deep marks of smallpox. An adventure so new, and so unexpected, presently overcame the effects of the wine. It was too late to disturb anybody either in the palace or at the house of the Ras. A hundred opinions were immediately started; some were for sending us up to the king, as we were actually in the precincts of the palace, where lifting a hand is death. Ayto Heikel advised that I should go, late as it was, to Koscam, and Petros, that I should repair immediately to the house of Ayto Aylo, while the Baalomaals were for taking me to sleep in the palace. Authule, in whose house I was, and who was therefore most shocked at the outrage, wished me to stay in his house, where I was, from a supposition that I was seriously wounded, which all of them, seeing the blood fall over my eyes, seemed to think was the case; and he, in the morning, at the king's rising, was to state the matter as it happened. All these advices appeared good when they were proposed; for my part, I thought they were only tended to make bad worse, and bore the appearance of guilt, of which I was not conscious.

I now determined to go home, and to bed in my own house. With that intention, I washed my face and wound with vinegar, and found the blood to be already staunched. I then wrapt myself up in my cloak and returned home without accident, and went to bed. But this would neither satisfy Ayto

Heikel nor Petros, who went to the house of Ayto Aylo, then past midnight, so that early in the morning when scarce light, I saw him come into my chamber. Guebra Mascal had fled to the house of Kefla Yasous his relation; and the first news we heard in the morning after Ayto Aylo arrived, were, that Guebra Mascal was in irons at the Ras's house.

Every person that came afterward brought up some new account; the whole people present had been examined and had given, without variation, the true particulars of my forbearance, and his insolent behaviour. Everybody trembled for some violent resolution the Ras was to take on my first complaint. The town was full of Tigre soldiers, and nobody saw clearer than I did, however favourable a turn this had taken for me in the beginning, it might be my destruction in the end.

I asked Ayto Aylo his opinion. He seemed at a loss to give it to me; but said, in an uncertain tone of voice, he could wish that I would not complain of Guebra Mascal while I was angry, or while the Ras was so inveterate against him, till some of his friends had spoken, and appeased, at least, his first resentment. I answered, "That I was of a contrary opinion, and that no time was to be lost: remember the letter of Mahomet Gibberti; remember his confidence yesterday of my being safe where he was; remember the influence of Ozoro Esther,* and do not let us lose a moment."

"What," says Aylo to me in great surprise, "are you mad? Would you have him cut to pieces in the midst of twenty thousand of his countrymen? Would you be *dimmenia*, that is guilty of the blood of all the province of Tigre, through which you must go in your way home?"

"Just the contrary," said I; "nobody has so great a right over the Ras's anger as I have, being the person injured; and, as you and I can get access to Ozoro Esther when we please,

---

*Ras Michael's young and beautiful wife, who befriended Bruce after he had helped to cure her son of smallpox.

let us go immediately thither, and stop the progress of this affair while it is not yet generally known. People that talk of my being wounded expect to see me, I suppose, without a leg or an arm. When they see me so early riding in the street, all will pass for a story as it should do. Would you wish to pardon him entirely?"

"That goes against my heart, too," says Aylo: "he is a bad man."

"My good friend," said I, "be in this guided by me; I know we both think the same thing. If he is a bad man, he was a bad man before I knew him. You know what you told me yourself of the Ras's jealousy of him. What if he was to revenge his own wrongs, under pretense of giving me satisfaction for mine? Come, lose no time, get upon your mule, go with me to Ozoro Esther, I will answer for the consequences."

We arrived there; the Ras was not sitting in judgement; he had drank hard the night before, on occasion of Powussen's marriage, and was not in bed when the story of the fray reached him. We found Ozoro Esther in a violent anger and agitation, which was much alleviated by my laughing. On her asking me about my wound, which had been represented to her as dangerous, "I am afraid," said I, "poor Guebra Mascal is worse wounded than I." "Is he wounded too?" says she; "I hope it is in his heart." "Indeed," replied I, "madam, there are no wounds on either side. He was very drunk, and I gave him several blows upon the face as he deserved, and he has already got all the chastisement he ought to have; it was all a piece of folly." "Prodigious!" says she, "is this so?" "It is so," says Aylo, "and you shall hear it all by-and-by; only let us stop the propagation of this foolish story."

The Ras in the instant sent for us. He was naked, sitting on a stool, and a slave swathing up his lame leg with a broad belt or bandage. I asked him, calmly and pleasantly, if I could be of any service to him. He looked at me with a grin, the most ghastly I ever saw, as half displeased.

"What," says he, "are you all mad? Aylo, what is the matter between him and that miscreant Guebra Mascal?"

"Why," said I, "I am come to tell you that myself; why do you ask Ayto Aylo? Guebra Mascal got drunk, was insolent, and struck me. I was sober and beat him, as you will see by his face; and I have not come to you to say I am sorry that I lifted my hand against your nephew; but he was in the wrong, and drunk; and I thought it was better to chastise him on the spot, than trust him to you, who perhaps might take the affair to heart; for we all know your justice, and that being your relation is no excuse when you judge between man and man."

"I order you, Aylo," says Michael, "as you esteem my friendship to tell me the truth, really as it was, and without disguise or concealment."

Aylo began accordingly to relate the whole history, when a servant called me out to Ozoro Esther. I found with her another nephew of the Ras, a much better man, called Welleta Selasse, who came from Kefla Yasous, and Guebra Mascal himself, desiring I would forgive and intecede for him, for it was a drunken quarrel without malice. Ozoro Esther had told him part. "Come in with me," said I, "and you shall see I never will leave the Ras till he forgive him." "Let him punish him," says Welleta Selasse; "he is a bad man, but don't let the Ras either kill or maim him." "Come," said I, "let us go to the Ras, and he shall neither kill, maim, nor punish him if I can help it. It is my first request; if he refuses me, I will return to Jidda [in Arabia, across the Red Sea]; come and hear."

Aylo had urged the thing home to the Ras in the proper light—that of my safety. "You are a wise man," says Michael, now perfectly cool, as soon as he saw me and Welleta Selasse. "It is a man like you that goes far in safety, which is the end we all aim at. I feel the affront offered you more than you do, but will not have the punishment attributed to you; this affair shall turn to your honour and security, and in that light only I can pass over his insolence."

"Welleta Selasse," says he, falling into a violent passion in an instant, "what sort of behaviour is this my men have adopted with strangers; and my stranger, too, and in the king's palace, and the king's servant? What! am I dead? or become incapable of governing longer?" Welleta Selasse bowed, but was afraid to speak, and indeed the Ras looked like a fiend.

"Come," says the Ras, "let me see your head." I shewed him where the blood was already hardened, and said it was a very slight cut. "A cut," continued Michael, "over that part, with one of our knives, is mortal."

"You see, sir," said I, "I have not even clipt the hair about the wound; it is nothing. Now give me your promise you will set Guebra Mascal at liberty; and not only that, but you are not to reproach him with the affair further than that he was drunk, not a crime in this country."

"No, truly," says he, "it is not, but that is, because it is very rare that people fight with knives when they are drunk. I scarce ever heard of it, even in the camp."

"I fancy," said I, endeavouring to give a light turn to the conversation, "they have not often wherewithal to get drunk in your camp." "Not this last year," says he, laughing, "there were no houses in the country." "But let me only merit," said I, "Welleta Selasse's friendship, by making him the messenger of good news to Guebra Mascal, that he is at liberty, and you have forgiven him." "At liberty!" says he, "where is he?" "In your house," said I, "somewhere, in irons." "That is Esther's intelligence," continued the Ras; "these women tell you all their secrets, but when I remember your behaviour to them, I do not wonder at it; and that consideration likewise obliges me to grant what you ask. Go, Welleta Selasse, and free that dog from his collar, and direct him to go to Welleta Michael, who will give him his orders to levy the meery in Woggora; let him not see my face till he returns."

The Civil Wars

The king's army halted upon the same ground they had done on their return to Gondar. They were then supposed to be near twenty thousand foot, belonging to Tigre and its dependencies, incomparably the best troops of the empire, six thousand of which were armed with musquets, six times the number that all the rest of Abyssinia could furnish, and, considering they were all matchlocks, very expert in the management of them. The rest of the foot which joined them since he passed the Tacazze [Atbara] were about ten thousand, besides two thousand of the king's household, five hundred of which were horsemen; of these, few short of two hundred were his black servants, armed with coats of mail, the horses with plates of brass on their cheeks and faces, with a sharp iron spike of about five inches in length, which stuck out in the middle of their forehead, a very troublesome, useless piece of their armour; their bridles were iron chains; the body of the horse covered with a kind of thin quilt stuffed with cotton, with two openings made above the flaps of the saddle, into which the horseman put his thighs and legs, and which covered him from his hip (where his shirt of mail ended) down to a little above his ancle: his feet were covered with slippers of thin leather, without heels, and his stirrups were of the Turkish or Moorish form, into which his whole foot entered, and, being hung very short, he could raise himself, and stand as firmly as if he was upon plain ground.

The saddles were in the Moorish form likewise, high before and behind; a strong lace made fast to the coat of mail by the one end, the other passed through a small hole in the back of the saddle, kept it close down, so that the back was never exposed by the coat of mail rising over the hinder part of the saddle. Each had a small ax in the furcingle of his saddle, and a pike about fourteen feet long, the weapon with which he charged; it was made of very light wood, brought from the banks of the Nile, with a small four-edged head, and the butt end balanced by a long spike of iron; this entered a leather case fastened by a thong to the saddle, and was rested sometimes below the thigh, and sometimes above, and guided by the right hand at the height the point was intended to strike at. The horseman's head was covered with a helmet of copper, or block tin, much like those of our light horse, with large crests of black horse tail.

The officers were distinguished from the soldiers by locks of hair dyed yellow, interspersed with the black. Upon the front of each helmet was a silver star, at least a white-metal one, and before the face, down to the top of the nose, a flap of iron chain, made in the same manner as the coat of mail, but only lighter, which served as a vizier. This was the most troublesome part of the whole, it was hot and heavy and constantly fretted the cheek and the nose, when either the man or the horse were in motion; and therefore I always substituted a black silk net, which concealed my colour better, and for the rest of my face I committed it to the care of Providence. . . .

The horsemen of the king's army were about seven thousand, mostly very indifferent troops; so that his whole muster was nearly seven thousand musqueteers, twenty-five thousand foot, armed with lances and shields, and about seventy-five hundred horsemen; in round numbers about forty thousand men. It is not possible, I believe, to know, with greater precision, the number, such is the confusion of barbarous armies on these occasions, and such the inclination of their leaders to magnify and increase their quotas. Besides these, Ayto Confu and Sanuda were left with about six hundred men each, to protect Gondar from flying, pillaging parties, and to keep the communication open between the army and the capital, from whence the provisions were to be supplied.

This army was furnished with a number of excellant officers, veterans of noble families, who had spent their whole life in war, which we may say, for these last four hundred years, has never ceased to lay desolate this unhappy country; the principal were Ras Michael, who, arrived at the age of seventy-four, had passed the last fifty years of his life in a course of continued victories. . . .

[Several battles are now fought between the king's army and the rebel army.]

The fire increasing on the hill, and several musquets having been heard, it was plain the enemy, in all the camps, were alarmed, and our further stay became every moment more dangerous. Kefla Yafous now beat a retreat, and sent the horsemen all round to force the foot to make the best of their way back, ordering also all mules taken to be hamstringed and left, not to retard our return. Trumpets and drums were heard from our camp, to warn us not to stay, as it was not doubted but mischief would follow, and accordingly we were scarce arrived within the limits of our camp when we heard the sound of horse in the valley.

Michael, always watchful upon every accident, no sooner saw the fires lighted on the hill, than he ordered Guebra Mascal to place a good body of musqueteers about half way down the hill, as near as possible to the ford of Mariam, thinking it probable that the enemy would enter at both ends of the long hill, in order to surround those who were destroying their camp, which they accordingly did, whilst those of our people, who had taken to drinking, fell into the hands of the troops that came by the lower road, and were all put to death. Those that reached the upper ford served to afford us a severe revenge, for Guebra Mascal, after having seen them pass between him and the river, though it was a dark and very windy night, guessed very luckily their position, and gave them so happy a fire, that most of those who were not slain returned back without seeing Ayto Tesfos's camp, being afraid that some other trap might still be in their way. . . .

Provisions were now become scarce in the camp, and there was a prospect that they would be every day scarcer; and, what was still worse, Deg-Ohha, which long had stood in pools, was now almost dry, and, from the frequent use made of it by the number of beasts, began to have both an offensive smell and taste; whilst, every time we attempted to water at the Mariam river, a battle was to be fought with Tesfos's horse in the valley. On the other hand, an epidemical fever raged in the rebels camp on the plain, especially in that of Gufho and Ayabdar. The rain, moreover, was now coming on daily, and something decisive became necessary for all parties. . . .

The hill of Serbraxos, when we first took post on it, was rugged and uneven, full of acacia and other ill-thriving trees, and various stumps of these had been broken by the wind, or undermined by the torrents. The great need the soldiers had of fuel to roast the miserable pittance of barley (which was all their food), had cleared away these encumbrances from the side of the hill, and the constant resort of men going up and down, had rendered the surface perfectly smooth and slippery; so that our camp did not appear as placed so high, nor nearly so inaccessible as it was at first. For this reason, Ras Michael had ordered the soldiers to gather all the stones on the hill, and range them in small walls, at proper places, in a kind of zigzag, under which the soldiers lay concealed, and with their firearms protected the mules which went down to drink. Michael had lined all these little fortifications with musquetry, from the bottom of the hill to the door of his tent and the king's.

About noon the hill was assaulted on all sides that were accessible, and the ancient spirit of the troops seemed to revive upon seeing the enemy were the aggressors. Without any aid of musquetry, the king's foot repulsed Coque Abou Barea, and drove him from the hill into the plain, without any considerable stand on his part: the same success followed against Mammo and Heraclius; there were chased down the hill, and several of their men pursued and slain on the plain; but a large reinforcement coming from the camp, the king's troops were driven up the hill again, and Tesfos, with his musquetry, had made a lodgment in a pit on the low side of one of these stone walls Ras Michael had built for his own defense, from which he fired with great effect, and the king's troops were obliged to fall back to the brow of the hill immediately below the tent, and that of the Ras. In a moment appeared Woodage Asahel, with a large body of horse, supported likewise with a considerable number of foot. This was the most accessible part of the hill, and under the cover of Tesfos's continued fire: they mounted it with great gallantry. . . .

Woodage Asahel had now advanced within about thirty yards of the musquetry that were expecting him, when unluckily the hill became more steep, and Ayto Tesfos (for some reason not then known) ceased firing. The king was now close to the very brow of the hill, nor could any one persuade him to keep at a greater distance. I was not far from him, and had no sort of doubt but that I should presently see the whole body of the enemy destroyed by the fire awaiting them, and blown into the air. Woodage Asahel was very conspicuous by a red fillet, or bandage, wrapt about his head, the two ends hanging over his ears, whilst he was waving with his hands for the troops below to follow briskly, and support those near him, who were impeded by the roughness and mossy quality of the ground. At this instant the king's troops fired, and I expected to see the enemy strewed dead along the face of the hill. Indeed we saw them speedily disappear, but like living men, riding and running down the declivity so as even to excite laughter. Woodage Asahel, with two men only, bravely gained the top of the mountain, and, as he passed the king's tent, pulled off his red fillet, making a sign as of saluting it, and then galloped through the middle of the camp.

He was now descending unhurt upon the left, where Abou Barea had been engaged and beaten, when Sebastos, a Greek, the king's cook, seventy-five years of age, of whom I have already spoken in the campaign of Maitfha, lying behind a stone, with his gun in his hand, seeing the troops engaged below, fired at him as he passed: the ball took place in the left side of his belly. He was seen stooping forward upon the tore of his saddle, with some men supporting him on each side, in his way to his tent, where he died in the evening, having, by his behaviour that day, deserved a better fate. Sebastos reported this feat of his to the king, but it was not believed, till a confirmation of the fact came in the evening, when Sebastos was cloathed, and received a reward from the king.

. . . .

[Bruce leaves Ethiopia and returns home by way of the Blue Nile. He tarries at Sennar, and visits one of the rulers of the Fung Confederacy founded two centuries earlier.]

Cavalry of Sennar

It was not till the eighth of May I had my audience of Sheikh Adelan at Aira, which is three miles and a half from Sennaar; we walked out early in the morning, for the greatest part of the way along the side of the Nile, which had no beauty, being totally divested of trees, the bottom foul and muddy, and edges of the water white with small concretions of calcarious earth, which, with the bright sun upon them, dazzled and affected our eyes very much.

We then struck across a large sandy plain without trees or bushes, and came to Adelan's habitation; two or three, very considerable houses of one story occupied the middle of a large square, each of whose sides was at least of an English mile. Instead of a wall to inclose this square, was a high fence of impalement of strong reeds, canes, or stalks of dora, (I do not know which) in fascines strongly joined together by stakes and cords.

On the outside of the gate, on each hand, were six houses of a slighter construction than the rest; close upon the fence were sheds where the soldiers lay, the horses picqueted before them with their heads turned towards the sheds, and their food laid before them on the ground; above each soldier's sleeping-place, covered only on the top and open in the sides, were hung a lance, a small oval shield, and a large broadsword. These, I understood, were chiefly quarters for couriers, who, being Arabs, were not taken into the court or square, but shut out at night.

Within the gate was a number of horses, with the soldiers' barracks behind them; they were all picqueted in ranks, their faces to their masters' barracks. It was one of the finest sights I ever saw of the kind. They were all above sixteen hands high, of the breed of the old Saracen horses, all finely made, and as strong as our coach-horses, but exceedingly nimble in their motion; rather thick and short in the forehand, but with the most beautiful eyes, ears, and heads in the world; they were mostly black, some of them black and white, some of them milk-white foaled, so not white by age, with white eyes and white hoofs, not perhaps a great recommendation.

A steel shirt of mail hung upon each man's quarters opposite to his horse, and by it an antelope's skin made soft like shamoy, with which it was covered from the dew of the night. A headpiece of copper, without crest or plumage, was suspended by a lace above the shirt of mail, and was the most picturesque part of the trophy. To these was added an enormous broadsword in a red leather scabbard; and upon the pummel hung two thick gloves, their fingers in one poke. They told me, that, within that inclosure at Aira, there were four hundred horses, which, with the riders, and armour complete for each of them, were all the property of Sheikh Adelan, every horseman being his slave, and bought with his money. . . .

Ruins of Meroe

[Beyond Shendi, about one hundred miles north of modern Khartoum, we saw] heaps of broken pedastals, like those of Axum, all plainly designed for the statues of the dog; some pieces of obelisk, likewise, with hieroglyphics, almost totally obliterated. The Arabs told us these ruins were very extensive; and that many pieces of statues, both of men and animals, had been dug up there; the statues of the men were mostly of black stone. It is impossible to avoid risking a guess that this is the ancient city of Meroe. . . .

From James Bruce, *Travels to Discover the Source of the Blue Nile, 1768-1773* (5 vols., London: 1790). The first extract is from vol. 3, p. 233; the second from vol. 4, p. 116 and p. 194; the third from vol. 4, p. 437; and the fourth from vol. 4, p. 538.

ANDREW SPARRMAN

The Hottentots

A Swede who had studied medicine at Uppsala, Andrew Sparrman sailed to the Antarctic as assistant naturalist on board the *Resolution* with Captain James Cook, and afterwards (1772-1776) saw much of life in what is now the Cape Province of South Africa.

The Hottentots who live in these parts, or within the boundaries of the Dutch colonies, seldom make use of any weapons. Here and there, indeed, a man will furnish himself with a javelin, by way of defence against the wolves: this is called a hassagai.

Their habitations are as simple as their dress, and equally adapted to the wandering pastoral life they lead in those parts. In fact, they scarcely merit any other name than that of huts; though not, perhaps, as spacious and eligible as the tents and dwelling-places of the patriarchs, at least they are sufficient for the Hottentots wants and desires; who may therefore be considered as a happy man, in being able in this point likewise so easily to satisfy them. The great simplicity of them is, perhaps, the reason, why in a Hottentot's craal, or village, the huts are all built exactly alike; and that one meets there with a species of architecture, that does not a little contribute to keep envy from insinuating itself under their roofs. The equality of fortune and happiness in some measure enjoyed by these people, cannot but have a singular effect in preventing their breasts from being disturbed by this baneful passion.

Every hut is disposed in the following manner. Some of them are of a circular, and others of an oblong shape, resembling a round beehive or a vault. The ground-plot is from eighteen to twenty-four feet in diameter. The highest of them are so low, that even in the centre of the arch, it is scarcely ever possible for a middle-sized man to stand upright. But neither the lowness thereof, nor that of the door, which is but just three feet high, can perhaps be considered evidence as any inconvenience to a Hottentot, who finds no difficulty in stooping and crawling on all fours, and who is at any time more inclined to lie down than stand.

The fireplace is in the middle of each hut, by which means the walls are not so much exposed to danger from fire. From this situation of their fireplace, the Hottentots likewise have this additional advantage, that when they sit or lie in a circle round the fire, the whole company equally enjoys benefit of its warmth.

The door, low as it is, is the only place that lets in the daylight; and at the same time, the only outlet that is left for the smoke. The Hottentot, inured to it from his infancy, sees it hover round him, without feeling the least inconvenience arising from it to his eyes; while lying at the bottom of his hut in the midst of the cloud rolled up like a hedgehog, and wrapped up snug in his sheepskin, he is now and then obliged to peep out from beneath it in order to stir the fire, or perhaps light his pipe, or else sometimes to turn the steak he is broiling over the coals.

The materials for these huts are by no means difficult to be procured; and the manner of putting them together being both neat and inartificial, merits commendation in a Hottentot, and is very suitable to his character. The frame of this arched roof, as I have described it above, is composed of slender rods or sprays of trees. These rods, being previously bent into a proper form, are laid, either whole or pierced, some parallel with each other, others crosswise; they are then strengthened, by binding others round them in a circular form with withies. These withies, as well as the rods themselves, are taken, as well as I can recollect, chiefly from the *cliffortia conoides*, which grows plentifully in this country near the rivers. Large mats are then placed very neatly over this latticework, so as perfectly to cover the whole. The aperture which is left for the door is closed, whenever there is occasion for it, with a skin fitted to it, or a piece of matting. These mats are made of a kind of cane or reed. These reeds, being laid parallel to each other, are fastened together with sinews or catgut, or else some kind of packthread, such as they have had an opportunity of getting them from Europeans. They have it therefore, in their power, to make their mats as long as they chuse, and at the same time as broad as the length of the rush will admit of, viz., from six to ten feet. This same kind of matting is now made use of likewise by the colonists, next to the tilts of their wagons, by way of preventing the sailcloth from being rubbed and worn by them, as well as by helping to keep out the rain.

When a Hottentot has a mind to take his house down and remove his dwelling, he lays all his mats, skins, and sprays on the back of his cattle, which to a stranger makes a monstrous, unwieldy, and, indeed, ridiculous appearance. . . .

The Bushmen (Khoi)

There is another species of Hottentots, who have got the name of boshies-men, from dwelling in woody or mountainous places.   These, particularly such as live round about the Camdebo and Sneeberg, are sworn enemies to the pastoral life. Some of their maxims are, to live on hunting and plunder, and never to keep any animal alive for the space of one night. By this means they render themselves odious to the rest of mankind, and are pursued and exterminated like the wild beasts, whose manners they have assumed. Others of them again are kept alive, and made slaves of. Their weapons are poison arrows, which, shot out of a small bow, will fly to the distance of two hundred paces; and will hit a mark with a tolerable degree of certainty, at the distance of fifty, or even a hundred paces. From this distance they can by stealth, as it were, convey death to the game they hunt for food, as well as to their foes, and even to so large and tremendous a beast as the lion: this noble animal thus falling by a weapon which, perhaps, is despised, or even did not take notice of. The Hottentot, in the meantime, concealed and safe in his ambush, is absolutely certain of the operation of his poison, which he always culls of the most virulent kind; and it is said, he has only to wait a few minutes, in order to see the wild beast languish and die.

I mentioned that their bows were small; they are, in fact, hardly a yard long, being at the same time scarcely of the thickness of an inch in the middle, and very much pointed at both ends. What kind of wood they are made of I cannot say, but it does not seem to be of a remarkably elastic nature. The strings of the bows that I saw were made some of them of sinews, others of a kind of hemp, or the inner bark of some vegetable, and most of them are made in a very slovenly manner; which shows, that these archers depend more on the poison of their weapons, than on any exactness in the formation of them or in other perfection in them.

Their arrows are a foot and a half long, and of the same thickness. They are made of a reed one foot in length, which, at the base, or the end that receives the bowstring, has a notch of a proper size to fit it. Just above this notch there is a joint in the reed, about which strings made of sinews are wound, in order to strengthen it. The other end of the reed is armed with a highly polished bone, five or six inches long. At the distance of an inch or two from the tip of this bone, a piece of a quill is bound on very fast with sinews. This is done, in order that the arrow shall not be easily drawn out of the flesh; and thus there may be so much longer time for the poison, which is spread on of a thick consistence like that of an extract, to be dissolved, and infect the wound. . . .

The capture of slaves from among this race of men is by no means difficult, and is effected in the following manner. Several farmers, that are in want of servants, join together, and take a journey to that part of the country where the Boshies-men live. They themselves, as well as their Lego-Hottentots, or else such Boshies-men as have been caught some time before, and have been trained up in fidelity in their service, endeavour to spy out where the wild Boshies-men have their haunts. This is best discovered by the smoke of their fires. They are found in societies from ten to fifty and a hundred, reckoning great and small together. Notwithstanding this, the farmers will venture on a dark night to set upon them with six or eight people, which they contrive to do, by previously stationing themselves at some distance round about the craal. They then give the alarm by firing a gun or two. By this means there is such a consternation spread over the whole body of these savages, that it is only the most bold and intelligent among them, that have the courage to break through the circle and steal off. . . .

From Andrew Sparrman, *A Voyage to the Cape of Good Hope, etc., 1772-1776* (London: 1785), vol. 1. For earlier—seventeenth century—accounts of the Hottentots, see *The Early Cape Hottentots*, ed., I. Schapera and B. Farrington (1933), which prints selections from Dapper (1668), Willem ten Rhyne (1686), and Johannes de Grevenbrock (1695).

The Nineteenth Century

*T*HE CONCEPT OF AFRICAN HISTORY specific to the nineteenth century, as distinct from the eighteenth, can be justified by more than mere convenience. At least three arenas of evidence may be called in witness, each of them the scene of crucial change. The first is the Western Sudan, the second is Southern Africa, and the third is the widening range of European presence which gathered after the 1880s into the race for imperialist partition. All these support a story of enormous scope and drama; and it is one to which the records give voluminous and pointful meaning. The following selection is designed to project the general shape and outline of these vast events.

To the Western Sudan, as a British Islamic scholar, H. F. C. Smith, has written, the nineteenth century brought "political revolution on a remarkable scale."* Into the "power vacuum" left by the collapse of the Songhay imperial system, by the challenge to Muslim orthodoxy of new and subversive schools of Islamic thought, and by the general chaos that remained in many regions after the disruptive pressures of the oversea slave trade (the overland slave trade being never a dominant factor), there plunged visionaries and reformers, adventurers and statesmen, soldiers and captains with devout armies at

*H. F. C. Smith, "A Neglected Theme of West African History: The Islamic Revolutions of the 19th Century," in *Journal of the Historical Society of Nigeria*, 2 of 2, 1961, p. 169.

their backs or raised at their inspiring call: Uthman dan Fodio and his memorable son Muhammad Bello, al Hajj Umar, Ahmadu, Samory Toure, Rabeh and others of their kind whose names and titles, better understood today, drum like a roster of pioneers who spoke and acted, whether for better or for worse, in the name of idealized faith and practical ambition. This ambition, as we can begin to apprehend it now, was nothing less than to settle the "problem of power" in broad grassland regions of the Sudan after the ravaging decades of the previous two centuries. Their efforts to resolve this problem make a vital part of the documentary record; and it is a part, most happily, that may be read quite often in their own writings.

This was a phase of rebirth and new directions. Until recent years, historians have passed over it, even ignored it altogether. For this the fault has lain with the lack of balance in imperialist attitudes. Painfully detailed attention has been given to the "subjects" of colonial conquest and reorganization, to the Faidherbes and Rhodeses and Lugards, while the "objects" of this sprawling enterprise have suffered a corresponding diminishment or eclipse. Men like al Hajj Umar appear in the European story as nothing more than wild fanatics or frantic nuisances, leaders like Samory as bloodthirsty bandits or mere adventurers. In truth, these men responded, as outstanding leaders always will, to the most profound movements of social need and thought of their time. They followed an impulse that came from revolutionary trends within Islamic thought, particularly through the *tariqa* or discipleship of the Tijaniyya brotherhood.

The Tijaniyya may be likened in a general sense to the Puritan movement in seventeenth-century England, or, within a narrower and perhaps more accurate comparison, to England's later "low church" revolt against the upper-class establishment of Church of England conformity. For while the older brotherhoods of the Sudan had settled into stratified orders of privilege and grace, "the Tijaniyya broke through these barriers and established direct contact between simple folk and the Caliph, opening to everyone, by courage or by learning, the road to the highest destinies. . . . It is this that accounts for the prodigious success of al Hajj Umar, as well as for the respect and even fear that he inspired among men of power."* This Tijaniyya brotherhood, of which al Hajj Umar became Caliph, was "something new and sensational. Sheikh Ahmed al-Tijani (1737-1815) taught a complete break with the old orders, and a new way of spiritual salvation through strict moral discipline..."**

Yet Umar was no isolated figure. Before embarking on his own holy war of religious and political reconstruction in the westerly regions of the Western Sudan, he had passed twelve years at the Fulani court of Sultan Bello in the easterly regions. There he had written an important book, the *Suyuf al-Said*; and "it is clear that he collected many followers in the Hausa country, some of whom occupied prominent positions in his organization."*** Like his great contemporaries, Umar was concerned with the reframing of social life throughout the Sudan: he stepped, as they did, far across the boundaries of narrow ethnic loyalty, considering, no differently from the leaders of much older states in these grasslands, that this was a cause which could and should unite every Muslim people. He failed a long way short of that mark. But it was not for want of trying.

None of this had anything to do with Europe except by pressure from the distant coastland. It was more than twenty years after the Fulani reorganization of Hausaland that the first European travellers reached Sultan Bello and, as Clapperton

---

*J. Suret-Canale, *Afrique Noire* (2nd ed., Paris: 1961), p. 191.

**H. F. C. Smith, *loc. cit.*

***Ibid.

afterwards recalled, found him reading Euclid. Barth, thirty years later, began to sketch what may reasonably be called the grand design of all that effort. But not until the 1870s, with the pioneering figure of Edward Blyden, do we come upon a clear external recognition of what it meant or was intended to mean. Speaking in a London suburb on the anniversary of Liberian independence, the Afro-West Indian Blyden had this to say in 1874 of the Muslim leaders and states of the Sudan:

> They read constantly the same books, and from this they derive that community of ideas and that understanding of each other . . . which gives them the power of ready organization and effective action. . . . Without the aid or hindrance of foreigners, then, they are growing up gradually and normally to take their place in the great family of nations, a distinct but integral part of the great human body, who will neither be spurious Europeans, bastard Americans, nor savage Africans, but men developed upon the basis of their own idiosyncrasies and according to the exigencies of the climate and country.*

It was of course to this complex of ideas and beliefs that the Mahdi of the Eastern (Anglo-Egyptian) Sudan adhered, a vivid personality to whom, for lack of space, no justice can be done here.

Switching to Southern Africa, we can see that the quenching of Rozwi-Karanga power, in the plateau lands between the Limpopo and Zambezi, also had its origin in European penetration only by remote effect. These social structures were thrown down by African invaders from the far southeast. No doubt it may be true that those Ngoni regiments had been set in motion by the shock of European invasion from the Cape of

*E. W. Blyden, *The Prospects of the African* (London: 1874), quoted by J. F. Ade Ajayi in *Journal of Negro Education*, 3, 1961, p. 206.

Good Hope; none of that was clear at the time. In this respect the nineteenth-century records are of little help. Nor do we know why the Karanga state collapsed so easily; we can only suppose that long security and prosperity had disarmed it beyond any chance of real resistance to invading bands determined to settle, as they hoped, in lands belonging to other (Shona) peoples but beyond the reach of white racist pressures from South Africa.

About European motives and actions, however, the records are copious. And with reason. The eighteenth century had opened the way for the men of property; in the nineteenth they set forth and followed it. They journeyed along it to such purpose that by 1900 there was hardly any part of Africa which had yet to feel the impact of Europe's drive for material possession. They strode into an epoch of ownership considered as the *summum bonum*, as the touchstone of happiness, as the token of a money-gathering ambition so compelling that even now, in the wake of two tremendous wars, the world is still dazed or dazzled by it. The records are enormously concerned with the question of possession.

Conquest followed hard on geographical discovery. This is not to say that the second must in any case have led to the first, nor even that the explorers always had conquest in mind (though most of the later ones did). But it is to say that the geographical enterprises of the period were part and parcel of an expansive movement which already nourished ambitions of African empire. One school of British historians, pointing to the well-known reluctance of most British governments in the nineteenth century to accept a policy of imperial annexation, have argued that "the scramble for Africa" should be explained merely by diplomatic and strategic motives.* These motives

---

*See R. Robinson, J. Gallagher, A. Denny: *Africa and the Victorians* (New York: Macmillan, 1961); and, for an opposing and to me convincing view, J. Stengers, "L'Imperialisme Colonial, etc.," in *Journal*

certainly existed, especially in relation to England's command of Egypt and therefore of the Isthmus of Suez. But they could have counted for little in promoting the colonial partition of Africa had it not been for other pressures, economic and commercial, which formed part of all that vast combination of capital investment and accumulation which now gave world leadership to Western Europe, and, after 1945, would give it to the USA. The motives and the men who really moved "the scramble" were those who were represented, at the point of parliamentary and city politics, by what Mary Kingsley was to call "our great solid understuff—the Merchant Adventurers."

To all this, national pride soon added a new frenzy. This bore down all barriers of discretion. Discussing partition west of the Niger in 1883, a senior official of the British Foreign Office wrote that "protectorates are unwelcome burdens, but in this case it is . . . a question between British protectorates, which would be unwelcome, and French protectorates, which would be fatal." Commenting on a similar attitude in France, an elderly economist remarked more in sorrow than in anger that the French no longer calculated their steps in Africa nor thought about them without passion. "We want annexations, and we care only for their size, not troubling about their quality." Such was the mental background against which most of the later writers of the nineteenth century composed their memoirs of Africa. It explains a great deal about their contempt for the African peoples whom they encountered.

But the "scramble" was still far ahead when the century opened. The great questions then were the ending of the oversea slave trade and, imminently, the discovery of what lay behind the coastal barriers erected by slave-dealing African kings and middleman chiefs. The year 1807 brought the end of the slave trade in British ships. After that, another eighty years would have to pass before the last slaving ships crossed the

of African History, 3, 1962, p. 469.

Atlantic. But even by 1807 the work of discovery had already begun. We can conveniently divide this work of geographical discovery into parts concerning west, east and central-south Africa.

Mungo Park, a young Scots surgeon, settled the main problem of the Niger river—whether it flowed westward or eastward—in two great journeys from the Gambia river in 1795-1797 and 1805-1806; if I have given him what may appear an undue share of space, it is because his moral qualities were such that no anthology of African discovery could be complete without the note they strike so clearly and so bravely. Then in eight epoch-making years, between 1823 and 1830, the inland country of West Africa was widely opened by six notable men, one French and five English: Dixon Denham, Hugh Clapperton, Dr. Walter Oudney, Rene Caillié and Richard and John Lander.* The Englishmen explored the lower course of the Niger, established its true direction and outflow, and encountered many rulers and peoples; little is said of them here because their books have been much anthologized and their discoveries were mainly geographical. Caillié's contribution was a remarkable feat of patient endurance in Muslim disguise: entering West Africa from the far southwest he emerged at last in Tangier, the first European of modern times to reach Timbuktu, where he was disappointed in its golden legend by finding only "a mass of ill-looking houses, built of earth."

*For the first three see *Narrative of Travels and Discoveries in Northern and Central Africa* (London: 1826); Clapperton's *Journal of a Second Expedition into the Interior of Africa* (London: 1829); R. and J. Lander, *Journal of an Expedition to . . . the Niger* (London: 1832).

For Caillié in English translation see *Travels through Central Africa to Timbuctoo* (London: 1830).

Valuable extracts from all these, and others, will be found in *West African Explorers*, ed. C. Howard with introduction by J. H. Plumb (Oxford: 1951).

Like the others, Caillie was nonetheless impressed by the many-sided quality of Western Sudanese civilization, mingling at Djenne with "a concourse of strangers from all parts of the Sudan." Denham, a few years earlier, had noted of Bornu (northeastern Nigeria) that there "are many hajjis, who have made the pilgrimage to Mecca, and excel in writing Arabic characters, as well as teaching the art to others"; while Clapperton, introduced to Sultan Bello at Sokoto in 1824, was at once asked "a great many questions about Europe" and found himself plunged into an erudite discussion on Christianity. The Sultan "continued to ask several other theological questions, until I was obliged to confess myself not sufficiently versed in religious subtleties to resolve these knotty points. . . ." Only in 1849, with the arrival of a remarkable German traveller, Heinrich Barth, was there to be a European in these countries with an intellectual formation adequate to the task of political, social and economic analysis that Europe now required.

After the travels of Bruce in Ethiopia and along the Middle Nile, the exploring of East Africa really begins with two German missionaries, Johann Krapf and Johannes Rebmann, in the 1840s, notably with Rebmann's journey to the Chagga of Kilimanjaro and Krapf's to Usumbura. Their journals are well worth reading. Then the 1850s and 1860s did for the inland country of East Africa what the 1820s had accomplished in the west. Richard Burton walked to Lake Tanganyika in 1857; John Hanning Speke went on to the southern shores of Lake Victoria, and, with James Grant a few years later, pushed northward to the White Nile; while Samuel Baker, coming south from Egypt at the same time, continued into what is now Western Uganda.*

*For Krapf and Rebmann in English translation see *Travels, Researches and Missionary Labours* (London: 1860).

For Burton, *First Footsteps in East Africa* (London: 1856; reprinted in Everyman Ed., London, 1910); *The Lake Regions of Equatorial Africa* (London: 1860, reprinted 1961).

Meanwhile other men were riding or walking up from the Cape Province of South Africa, hunters and prospectors who have left us little of their stories, and missionaries who have left us much. Fifteen years of pioneer travel took David Livingstone, between 1841 and 1856, from Kuruman in Bechuanaland north to the Zambezi, west through Angola to its capital city of Luanda on the Atlantic coast, and thence back again eastward to the lower course of the Zambezi. Eager to open a route from the eastern seaboard, he set out once more in 1858 and a third time in 1866, coming now up the course of the Ruvuma river to Lake Nyasa and onward to the upper waters of the Congo.* Henry Stanley went to find him and succeeded; but Stanley's real achievement came during 1874-1877 when he crossed the whole Congo basin in a thousand quelling days from Bagamoyo on the coast of Tanganyika to Boma at the mouth of the Congo. His long book about this journey, *Through the Dark Continent*, may still be read with perseverance if not with much enjoyment, for his prose was awkward and pretentious; those who want to know more of the man and what he did will probably do better with his much shorter and unvarnished *Exploration Diaries*, lately discovered

For Speke, *What Led to the Discovery of the Source of the Nile?* (London: 1864).

For Grant, *A Walk Across Africa* (London: 1864).

See also G. Schweinfurth, *Im Herzen von Afrika* (Leipzig: 1874); English translation, *The Heart of Africa* (London: 1873). Selections from the books of eighteen of these travelers are in *East African Explorers*, C. Richards and J. Place (Oxford: 1960).

*For Livingstone, see especially *Missionary Travels, etc.* (London: 1857); *Private Journals 1851-1853*, ed. I. Schapera (London: 1960); and *Missionary Correspondence 1841-1856*, ed. I. Schapera (London: 1961).

by his grandson in a box-file containing "four closely written reporter's pads."*

How much, in the light of what we know today, may it be said that these men understood of what they saw and found? They varied as greatly in their capacity as in their morality. Faced by systems and situations more or less strange to the Europe from which they came, they reacted according to their individual formation without having much chance to correct its shortcomings, or even of knowing that it should be corrected. Some made a tremendous and successful effort to come to grips with African reality; Barth and Livingstone stand at the head of these. Others made little or none, and the books they wrote are practically unreadable today. Others again made an effort, but were unable to escape the mould of their own preconceptions: few exerted themselves more than Burton, for example, yet Burton could seldom bring himself into any constructive sympathy with Africans who were so clearly different from English gentlemen. Consequently, as Henry Nevinson wrote of him in 1910, Burton "saw everything clearly, but everything on the flat." Few risked more than Stanley, but Stanley was already involved in dreams of commercial enterprise which could be no different from imperial conquest: he travelled much, but thought little. Few covered more ground than Baker, yet Baker was nothing if not a product of England's Victorian Age, confident from sheer technical superiority that

*The Exploration Diaries of H. M. Stanley, ed. R. Stanley and A. Neame (London: 1961).

See also V. L. Cameron, Across Africa (1877); and, for a most useful selection from Southern African explorers' books, South African Explorers, ed., E. Axelson (Oxford: 1964).

For early times in Southern Rhodesia (Matabeleland and Mashonaland) the reader will enjoy F. C. Selous, Travel and Adventure in South-east Africa (London: 1893); see also H. M. Hole, Old Rhodesian Days (London: 1928).

Africans were "Nature's children" and, as such, doomed to no good if left in charge of themselves.

Besides, as we have seen at another point in this book, they entered a continent in crisis. They met with situations of large instability and, often enough, ferocious chaos. Throughout much of East Africa the advent of a massive Arab-Swahili slave trade in the 1830s had thrown whole regions and peoples into violent collision and political disruption, forming the main reason why Stanley had to fight his way down the Congo. Each people had come to fear the intended evil of its neighbors. That was not yet true a little to the southward, along the course of the Middle Zambezi, where Livingstone found an agreeable security of life. But southward again, on the plateau lands of what was to become Southern Rhodesia, the same disruption had followed on the recent incursion of African invaders from Natal in the far southeast. The more intelligent explorers were aware that much of this confusion and fear formed relatively new factors in African life, but—understandably—they could not see back beyond it, and they tended to assume that life had "always been like this." The colonial period, which now followed, was born under the philanthropic banner of "trusteeship"; the poor savages, unable to help themselves, should be taken in hand by their betters, and shown the way they should go. Reaching out for his share of what he called "this magnificent African cake," Leopold of Belgium blew loud trumpet voluntaries to the cause of charity and good will. He was soon well satisfied with the profits.

Formally, the colonial period may be thought to have begun with the international "share-out" conference of 1884-1885 in Berlin. From around this time, in any case, books and memoirs about Africa become so abundant that a lifetime's reading would scarcely avail to know them all. Spurred by the desire for possession, jostled by their rivals, driven by the furies of an extreme nationalism, each of the imperialist powers strove to outdo its rivals. The newspapers of the period show that any argument, true or false, was pressed into service of this colossal adventure.

All that makes sad reading today. Fortunately, with the colonial period over and done with, rather little of this ocean of words need be navigated by those who wish to understand African as distinct from European history. So I make no excuse for mentioning only a few of the books of the late nineteenth century, and I conclude this section with some passages from the work of the English sociologist Mary Kingsley because, as Thomas Hodgkin has rightly said, she was the last great European traveller-reporter "who could go where her genius led her, accepting Africans and accepted by them as a person among persons, without the privileges and embarrassments associated with membership of an imperial nation, and with a total disregard of what a European administration might think of her way of life."* Kingsley, too, was an outstanding woman of her time; and I only regret that relevant texts by African women are not to hand. Finally, I add a comment from one of those Africans who faced the colonial onslaught but could not see—as who could have seen?—how it all would end.

---

*For a wide selection of late nineteenth-century extracts for various regions, see Thomas Hodgkin, *Nigerian Perspectives* (Oxford: 1960); F. Wolfwon, *Pageant of Ghana* (Oxford: 1958). See also Howard, ed., *West African Explorers*; Richards and Place, eds., *East African Explorers*; and Axelson, ed., *South African Explorers*, cited in footnotes above. For "French West Africa" see M. E. Mage, *Voyage dans le Soudan Occidental* (Paris: 1868); and L. G. Binger, *Du Niger au Golfe de Guinee* (2 vols., Paris: 1892).

FRÉDÉRIC CAILLAUD

Rediscovering Kush

Since this was the century of Europe's discovery of the African interior, it seems appropriate to begin with Meroe, although it would still be many years before Kushite civilization was to be recognized in its true historical importance. Bruce had glimpsed the ruins of Meroe in 1772, but the first clear descriptions are the work of two French explorers, Linant de Bellefonds and Frederic Caillaud. They extended to the southward that great field of research in the Nile Valley which French scholars had opened two decades earlier as a happy byproduct of Napoleon's invasion of Egypt. Just as Vivant Denon and others had then given Europe its first effective view of the civilization of ancient Egypt, so now his fellow-countrymen surveyed the physical remains of Kush.

[1822: On first crossing the Nile from the western bank, he failed to see any ruins and came to the conclusion that he was "chasing a chimera." But the next day went better:] Imagine my joy when I saw the tops of a crowd of pyramids raised a little on the horizon, and tipped by the rays of the sun. . . . I climbed to the summit of the highest of them and there, wishing to pay my small tribute to the illustrious geographer whose genius had guided me to this place, I carved the name of d'Anville in the stone [this great eighteenth-century French geographer had made a near guess at Meroe's true position]. Looking round, I saw a second group of pyramids to the west, and, not far from the river, a huge field of ruins and remains indicating the site of an ancient city. . . .

From Frederic Caillaud, *Voyage a Meroe, etc., 1819-1822* (2 vols. Paris), vol. 2, p. 142. Translated here by B. Davidson.

JOHN BARROW

Beyond the Orange River

As Mungo Park was discovering the Niger, others, far away in the south, came pushing northward into the lands beyond the Orange. The following account of the peoples of what is now Botswana (or Bechuanaland in colonial times) was set down at second hand by John Barrow, who had gone to South Africa as secretary to the governor, and who was afterwards one of the founders of Britain's Royal Geographical Society.

[1801] The town of Leetakoo, according to the direction and the distance travelled by the expedition from the Roggeveld, is situated in latitude 26° 30' south, and longitude 27° east. A river, which from the width of the channel must occasionally be of considerable size, runs through the midst of it. The town, in its circumference, was estimated to be fully as large as Cape Town, including all the gardens of Table Valley; but from the irregularity of the streets, and the lowness of the buildings, it was impossible to ascertain, with any degree of accuracy, the number of houses; it was concluded, however, that they could not be less than two nor more than three thousand, all nearly of the same size and construction, and differing in nothing from that of the chief except that his was a little larger than the others. The whole population, including men, women and children, they considered to be from ten to fifteen thousand persons. Round numbers are rarely exact. The two commissioners, it seems, at the end of fifteen days, on comparing notes, found that the estimate of one was ten, of the other fifteen thousand. The truth may probably lie in the middle. The ground plan of every house was a complete circle, from twelve to fifteen feet in diameter; the floor of hard beaten clay, raised about four inches above the general surface of the enclosure. About one fourth part of the circle, which was the front of the house and observed generally to face the east, was entirely open; the other three fourths were walled up with clay and stones, to the height of about five feet. . . .

The dwelling of a Booshuana is not ill calculated for the climate. In elegance and solidity it may probably be as good as the *Casae* or first houses that were built in imperial Rome, and may be considered in every respect superior in its construction and in comfort to most of the Irish cabins, into which the miserable peasantry are ofttimes obliged to crawl through puddles of water. The hut of a Booshuana is not only raised upon an elevated clay flooring, but the ground of the whole enclosure is so prepared that the water may run off through the gateway; and the whole of their cookery being carried on in this open area, the inside of the dwelling is free from smoke and soot. So well is he acquainted with the comfort and convenience of shade, that his hut is usually built under the branches of a spreading mimosa, every twig of which is preserved with a religious care, and not a bough suffered to be broken off on any emergency, though the article of fuel must sometimes be sought at a very considerable distance.

So large a population collected together on one spot, surrounded by barren deserts occasionally inhabited by a few savages, and cut off from all communication with other civilized societies, necessarily implies the adequate means of subsistence within themselves. One great source from which they draw their support is their cattle, whose flesh, however, they eat but very sparingly; milk is mostly used in a curdled state, which they keep not in grass baskets, like the Eastern Kaffers, but in leathern bags and clay pots. . . .

The grain chiefly cultivated, as appeared by the samples brought back by the commissioners, consisted of the holcus sorghum, a small species of the same genus which from the reddish coloured seed appeared to be the Saccharatus, a Dolichos not unlike the cadjan, and a small spotted Phaseolus or kidney bean. These different kinds of grain and pulse appear to be sown promiscuously and, when reaped, to be thrown indiscriminately into their earthen granaries; from whence they are taken and used without selection, sometimes by broiling, but more generally boiling in milk. It will readily be supposed that the art of agriculture among this people is yet in its lowest stage. In fact, the only labour bestowed on the ground is performed by women, and with a rude instrument, something like the hoe. It is a flat piece of iron fixed into the knob of the Kaffer *keerie*. When its horizontal edge is so fitted that it stands at right angles with the handle, it serves as a hoe; when turned round so as to be parallel with the handle, it is then a hatchet.

But the Booshuanas are arrived at that stage of civilization which is not satisfied with the mere necessities of life supplied to them abundantly from the three sources of agriculture, grazing, and hunting; they are by no means insensible of its conveniences and its luxuries. Their skin cloaks for the winter are pliant, soft and warm, being frequently lined with the fur-skins of tyger-cats, viverras and other small animals; and when in summer they go without clothing, they rarely expose their bodies to the rays of the sun, but carry umbrellas made of the broad feathers of the ostrich fixed to the end of a stick. They vary their mode of dressing both animal food and grain, occasionally boiling, broiling, or roasting the former, and simply broiling the latter, or bruising it into flour and boiling it up with milk. Among the luxuries of the appetite tobacco seems to hold the highest estimation. . . .

Every man had a knife slung about the neck by a leather thong, and fitted into a scabbard. The blade is generally about six inches long, an inch broad, rounded at the end, and brought to an edge on each side; the handle sometimes of wood, and sometimes of ivory; in the latter case, it is usually carved into the shape of the elephant's proboscis. The party had with them a quantity of common knives intended for barter, but the Booshuanas held them very cheap, observing that their own were at least twice as good, because they were made to cut with two edges, whereas those of the white people only cut with one. The knife, in fact, is so useful an instrument to such as live by the chase and on roots, that it may almost be considered as an article of the first necessity, and is valued accordingly. A Booshuana is accounted wealthy according to the number of cattle, knives and beads he may possess: these are the money and the currency of Leetakoo. . . .

The system on which their government is founded appears to be completely patriarchal, and the chief must of course be a man idolized by the people; and the consequence is, that he has the nomination of his successor. From the elders of the society he is informed of the general sentiments of the people; and with their advice such rules and regulations are framed or altered as are best calculated to give general satisfaction, and consequently to make himself popular. No young man can be admitted into the king's council, which is established on the principles of true primitive simplicity, when, in almost every nation and language, age and authority were synonymous terms. If any man in the society feels himself aggrieved, and is not satisfied with the decision of the council, he is at full liberty to settle his affairs and leave the horde with his whole property.

From John Barrow, *Voyage to Cochinchina, etc.* (London: 1806). To this volume Barrow added an account of travels beyond the Orange River by his father-in-law, Pieter Trater, and a surgeon called William Sullivan, in 1801-1802.

HENRY FYNN

Shaka the Zulu

A surgeon's assistant who went to South Africa in 1818, Henry Fynn six years later visited the famous Zulu monarch who had formed and militarized the Zulu nation.

[1824] On the following morning we were requested to mount our horses and ride to the king's kraal. On our arrival we found him sitting under a tree, in the act of decorating himself. He was surrounded by about two hundred people, a servant standing at his side, and holding a shield over him to keep the glare of the sun from him. Round his forehead he wore a turban of otterskin, with a feather of a crane erect in front, full two feet long. Earrings of dried sugar cane, carved round the edge, with white ends, and an inch in diameter, were let into the lobes of the ears, which had been cut to admit them. From shoulder to shoulder he wore bunches, three inches in length, of the skins of monkeys and genets, twisted like the tails of these animals, and hanging half down the body.

Round the ring on the head ... were a dozen bunches of the red feathers of the loorie, tastefully tied to thorns which were stuck into the hair. Round his arms were white ox-tails, cut down the middle so as to allow the hairs to hang about the arm, to the number of four for each. Round the waist a petticoat, resembling the Highland plaid, made of skins of monkeys and genets, and twisted as before described, having small tassels round the top, the petticoat reaching to the knees, below which were white ox-tails to fit round the legs, so as to hang to the ankles. He had a white shield with a single black spot, and an assagai. While he was thus dressing himself, the natives proceeded, as on the day before, to show droves of cattle, which were still flocking in, and repeatedly varying the scene by dancing and singing. Meanwhile it became known to us that Shaka had ordered that a man standing near us should be put to death, for what crime we could not learn: but we soon found it to be one of the common occurrences in the course of the day. . . .

From an account of Henry Fynn's travels in J. Bird, *Annals of Natal* (Pietermaritzburg: 1888). For Zulu history see A. T. Bryant, *Olden Times in Zululand and Natal* (London: 1929 but reprinted by C. Struik,

Cape Town: 1965); E. A. Ritter, *Shaka Zulu* (London: 1955); and J. D. Omer-Cooper, *The Zulu Aftermath*, Longman (London: 1966).

EDOUARD CASALIS

In the Wake of Many Wars

Of Shaka's great and very different contemporary, Moshesh of the Basuto, we are fortunate in having an early firsthand account by Casalis, who was a member of the Paris Evangelical Missionary Society. Casalis arrived in the wake of what the Basuto traditionally call the *Lifaqane*, the "wars of wandering" around 1822, on which see J. Cobbing, in *Journal of African History*, 29, 1988, p. 487, an important work of historical revision.

[1833] Six months after leaving Paris we entered the country of the Basuto two hundred leagues from the Cape, and saw with astonishment the majestic chain of the Maluti [mountains] which separate Bechuanasie [i.e., later Orange Free State] from the land of Natal . . . . Up to forty or fifty kilometres from this chain our wagon had encountered no serious obstacle. Pulled by twelve oxen driven by a patient native of the country, it advanced a few leagues every day across interminable plains while we amused ourselves in pursuit of multitudes of gazelles, elands and zebras. But when we were only two days' travel from our destination, everything changed. Isolated hills five or six hundred metres high stood across our passage. . . .

Arriving here, what struck us most was the solitary and desolate aspect of the country. We looked in vain for hamlets, for those groups of cultivators whose presence we associated with a fertile and varied soil. On every side we saw human bones whitening in the sun and rain, and more than once we had to turn our wagon out of its course so as to avoid passing over these sad remains. When we asked our guides where the owners of the country lived they pointed a finger towards a few wretched huts on the top of the steepest hills. And whenever we chanced to meet a hunter, the unfortunate man no sooner saw our caravan than he threw himself to the ground so as to hide in the grass.

Yet as we came nearer to the residence of the chief [Moshesh], appearances changed encouragingly. We began to meet fairly big herds pasturing under the care of well-armed herdsmen. We saw fields in what looked like careful cultivation. . . .

Moshesh of the Basuto

We found that it was not without reason that the king of the Basuto was known as the *chief of the mountain*. His main town was and still is placed on the plateau of Thaba Bosiu, a pentagon-shaped hill which is perfectly fortified by nature. We were received with the greatest expressions of joy. The first days [after our arrival] were taken up in explaining to our new acquaintances the object we had in view. It was no easy thing to do . . . . But when God wills a thing, all obstacles are overcome. He inspired in the Basuto and their chief a deep confidence in our good intentions. This population had passed through many evil years. There was a gleam of hope in their eyes; they received us eagerly. . . .

Moshesh has a pleasant and intelligent appearance. His bearing is noble and assured. One can see in his face the habit of thought and of command, but this does not prevent him from having a smile of great good will. At the time of his birth,* the country of the Basutos was densely populated. In

---

*In about 1790, according to G. Lagden, *The Basutos* (New York: 1910), vol. 2, p. 463.

miniature form the tribe presented the aspect of our own country [France] in feudal times. In principle the supremacy of the house of Monahing was recognized, Moshesh being one of its representatives; but each chief tried to win as much independence as possible. There were quarrels at one time or another between the various communities, but generally little blood was spilt, and the whole affair usually came down to the raiding of a few herds.

This state of things lasted until 1820. Moshesh was then living in his native country two days towards the north from Thaba Bosiu. The national songs still celebrate the green pastures of Butabute and the steep hills where the son of Mokachane and his companions hunted the eland and the wild boar. In a moment least expected, disastrous invasion put an end to these pastimes. It came from Natal, whence we have already seen the emergence of the terrible Moselekatse. An iron yoke weighed on the peoples of that country. Shaka, a chief as clever as he was cruel, had subjugated them and kept them in obedience. . . . One of his strongest vassals, Matewane, tired of that regime, secretly left the country with several thousand warriors faithful to himself. On his way he met Pakalita, chief of the Fingos, and drove him into flight after several battles. Hotly pursued, Pakalita crossed the Maluti mountains and turned towards the Mantatees . . . and these people, helped by their knowledge of the country, pushed into the gorges of the mountains and moved rapidly towards the south, carrying desolation into the heart of the peaceful valleys of Lesuto (the name that the Basutos give their country). After that this land became the scene of continual massacres. Matewane, believing himself safe at last from Shaka, settled on the banks of the Caledon River. Pakalita did the same. The two peoples continued to harass one another; and the Mantatees and Basutos, always involved, felt the terrible effects of their presence. This state of things continued for years. Fields lay fallow and famine piled fresh horrors on those of war. Whole populations succumbed. . . .

Moshesh resisted.   Gifted with remarkable powers of observation, with much subtlety, with great force of character, he knew how to resist or give way at the right moment, how to win allies even among the invaders of his territory, how to set his enemies at odds with one another, and, by acts of good will, how to gain the respect even of those who had sworn his ruin. . . .

From Edouard Casalis, *Les Bassoutos, etc.* (Paris: 1859). Translated by B. Davidson. For Basuto history, see also D. F. Ellenberger, *History of the Basuto* (London: 1912); and G. Lagden, *The Basutos*, 2 vols. (London and New York: 1910).

ROBERT MOFFAT

Chief Moselekatse

To complete the triptych, here is Robert Moffat's famous description of the warrior chief of those predatory Matabele who, breaking away from their Zulu fellow-countrymen and then finding themselves in conflict with Boer settlers, swept northward in 1837 across the Limpopo, where they finished off the ruin of the Karanga, finding a new home for themselves but terrorizing the country far and wide. Moffat finds them before they embarked on that enterprise. Cobbing's research (see reference on p. 331) shows that Moffat's writings, like those of Fynn and others at this time, were heavily biassed in favour of European military and/or commercial interests, Casalis less so.

[1829] At Sitlagole River, about 160 miles from the Kuruman, we halted in the afternoon, and allowed our oxen to graze on a rising bank opposite our wagons, and somewhat farther than a gunshot from them. Having but just halted, and not having loosened a gun, we were taken by surprise by two lions rushing out from the neighbouring thicket. The oldest one, of enormous size, approached within ten yards of the oxen, and bounding on one of my best, killed him in a moment, by sending his great teeth through the vertebrae of the neck. The younger lion couched at a distance, while the elder licked his prey, turning his head occasionally towards the other oxen, which had caught his scent and scampered off; then, with his forefeet upon the carcass, he looked and roared at us, who were all in a scuffle to loosen our guns, and attack his majesty. Two of our number, more eager to frighten than to kill, discharged their muskets; and, probably, a ball whistling past his ear, induced him to retire to the thicket whence he had come, leaving us in quiet possession of the meat. At Meritsane, the bed of another dry river, we had a serenade of desert music, composed of the treble, counter, and bass voices of jackals, hyenas, and lions. . . .

Having travelled one hundred miles, five days after leaving Mosega we came to the first cattle outposts of the Matebele, when we halted by a fine rivulet. . . .

We now travelled along a range of mountains running near eastsoutheast [the Magaliesberg], while the country to the north and east became more level, but beautifully studded with ranges of little hills, many isolated, of a conical form, along the bases of which lay the ruins of innumerable towns, some of which were of amazing extent. The soil of the valleys and extended plains was of the richest description. The torrents from the adjacent heights had, from year to year, carried away immense masses, in some places laying bare the substratum of granite rocks, exhibiting a mass of rich soil from ten to twenty feet deep, where it was evident native grain had formerly waved; and watermelons, pumpkins, kidney beans, and sweet reed had once flourished.

The ruins of many towns showed signs of immense labour and perseverance; stone fences, averaging from four to seven feet high, raised apparently without mortar, hammer, or line. Everything was circular, from the inner walls which surrounded each dwelling or family residence, to those which encircled a town. In traversing these ruins, I found the remains of some houses which had escaped the flames of the marauders. These were large, and displayed a far superior style to anything I had witnessed among the aboriginal tribes of Southern Africa. The circular walls were generally composed of hard clay, with a small mixture of cow-dung, so well plastered and polished, a refined portion of the former mixed with a kind of ore, that the interior of the house had the appearance of being varnished. The walls and doorways were also neatly ornamented with a kind of architraves and cornices. The pillars supporting the roof in the form of pilasters, projecting from the walls, and adorned with flutings and other designs, showed much taste in the architectresses. This taste, however, was exercised on fragile materials, for there was nothing in the building like stone, except the foundations. The houses, like all others in the interior, were round, with conical roofs, extending beyond the walls, so as to afford considerable shade, or what might be called a verandah. The raising of the stone fences must have been a work of immense labour, for the materials had all to be brought on the shoulders of men, and the quarries where these materials were probably obtained, were at a considerable distance. The neighbouring hills also gave ample demonstrations of human perseverance, with instruments of the most paltry description. . . .

Nothing now remained but dilapidated walls, heaps of stones, and rubbish, mingled with human skulls, which, to a contemplative mind, told their ghastly tale. These are now the abodes of reptiles and beasts of prey. Occasionally a large stone-fold might be seen occupied by the cattle of the Matabele, who had caused the land thus to mourn. Having Matebele with me, I found it extremely difficult to elicit local information from the dejected and scattered aborigines who occasionally came in our way. These trembled before the nobles, who ruled them with a rod of iron.

It was soon evident that the usurpers were anxious to keep me in the dark about the devastations which everywhere met our eyes, and they always endeavoured to be present when I came in contact with the aborigines of the country, but as I could speak the language some opportunities were afforded. One of the three servants who accompanied the two ambassadors to the Kuruman was a captive among the Mantatees, who had been defeated at Old Lithako. He, as well as his fellow-servants, felt a pleasure in speaking with us in Sechuana, their native language. He, and many hundreds more of that people, were, on their return from the defeat, taken prisoners by Moselekatse. This individual, though an athletic and stern-looking being, was also a shrewd observer of character, and possessed a noble mind, which revolted at the tyranny of his new masters. He was a native of the regions through which we were now passing, and would sometimes whisper to me events connected with the desolations of his fatherland.

These nations he described as being once numerous as the locusts, rich in cattle, and traffickers, to a great extent, with the distant tribes of the north. My informant, with his fellow Bakones, had witnessed the desolation of many of the towns around us—the sweeping away of the cattle and valuables—the butchering of the inhabitants, and their being enveloped in smoke and flames. Commandos of Shaka, the once bloody monarch of the Zoolus, had made frightful havoc; but all these were nothing to the final overthrow of the Bakone tribes by the arms of Moselekatse. The former inhabitants of these luxuriant hills and fertile plains had, from peace and plenty, become effeminate—while the Matebele, under the barbarous reign of the monster Shaka, from whose iron grasp they had made their escape, like an overwhelming torrent, rushed onward to the north, marking their course with blood and carnage. . . .

[Arriving at their destination, they] proceeded directly to the town, and on riding into the centre of the large fold, which was capable of holding ten thousand head of cattle, we were rather taken by surprise to find it lined by eight hundred warriors, besides two hundred who were concealed in each side of the entrance, as if in ambush. We were beckoned to dismount, which we did, holding our horses' bridles in our hands. The warriors at the gate instantly rushed in with hideous yells, and leaping from the earth with a kind of kilt around their bodies, hanging like loose tails, and their large shields, frightened our horses. They then joined the circle, falling into rank with as much order as if they had been accustomed to European tactics. Here we stood surrounded by warriors, whose kilts were of ape skins, and their legs and arms adorned with the hair and tails of oxen, their shields reaching to their chins, and their heads adorned with feathers.

Although in the centre of a town, all was silent as the midnight hour, while the men were motionless as statues. Eyes only were seen to move, and there was a rich display of fine white teeth. After some minutes of profound silence, which was only interrupted by the breathing of our horses, the war song burst forth. There was harmony, it is true, and they beat time with their feet, producing a sound like hollow thunder, but some parts of it was music befitting the nether regions, especially when they imitated the groanings of the dying on the field of battle, and the yells and hissings of the conquerors. Another simultaneous pause ensued, and still we wondered what was intended, till out marched the monarch from behind the lines, followed by a number of men bearing baskets and bowls of food. He came up to us, and having been instructed in our mode of salutation, gave each a clumsy but hearty shake of the hand. He then politely turned to the food, which was placed at our feet, and invited us to partake. By this time the wagons were seen in the distance, and having intimated our wish to be directed to a place where we might encamp in the outskirts of the town, he accompanied us, keeping fast hold of my right arm, though not in the most gracious manner, yet with perfect familiarity. "The land is before you; you are come to your son. You must sleep where you please." . . .

During one of my first interviews with Moselekatse, the following incident took place, which shows that, however degraded and cruel man may become, he is capable of being subdued by kindness. He drew near to the spot where I stood, with some attendants bearing dishes of food; the two chiefs who had been at the Kuruman were with me, but on the approach of their sovereign, they bowed and withdrew, shouting, as usual, "*Baaite 'nkhosi enkolu*," but were instantly desired to return. Moselekatse, placing his left hand on my shoulder, and his right on his breast, addressed me in the following language: "Machobane, I call you such because you have been my father. You have made my heart as white as milk; milk is not white today, my heart is white. I cease not to wonder at the love of a stranger. You never saw me before, but you love me more than my own people. You fed me when I was hungry; you clothed me when I was naked; you carried my in your bosom"; and, raising my right arm with his, added, "that arm shielded me from my enemies." On my replying, I was unconscious of having done him any such services, he instantly pointed to the two ambassadors who were sitting at my feet, saying, "These are great men; 'Umbate is my right hand. When I sent them from my presence to see the land of the white men, I sent my ears, my eyes, my mouth; what they heard I heard, what they saw I saw, and what they said, it was Moselekatse who said it. You fed them and clothed them, and when they were to be slain, you were their shield. You did it unto me. You did it unto Moselekatse, the son of Machobane."

From Robert Moffat, *Missionary Labours and Scenes in South Africa* (London: 1842). His strong bias needs to be kept in mind.

ANTONIO GAMITTO

The Land of Kazembe

By the beginning of the century, the central regions of Africa had become organized into a number of important states and confederations, with those of the Marave (Malawi) and of the Western Lunda and Eastern Lunda prominent among them. The Western Lunda were ruled by a supreme chief whose title was the *Muata* Yamvo, while the Eastern Lunda owed allegiance to a vassal of the *Muata* Yamvo, whose title was the *Kazembe* and whose territory was in that of the modern Katanga.

These Central African states and rulers were possibly visited by a handful of Portuguese traders; and the first account of this broad belt of central African land comes with the notes and journals of two *pombeiros*—Afro-Portuguese traders—Pedro Joao Baptista and Amaro Jose, who crossed Africa from Angola to Mozambique between 1806 and 1811. Their notes and journals were published in London in 1873 in a translation by Richard Burton, and form an important if slim addition to the record. Obliged to live for four years at the court of the *Kazembe*, the two *pombeiros* found that country "supplied with provisions all the year round and every year: manioc flour, millet, maize, large haricot beans, small and round beans . . . bananas, sugar cames, yams, gourds . . . and much fish. . . ."

Captain Antonio Gamitto visited the *Kazembe*, passing northwestward from Tete on the Zambezi through the country of the Marave (Malawi), in the year 1831-1832, as second-in command of a Portuguese expedition headed by Major Jose Monteiro. Gamitto is among the most satisfactory of nineteenth-century travellers: patient, curious, long-suffering, and gifted with strong powers of observation. A brief resume of his book was made available in English in 1873; but an admirably produced full-scale translation by Ian Cunnison appeared in 1960.

Marave Bridges

The Luangwa-Pire or Luangwa-Jaua which we crossed today has very little water in this dry season but swells greatly in the rains, and such is the velocity of the current then that it does not afford passage even to canoes, for great stones and tree trunks are washed down with it; and the water reaches such a height that the Marave are forced to erect bridges, which they call Uraro, in the most frequent places.

They are constructed with bamboos laid parallel and tied together with bark (which they call Maruze), the first lengths at each end being fixed firmly to some tree already there. Other bamboos are tied athwart these, six spans in length, which is the width of the bridge, the top of them being the path one crosses by. The bridge dips to make an obtuse angle at the centre, being eighty spans high at this point, and it has no support except at the two banks. Crossing it produces such an extraordinary movement that it seems to be coming apart at every moment; but the Marave are very careful in securing them although they do not cross them unless it is absolutely essential. To disabuse myself I crossed one, although I would not have done it if they had not placed two bamboos high on it, which, although slender, served as a balustrade and support on each side. These are the only people whom I have seen to construct such a thing.

Metallurgy

Joao Pedro told me, and I do not doubt it, that he has nine hundred negro women mining gold, of which he gets 42 *pastas* a year. Many years ago this Bar had slaves of Tete citizens employed in mining, but few in number; Botelho extended the mining and made this the principal part of his establishment. Mining aside, he augments his income and furthers his interest by trading in ivory, for the road here is frequented by Bisa. . . .

I gave him to understand that I wanted to see the African women at work mining, but he excused himself and said they did not work at this time. I learned later what I had not known, that there is a superstition that the work may be seen only by those who actually perform it, for otherwise the metal would be lost. The metals known here are gold, tin, which they do not care about, and iron: the latter is found in such quantities on the surface that they do not need to dig for it; they collect it and put it into a funnel built of clay, forty spans high and one in diameter; the lower part has a wood fire which they blow with goatskin bellows like those of our wandering tinkers. The iron comes out through holes in the bottom of the funnel; and with this simple operation they draw off the smelted metal, which they then use in their manufactures. These are principally hoes, axes, knives, arrows and spears. For this the tools used are: bellows of the same kind to make a forge on the ground, a stone serving as an anvil, another smaller one as a hammer, and two pieces of wood as pincers; and it is with this set of tools that they make all their work, which is as polished as if it were done by European instruments. The people making them are the Marave blacksmiths. Our blacksmiths of Tete work in our way with proper tools but not so well. When the iron is hot it is malleable like lead, and like it does not crack; but when cold it is hard as steel. . . .

Botelho is said to have announced that he would behead any slave who sold gold to the expedition.

The slaves employed at the mine are divided into *Insakas* as usual, but each of these has six negresses, it being, as I have said, only women who mine. Each *Insaka* is under the charge of a Nyakoda who gives a weekly account of the work of her people. These weeks are of four days, and each woman has to account for six Tangas a week; this satisfied, the rest is hers. It often happens that a woman gets enough on the first day to pay the quota and in this case she is not required to turn up on the following days. Owners of Bars usually have imported cloths, beads, etc., at them to sell to their slaves at exorbitant prices; and so these slaves buy from any passing merchant, secretly, what they need; and this was why Botelho forbade the sale of gold to members of the expedition. In spite of this they kept selling it.

Devastation

In remote times, perhaps at the period of Portuguese conquests in this part of Africa, there existed two great *Mambos*, one of whom ruled the Marave, a people who inhabited the left or eastern bank of the Zambezi; and the other of whom dominated the Munhaes, who occupied its right or western margin.* The Mozungos, or Portuguese, caused these *Mambos* to lose all their ancient power; and today they exist in the form we have indicated, their decadence still continuing. Meanwhile the main cause of this is the devastation of the country, a result of the continual warfare in which they are engaged. In other times, there was great commerce in gold, ivory and cereals, but today there is hardly any, and this results from the same cause.

King Kazembe

[1831] All five Whites with the expedition have let their hair and beards grow; my hair, falling over my shoulders, comes down to the level of my thick beard, which reaches my chest. My uniform is a tunic of blue nankeen and white breeches; as a sash I have scarlet cords and tassels about my waist. On my head I have an otter-skin cap, and from my side hangs a fine sword, whose metal sheath the climate has turned the colour of the local inhabitants. Dressed in this array and mounted on a donkey as I have described, I made solemn entry into what is perhaps the greatest town of Central Africa.

Continuing our march we entered, at some distance from the place we had stopped, a long street of enclosures made

---

*A memory, of course, of the great period of the Monomotapa rulers.

with posts fixed into the ground and interlaced with grass to a height of ten or twelve spans and which, by the regularity of their construction, looked like walls. On each side were small gates opening into a straight grass fence bordering the road, which would be about a mile long. At the end of this road was a small rectangular hut, open only on the part facing west, in the centre of which on a wooden base was a bust of a human figure made roughly of wood, about three spans high; and outside in front of the hut door was a heap of more than three hundred skulls. . . .

This morning we were advised to present ourselves before the Mwata Kazembe, who was expecting the principal persons of the expedition. As we had previously been advised, we marched with all possible ceremony, each detachment going armed under the command of its respective leader; and each of us took something to offer the Mwata, so that he might know thereby how many and who were the persons with whom he had to deal. We each took a piece of cloth.

Arriving at the Musumba [the Mwata's residence] we found the great square filled with a throng of people, so arranged as to leave empty a small area in front of the eastern gate of the Chipango. This is the name given to a fence enclosing a dwelling; but when they speak of the Chipango, by itself, they are referring to the Mwata's residence; others they would specify by saying "the Chipango of so-and-so." The Mwata's is very big, and higher and better built than the others.

The warriors in the square were the Lunda army, which would comprise some five or six thousand men, all armed with bows and arrows, Mpok and spears. They were standing about without any appearance of military discipline. The Mwata was seated on the left side of the eastern gate of the Musumba; many leopard skins served him as a carpet, the tails pointing outwards to form a star; over these was an enormous lion skin, and on this a stool covered with a big green cloth. On this throne the Mwata was seated, in greater elegance and state than any other *Mambo* I have seen.

His head was ornamented with a kind of mitre, pyramidal in shape and two spans high, made of brilliant scarlet feathers; round his forehead was a dazzling diadem of beads of various kinds and colours. Behind his head a band of green cloth, supported by two small ivory needles, fanned out from the back of his neck. Neck and shoulders were covered with a kind of capuchin the upper part of which was covered with up-turned cowries; there followed a band of pretty imitation jewels, made of glass, and the lower part had a string of alternately placed little round and square mirrors, in symmetry. This fell round his shoulders and over his chest, and when struck by the sun's rays it was too bright to look upon. Above each elbow was a band of blue feathers four inches wide, edged with what looked like a fringe, but which was in fact very fine strips of hide, the hair of which, four or five inches long, was black and white in colour. This ornament only Kazembe and his closest relatives may use, for it is a royal emblem. The arm from elbow to wrist was decorated with a string of bright blue beads. . . .

From beside the Mwata's seat two curved lines went out and met some twenty paces in front of him. The left-hand line was indicated by a scratch on the ground, and the right-hand one by means of Mpemba, a kind of gypsum. In front of Kazembe were various figurines in two parallel files beginning from the ends of the curved lines. They formed wings about three spans wide. These figurines were attached to sticks thrust into the ground, they all had Kaffir features, and were adorned with animals' horns. In the centre of the wing, and at the end nearest Kazembe, was a cage in the shape of a barrel, and inside this was another figurine. Two negroes sat beside the two end figurines, facing them, and each had before him a small clay pot of embers into which he threw leaves which produced a thick aromatic smoke. All these figurines had their backs turned to Kazembe. From under the end one on the right, nearest the censer, a string extended to the Mwata's feet, but I do not know its purpose.

The gate of the Chipango was open, and seated in it were the two principal wives of Kazembe. The first was to the right, sitting on a stool and mantled in a large green cloth; her arms, neck and forehead were ornamented with differently coloured beads, while on her head was an ornament of scarlet feathers like Kazembe's only smaller. This first wife is called Mwadi-Ngombe. The second wife, who was to the left sitting on a lion skin on the ground, was simply dressed in a cloth, without ornament; she was called Ntemena. Behind them stood more than four hundred wives of various ages dressed in Nyandas, all of them being the wives of the Chipango, or harem, that being the meaning of the word. These women are divided among the four great wives as servants. . . .

Mwata Kazembe looks fifty years old but we were told he is much older. He has a long beard, already turning gray. He is well built and tall, and has a robustness and agility which promises a long life; his look is agreeable and majestic, and his style splendid in its fashion. We certainly never expected to find so much ceremonial, pomp and ostentation in the potentate of a region so remote from the seacoast, and in a nation which appears so barbarous and savage.

From A. C. P. Gamitto, *O Muata Kazembe, etc., 1831-1832* (Lisbon: 1854), in the translation of Ian Cunnison, *King Kazembe, etc.* (2 vols., Lisbon: 1960). The first extract is from vol. 1, p. 50; the second from vol. 1, p. 55; the third from vol. 1, p. 109; and the fourth from vol. 2, p. 15.

DAVID LIVINGSTONE

Central Africa in the 1840s

There is no need to introduce David Livingstone except, in this context, to situate these extracts from his *Missionary Travels and Researches.* They refer to his labors and journeys in what are now the northern part of South Africa, Botswana, and Zimbabwe.

The Roots of Apartheid

The word Boer simply means "farmer," and is not synonymous with our word boor. Indeed, to the Boers generally the latter term would be quite inappropriate, for they are a sober, industrious, and most hospitable body of peasantry. Those, however, who have fled from English law on various pretexts, and have been joined by English deserters and every other variety of bad character in their distant localities, are unfortunately of a very different stamp. The great objection many of the Boers had, and still have, to English law is that it makes no distinction between black men and white. They felt aggrieved by their supposed losses in the emancipation of their Hottentot slaves, and determined to erect themselves into a republic, in which they might pursue without molestation the "proper treatment of the blacks." It is almost needless to add that the "proper treatment" has always contained in it the essential element of slavery, namely, compulsory unpaid labour.

One section of this body, under the late Mr. Hendrick Potgeiter, penetrated the interior as far as the Cashan Mountains, whence a Zulu or Caffre chief, named Moselekatse, had been expelled by the well-known Caffre Dingaan; and a glad welcome was given them by the Bechuana tribes, who had just escaped the hard sway of that cruel chieftain. [These Boers] came with the prestige of white men and deliverers; but the Bechuanas soon found, as they expressed it, "that Moselekatse was cruel to his enemies, and kind to those he conquered; but that the Boers destroyed their enemies, and made slaves of their friends." The tribes who still retain the semblance of independence are forced to perform all the labour of the fields, such as manuring the land, weeding, reaping, building, making dams and canals, and at the same time to support themselves.

I have myself been an eyewitness of Boers coming to a village, and, according to their usual custom, demanding twenty or thirty women to weed their gardens, and have seen these women proceed to the scene of unrequited toil, carrying their own food on their heads, their children on their backs, and instruments of labour on their shoulders. Nor have the Boers any wish to conceal the meanness of thus employing unpaid labour; on the contrary, every one of them, from Mr. Potgeiter and Mr. Gert Kreiger, and the commandants, downwards, lauded his own humanity and justice in making such an equitable regulation. "We make the people work for us, in consideration of allowing them to live in our country."

Boer Policy

The Boers, four hundred in number, were sent by the late Mr. Pretorius to attack the Bakwains in 1852. Boasting that the English had given up all the blacks into their power, and had agreed to aid them in their subjugation by preventing all supplies of ammunition from coming into the Bechuana country, they assaulted the Bakwains, and, besides killing a considerable number of adults, carried off two hundred of our school children into slavery. The natives under Sechele defended themselves till the approach of night enabled them to flee to the mountains; and having in that defence killed a number of the enemy, the very first ever slain this country by Bechuanas, I received the credit of having taught the tribe to kill Boers!*

My house, which had stood perfectly secure for years under the protection of the natives, was plundered in revenge. English gentlemen, who had come in the footsteps of Mr.

*Livingstone does not mean, of course, that he did the killing himself.

Cumming to hunt in the country beyond, and had deposited large quantities of stores in the same keeping, and upwards of eighty head of cattle as relays for the return journeys, were robbed of all; and when they came back to Kolobeng found the skeletons of the guardians strewed all over the place. The books of a good library—my solace in our solitude—were not taken away, but handfuls of the leaves were torn out and scattered over the place. My stock of medicines was smashed; and all our furniture and clothing carried off and sold at public auction to pay the expenses of the foray.

African Justice

The complainant [in the common cases] asks the man, against whom he means to lodge his complaint, to come with him to the chief. This is never refused. When both are in the *kotla*, the complainant stands up and states the whole case before the chief and the people usually assembled there. He stands a few seconds after he has done this, to recollect if he has forgotten anything. The witnesses to whom he has referred then rise up and tell all they themselves have seen or heard, but not anything that they have heard from others.

The defendant, after allowing some minutes to elapse so that he may not interrupt any of the opposite party, slowly rises, folds his cloak around him, and, in the most quiet, deliberate way he can assume—yawning, blowing his nose, etc.—begins to explain the affair, denying the charge or admitting it, as the case may be. Sometimes, when galled by his remarks, the complainant utters a sentence of dissent; the accused turns quietly to him, and says, "Be silent: I sat still while you were speaking; can't you do the same? Do you want to have it all to yourself?" And as the audience acquiesce in this bantering, and enforce silence, he goes on till he has finished all he wishes to say in his defence. If he has any witnesses to the truth of the facts of his defence, they give their evidence.

No oath is administered; but occasionally, when a statement is questioned, a man will say, "By my father," or "By the chief, it is so." Their truthfulness among each other is quite remarkable; but their system of government is such that Europeans are not in a position to realize it readily. A poor man will say, in his defence against a rich one, "I am astonished to hear a man so great as he make a false accusation"; as if the offence of falsehood were felt to be one against the society which the individual referred to had the greatest interest in upholding.

If the case is one of no importance, the chief decides it at once; if frivolous, he may give the complainant a scolding, and put a stop to the case in the middle of the complaint, or he may allow it to go on without paying any attention to it whatever. Family quarrels are often treated in this way, and then a man may be seen stating his case with great fluency, and not a soul listening to him. But if it is a case between influential men, or brought on by under-chiefs, then the greatest decorum prevails. If the chief does not see his way clearly to a decision, he remains silent; the elders then rise one by one and give their opinions, often in the way of advice rather than as decisions; and when the chief finds the general sentiment agreeing in one view, he delivers his judgment accordingly. He alone speaks sitting: all others stand.

No one refuses to acquiesce in the decision of the chief, as he has the power of life and death in his hands, and can enforce the law to that extent if he chooses; but grumbling is allowed, and, when marked favouritism is shown to any relative of the chief, the people generally are not so astonished at the partiality as we would be in England.

Security

I believe that the interior of this country presents a much more inviting field for the philanthropist than does the west coast. . . .

But I am not to be understood as intimating that any of the numerous tribes are anxious for instruction: they are not the inquiring spirits we read of in other countries; they do not desire the gospel, because they know nothing about either it, or its benefits; but there is no impediment in the way of instruction. Every headman would be proud of a European visitor or resident in his territory, and there is perfect security for life and property all over the interior country. The great barriers which have kept Africa shut are the unhealthiness of the coast, and the exclusive, illiberal disposition of the border tribes.

Gold and Iron

The fort of Tete [on the middle Zambezi] has been the salvation of the Portuguese power in this quarter. It is a small square building, with a thatched apartment for the residence of the troops; and though there are but few guns, they are in a much better state than those of any fort in the interior of Angola. The cause of the decadence of the Portuguese power in this region is simply this. In former times considerable quantities of grain, as wheat, millet, and maize, were exported, also coffee, sugar, oil, and indigo, besides gold dust and ivory. The cultivation of grain was carried on by means of slaves, of whom the Portuguese possessed a large number. The gold dust was procured by washing at various points on the north, south, and west of Tete. A merchant took all his slaves with him to the washings, carrying as much calico and other goods as he could muster. On arriving at the washing-place he made a present to the chief, of the value of about a pound sterling. The slaves were then divided into parties, each headed by a confidential servant, who not only had the supervision of his squad while the washing went on, but bought dust from the inhabitants, and made a weekly return to his master.

When several masters united at one spot, it was called a "Bara," and they then erected a temporary church, in which a priest from one of the missions performed mass. Both chiefs and people were favourable to these visits, because the traders purchased grain for the sustenance of the slaves with the goods they had brought. They continued at this labour until the whole of the goods were expended, and by this means about 130 pounds of gold were annually produced. Probably more than this was actually obtained, but, as it was an article easily secreted, this alone was submitted to the authorities for taxation. At present the whole amount of gold obtained annually by the Portuguese is from eight to ten pounds only.

When the slave trade began, it seemed to many of the merchants a more speedy mode of becoming rich, to sell off the slaves, than to pursue the slow mode of gold-washing and agriculture, and they continued to export them, until they had neither hands to labour nor to fight for them. It was just the story of the goose and the golden egg. The coffee and sugar plantations and gold-washings were abandoned, because the labour had been exported to the Brazils. Many of the Portuguese then followed their slaves, and the Government was obliged to pass a law to prevent further emigration, which, had it gone on, would have depopulated the Portuguese possessions altogether. . . .

The only other metal, besides gold, we have in abundance in this region, is iron, and that is of excellent quality. In some places it is obtained from what is called the specular iron ore, and also from black oxide. The latter has been well roasted in the operations of nature, and contains a large proportion of the metal. It occurs generally in tears or rounded lumps, and is but slightly magnetic. When found in the beds of rivers, the natives know of its existence by the quantity of oxide on the surface, and they find no difficulty in digging it with pointed sticks. They consider English iron as "rotten"; and I have seen, when a javelin of their own iron lighted on the cranium of a hippopotamus, it curled up like the proboscis of a butterfly, and the owner would prepare it for future use by straightening it cold with two stones. I brought home some of the hoes which Sekeletu gave me to purchase a canoe, also some others obtained in Kilimane, and they have been found of such good quality that a friend of mine in Birmingham has made an Enfield rifle of them.

From David Livingstone, *Missionary Travels and Researches in South Africa* (London: 1857); extracts: pp. 29, 39, 184, 505, 630-650.

JAMES PRIOR

Kilwa in Ruins

Although the once wealthy and prestigious city-port of Kilwa still had a sultan, its renown and power were long since gone. Anyone today who visits the island and its neighbouring sites will have much the same impression as James Prior, surgeon of the *Nisus* frigate, and his commander Captain Beaver, although, thanks to the work of the late Neville Chittick, the modern visitor can refer as well to an excellent archaeological guidebook. Chittick's excavation and historical record of the city, *Kilwa* (Nairobi: 1974) is indispensable for those who wish to specialize.

[1812] Quitting the ship next morning with three boats and forty men, a variety of fresh obstacles were started by the old minister [of the sultan of Kilwa], while Captain B———— and I, during the interval, rambled through the greatest part of the village. It is larger than could be at first conjectured, extending from the shore inland, by winding footpaths, between enclosures of plantain, banana, tamarind, and cocoa-nut trees. The huts are generally unconnected, and formed of these convenient materials, combined with bamboo, twigs, and thatch; footpaths form the only streets, and abundant foliage gives it the appearance of a wood. We saw but two or three stone houses, one of which belongs to the sultan. It is a large irregular ill-built edifice, tolerably high, and partly surrounded with walls. I had penetrated through the courtyard to the outer door, when some females, looking carelessly out of a latticed window above, beckoned me not to enter. . . .

The remains of the wall that formerly encircled the town are still partially visible, though overgrown with weeds. We traced it to some distance; it has been above two feet thick, and seems to have enclosed a very considerable space. Captain B—— justly remarked, as we walked along, turning the grass to one side, in following the line of the foundation, that the older writers gave such flattering accounts of the importance of this city in the days of Da Gama, as, from present appearances, to be scarcely worthy of credit. The people were said to be numerous, civilized and wealthy; the city extensive and fortified, its habitations elegant, and public building numerous. This picture, though partly true, was probably exaggerated, like some others of the early discoveries; yet there are several heaps of ruins. . . .

Songo Mnara

Within these few days we made a small party in an excursion on the main in a new direction. The tide being low, we landed at a short distance from the ship, on a flat of mud, which, at its junction with the shore, was so thickly bound with mangroves, that we had to walk above a mile, sinking to the calf of the leg, to gain a fair opening into the country. . . .

The country preserves the same aspect of an uncultivated waste; man, as he exists here, seems neither to have the taste nor talent to tenant it. Yet we fancied there were faint traces of former industry and population scattered here and there, and that wars, or the detestable slave trade, had carried off the wretched inhabitants, whom it will now be impossible to replace. . . .

In returning we discovered a large well, situated in an extensive copse, which had been formerly enclosed by a wall, part of which was still standing. The well seemed about twenty-five feet in depth and ten in diameter, apparently hollowed out of a soft, calcareous rock, while from the bottom grew a tree, now in a great measure decayed, affording steps by which an attendant descended, and found the water dirty, ill-tasted, and small in quantity, though bearing traces of having been formerly of much more importance. Further on, towards Pagoda Point, appeared several decayed huts, tenanted by bats and reptiles, two small burying-grounds amid a cluster of small trees, and, about a mile distant, the ruins of regular stone edifices, which, appearing unexpectedly, induced Captain B———, Mons. S———, and myself, to revisit them next day.

The first object was a small cemetery, about forty feet square, enclosed with stone, and raised two feet above the ground; the graves were convexly raised, as in Europe, with stones at the head and feet, the bodies lying east and west, but no trace that we could find of inscriptions. To the eastern end of this enclosure was attached the remains of what appeared to have been a place of worship, about twenty-three feet by twelve. The walls now remaining seemed about sixteen feet high, built of stone, cemented by mortar formed of the bastard coral, or madrepore, and in which were wedged many pieces of cocoa-nut shell, that seemed of no other use than as emblems, probably of the value of the divine gifts, as they crumbled into dust on being touched. An arched door in front, and two in the rear, formed the entrances, and a circular white stone raised above the ground may, perhaps, have received the inclined knee of many an humble suppliant for divine mercy. Behind the ruin is a steep descent to a bed of mud, thickly lined with mangroves, which, though seemingly dry, forms an island at high-water, that, at the conclusion of the first day's excursion, occasioned us some uneasiness.

Two or three hundred yards from this spot lie the ruins of a stone building, larger than any at present possessed by the Quiloans [the people of Kilwa], except the residence of the sultan. Its apartments have been numerous, some large, others smaller, and a third class, with still minuter divisions, separated by thick walls, but opening at one end into a passage common to all. The walls, at least the present remains, are broad, though not so firmly built as those of the smaller edifice, and judging from the quantity of rubbish, their height must have been considerable. Several thick trees, of a spungy texture, issue not only from among the fallen ruins, but from the substance of the walls which seem held together merely by clay. These form various convolutions, and, by a kind of heterogeneous union, living wood seems inseparably combined and coexistent with stone. Captain B—— thought he could distinguish the remains of Saxon arches; but this resemblance is probably accidental. . . .

From James Prior, *Voyage along the Eastern Coast of Africa, etc.* (London: 1819).

W. F. W. OWEN

After the Deluge

Captain W. F. W. Owen, British Navy, has a place of his own in the nineteenth-century history of the East Coast, but it refers much more to the British than the African side of it. He began his service on the Coast with the making of Admiralty surveys and noticed, as had Prior and Beaver, how sadly the seaward country had declined from a former prosperity.

[1821-1826] Quilimane [on the coast of modern Mozambique] is now the greatest mart for slaves on the east coast. They are purchased with blue dangarees, coloured cloths, arms, gunpowder, brass and pewter, red coloured beads in imitation of coral, cutlery, and various other articles. . . .

The riches of Quilimane consisted, in a trifling degree, of gold and silver, but principally of grain, which was produced in such quantities as to supply Mozambique. But the introduction of the slave trade stopped the pursuits of industry, and changed those places where peace and agriculture had formerly reigned into a seat of war and bloodshed. Contending tribes are now constantly striving to obtain by mutual conflict prisoners as slaves for sale to the Portuguese, who excite these wars and fatten on the blood and wretchedness they produce. The slave trade has been a blight on its prosperity; for at present Quilimane and the Portuguese possessions in the whole colony of the Rios de Senna [i.e., the Lower Zambezi] do not supply themselves with sufficient corn for their own consumption. . . .

[Of Kilwa:] A miserable village, scarcely visited or known, occupies its site, and the wretched Arab hovels of the present day are blended among the ruins of the once respectable and opulent city of former years. . . .

It is really melancholy to contemplate the devastations that the monopolizing spirit of mankind has produced on the east coast of Africa; wherever we went, even in the most obscure harbours, we could trace the remains of former wealth and civilization, contrasted strongly with present poverty and barbarism.

From Capt. W. F. W. Owen, R.N.: *Narrative of Voyages to Explore the Shores of Africa, Arabia and Madagascar* (2 vols., London: 1833).

ABDULLAH BIN NASIR

Lament for Greatness

Composed between about 1810 and 1820, the *Utendi wa Inkishafi* of Abdullah bin Nasir of Pate has become the best known—or rather the least ill-known—of Swahili poems. Translated into English by Hichens as "The Soul's Awakening," the poem has been rendered anew by Dr. Lyndon Harries, from whose version I draw this extract. *Al Inkishafi* is not only a lament for the past glory of Swahili civilization but a warning to all who seek their salvation by laying up treasure on Earth.

How many rich men have you seen
who shone like the sun
who had control of the weapons of war
and stored up silver and gold?

All the world paid them homage
and their world was straight ahead of them
they walked with heads held disdainfully
and eyes closed in scorn.

Swinging their arms and arching their necks
while behind and in front crowds accompanied them
everywhere they live there are seats of honour
and troops of soldiers attend them.

Their lighted houses were aglow
with lamps of crystal and brass
the nights were as the day
beauty and honour surrounded them.

They decorated (their houses) with choice porcelain
and every goblet was engraved
and in the midst they put crystal pitchers
amongst the decorations that glittered. . .

Now they lie in a town of finger's span
with no fine curtains nor cushions
and their bodies are destroyed
for the constraint of the grave has come upon them. . .

Their lighted mansions are uninhabited
the young of bats cling up above
you hear no whisperings nor shoutings
spiders crawl over the beds.

The wall-niches for porcelain in the houses
are now the resting-place for nestlings
owls hoot within the house. . .

From Abdullah bin Nasir, *Utendi wa Inkishafi*, translated in Lyndon
Harries, *Swahili Poetry* (Oxford: 1962).

ARNAULD D'ABBADIE

On the Meaning of Gifts

Arnauld d'Abbadie reached Abyssinia in 1837, some sixty
years after Bruce. His memoirs share much of Bruce's vivacity and
savour, and make a valuable picture of the Abyssinians and their
country. The later generalized name of Ethiopia belongs more
properly to the period of the Ethiopian Empire formed during the
colonialist "scramble."

One morning the Prince asked me to choose a horse from among those he daily received in tribute. . . .

"In Gojam," he said to me, "every self-respecting man has a war horse except for the priests, and it is wrong that you should be without one." . . . I noticed several fine horses but by a remnant of European reticence, made no sign that any of them pleased me. I should much rather have learned how to handle them like their own cavaliers, but that was more than the Prince's liberality could do for me. . . . [In the evening the Prince sent d'Abbadie an excellent horse.] My acquaintances now came to congratulate me [on receiving this horse]. I was of course grateful to the Prince for his generosity and courtesy, but as yet I did not understand their meaning, nor the eagerness of those about me who now adopted a more affectionate familiarity.

In this feudal country, however, men are united by an infinity of ties which would count for nothing in Europe. They live together in a reciprocal dependence and solidarity which they value highly and consider a matter of pride, and which influence all they do. A man freed from all subjection is in their eyes outside the social order; that is how they consider a stranger. In accepting a mule from Dedjasmatch I had already, by the customs of the country, entered into a moral obligation towards him. But in receiving a war horse I became, in the eyes of his men, the man of their master; I was obliged to follow him, and at least for a certain time to share in his fortunes, bad or good. No matter how much good will they might have shown me until now, I had nonetheless been for them like a being apart, like one without any social relationship with them. But from now on I was going to share in their duties and their rights. I was no longer for them a stranger in the old and hostile sense of the word. I became their comrade, their companion. . . .

From Arnauld d'Abbadie, *Douze Ans dans la Haute-Ethiopie* (Paris: 1868), vol. 1, p. 263. Translated by B. Davidson.

MUNGO PARK

To the Niger

"My dear friend Mr. Anderson and likewise Mr. Scott are both dead, but though all the Europeans who are with me should die, and though I were myself half dead, I would still persevere; and if I could not succeed in the object of my journey, I would at least die on the Niger." Thus Mungo Park in 1805, writing back to London from the heart of West Africa before departing on the final and fatal part of his quest for the river's mouth. Of the heroes of that cataclysmic year, England has placed Nelson, dying in the battle of Trafalgar, at the head of her list; yet if courage and self-sacrifice are any test of greatness, Park surely deserves to stand beside Nelson. He had left the Gambia with forty-three Europeans; at Sansanding on the Upper Niger he had only four, and one of these was no longer fully sane. All the rest had died on the journey. Yet Park persisted. A few weeks later—or was it months? there is no means of being sure—he and his companions were also dead.

Park must have a leading place in any anthology of West African memoirs for the quality of his writing, the importance of what he had to say, and the initiating stimulus of what he did. In a real sense he opened the nineteenth century with an unforgettable challenge to his fellow-countrymen—and hence to other Europeans—that they should at last penetrate the mysteries of inner Africa; and it is safe to say that no European observer of West Africa during the period now opening will have made his journeys without a more than occasional thought of Mungo Park to carry with him and encourage him. Park has therefore a special importance to a period in African history when the interest and influence of Europe were increasingly felt.

The following extracts are from the first of his two journeys, completed in 1797. We find him as he leaves the Gambia and proceeds eastward to what is now the Republic of Mali.

The King of Bondou

[1795] I took my interpreter with me, and followed the messenger till we got quite out of the town, and crossed some cornfields: when, suspecting some trick, I stopped, and asked the guide whither he was going. Upon which he pointed to a man sitting under a tree at some little distance, and told me that the king frequently gave audience in that retired manner, in order to avoid a crowd of people; and that nobody but myself and my interpreter must approach him.   When I advanced, the king desired me to come and sit by him upon the mat; and after hearing my story, on which he made no observation, he asked if I wished to purchase any slaves, or gold: being answered in the negative, he seemed rather surprised, but desired me to come to him in the evening, and he would give me some provisions.

This monarch was called Almami, a Moorish name, though I was told that he was not a Mahomedan, but a Kafir, or Pagan. I had heard that he had acted towards Major Houghton with great unkindness, and caused him to be plundered.   His behaviour, therefore, towards myself at this interview, though much more civil than I expected, was far from freeing me from uneasiness. I still apprehended some double dealing; and as I was now entirely in his power, I thought it best to smooth the way by a present; accordingly I took with me in the evening one canister of gunpowder, some amber, tobacco, and my umbrella; and, as I considered that my bundles would inevitably be searched, I concealed some few articles in the roof of the hut where I lodged, and I put on my new blue coat, in order to preserve it.

All the houses belonging to the king and his family are surrounded by a lofty mud wall, which converts the whole into a kind of citadel.   The interior is subdivided into different courts. At the first place of entrance I observed a man standing with a musket on his shoulder; and I found the way to the presence very intricate, leading through many passages, with sentinels placed at the different doors.   When we came to the entrance of the court in which the king resides, both my guide and interpreter, according to custom, took off their sandals; and the former pronounced the king's name aloud, repeating it till he was answered from within.

We found the monarch sitting upon a mat, and two attendants with him. I repeated what I had told him concerning the object of my journey, and my reasons for passing through his country. He seemed, however, but half satisfied. The notion of travelling for curiosity was quite new to him. He thought it impossible, he said, that any man in his senses would undertake so dangerous a journey, merely to look at the country and its inhabitants; however, when I offered to show him the contents of my portmanteau, and everything belonging to me, he was convinced; and it was evident that his suspicion had arisen from a belief that every white man must of necessity be a trader. When I had delivered my presents, he seemed well pleased, and was particularly delighted with the umbrella, which he repeatedly furled and unfurled, to the great admiration of himself and his two attendants, who could not for some time comprehend the use of this wonderful machine. After this I was about to take my leave, when the king, desiring me to stop awhile, began a long preamble in favour of the whites, extolling their immense wealth and good dispositions. He next proceeded to an eulogium on my blue coat, of which the yellow buttons seemed particularly to catch his fancy: and he concluded by entreating me to present him with it; assuring me, for my consolation under the loss of it, that he would wear it on all public occasions, and inform every one who saw it of my great liberality towards him. The request of an African prince, in his own dominions, particularly when made to a stranger, comes little short of a command. It is only a way of obtaining by gentle means what he can, if he pleases, take by force; and, as it was against my interest to offend him by a refusal, I very quietly took off my coat, the only good one in my possession, and laid it at his feet.

In return for my compliance, he presented me with great plenty of provisions, and desired to see me again in the morning. I accordingly attended, and found him sitting upon his bed. He told me he was sick, and wished to have a little blood taken from him; but I had no sooner tied up his arm, and displayed the lancet, than his courage failed, and he begged me to postpone the operation till the afternoon, as he felt himself, he said, much better than he had been, and thanked me kindly for my readiness to serve him. He then observed that his women were very desirous to see me, and requested that I would favour them with a visit. An attendant was ordered to conduct me, and I had no sooner entered the court appropriated to the ladies, than the whole seraglio surrounded me, some begging for physic, some for amber, and all of them desirous of trying that great African specific, blood-letting. They were ten or twelve in number, most of them young and handsome, and wearing on their heads ornaments of gold, and beads of amber.

They rallied me with a good deal of gaiety on different subjects, particularly upon the whiteness of my skin, and the prominency of my nose. They insisted that both were artificial. The first, they said, was produced when I was an infant, by dipping me in milk; and they insisted that my nose had been pinched every day till it had acquired its present unsightly and unnatural conformation. On my part, without disputing my own deformity, I paid them many compliments on African beauty. I praised the glossy jet of their skins, and the lovely depression of their noses; but they said that flattery, or (as they emphatically termed it) honey mouth, was not esteemed in Bondou. In return, however, for my company or my compliments (to which, by the way, they seemed not so insensible as they affected to be), they presented me with a jar of honey and some fish, which were sent to my lodging, and I was desired to come again to the king a little before sunset.

"Broad as the Thames at Westminster"

[1796] Early in the morning we again set forward. [Park is now in the country of the Bambara, and about to reach the Niger, the great aim of his journey.] The roads were wet and slippery; but the country was very beautiful, abounding with rivulets, which were increased by the rain into rapid streams. About ten o'clock we came to the ruins of a village, which had been destroyed by war about six months before; and in order to prevent any town from being built there in future, the large Bentang tree, under which the natives spent the day, had been burned down, the wells filled up, and everything that could make the spot desirable completely destroyed.

About noon my horse was so much fatigued that I could not keep up with my companions; I therefore dismounted, and desired them to ride on, telling them that I would follow as soon as my horse had rested a little. But I found them unwilling to leave me. The lions, they said, were very numerous in those parts, and though they might not so readily attack a body of people, they would soon find out an individual. It was therefore agreed that one of the company should stay with me to assist in driving my horse, while the others passed on to Galloo to procure lodgings, and collect grass for the horses before night. Accompanied by this worthy Negro, I drove my horse before me, until about four o'clock, when we came in sight of Galloo, a considerable town, standing in a fertile and beautiful valley surrounded with high rocks.

As my companions had thoughts of settling in this neighbourhood, they had a fine sheep given them by the Dooty; and I was fortunate enough to procure plenty of corn for my horse. Here they blow upon elephants' teeth when they announce evening prayers, in the same manner as at Kemmoo.

Early next morning [July 14], having first returned many thanks to our landlord for his hospitality, while my fellow travellers offered up their prayers that he might never want, we set forward, and about three o'clock arrived at Moorja, a large town, famous for its trade in salt, which the Moors bring here in great quantities to exchange for corn and cotton cloth. As most of the people here are Mahomedans, it is not allowed to the Kaffirs to drink beer, which they call Neo-dello (corn spirit), except in certain houses. In one of these I saw about twenty people sitting round large vessels of this beer with the greatest conviviality, many of them in a state of intoxication. As corn is plentiful, the inhabitants are very liberal to strangers. I believe we had as much corn and milk sent us by different people as would have been sufficient for three times our number; and though we remained here two days, we experienced no diminution of their hospitality.

On the morning of the 16th we again set forward, accompanied by a coffle of fourteen asses, loaded with salt, bound for Sansanding. The road was particularly romantic, between two rocky hills; but the Moors sometimes lie in wait here to plunder strangers. As soon as we had reached the open country, the master of the salt coffle thanked us for having staid with him so long, and now desired us to ride on. The sun was almost set before we reached Datliboo. In the evening we had a most tremendous tornado. The house in which we lodged being flat-roofed, admitted the rain in streams. The floor was soon ankle deep, the fire extinguished and we were left to pass the night upon some bundles of firewood that happened to lie in a corner. . . .

We departed from Datliboo, and about ten o'clock passed a large coffle returning from Segu with corn, hoes, mats, and other household utensils. At five o'clock we came to a large village, where we intended to pass the night, but the Dooty would not receive us. When we departed from this place, my horse was so much fatigued that I was under the necessity of driving him, and it was dark before we reached Fanimboo, a small village; the Dooty of which no sooner heard that I was a white man than he brought out three old muskets, and was much disappointed when he was told that I could not repair them. . . .

We continued our journey; but, owing to a light supper the preceding night, we felt ourselves rather hungry this morning, and endeavoured to procure some corn at a village, but without success. The towns were now more numerous, and the land that is not employed in cultivation affords excellent pasturage for large herds of cattle; but owing to the great concourse of people daily going to and returning from Segu, the inhabitants are less hospitable to strangers.

My horse becoming weaker and weaker every day, was now of very little service to me; I was obliged to drive him before me for the greater part of the day, and did not reach Geosorro until eight o'clock in the evening. . . . I found my companions wrangling with the Dooty, who had absolutely refused to give or sell them any provisions; and as none of us had tasted victuals for the last twenty-four hours, we were by no means disposed to fast another day, if we could help it. But finding our entreaties without effect, and being very much fatigued, I fell asleep, from which I was awakened, about midnight, with the joyful information, "*kinnenata*" (the victuals is come). This made the remainder of the night pass away pleasantly; and at daybreak, July 19th, we resumed our journey, proposing to stop at a village called Doolinkeaboo, for the night following. My fellow-travellers, having better horses than myself, soon left me, and I was walking barefoot, driving my horse, when I was met by a coffle of slaves, about seventy in number, coming from Segu. They were tied together by their necks with thongs of a bullock's hide, twisted like a rope; seven slaves upon a thong, and a man with a musket between every seven. Many of the slaves were ill-conditioned, and a great number of them women. In the rear came Sidi Mahomed's servant, whom I remembered to have seen at the camp of Benowm; he presently knew me, and told me that these slaves were going to Morocco, by the way of Ludamar, and the Great Desert.

In the afternoon, as I approached Doolinkeaboo, I met about twenty Moors on horseback, the owners of the slaves I had seen in the morning; they were well armed with muskets, and were very inquisitive concerning me, but not so rude as their countrymen generally are. From them I learned that Sidi Mahomed was not at Segu, but had gone to Kancaba for gold dust.

When I arrived at Doolinkeaboo, I was informed that my fellow-travellers had gone on, but my horse was so much fatigued that I could not possibly proceed after them. The Dooty of the town, at my request, gave me a draught of water, which is generally looked upon as an earnest of greater hospitality; and I had no doubt of making up for the toils of the day by a good supper and a sound sleep; unfortunately I had neither one nor the other. The night was rainy and tempestuous, and the Dooty limited his hospitality to the draught of water. . . .

In the morning I endeavoured, both by entreaties and threats, to procure some victuals from the Dooty, but in vain. I even begged some corn from one of his female slaves, as she was washing it at the well, and had the mortification to be refused. However, when the Dooty was gone to the fields, his wife sent me a handful of meal, which I mixed with water, and drank for breakfast. About eight o'clock I departed from Doolinkeaboo, and at noon stopped a few minutes at a large *korree*, where I had some milk given me by the Foulahs. And hearing that two Negroes were going from thence to Segu, I was happy to have their company, and we set out immediately. About four o'clock we stopped at a small village, where one of the Negroes met with an acquaintance, who invited us to a sort of public entertainment, which was conducted with more than common propriety. A dish made of sour milk and meal, called Sinkatoo, and beer made from their corn, was distributed with great liberality, and the women were admitted into the society—a circumstance I had never before observed in Africa. There was no compulsion, every one was at liberty to drink as he pleased; they nodded to each other when about to drink, and on setting down the calabash, commonly said *berka* (thank you).   Both men and women appeared to be somewhat intoxicated, but they were far from being quarrelsome.

Departing from thence, we passed several large villages, where I was constantly taken for a Moor, and became the subject of much merriment to the Bambarrans; who seeing me drive my horse before me, laughed at my appearance. He has been at Mecca, says one, you may see that by his clothes; another asked me if my horse was sick; a third wished to purchase it, etc.; so that I believe the very slaves were ashamed to be seen in my company. Just before it was dark, we took up our lodging for the night at a small village, where I procured some victuals for myself, and some corn for my horse, at the moderate price of a button, and was told that I should see the Niger (which the Negroes called Jolliba, or the great water) early the next day. The lions are here very numerous; the gates are shut a little after sunset, and nobody allowed to go out. The thoughts of seeing the Niger in the morning, and the troublesome buzzing of mosquitoes, prevented me from shutting my eyes during the night; and I had saddled my horse and was in readiness before daylight; but, on account of the wild beasts, we were obliged to wait until the people were stirring, and the gates opened. This happened to be a market-day at Segu, and the roads were everywhere filled with people carrying different articles to sell. We passed four large villages, and at eight o'clock saw the smoke over Segu.

As we approached the town, I was fortunate enough to overtake the fugitive Kaartans, to whose kindness I had been so much indebted in my journey through Bambarra. They readily agreed to introduce me to the king; and we rode together through some marshy ground, where, as I was anxiously looking around for the river, one of them called out, *geo affili* (see the water), and looking forwards, I saw with infinite pleasure the great object of my mission—the long sought-for majestic Niger, glittering to the morning sun, as broad as the

Thames at Westminster, and flowing slowly *to the eastward.**
I hastened to the brink, and, having drank of the water, lifted
up my fervent thanks in prayer to the Great Ruler of all things,
for having thus far crowned my endeavours with success. . . .

Segu

Segu, the capital of Bambarra, at which I had now arrived,
consists, properly speaking, of four distinct towns; two on the
northern bank of the Niger, called Segu Korro and Segu Boo;
and two on the southern bank, called Segu Soo Korro and Segu
See Korro. They are all surrounded with high mud walls; the
houses are built of clay, of a square form, with flat roofs; some
of them have two stories, and many of them are whitewashed.
Besides these buildings, Moorish mosques are seen in every
quarter; and the streets, though narrow, are broad enough for
every useful purpose, in a country where wheel-carriages are
entirely unknown.

From the best inquiries I could make, I have reason to
believe that Segu contains altogether about thirty thousand
inhabitants. The king of Bambarra constantly resides at Segu
See Korro; he employs a great many slaves in conveying people
over the river, and the money they receive (though the fare is
only ten cowrie shells for each individual) furnishes a considerable revenue to the king in the course of a year. The canoes
are of a singular construction, each of them being formed of the
trunks of two large trees, rendered concave, and joined
together, not side by side, but endways; the junction being
exactly across the middle of the canoe; they are therefore very
long and disproportionably narrow, and have neither decks nor
masts; they are, however, very roomy; for I observed in one of
them four horses, and several people crossing over the river.

*Emphasis by Park, who well knew that his readers would expect
that the Niger, as was then generally believed in Europe, should flow
to the westward.

When we arrived at this ferry, with a view to pass over to that part of the town in which the king resides, we found a great number waiting for a passage; they looked at me with silent wonder, and I distinguished, with concern, many Moors among them. There were three different places of embarkation, and the ferrymen were very diligent and expeditious; but, from the crowd of people, I could not immediately obtain a passage; and sat down upon the bank of the river, to wait for a more favourable opportunity. The view of this extensive city; the numerous canoes upon the river; the crowded population, and the cultivated state of the surrounding country, formed altogether a prospect of civilization and magnificence, which I little expected to find in the bosom of Africa.

I waited more than two hours without having an opportunity of crossing the river; during which time, the people who had crossed carried information to Mansong, the king, that a white man was waiting for a passage, and was coming to see him. He immediately sent over one of his chief men, who informed me that the king could not possibly see me, until he knew what had brought me into his country; and that I must not presume to cross the river without the king's permission. He therefore advised me to lodge at a distant village, to which he pointed, for the night; and said that in the morning he would give me further instructions how to conduct myself. This was very discouraging. However, as there was no remedy, I set off for the village; where I found to my great mortification, that no person would admit me into his house. I was regarded with astonishment and fear, and was obliged to sit all day without victuals, in the shade of tree; and the night threatened to be very uncomfortable, for the wind rose, and there was great appearance of a heavy rain; and the wild beasts are so very numerous in the neighbourhood, that I should have been under the necessity of climbing up the tree, and resting among the branches.

"Pity the White Man, Faint and Weary . . ."

About sunset, however, as I was preparing to pass the night in this manner, and had turned my horse loose, that he might graze at liberty, a woman, returning from the labours of the field, stopped to observe me, and perceiving that I was weary and dejected, inquired into my situation, which I briefly explained to her; whereupon, with looks of great compassion, she took up my saddle and bridle, and told me to follow her. Having conducted me into her hut, she lighted up a lamp, spread a mat on the floor, and told me I might remain there for the night. Finding that I was very hungry, she said she would procure me something to eat. She accordingly went out, and returned in a short time with a very fine fish; which having caused to be half-broiled upon some embers, she gave me for supper.

The rites of hospitality being thus performed towards a stranger in distress, my worthy benefactress (pointing to the mat, and telling me I might sleep there without apprehension) called to the female part of her family, who had stood gazing on me all the while in fixed astonishment, to resume their task of spinning cotton; in which they continued to employ themselves [a] great part of the night. They lightened their labour by songs, one of which was composed extempore; for I was myself the subject of it. It was sung by one of the young women, the rest joining in a sort of chorus. The air was sweet and plaintive, and the words, literally translated, were these:—"the winds roared, and the rains fell. The poor white man, faint and weary, came and sat under our tree. He has no mother to bring him milk; no wife to grind his corn." Chorus—"Let us pity the white man; no mother has he," etc., etc. Trifling as this recital may appear to the reader, to a person in my situation, the circumstance was affecting in the highest degree. I was oppressed by such unexpected kindness; and sleep fled from my eyes. In the morning I presented my compassionate landlady with two of the four brass buttons which remained on my waistcoat; the only recompense I could make her.

A Slave Coffle

[1797] My clothes were by this time become so very ragged, that I was almost ashamed to appear out of doors; but Karfa, on the day after his arrival, generously presented me with a garment and trousers as are commonly worn in the country.

The slaves which Karfa had brought with him were all of them prisoners of war; they had been taken by the Bambarran army in the kingdoms of Wassela and Kaarta, and carried to Segu, where some of them had remained three years in irons. From Segu they were sent, in company with a number of other captives, up the Niger in two large canoes, and offered for sale at Yamina, Bammakoo, and Kancaba, at which places the greater number of the captives were bartered for gold dust, and the remainder sent forward to Kankaree.

Eleven of them confessed to me that they had been slaves from their infancy; but the other two refused to give any account of their former condition. They were all very inquisitive; but they viewed me at first with looks of horror, and repeatedly asked if my countrymen were cannibals. They were very desirous to know what became of the slaves after they had crossed the salt water. I told them that they were employed in cultivating the land, but they would not believe me; and one of them, putting his hand upon the ground, said, with great simplicity, "Have you really got such ground as this to set your feet upon?" A deeply rooted idea that the whites purchase Negroes for the purpose of devouring them, or of selling them to others, that they may be devoured hereafter, naturally makes the slaves contemplate a journey towards the coast with great terror, insomuch that the Slatees are forced to keep them constantly in irons, and watch them very closely to prevent their escape. They are commonly secured by putting the right leg of one and the left of another into the same pair of fetters. By supporting the fetters with a string, they can walk, though very slowly. Every four slaves are likewise fastened together by the necks with a strong rope or twisted thongs; and in the night

an additional pair of fetters is put on their hands, and sometimes a light iron chain passed round their necks.

Such of them as evince marks of discontent, are secured
in a different manner. A thick billet of wood is cut about three
feet long, and a smooth notch being made upon one side of it,
the ankle of the slave is bolted to the smooth part by means of
a strong iron staple, one prong of which passes on each side of
the ankle. All these fetters and bolts are made from native
iron; in the present case they were put on by the blacksmith as
soon as the slaves arrived from Kancaba, and were not taken
off until the morning on which the coffle departed for Gambia. . . .

From Mungo Park, *Travels in the Interior Districts of Africa, etc.* (London:
1799). Long extracts are reproduced in a good cheap abridgment by
the Everyman Library (London: 1954).

UTHMAN DAN FODIO

Reformation

The great upheavals of the Western Sudan in the first half of
the century may be said to have begun, at least in their main part,
with the rebellion of Fulani people (in modern Niger and Northern
Nigeria) against their Hausa or Habe overlords. This rebellion had
many social motivations but took the form, characteristic of the
place and period, of jihad, a war of religion. It began in 1804 and
was associated with three outstanding men in the Hausa state of
Gobir: *Shehu* (or Sheikh) Uthman dan Fodio (died 1817), his
brother Abdullahu (died 1829), and his son Muhammad Bello (died
1837).

These reformers wrote enormously. Many of their works
have been preserved. As many as 258 surviving books and

pamphlets on a wide variety of topics—Koranic study, medicine, diplomacy, rules for good government—are attributed to these distinguished men, and more may yet be found. Only in the 1960s did students of West African history begin to turn a consistent attention to this copious literature. "At present," wrote H. F. C. Smith, "it is possible to say that in outline the thought of the leaders followed a classical pattern of Islamic revivalism. In their search for the ideal society and the just ruler, they looked back to a previous golden age in the history of *dar al-Islam* [*Pax Islamica* as we might call it], and their aim was to re-create in the Western Sudan the society of the rightly guided caliphate." They were trying, that is, to reconstruct the political and social order of the Western Sudan in line with the great precedents of the distant past of Islam. Severe moralists, they repeatedly attacked their Hausa (Habe) opponents, whom they overthrew, for "corruption and misgovernment," as the following extracts interestingly show.

Much that these men and their contemporaries had to say is historically of the highest possible interest, obscure though it may often seem. Here then are three fragments to whet the appetite for more: the first from one of Uthman dan Fodio's minor works, the second from the *Tazyin al-Waraqat* of Abdullah Ibn Muhammad, and the third from Muhammad Bello. Each, of course, is arguing a case.

The Old Habe Kingdoms

One of the ways of their government [that is, of the Hausa or Habe kings] is succession to the emirate by hereditary right and by force to the exclusion of consultation. And one of the ways of their government is the building of their sovereignty upon three things: the people's persons, their honour, and their possessions; and whomsoever they wish to kill or exile or violate his honour or devour his wealth they do so in pursuit of their lusts, without any right in the Shari'a. One of the ways of their government is their imposing on the people monies not laid down by the Shari'a, being those which they call *janghali* and *kurdin ghari* and *kurdin salla*. One of the ways of their governments is their intentionally eating whatever food they wish, whether it is religiously permitted or forbidden, and drinking what beverages [ta'am] they wish, whether religiously permitted or forbidden, and riding whatever riding beasts they wish, whether religiously permitted or forbidden, and taking what women they wish without marriage contract, and living in decorated palaces, whether religiously permitted or forbidden, and spreading soft (decorated) carpets as they wish, whether religiously permitted or forbidden. . . .

One of the ways of their governments is to compel the people to serve in their armies, even though they are Muslims, and they call it *gharghadi*, and whosoever does not go, they impose upon him a money payment, not imposed by the Shari'a. One of the ways of their government which is also well known, is that if you have an adversary (in law) and he precedes you to them, and gives them some money, then your word will not be accepted by them, even though they know for a certainty of your truthfulness, unless you give them more than your adversary gave. One of the ways of their government is to shut the door in the face of the needy. One of the ways of their governments is their forbidding to the worshippers of God part of that which is legal for them, such as the veiling of women, which is incumbent upon them, and turbans for men, which is *sunna* for them, and they call this forbidding *duka*. One of the ways of their government which is also well known is that they will not abandon the custom which they found their forebears practising, even though it is evil. One of the ways of their government is the putting of dust upon their heads when giving a greeting, and it is an evil custom, as in *al-Kibrit al-ahmar*, where the author says "because it is a sign of excess."

One of the ways of their government is their being occupied with doing vain things (continuously) by night or by day, without legal purpose, such as beating drums, and lutes, and kettledrums. The Muslims only beat the kettledrum, and similar instruments for a legal purpose, such as wishing to gather the army together, or to signify its departure, or the setting up of camp, and its arrival, and as a sign of the advent of the festival, as the kettledrum is beaten for the advent of *'Id al-adha*, and they confine themselves to what necessity requires. One of the ways of their governments is the giving of a gift to one who conducts them before the ruler. . . .

Five Rules of Government (Continuing Dan Fodio)

. . . and I say—and help is with God—the foundations of government are five things: the first is that authority shall not be given to one who seeks it. The second is the necessity for consultation. The third is the abandoning of harshness. The fourth is justice. The fifth is good works. And as for its ministers, they are four. (The first) is a trustworthy wazir to wake the ruler if he sleeps, to make him see if he is blind, and to remind him if he forgets, and the greatest misfortune for the government and the subjects is that they should be denied honest wazirs. And among the conditions pertaining to the wazir is that he should be steadfast in compassion to the people, and merciful towards them. The second of the ministers of government is a judge whom the blame of a blamer cannot overtake concerning the affairs of God. The third is a chief of police who shall obtain justice for the weak from the strong. The fourth is a tax collector who shall discharge his duties and not oppress the subjects. . . .

From the *Kitab al-Farq*, attributed to Uthman dan Fodio, translated by M. Hiskett in *Bulletin* of the School of Oriental and African Studies (London: 1960), part 3, p. 558.

ABDULLAH IBN MUHAMMAD

Against Bad Rulers

Whose purpose is the ruling of the countries and
     their people
In order to obtain delights and acquire rank
According to the custom of the unbelievers and the
     titles of their sovereignty.
And the appointing of ignorant persons to the high-
     est offices
And the collecting of concubines and fine clothes.
And horses that run in the towns, not on the battle-
     fields.
And the devouring of the gifts of influence, booty,
     and bribery,
And lutes and flutes, and the beating of drums.
And their activities weaken those charged with
     managing affairs.
And the country people make off from every side.
Their purpose is fleeing from the judge. . .
And the selling of free men, while in the market.
And some of them are posing as *qadis*, in the cloth-
     ing of foxes. . .

From Abdullah Ibn Muhammad, *Tazyin al-Waraqat*, edited, with
translation and introductory study of the author's life and times, by
M. Hiskett (Ibadan: 1963), p. 121.

MUHAMMAD BELLO

Jihad

To the Emir of Bauchi, Ya'qub bin Dadi, a thousand valedictions and a thousand greetings.

After which, the reason for [this message] is to inform you of our circumstances, and of what we are engaged in today of the important affairs of Islam and of the Muslims. That is, that we have gone out in the direction of the North, because of the affair of the beasts, and the foray against Tadaghaw with al-Jilani. We have taken our equipment, consisting of tents of hide, and water-skins, and all that is required for a journey.

We have ordered the expedition for the twentieth of Sha'ban, and we commanded those of the brethren who adjoin us to follow us, and to march out with us bringing their beasts and military equipment. There is not to stay behind a single one of the owners of beasts [*ashabu 'l-dawwabi*], nor of the gahzis, whoever he may be, excepting those who have embarked upon the campaign against Banagha. The result is that we have imposed upon the community at the present time one of two alternatives; either they should join the ghazis on the Banagha front, and besiege it until we arrive, if Allah so wills; or for whoever may prefer the expedition to Tadaghaw to accompany us. As for the cattle-owning herdsmen [*al-ra'atu ashabu 'l-baqari*], not one of them must fail to join us, unless there is no help for it. . . .

As for what is required of you yourself, you must follow our example—when this reaches you—and gird up your skirts for the sacred war [*jihad*] against the infidels upon your most important fronts and "let them find strength in you," and do not give way, and "do not be discouraged, for you shall have the upper hand"; or rather "a morning upon the road of Allah, or a day's march is better than this world, and what is in it."

So do not turn aside from your resolve [*al-hazmi*] but be heroes of Allah [*rijjalu 'llahi*]. Incumbent on you too is the multiplication of your beasts, and the seeking out for them of grazing-grounds that are suited to them, since they are the instruments of the sacred war. Greetings.

From Muhammad Bello, Sultan of Sokoto (1817-1837), a letter to the Emir of Bauchi, translation of Arabic text by A. D. H. Bivar in *Bulletin of the School of Oriental and African Studies* (London: 1960), part 2, p. 339.

HUGH CLAPPERTON

Sultan Muhammad Bello

Still unknown to them save by rumour and distant report, the British followed Park into the interior of western Africa, by way of the Mediterranean Coast and the Sahara, with a three-man expedition of 1822. One of those three Englishmen, Captain Clapperton, was able to reach the capital of Sultan Muhammed Bello, ruler of much of what is now Northern Nigeria and prestigious *Amir al-Mumenin*, Commander of the Faithful of Islam. His writings convey vivid accounts of what he saw and heard, and are especially useful for his description of political and social life in the then newly-formed Fulani-ruled emirates of Nigeria.

[1824] . . . At noon we arrived at Sokoto where a great multitude of people was assembled to look at me, and I entered the city amid the hearty welcome of young and old. I was conducted to the house of the gadado or vizier, where apartments were provided for me and my servants. After being supplied with plenty of milk, I was left to repose myself. . . .

March 17th. After breakfast, the sultan sent for me; his residence was at no great distance. In front of it there is a large quadrangle, into which several of the principal streets of the city lead . . . [and we] were immediately ushered into the presence of Bello, the second sultan of the Felatahs [Fulani]. He was seated on a small carpet, between two pillars supporting the roof of a thatched house, not unlike one of our cottages. The walls and pillars were painted blue and white in the Moorish taste; and on the back wall was sketched a fire-screen, ornamented with a course painting of a flower-pot. An armchair, with an iron lamp standing on it, was placed on each side of the screen. The sultan bade me many hearty welcomes, and asked me if I was not much tired. . . .

He asked me a great many questions about Europe and our religious distinctions. He was acquainted with the names of some of the more ancient sects, and asked whether we were Nestorians or Socinians. To extricate myself from the embarrassment occasioned by this question, I bluntly replied we were called Protestants. "What are Protestants?" says he. I attempted to explain to him, as well as I was able, that having protested more than two centuries and a half ago against the superstitions, absurdities and abuses practised in those days, we had ever since professed to follow simply what was written 'in the book of our Lord Jesus,' as they [i.e., the Muslims] call the New Testament, and thence received the name of Protestants. He continued to ask several other theological questions, until I was obliged to confess myself not sufficiently versed in religious subtleties to resolve these knotty points, having always left that task to others more learned than myself. . . .

The sultan is a noble-looking man, forty-four years of age although much younger in appearance, five feet ten inches high, portly in person, with a short curling black beard, a small mouth, a fine forehead, a Grecian nose, and large black eyes. He was dressed in a light blue cotton *tobe*, with a white muslin turban, the shawl of which he wore over the nose and mouth in the Tuareg fashion.

[On a second expedition of 1826-7, Clapperton again found a welcome in Sultan Bello's capital of Sokoto.] Saw the sultan this morning, who was sitting in the inner apartment of his house, with the Arabic copy of Euclid before him that I had given him as a present. He said that his family had a copy of Euclid brought by one of their relations, who had procured it at Mecca; that it was destroyed when part of his house was burnt down last year; and he observed that he could not feel but very much obliged to the king of England for sending him so valuable a present. . . .

From D. Denham, H. Clapperton, and W. Oudney, *Narrative of Travels and Discoveries in Northern and Central Africa* (London: 1826). The last extract is from H. Clapperton, *Journal of a Second Expedition into the Interior of Africa from the Bight of Benin to Sokoto* (London: 1829); on this second journey, in which he eventually perished of sickness, Clapperton had gone inland from the West Coast, and not, as on the first expedition, from the Mediterranean.

———

AL HAJJI SA'ID

Muhammad Bello

The Hausa country flourished greatly under his rule. He spread respect for learning, and scholars came from different countries. He was very solicitous for their welfare . . . whether they came from east, west, south or north. . . . He spent much time in writing; every time he finished one of his works he made it known to the public and had them read it, and then set himself to writing another volume. . . . If anyone posed him a problem he made it at once the subject of a publication. If he found that such and such persons were in disagreement on a point, he at once composed a treatise on it. . . . He supported himself by the fruits of his work, without asking for upkeep from the public purse. . . . He was sympathetic to the people and full of care for them, calm, patient, indifferent to the wealth of other men. A skillful administrator, he watched over the work of the *qadis*, quashed their judgments if these had been given under the influence of passion, never allowing them to grow slack in their work. . . . Ruddy of complexion, tall, bald of head, wearing a long and tufted beard, such was his appearance. . . .

From al Hajji Sa'id, *A History of Sokoto*, translated here from the French version of the Arabic text of O. Houdas (Paris: 1901), p. 318. This writer was a Koranic official under Sultan Ali, son of Muhammad Bello, who reigned from 1837 to 1849. Houdas thought that Sa'id was possibly from the Masina region on the Middle Niger.

THOMAS BOWDICH

At Kumasi

Early in the 19th century the English on the Gold Coast became interested in the greatest inland power they knew, which was then Ashanti (Asante). Bowdich was sent on an official British mission to Kumasi, and saw this capital at the zenith of its wealth and influence.

[1817] We entered Kumasi at two o'clock . . . . Upwards of five thousand people, the greater part warriors, met us with awful bursts of martial music. . . . The smoke which encircled us from the incessant discharges of musquetry confined our glimpses to the foreground; and we were halted, while the captains performed their pyrrhic dance, in the centre of a circle formed by their warriors; where a confusion of flags, English, Dutch, and Danish, were waved and flourished in all directions. . . . The dress of the captains was a war cap, with gilded rams' horns projecting in front, the sides extended beyond all proportion by immense plumes of eagles' feathers. . . . Their vest was of red cloth, covered with fetishes and saphies in gold and silver. . . . They wore loose cotton trowsers, with immense boots of a dull red leather, coming half way up the thigh. . . .

Our observations *en passant* had taught us to conceive a spectacle far exceeding our original expectations; but they had not prepared us for the extent and display of the scene which here burst upon us: an area of nearly a mile in circumference was crowded with magnificence and novelty. The king, his tributaries, and captains, were resplendent in the distance, surrounded by attendants of every description. . . . More than a hundred bands burst [out] at once on our arrival, with the peculiar airs of their several chiefs; the horns flourished their defiances, with beating of innumerable drums and metal instruments, and then yielded for a while to the soft breathings of their long flutes. . . . At least a hundred large umbrellas, or canopies, which could shelter thirty persons, were sprung up and down by the bearers with brilliant effect, being made of scarlet, yellow, and the most shewy cloths and silks, and crowned on the top with crescents, pelicans, elephants, barrels, and arms and swords of gold. . . .

The caboceers, as did their superior captains and attendants, wore Ashanti cloths, of extravagant price from the costly foreign silks which had been unravelled to weave them in all the varieties of colour, as well as pattern; [these cloths] were of an incredible size and weight, and thrown over the shoulder exactly like a Roman toga; a small silk fillet generally encircles their temples, and massy gold necklaces, intricately wrought. . . .

Four of the principal streets [of Kumasi] are half a mile long, and from fifty to one hundred yards wide. I observed them building one, and a line was stretched on each side to make it regular. The streets were all named, and a superior captain in charge of each . . . . The Ashantis persisted that the population of Kumasi, when collected, was upwards of one hundred thousand. . . . Perhaps [its] average resident population . . . is not more than from twelve to fifteen thousand . . . . What surprised me most . . . was the discovery that every house had its cloacae, besides the common ones for the lower orders without the town. They were generally situated under a small archway in the most retired angle of the building, but not unfrequently upstairs, within a separate room like a small closet . . . the holes are of a small circumference, but dug to a surprising depth, and boiling water is daily poured down, which effectually prevents the least offence. The rubbish and offal of each house was burnt every morning at the back of the street, and they were as nice and cleanly in their dwellings as in their persons. . . .

From T. E. Bowdich, *Mission from Cape Coast to Ashantee* (London: 1819).

BRODIE CRUICKSHANK

Political Background

Arriving on the Gold Coast in 1834, Brodie Cruickshank remained there for eighteen years, and served as a magistrate and as British lieutenant-governor in 1853-1854. A Scottish merchant by origin and formation, he became interested in African political affairs and went to great pains, as his book reveals, to find out what they really implied and meant. His account of some forms of government in the interior and along the seaboard of the Gold Coast remains especially interesting, for it throws a broad light on the situation which had flowed from the pressures of two centuries of great involvement in the European slave trade; and it opens an early discussion on the nature of African forms of kingship and government, which Cruickshank, though mistakenly, thought akin to the feudalism of Europe. But his direct impressions are very instructive.

. . . By the treaty concluded with the king of Ashantee at the close of the war, the English [on the Gold Coast] obtained for their allies an acknowledgment of entire independence [from Ashantee overlordship]. Those countries . . . returned to the simple and original form of government, which had been in force previous to the subjection of their country by the Ashantees. It would be difficult, however, to define the nature of that government.

It was not a despotism, nor a constitutional monarchy, nor an oligarchy, nor a republic, but partook something of the qualities of each of these different forms, and depended much upon the individual character and riches of the chief. It was, moreover, greatly modified by traditionary customs and precedents, which appear to define the extent of the chiefs' authority, as well as the privileges of the people, and to be equally binding on both. From this cause it is that we see a strange combination of despotic acts, with occasional instances of great freedom and equality, in which the authority of the chief seems nearly lost. . . . But while the chief is thus checked in the general government of his country, his authority over his immediate retainers is absolute. . . . The same feudal system prevails among the Denkeras . . . the Assins . . . the Abrahs . . . the Akims, Aquapims, and others. . . .

Observation shows that in this country the principal source of feudal retainers has arisen from the necessity of obtaining a protector. Families and whole tribes, to avoid extirpation by war, have placed themselves under the wing of some powerful chief, who perhaps supported them in famine and shielded them in battle. Only a personal interest in the individuals whom he thus supported would have induced him to burden himself with their care; and he consequently expects, as a return for his protection, their ready and willing obedience as vassals. There are also instances of whole towns undergoing this vassalage, in return for money advanced to help them out of difficulties. . . .

[Writing of the town governments of the Gold Coast seaboard, which have "an infinitely greater share of political liberty"—as did, in Cruickshank's comparison, the "free towns" of medieval Europe—he points out that] in the towns of Cape Coast, Anamaboe, Accra, and others situated under the guns of the European forts, or in the immediate vicinity of the sea, we find, as among the chiefs of the interior, an hereditary power vested in an individual, indiscriminately called king, chief, or principal cabboceer. He is the acknowledged head of the town, but has not, like the bush chief, any claim to the services of the inhabitants as vassals. . . . He is, in fact, the chief magistrate of the town, presiding and assisting in council and in the judgment hall, but with a voice no whit more potential than his fellow-counsellors and judges. These consist first of hereditary cabboceers, men of the principal rank in town, whose authority has been originally derived from the consequence which wealth has given to the first distinguished founder of the family. . . .

In addition to the king and cabboceers, both the council and judgment seat are composed of the representatives of the people. The towns are invariably divided into departments or wards, and those residing within these divisions are formed into companies, who have each their distinctive flags, drums, and other equipments. . . . There are instances of women, from some particular services, either of themselves or of their family, being promoted to the rank of captain [of a company] . . . .

From Brodie Cruickshank, *Eighteen Years on the Gold Coast* (2 vols., London: 1853), vol. 1, p. 232.

HEINRICH BARTH

The Western Sudan

For long years after its appearance Barth's great work was appreciated only by a handful of specialists. This curious public attitude to an outstanding explorer may probably be best explained in terms of the peculiar slant of European interest in Africa at that time, concentrated as this so greatly was on missionary enterprise. Three of the five volumes of his principal book appeared in 1857, the same year as Livingstone's *Missionary Travels*, but whereas Livingstone's single though substantial volume ran through twenty-two thousand copies in six months, Barth's first three volumes were published in an initial edition of only twelve hundred copies followed by another of one thousand, while one thousand copies were found to be enough for the fourth and fifth volumes (perhaps the most interesting and exciting of them all), which appeared in July 1858.* It may be added that Barth suffered an eclipse in Germany, his native land, as well. Even the 1952 edition of *Der Grosse Brockhaus*, appearing at a time when Barth's importance was widely recognized, gives him no more than fourteen lines. And we still await a complete republication of his West African travels.

---

*I am indebted for these figures to Longmans, Green & Co. Ltd., and John Murray Ltd., respectively the publishers of Barth and Livingstone.

Born in Hamburg in 1821, Heinrich Barth died at the age of forty-four. He travelled in North Africa and the Near East in 1845-1847, and went to the Western Sudan as a member of a British expedition in 1849, returning in 1855 with the first scholarly and comprehensive understanding of this vast region that any European had ever secured. We take up his story with his first arrival in the famous city of Kano, then known to the outside world only by vague report.

Kano in Mid-Century

[1851] Kano had been sounding in my ears now for more than a year; it had been one of the great objects of our journey as the central point of commerce, as a great storehouse of information, and as the point whence more distant regions might be most successfully attempted. At length, after nearly a year's exertions, I had reached it. . . .

With regard to the growth of the town, we have express testimony that Dala was the most ancient quarter. The steep rocky hill, about 120 feet high, naturally afforded a secure retreat to the ancient inhabitants in case of sudden attack; but it is most probable that there was another or several separate villages within the wide expanse now encompassed by the wall, which rather exceeds than falls short of fifteen English miles. . . .

The wall, just as it has been described by Captain Clapperton, is still kept in the best repair, and is an imposing piece of workmanship in this quarter of the world. . . .

In estimating the population of the town at thirty thousand, I am certainly not above the truth. Captain Clapperton estimated it at from thirty thousand to forty thousand. The population, as might be expected in a place of great commercial resort, is of a rather mixed nature; but the chief elements in it are Kanuri or Bornu people, Hausawa, Fulbe or Fellani, and Nyffawa or Nupe; a good many Arabs also reside there, who by their commerce and their handicraft contribute a great deal to the importance of the place. The influx of foreigners and temporary residents is occasionally very great, so that the whole number of residents during the most busy time of the year (that is to say from January to April) may often amount to sixty thousand. The number of domestic slaves, of course, is very considerable; but I think it hardly equals, certainly does not exceed, that of the free men, for, while the wealthy have many slaves, the poorer class, which is far more numerous, have few or none. It would be very interesting to arrive at an exact estimate of the numbers of the conquering nation, in order to see the proportion in which they stand to the conquered. As for the town itself, their whole number, of every sex and age, does not, in my opinion, exceed four thousand; but with regard to the whole country I can give no opinion. [Barth is referring here to the Fulani and the Hausa peoples.]

The principal commerce of Kano consists in native produce, namely, the cotton cloth woven and dyed here or in the neighbouring towns, in the form of tobes or *rigona* (sing. *riga*); *turkedi*, or the oblong piece of dress of dark-blue colour worn by women; the *zenne* or plaid, of various colours; and the *rawani baki*, or black litham.

The great advantage of Kano is, that commerce and manufactures go hand in hand, and that almost every family has its share in them. There is really something grand in this kind of industry, which spreads to the north as far as Murzuk, Ghat, and even Tripoli; to the west, not only to Timubuktu, but in some degree even as far as the shores of the Atlantic, the very inhabitants of Arguin dressin in the cloth woven and dyed in Kano; to the east, all over Bornu, although there it comes into contact with the native industry of the country; and to the south it maintains a rivalry with the native industry of the I'gbira and I'gbo, while towards the southeast it invades the whole of 'Adamawa, and is only limited by the nakedness of the pagan sans-culottes, who do not wear clothing.

As for the supply sent to Timbuktu, this is a fact entirely overlooked in Europe, where people speak continually of the fine cotton cloth produced in that town, while in truth all the apparel of a decent character in Timbuktu is brought either from Kano of from Sansandi; and how urgently this article is there demanded is amply shown by the immense circuit which the merchandise makes to avoid the great dangers [from Tuareg raiding] of the direct road from Kano to Timubuktu travelled by me, the merchandise of Kano being first carried up to Ghat and even Ghadames [in the Northern Sahara], and thence taking its way to Timbuktu by Tawat.

I make the lowest estimate in rating this export to Timbuktu alone at three hundred camel-loads annually, worth sixty million *kurdi* in Kano—an amount which entirely remains in the country, and rebounds to the benefit of the whole population, both cotton and indigo being produced and prepared in the country.

In taking a general view of the subject, I think myself justified in estimating the whole produce of this manufacture, as far as it is sold abroad, at the very least at about three hundred million; and how great this national wealth is, will be understood by my readers when they know that, with from fifty to sixty thousand *kurdi*, or from four to five pounds sterling a year, a whole family may live in that country with ease, including every expense, even that of their clothing: and we must remember that the province is one of the most fertile spots on the earth, and is able to produce not only the supply of corn necessary for its population, but can also export, and that is possesses, besides, the finest pasture-grounds. In fact, if we consider that this industry is not carried on here as in Europe, in immense establishments, degrading man to the meanest condition of life, but that it gives employment and support to families without compelling them to sacrifice their domestic habits, we must presume that Kano ought to be one of the happiest countries in the world; and so it is as long as its governor, too often lazy and indolent, is able to defend its inhabitants from the cupidity of their neighbours, which of course is constantly stimulated by the very wealth of this country. . . .

Finding the Tarikh al-Sudan

[1853] . . . I passed the time during my residence in this place [Gando] not quite uselessly, especially as I was so fortunate as to obtain here from a learned man of the name Bokhari, a son of the late Mohammed Wani, a copy of that most valuable historical work of Ahmed Baba,* to which my friend 'Abd el Kader, in Sokoto, had first called my attention, but without being able to satisfy my curiosity; and I spent three or four days most pleasantly in extracting the more important historical data of this work, which opened to me quite a new insight into the history of the regions on the middle course of the Niger, whither I was bending my steps, exciting in me a far more lively interest than I had previously felt in a kingdom the great power of which, in former times, I here found set forth in very clear and distinct outlines, and I only lamented that I had not time enough to copy the whole.

Timbuktu

[1853] Thus the day broke which, after so many months' exertion was to carry me [up the Niger] to the harbour of Timbuktu. We started at a tolerably early hour, crossing the broad sheet of the river, first in a northeasterly, then in an almost northerly direction, till finding ourselves opposite the small hamlet Tasakal, mentioned by Caillie, we began to keep along the windings of the northern bank which, from its low character, presented a very varying appearance, while a creek, separating from the trunk, entered the low ground. . . .

We entered the branch of Korome, keeping along the grass which here grows in the river to a great extent, till we reached the village, consisting of nothing but temporary huts of reed, which, in the course of a few weeks, with the rising of the waters, were to be removed further inland. Notwithstanding its

---

*Barth was mistaken. The author was al-Sa'di.

fail character, this poor little village was interesting on account of its wharfs, where a number of boats were repairing. The master of our own craft residing here (for all boatmen on this river are serfs, or nearly in that condition), we were obliged to halt almost an hour and a half; but in order not to excite the curiosity of the people, I thought it prudent to remain in my boat. But even there I was incommoded with a great number of visitors, who were very anxious to know exactly what sort of person I was. . . .

At length we lay to, and sending two of my people on shore, in order to obtain quarters, I followed them as soon as possible, when I was informed that they had procured a comfortable dwelling for me. The house where I was lodged was a large and grand building (if we take into account the general relations of this country), standing on the very top of the mound on the slope of which the town is situated. It was of an oblong shape, consisting of very massive clay walls, which were even adorned, in a slight degree, with a rude kind of relief; and it included, besides two anterooms, an inner courtyard, with a good many smaller chambers, and an upper story. The interior, with its small stores of every kind, and its assortment of sheep, ducks, fowls, and pigeons, in different departments, resembled Noah's ark, and afforded a cheerful sight of homely comfort which had been preserved here from more ancient and better times, notwithstanding the exactions of Fulbe [Fulani] and Imoshagh [Tuareg of the Sahara].

Having taken possession of the two anterooms for my people and luggage, I endeavoured to make myself as comfortable as possible; while the busy landlady, a tall and stout personage, in the absence of her husband, a wealthy Songhay merchant, endeavoured to make herself agreeable, and offered me the various delicacies of her store for sale; but these were extremely scanty, the chief attaction to us, besides a small bowl of milk seasoned with honey, being some onions, of which I myself was not less in want than my people for seasoning our simple food; but fresh ones were not even to be got here, the article sold being a peculiar preparation which is imported from Sansandi, the onions, which are of very small size, being cut into slices and put in water, then pounded in a wooden mortar, dried again, and, by means of some butter, made up into a sort of round ball, which is sold in small pats of an inch and a half in diameter for five shells each: these are called *lawashi* in Fulfulde, or *gabu* in the Songhay language. Besides this article, so necessary for seasoning the food, I bought a little *bulanga*, or vegetable butter, in order to light up the dark room where I had taken up my quarters; but the night which I passed here was a very uncomfortable one, on account of the number of mosquitoes which infest the whole place.

Thus broke the 6th of September, a very important day for me, as it was to determine the kind of reception I was to meet in this quarter. But notwithstanding the uncertainty of my prospects, I felt cheerful and full of confidence; and, as I was now again firmly established on dry soil, I went early in the morning to see my horse, which had successfully crossed all the different branches lying between Kabara and Sarayamo; but I was sorry to find him in a very weak and emaciated condition.

While traversing the village, I was surprised at the many clay buildings which are to be seen here, amounting to between one hundred fifty and two hundred; however, these are not so much the dwellings of the inhabitants of Kabara themselves, but serve rather as magazines for storing up the merchandise belonging to the people of, and the foreign merchants residing in, Timbuktu and Sansandi. There are two small market places, one containing about twelve stalls or sheds, where all sorts of articles are sold, the other being used exclusively for meat. Although it was still early in the day, women were already busy boiling rice, which is sold in small portions, or made up into thin cakes boiled with *bulanga*, and sold for five shells each.

Almost all the inhabitants, who may muster about two thousand, are Songhay; but the authorities belong to the tribe of the Fulbe, whose principal wealth consists of cattle, the only exception being the office of the inspector of the harbour,—a very ancient office, repeatedly mentioned by Ahmed Baba—which at present is in the hands of Mulay Kasim, a sherif whose family is said to have emigrated originally from the Gharb or Morocco, but who has become so Sudanized that he has forgotten all his former knowledge of Arabic. On account of the cattle being driven to a great distance, I found that milk was very scarce and dear. The inhabitants cultivate a little rice, but have some cotton, besides *bamia*, or *Corchorus olitorius*, and melons of various descriptions.

Having returned to my quarters from my walk through the town, I had to distribute several presents to some people whom El Walati chose to represent as his brothers and friends. Having then given to himself a new, glittering, black tobe of Nupe manufacture, a new "haf," and the white bernus which I wore myself, I at length prevailed upon him to set out for the town [of Timbuktu], in order to obtain protection for me; for as yet I was an outlaw in the country, and any ruffian who suspected my character might have slain me, without scarcely anybody caring anything about it; and circumstances seemed to assume a very unfavourable aspect: for there was a great movement among the Tawarek [Tuareg] in the neighbourhood when it almost seemed as if some news of my real character had transpired.

Not long after my two messengers were gone, a Tarki* chief, of the name of Kneha, with tall and stately figure, and of noble expressive features, as far as his shawl around the face allowed them to be seen, but, like the whole tribe of the Kel-hekikan to which he belongs, bearing a very bad character as a freebooter, made his appearance, armed with spear and sword, and obtruded himself upon me while I was partaking of my simple dish of rice; notwithstanding which, he took his seat at a short distance opposite to me. Not wishing to invite him to a share in my poor frugal repast by the usual *bismillah*, I told

*Targui, sing. of Tuareg, the name of a Saharan (Berber) people.

him, first in Arabic and then in Fulfulde, that I was dining, and had no leisure to speak with him at present. Whereupon he took his leave, but returned after a short while, and, in a rather peremptory manner, solicited a present from me, being, as he said, a great chief of the country; but as I was not aware of the extent of his power, and being also afraid that others might imitate his example, I told him that I could not give him anything before I had made due inquiries respecting his real importance from my companion who had just gone to the town. But he was not at all satisfied with my argument; representing himself as a great *dhalem*, or evildoer, and that as such he might do me much harm; till at length, after a very spirited altercation, I got rid of him.

He was scarcely gone, when the whole house was filled with armed men, horse and foot, from Timbuktu, most of them clad in light blue tobes, tightly girt round the waist with a shawl, and dressed in short breeches reaching only to the knees, as if they were going to fight, their head being covered with a straw hat of the peculiar shape of a little hut with regular thatchwork, such as is fashionable among the inhabitants of Masina and of the provinces further west. They were armed with spears, besides which some of them wore also a sword: only a few of them had muskets. Entering the house rather abruptly, and squatting down in the antechambers and courtyard, just where they could find a place, they stared at me not a little, and began asking of each other who this strange-looking fellow might be, while I was reclining on my two smaller boxes, having my larger ones and my other luggage behind me. I was rather at a loss to account for their intrusion, until I learned, upon inquiry from my landlady, that they were come in order to protect their cattle from the Tawarek, who at the time were passing through the place, and who had driven away some of their property. The very person whom they dreaded was the chief Kneha, who had just left me, though they could not make out his whereabouts. Having refreshed themselves during the hot hours of the day, these people started off; but the alarm about the cattle continued the whole of the after-noon, and not less than two hundred armed men came into my apartments in the course of an hour.

My messengers not returning at the appointed time from their errand to the town, I had at length retired to rest in the evening, when shortly before midnight they arrived, together with Sidi A'lawate, the Sheikh El Bakay's brother, and several of his followers, who took up their quarters on the terrace of my house in order to be out of reach of the mosquitoes; and after they had been regaled with a good supper, which had been provided beforehand by some of the townspeople, I went to pay my respects to them.

It was an important interview; for, although this was not the person for whom my visit was specially intended, and whose favourable or unfavourable disposition would influence the whole success of my arduous undertaking, yet for the present I was entirely in his hands, and all depended upon the manner in which he received me. Now my two messengers had only disclosed to himself personally, that I was a Christian, while at the same time they had laid great stress upon the circumstance that, although a Christian, I was under the special protection of the Sultan of Stambul; and Sidi A'lawate inquired therefore of me, with great earnestness and anxiety, as to the peculiar manner in which I enjoyed the protection of that great Mohammedan sovereign.

Now it was most unfortunate for me that I had no direct letter from that quarter. Even the *firman* with which we had been provided by the Basha of Tripoli had been delivered to the governor from whom it was destined, so that at the time I had nothing with me to show but a *firman* which I had used on my journey in Egypt, and which of course had no especial relation to the case in question. The want of such a general letter of protection from the Sultan of Constantinople, which I had solicited with so much anxiety to be sent after me, was in the sequel the chief cause of my difficult and dangerous position in Timbuktu; for, furnished with such a letter, it would have been easy to have imposed silence upon my adversaries and enemies there, and especially upon the merchants from Morocco, who were instigated by the most selfish jealousy to raise all sorts of intrigues against me.

Having heard my address with attention, although I was not able to establish every point so clearly as I could have wished, the sheikh's brother promised me protection, and desired me to be without any apprehension with regard to my safety. . . .

After a rather restless night, the day broke when I was at length to enter Timbuktu. It was ten o'clock when our cavalcade at length put itself in motion, ascending the sandhills which rise close behind the village of Kabara, and which, to my great regret, had prevented my obtaining a view of the town from the top of our terrace. The contrast of this desolate scenery with the character of fertile banks of the river which I had just left behind was remarkable. . . . Having traversed two sunken spots designated by especial names, where in certain years when the river rises to an unusual height . . . we approached the town: but its dark masses of clay not being illuminated by bright sunshine, for the sky was thickly overcast and the atmosphere filled with sand, were scarcely to be distinguished from the sand and rubbish heaped all round; and there was no opportunity for looking attentively about, as a body of people were coming towards us in order to pay their compliments to the stranger and bid him welcome. This was a very important moment, as, if they had felt the slightest suspicion with regard to my character, they might easily have prevented my entering the town at all, and thus even endangered my life.

I therefore took the hint of A'lawate, who recommended me to make a start in advance in order to anticipate the salute of these people who had come to meet us; and putting my horse to a gallop, and gun in hand, I galloped up to meet them, when I was received with many salams. But a circumstance occurred which might have proved fatal, not only to my enterprise, but even to my own personal safety, as there was a man among the group who addressed me in Turkish, which I had almost entirely forgotten; so that I could with difficulty make a suitable answer to his compliment; but avoiding further indiscreet questions, I pushed on in order to get under safe cover.

Having then traversed the rubbish which has accumulated round the ruined clay wall of the town, and left on one side a row of dirty reed huts which encompass the whole of the place, we entered the narrow streets and lanes, or, as the people of Timbuktu say, the *tijeraten*, which scarcely allowed two horses to proceed abreast. But I was not a little surprised at the populous and wealthy character which this quarter of the town, the Sane-Gungu, exhibited, many of the houses rising to the height of two stories, and in their facade evincing even an attempt at architectural adornment. Thus, taking a more westerly turn . . . we reached the house on the other side of the street, which was destined for my residence, and I was glad when I found myself safely in my new quarters. . . .

I was not allowed to stir about, but was confined within the walls of my house. In order to obviate the effect of this want of exercise as much as possible, to enjoy fresh air and at the same time to become familiar with the principal features of the town, through which I was not allowed to move about at pleasure, I ascended as often as possible the terrace of my house. This afforded an excellent view over the northern quarters of the town. On the north was the massive mosque of Sankore, which had just been restored to all its former grandeur through the influence of the Sheikh el Bakay, and gave the whole place an imposing character. Neither the mosque Sidi Yahia, nor the "great mosque," or Jingere-ber, was seen from this point; but towards the east the view extended over a wide expanse of the desert, and towards the south the elevated mansions of the Ghadamsiye merchants were visible. The style of the buildings was various. I could see clay houses of different characters, some low and unseemly, others rising with a second story in front to a greater elevation, and making even an attempt at architectural ornament, the whole being interrupted by a few round huts of matting. . . .

But while the terrace of my house served to make me well acquainted with the character of the town, it also had the disadvantage of exposing me fully to the gaze of the passers by, so that I could only slowly and with many interruptions, succeed in making a sketch of the scene thus offered to my view. . . . At the same time I became aware of the great inaccuracy which characterizes the view of the town as given by M. Caillie; still, on the whole, the character of the single dwellings was well represented by that traveller, the only error being that in his representation the whole town seems to consist of scattered and quite isolated houses, while, in reality, the streets are entirely shut in, as the dwellings form continuous and uninterrupted rows. But it must be taken into account that Timbuktu, at the time of Caillie's visit, was not so well off as it is at present, having been overrun by the Fulbe [Fulani] the preceding year, and he had no opportunity of making a drawing on the spot. . . .

The circumference of the city at the present time I reckon at a little more than two miles and a half; but it may approach closely to three miles, taking into account some of the projecting angles. . . . At present it is not walled. Its former wall, which seems never to have been of great magnitude, and was rather more of the nature of a rampart, was destroyed by the Fulbe [Fulani] on their first entering the place in the beginning of the year 1826. The town is laid out partly in rectangular, partly in winding, streets, or, as they are called here, *tijeraten*, which are not paved, but for the greater part consists of hard sand and gravel, and some of them have a sort of gutter in the middle. Besides the large and the small market there are few open areas, except a small square in front of the mosque of Yahia, called Tumbutu-bottema.

Small as it is, the city is tolerably well inhabited, and almost all the houses are in good repair. There are about 980 clay houses, and a couple of hundred conical huts of matting, the latter, with a few exceptions, constituting the outskirts of the town on the north and northeast sides, where a great deal of rubbish, which has been accumulating in the course of several centuries is formed into conspicuous mounds. . . .

The only remarkable public buildings in the town are the three large mosques: the Jingere-ber, built by *Mansa* Musa; the mosque of Sankore, built, at an early period, at the expense of a wealthy woman; and the mosque of Sidi Yahia, built at the expense of a *kadhi* of the town. There were three other mosques . . . . Besides these mosques, there are at present no distinguished public buildings in the town; and of the royal palace, or Ma-dugu, wherein the kings of Songhay used to reside occasionally, as well as the Kasbah, which was built in later times, in the southeastern quarter, or the "Sane-gungu," which already at that time was inhabited by the merchants from Ghadames, not a trace is to be seen. . . .

The whole number of the settled inhabitants of the town amounts to about thirteen thousand; while the floating population, during the months of the greatest traffic and intercourse, especially from November to January, may amount, on an average, to five thousand, and under favourable circumstances to as many as ten thousands.

Industry and Trade

The great feature which distinguishes the market of Timbuktu from that of Kano is the fact, that Timbuktu is not at all a manufacturing town, while the emporium of Hausa fully deserves to be classed as such. Almost the whole life of the city is based upon foreign commerce, which owing to the great northerly bend of the Niger, finds here the most favoured spot for intercourse, while at the same time that splendid river enables the inhabitants to supply all their wants from without; for native corn is not raised here in sufficient quantities to feed even a very small proportion of the population, and almost all the victuals are imported by water-carriage from Sansandi and the neighbourhood.

The only manufactures carried on in [Timbuktu], as far as fell under my observation, are confined to the art of the blacksmith, and to a little leatherwork. Some of these articles, such as provision or luggage bags, cushions, small leather pouches for tobacco, and gun-cloths, especially leather bags, are very neat but even these are mostly manufactured by Tawarek, and especially females, so that the industry of the city is hardly of any account. It was formerly supposed that Timbuktu was distinguished on account of its weaving, and that the export of dyed shirts from hence was considerable; but I have already had an opportunity of showing that this was entirely a mistake, almost the whole clothing of the natives themselves, especially that of the wealthier classes, being imported either from Kano or from Sansandi, besides the calico imported from England.

The export of the produce of Kano, especially by way of A'rawan, extends to the very border of the Atlantic, where it comes into contact with the considerable import of Malabar cloth by way of St. Louis, or Nder, on the Senegal, while the dyed shirts from Sansandi, which, as far as I had an opportunity of observing, seem to be made of foreign or English calico, and not of native cotton, do not appear to be exported to a greater distance. These shirts are generally distinguished by their rich ornament of coloured silk, and look very pretty; and I am sorry that I was obliged to give away, as a present, a specimen which I intended to bring home with me.

The people of Timbuktu are very experienced in the art of adorning their clothing with a fine stitching of silk, but this is done on a very small scale, and even these shirts are only used at home. There is, however, a very considerable degree of industry exercised by the natives of some of the neighbouring districts, especially Fermagha, who produce very excellent woollen blankets, and carpets of various colours, which form a most extensive article of consumption with the natives.

The foreign commerce has especially three great high-roads: that along the river from the southwest (for lower down the river there is at present scarcely any commerce at all), which comprises the trade proceeding from various points; and two roads from the north, that from Morocco on the one hand, and that from Ghadames on the other. In all this commerce, gold forms the chief staple, although the whole amount of the precious metal exported from this city appears to be exceedingly small, if compared with a European standard. It probably does not exceed an average of £20,000 sterling per year. The gold is brought either from Bambuk or from Bure, but from the former place in a larger quantity. The gold from the country of the Wangarawa does not reach this market, but, as it seems, at present is directly exported to that part of the southern coast which on this account is called the Gold Coast. The species of gold from Bambuk is of a more yellow colour; that from Bure is rather whitish; and that from Wangara has a greenish hue. Most of this gold, I think, is brought into the town in rings. I do not remember to have seen or heard of gold dust, or "tibber," being brought to market in small leathern bags, such as Shabini and other people describe, containing about one ounce, equal to twenty-five dollars in value. But, nevertheless, a considerable amount of this article must come into market, as most of the gold dust which comes to Ghadames and Tripoli passes through Timbuktu, while another portion goes directly from Sansandi to A'rawan.

It was evidently in consequence of the influence of the Arabs, that the scale of the *mithkal* was introduced in the trade of gold;* but it is a very general term, which may signify very different quantities, and thus we find various kinds of *mithkals* used in Negroland, especially those of A'gades, Timbuktu, and

---

*Initially, in the Middle Ages, the *mithcal* or *mitqal* was the standard weight of a gold *dinar*, or 4.233 grams; but this weight, as Barth shows, became greatly varied over time.

Mango, the Mandingo place between Yendi and the Niger, the former of which is the smallest, and equal, as I have stated in the proper place, to one thousand shells of Hausa standard, although in the present decayed state of the town of A'gades, where all the gold trade has ceased, it possesses rather an imaginary value. The *mithkal* of Timbuktu contains the weight of twenty-four grains of the kharub tree, or ninety-six of wheat, and is worth from three thousand to four thousand shells. The *mithkal* of Mango is equal to one and one-fourth of that of Timbuktu.   Besides rings, very handsome ornaments are worked of gold; but, as far as I could learn, most of this workmanship comes from Walata, which is still celebrated on this account.

The next article that forms one of the chief staples in Timbuktu, and in some respects even more so than gold, is salt, which, together with gold, formed articles of exchange all along the Niger from the most ancient times. It is brought from Taodenni, a place whose situation has been tolerably well established by M. Caillie's journey, and the mines of which have been worked, as we know from Ahmed Baba,* since the

*That is, the *Tarikh al-Sudan*, wrongly attributed by Barth to Ahmad Baba. But the error was forgivable. For the memorable scholar of Timbuktu Ahmad Baba (1556-1607) was the teacher of the actual writer of the *Tarikh al-Sudan*, al-Sadi, and was famous throughout the Western and Central Sudan as the author of notable works of Islamic scholarship, some of which, indeed, remain in use to this day.

A stubborn patriot of his chosen city, then a leading African center for Muslim studies, Ahmad Baba was among the prominent citizens of Timbuktu who suffered at the hands of the Moroccan invaders of 1591. Having denounced Moroccans for their invasion and occupation of Timbuktu, he was taken in chains across the Sahara to the Moroccan capital of Marrakesh, and detained there until 1607, after which he resumed his teaching and studies in Timbuktu. See an authoritative monograph by Mahmoud A. Zouber, *Ahmad Baba de* year 1596, when the former mines of Teghaza, situated some seventy miles further to the north, were given up. These salt mines of Teghaza appear to have been worked from very remote times, or at least before the eleventh century; and there can be little doubt that the mines of Tatental, described by the excellent geographer El Bekri as situated twenty days' journey from Sijilmesa, and two from the beginning of the desert, are identical with Teghaza. Even at that time both Sijilmesa and Ghanata were provided from here, while at least the eastern and original portion of Songhay was supplied at that early period from the mines of Tautek, six days from Tademekka. . . .

From Heinrich Barth, *Travels and Discoveries in North and Central Africa, etc.* (5 vols., London: 1857-1858). These extracts are from vols. 2, 4 and 5. A good modern introduction to Barth, and an anthology of his writings so far as they concern Nigeria, is A. H. M. Kirk-Greene's *Barth's Travels in Nigeria* (Oxford: 1962).

MARTIN DELANY

On Slavery

The first black American to be commissioned by President Lincoln with field rank in the United States Army, Martin R. Delany was a Harvard-trained physician who visited Africa in 1859-1860 by commission from the National Emigration Convention of Coloured Men which he had helped to form at Cleveland in 1854. With Edward Blyden, he was one of the earliest to understand the coming nationalist challenge, and to use the slogan of "Africa for

Tombouctou: sa Vie et son Oeuvre, Maisonneuve & Larose (Paris: 1977).

the Africans." Speaking at Philadelphia in 1852, he declared that:
"The claims of no people . . . are respected by any nation until
they are presented in a national capacity." A century later this
thought would sweep the whole African continent. His observations on the real facts of slavery in West Africa are of penetrating
and permanent value.

A word about slavery. It is simply preposterous to talk
about slavery, as that term is understood, either being legalized
or existing in this part of Africa. It is nonsense. The system is
a patriarchal one, there being no actual difference, socially,
between the slave (called by their protector son or daughter)
and the children of the person with whom they live. Such
persons intermarry and frequently become the heads of state;
indeed, generally so, as I do not remember at present a king or
chief with whom I became acquainted whose entire members
of the household, from the lowest domestic to the highest
official, did not sustain this relation to him, they calling him
baba or "father," and he treating them as children. And were
this not the case, it either arises from some innovation among
them or those exceptional cases of despotism to be found in
every country. Indeed, the term "slave" is unknown to them,
only as it has been introduced among them by whites from
Europe and America. So far from abject slavery, not even the
old feudal system, as known to exist until comparatively recent
times in enlightened and Christian Europe, exists in this part of
Africa.
Criminals and prisoners of war are legally sold into slavery
among themselves, just as was the custom in almost every
civilized country in the world till very lately, when nothing but
advanced intelligence and progressive Christianity among the
people put a stop to it. There is no place, however, but Ilorin,
a bona fide Mohammedan kingdom, where we ever witnessed
any exhibition of these facts.

Slaves are abducted by marauding, kidnapping, depraved natives, who, like the organized bands and gangs of robbers in Europe and America, go through the country thieving and stealing helpless women and children, and men who may be overpowered by numbers. Whole villages in this way sometimes fall victims to these human monsters, especially when the strong young men are out in the fields at work, the old of both sexes in such cases being put to death, whilst the young are hurried through some private way down to the slave factories usually kept by Europeans (generally Portuguese and Spaniards) and Americans, on some secluded part of the coast. And in no instances are the parents and relatives known to sell their own children or people into slavery, except, indeed, in cases of base depravity, and except such miserable despots as the kings of Dahomi and Ashantee; neither are the heads of countries known to sell their own people, but like the marauding kidnapper, obtain them by war on others.

From Martin R. Delany, *Official Report of the Niger Valley Exploring Party* (New York: 1861), p. 40.

ROBERT CAMPBELL

Yoruba Government

Although a Jamaican by origin, Robert Campbell may count, with Delany, as one of the earliest black Americans to visit and report on Africa. A teacher in chemistry at the Institute for Coloured Youth in Philadelphia, Campbell accompanied Martin Delany to Yorubaland in 1859-1860. He describes the politics of the Yoruba town of Abeokuta, and the importance of the Ogboni Society there. This was a device for the self-government of a community of people of different Yoruba loyalties that was typical of political development in these southern Nigerian lands, where the splintering impact of the slave trade, and the wars to which the trade had helped to give rise, had taken their full effect.*

    The government of Abeokuta is peculiar, combining the monarchical, the patriarchal, and no small share of the republican. Almost every free man, woman and child is a member of the Ogboni Lodge, of which there is one in every township or chiefdom. These lodges are presided over by elders of their own election, and the elders at the decease of the chief choose his successor from his relatives, generally his brother, seldom or never among his sons. . . . The successor of the king is also chosen by the chiefs and elders combined, their act being subsequently ratified by the people, assembled en masse. It is in this that the republican element of the government of Abeokuta is recognized. . . .

From Robert Campbell, *A Pilgrimage to my Motherland, etc.* (New York: 1861), p. 36.

---

    *For a detailed discussion of this trend, see K. O. Dike, *Trade and Politics in the Niger Delta* (Oxford: 1956), and B. Davidson, *Black Mother: The African Slave Trade* (Boston and London: 1961 and many reprints).

WINWOOD READE

In the Oil Rivers

By the middle of the nineteenth century the old but costly local prosperity of the slaving ports and little kingdoms of the Niger Delta had been replaced entirely by a still greater and altogether more acceptable prosperity from the sale of palm oil, then wanted in Europe as the only known basis for good soap. But by this time the long years of enmity, suspicion, violence and double-dealing had produced an atmosphere of bitter hostility between African and European traders. Winwood Reade was a radical-minded English landowner who travelled much in West Africa and wrote books that were widely read.

. . . We entered Bonny, the wealthiest of these rivers of corruption. Here the traders do not dare to live ashore, but inhabit the huge hulks of ancient merchantmen. . . . The trade [in oil] is active enough, but from its nature is attended with much delay. The Bonny natives go to market in the interior. The oil is brought to them little by little in calabashes. This they pour off into barrels. It is then brought on board one of the hulks, and is purchased with goods of European manufacture. . . . These black traders are now almost too much for the white ones in these matters of low cunning which enter so largely into commerce of a petty nature. The days have long gone by when charcoaled powder and coraline could be passed off [by European traders] upon the simple natives with impunity. A little can still be done with false weights and measures, but the good old days are gone for ever, and the natives have learnt to turn the dirty tables upon those who could once cheat them as they chose. . . . Among the whites there is no real unity: nobody trusts his neighbour. This gives the blacks a great advantage . . . . Rivals as they are, they [the blacks] can always combine with that honesty which is always the best policy. . . .

From W. Winwood Reade, *Savage Africa* (London: 1863), p. 53.

EDWARD BLYDEN

A West African Spartacus

Born of black parents in the West Indian island of St. Thomas, Edward Wilmot Blyden became one of the earliest and most distinguished spokesmen of the independent African spirit. He first went to Liberia at the age of seventeen, gained there an education at an American missionary school and, thanks to his brains and application, was awarded a professorship at the newly founded College of Liberia in 1862. Entering his adopted country's service, he became Liberian ambassador in London in 1877. Much of what he wrote is bone and sinew of the rise of West African nationalism, but a collected edition of his scattered books and papers has still to be published. What follows is an extract from his report to the governor of Sierra Leone on an expedition to the interior of that country, undertaken in 1872 during a period in British service at Freetown.

The present unsettled state of the [inland] country [of Sierra Leone] is owing to the influence of one Bilali, a native of the Kissy country, and formerly a slave among the Soosoos. About twenty seven years of age he ran away from his master, Almamy Mumineh, now residing at Kukuna, and founded a settlement between the Soosoo and Limba countries, to which numerous fugitives have, from time to time, betaken themselves.

By numerous accessions of that class of person, Bilali has succeeded in forming a powerful party, and in rousing a large portion of the servile population, not only to a devotion to the idea of liberty at any price, but a strong attachment to himself and a hatred of all who hold slaves; and he is by no means scrupulous as to the price he pays for their support.

On the other hand, the slave-holding chiefs, in various parts of the surrounding country, except those of the Limba district, have formed a combination against him, alleging, when appealed to in favour of Bilali on the ground of the abstract right of every man to personal liberty, the same argument that is always used by oppressors, viz., granting that Bilali has just cause for rebellion, granting that he is wise in perilling his personal ease and security for the sake of liberty, still his course (as they hold) is producing a confusion in the country, which will eventually beget a state of things much worse than that against which he and his allies have risen. Standing on the basis of this, to them conclusive argument, they are anxious to crush Bilali, but it seems that their combination is powerless against him. . . .

In the neighbourhood of Kukuna, the country gives sad evidence of the dire results of war. We were surrounded by lamentable illustrations of a war which had lasted during a whole generation; and it is difficult for one at a distance to frame any clear idea of a state of society induced by this protracted contest, kept up by determined slave-holders in the vain hope of reducing to servitude a man to whom there is no equal in the country for military prowess, tact, and ability.

Back to Africa

[1881] As those who have suffered affliction in a foreign land, we have no antecedents from which to gather inspiration. Now, if we are to make an independent nation—a strong nation—we must listen to the songs of our unsophisticated brethren as they sing of their history, as they tell of their traditions, of the wonderful and mysterious events of their tribal or national life, of the achievements of what we call their superstitions. We must lend a ready ear to the ditties of the Kroomen who pull our boats, of the Pessah and Golah men who till our farms. We must read the compositions, rude as we may think them, of the Mandingos and the Veys. We shall in this way get back the strength of the race, like the giant of the ancients, who always gained strength for his conflict with Hercules, whenever he touched his mother earth.

From Edward W. Blyden, M. A., "Report on the Expedition to Falaba, January to March 1872": *Proceedings of Royal Geographical Society 1872-1873*, vol. 17, p. 117. The second selection is from E. W. Blyden, *Christianity, Islam and the Negro Race*, inaugural address as President of Liberia College, Monrovia, January 5, 1881. I draw this extract from a valuable anthology edited with introductions by Wilfred Cartey and Martin Kilson, *Independent Africa* (Random House, New York: 1970). A masterly review of early West African nationalist thinkers such as Blyden will be found in D. Kimble's *Political History of Ghana* (Oxford: 1963), and J. Ayodele Langley, *Pan-Africanism and Nationalism in West Africa 1900-1945* (Oxford: 1972).

MARY KINGSLEY

In the Gaboon

Mary Kingsley wrote two important books which can still be read with enjoyment for their wit and understanding: *Travels in West Africa* (London: 1897), and *West African Studies* (London: 1899). Had she not died of typhoid while nursing Boer prisoners during the South African War, she would no doubt have written other books; and all who are interested in Africa must lament their loss. More than most Europeans of her day she was free of that stifling "paternalism" which saw in Africans a curiously "childish" branch of humanity. Although a British imperialist, she was shrewd and sympathetic at the same time. These extracts from her *Travels* give at least some notion of her wit and quality. They describe her wanderings in what is now the Republic of Gabon, or, as the English have generally written it, Gaboon.

Went alone for a long walk to the bend of the mangrove-swamp river to the east. It stank severely, but was most interesting, giving one the conditions of life in a mangrove-swamp in what you might call a pocket edition. Leaving this, I made my way northwest along native paths across stretches of trees growing on rolling hills and down through wooded valleys, each of which had a little stream in it, or a patch of swamp, with enormous arums and other water plants growing, and along through Fan villages, each with just one straight street, having a clubhouse at the alternative ends. I met in the forest a hunter, carrying home a deer he had shot; in addition to his musket, he carried a couple of long tufted spears, archaic in type. He was very chatty, and I gave him tobacco, and we talked sport, and on parting I gave him some more tobacco, because he kindly gave me a charm to enable me to see things in the forest. He was gratified, and said, "You ver nice," "Good-bye," "Good-day," "So long," "Good-night," which was very nice of him, as these phrases were evidently all the amiable greetings in English that he knew. The "So long" you often hear the natives in Gaboon say: it always sounds exceedingly quaint. They have of course picked it up from the American missionaries, who have been here upwards of thirty years.

Ascent of the Ogowe

About 9:30 we got into a savage rapid. We fought it inch by inch. The canoe jammed herself on some barely sunken rocks in it. We shoved her off over them. She tilted over and chucked us out. The rocks round being just awash, we survived and got her straight again, and got into her and drove her unmercifully; she struck again and bucked like a broncho, and we fell in heaps upon each other, but stayed inside that time—the men by the aid of their intelligent feet, I by clinching my hands into the bush rope lacing which ran round the rim of the canoe and the meaning of which I did not understand when I left Talagouga. We sorted ourselves out hastily and sent her at it again. Smash went a sorely tried pole and a paddle. Round and round we spun in an exultant whirlpool, which, in a light-hearted, maliciously joking way, hurled us tail first out of it into the current. Now the grand point in these canoes of having both ends alike declared itself; for at this juncture all we had to do was to revolve on our own axis and commence life anew with what had been the bow for the stern. Of course we were defeated, we could not go up any further without the aid of our lost poles and paddles, so we had to go down for shelter somewhere, anywhere, and down at a terrific pace in the white water we went. While hitched among the rocks the arrange-ment of our crew had been altered, Pierre joining M'bo in the bows; this piece of precaution was frustrated by our getting turned round; so our position was what you might call pre-carious, until we got into another whirlpool, when we persuad-ed nature to start us right end on. This was only a matter of minutes, whirlpools being plentiful, and then M'bo and Pierre, provided with our surviving poles, stood in the bows to fend us off rocks, as we shot towards them; while we midship paddles sat, helping to steer, and when occasion arose, which occasion did with lightning rapidity, to whack the whirlpools with the flat of our paddles, to break their force. Cook crouched in the stern concentrating his mind on steering only. A most excellent arrangement in theory and the safest practical one no doubt, but it did not work out what you might call brilliantly well; though each department did its best. We dashed full tilt towards high rocks, things twenty to fifty feet above water. Midship backed and flapped like fury; M'bo and Pierre received the shock on their poles; sometimes we glanced successfully aside and flew on; sometimes we didn't. The shock being too much for M'bo and Pierre they were driven back on me, who got flattened on to the cargo of bundles, which, being now firmly tied in, couldn't spread the confusion further aft; but the shock of the canoe's nose against the rock did so in style, and the rest of the crew fell forward on to the bundles, me, and themselves. . . .

Adventures in the Forest

I watched the gorillas with great interest for a few seconds, until I heard Wiki make a peculiar small sound, and looking at him saw his face was working in an awful way as he clutched his throat with his hands violently.

Heavens! think I, this gentleman's going to have a fit; it's lost we are entirely this time. He rolled his head to and fro, and then buried his face into a heap of dried rubbish at the foot of a plantain stem, clasped his hands over it, and gave an explosive sneeze. The gorillas let go all, raised themselves up for a second, gave a quaint sound between a bark and a howl, and then the ladies and the young gentleman started home. The old male rose to his full height (it struck me at the time this was a matter of ten feet at least, but for scientific purposes allowance must be made for a lady's emotions) and looked straight towards us, or rather towards where that sound came from. Wiki went off into a paroxysm of falsetto sneezes the like of which I have never heard; nor evidently had the gorilla, who doubtless thinking, as one of his black co-relatives would have thought, that the phenomenon favoured Duppy, went off after his family with a celerity that was amazing the moment he touched the forest, and disappeared as they had, swinging himself along through it from bough to bough, in a way that convinced me that, given the necessity of getting about in tropical forests, man has made a mistake in getting his arms shortened. I have seen many wild animals in their native wilds, but never have I seen anything to equal gorillas going through bush; it is a graceful, powerful, superbly perfect hand-trapeze performance.

Advantages of Wearing a Skirt

... But these Fans are a fine sporting tribe, and allowed they would risk it; besides, they were almost certain they had friends at Efoua; and, in addition, they showed me trees scratched in a way that was magnification of the condition of my own cat's pet table leg at home, demonstrating leopards in the vicinity. I kept going, as it was my only chance, because I found I stiffened if I sat down, and they always carefully told me the direction to go in when they sat down; with their superior pace they soon caught me up, and then passed me, leaving me and Ngouta and sometimes Singlet and Pagan behind, we, in our turn, overtaking them, with this difference that they were sitting down when we did so.

About five o'clock I was off ahead and noticed a path which I had been told I should meet with, and, when met with, I must follow. The path was slightly indistinct, but by keeping my eye on it I could see it. Presently I came to a place where it went out, but appeared again on the other side of a clump of underbrush fairly distinctly. I made a short cut for it and the next news was I was in a heap, on a lot of spikes, some fifteen feet or so below ground level, at the bottom of a bag-shaped game pit.

It is at these times you realize the blessing of a good thick skirt. Had I paid heed to the advice of many people in England, who ought to have known better, and did not do it themselves, and adopted masculine garments, I should have been spiked to the bone, and done for. Whereas, save for a good many bruises, here I was with the fullness of my skirt tucked under me, sitting on nine ebony spikes some twelve inches long, in comparative comfort, howling lustily to be hauled out. The Duke came along first, and looked down at me. I said, "Get a bush-rope and haul me out." He grunted and sat down on a log. The Passenger came next, and he looked down. "You kill?" says he. "Not much," say I; "get a bush-rope and haul me out." "No fit," says he, and sat down on the log. Presently however, Kiva and Wiki came up, and Wiki went and selected the one and only bush-rope suitable to haul an English lady, of my exact complexion, age, and size, out of that one particular pit. They seemed rare round there from the time he took; and I was just casting about in my mind as to what method would be best to employ in getting up the smooth, yellow, sandy clay, incurved walls, when he arrived with it, and I was out in a twinkling, and very much ashamed of myself, until Silence, who was then leading, disappeared through the path before us with a despairing yell. . . .

From Mary H. Kingsley, *Travels in West Africa* (London: 1897).

MACEMBA

Facing Invasion

By 1890 the invasion of many coastal and near-coastal regions was in full spate. It was bitterly resisted. In southern Tanganyika the main opponents were Hermann von Wissmann, commanding the German forces, and Macemba, ruling chief of the Yao people. When the empire-building Wissmann demanded submission by this ruler, Macemba wrote him—in Kiswahili—a memorable reply, and one that was characteristic of the African response. This letter has become known only in the last few years, thanks to the opening of the German colonial archives.

I have listened to your words but can find no reason why I should obey you—I would rather die first. I have no relations with you and cannot bring it to my mind that you have given me so much as a *pesa* [fraction of a rupee] or the quarter of a *pesa* or a needle or a thread. I look for some reason why I should obey you and find not the smallest. If it should be friendship that you desire, then I am ready for it, today and always; but to be your subject, that I cannot be. . . . If it should be war you desire, then I am ready, but never to be your subject. . . . I do not fall at your feet, for you are God's creature just as I am . . . . I am sultan here in my land. You are sultan there in yours. Yet listen, I do not say to you that you should obey me; for I know that you are a free man. . . . As for me, I will not come to you, and if you are strong enough, then come and fetch me. . . .

From the German version of the Kiswahili original in Archives of the *Reichskolonialamt*, No. 747, Deutschen Zentralarchiv, Potsdam, reprinted in F. F. Muller, *Deutschland-Zanzibar-Ostafrika* (Berlin: 1959), p. 455. Translated by B. Davidson.

SIR DAVID CHALMERS

The "Hut Tax War" in Sierra Leone

The Sierra Leone, largely Mende, rising in 1898 against British colonial taxation may be taken as characteristic in many ways of countless violent protests and upheavals that derived from the nature and consequences of colonial dispossession. It gave rise, as one should expect, to bitter controversies on the rights and wrongs of the matter; but I include an extract from the subsequent official report of a retired colonial judge, serving as the British Government's special commissioner, because it may serve as a good example of a European objectivity of judgment that was to become all too rare as early colonial enclosures fed into a rising anti-black racism after about 1900, at any rate in West Africa (European racism in East and Southern Africa went hand in hand, from late in the nineteenth century, with the advent of white settlers).

[1899] . . . In March [1898] a powerful chief, Momoh Jah, was arrested for not paying the Tax by a sergeant and twenty frontier police. Previous attempts had been made for his arrest, when he was not found, but the police seized goats, sheep, and cattle at his town, as many as they could find, and carried them off, some of which, it is said, they appropriated to their own use—an example likely to provoke retaliation.

I cannot doubt, therefore, that the lawless outrages and severities of the frontier police, when they were thus let loose, so to speak, in collecting the hut tax, materially contributed to bring about that angry discontent which, pent up and smouldering for a time, at last broke out in massacre and plunder.

The outbreak commenced on the April 26. Within less than a week, the male British subjects in Bandajuma, Kwallu and Sulaymah districts, with few exceptions, were murdered. A number of women also were murdered, and after an order went forth from the leaders staying the killing of women, they were treated as captive slaves. All property belonging to British subjects was plundered, except at Bonthe and York Island, which were saved by the arrival of the marines and troops. . . .

Whichever was the method, it seems clear that there was very definite prearrangement. Once started, the rebellious mob grew rapidly; at every place they came to, they were joined by their countrymen—those who were in sympathy and those who were compelled to join by threats; those who had paid their hut tax and those who had not paid. The more resolute pressed on the less resolute to join the war, and the stronger natures had their way. The police station, which was also the headquarters of the district commissioner at Bandajuma, was attacked, as was also that at Kwallu. The attacks, which seem to have had little system, were repelled with very little casualty on the side of the defenders.

The Mende rising, although really war, would be better understood as to many of its practical aspects if considered as a very aggravated riot. The riot once launched, various motives would come into operation. There was doubtless the all-pervading sense of the hostile treatment which had been meted out toward themselves, but it is in no ways necessary to suppose there was unity of aim among all who took part. . . .

The attack on the barracks at Bandajuma and Kwallu need have no more significance than the mad rush of a mob on a police barrack, which has occurred in our own country in less happy times than the present, when the mob was only guided by a temporary instinct for mischief or revenge . . . but the weight of the evidence very clearly points to the general and pervading motive to have been that the rioters, identifying all English-speaking people with the English government, and believing that in one way or other they [the English-speaking people] had taken part with and aided the government in bringing the hut tax, with its concomitant grievances, upon them, were wrought up to the desire of taking vengeance upon them.

A circumstance whither there is much reason to belive was connected with the murder of missionaries, seems in accordance with this view, and to confirm it. Missionaries had been in the Mende country for more than thirty years, and the native inhabitants had always been most friendly with them, so much so that in previous risings the mission stations had always been considered safe places of refuge. The animosity, so contrary to precedent, shown in the recent raid, has been attributed to the fact that the missionaries at some of the Mende stations had preached sermons shortly before the outbreak in support of the hut tax, and advising people to pay the tax. It is beyond doubt that such sermons were preached, nor does it seem improbable that the people considered the missionaries showed by these sermons that they identified themselves with the government in the enforcement of the hut tax. There is no evidence that the missionaries were disliked or feared as the introducers of a new religion or the enemies of old superstitions.

[The "disturbance" in the Mende country was quelled by two military expeditions; and of 158 persons brought to trial and found guilty, 96 were duly executed. For a detailed report and comment, see the monumental *History of Sierra Leone* by Christopher Fyfe (Oxford: 1962), *passim*. B.D.]

From Sir D. Chalmers, *Report by Her Majesty's Commissioner* . . . (London: 1899), vol. 2.

The Twentieth Century

A Few Signposts

*H*ERE WE MUST CALL A HALT. No brief guide to the literature of the twentieth century could be useful to the general reader, much less to the student. Far too much would have to be left out. For if books and papers about Africa become copious in the 1880s, in the years that follow they swell into a flood, and the tide is happily still rising. Yet the reader who has come with me as far as this may feel, as I do, the need for some rounding off and completion of the story, even though in summary and symbolic fashion.

The first fifty years of the twentieth century may be divided into three overlapping periods. From an African standpoint these may be labelled as the periods of subjection, stagnation, and struggles for liberation. The first begins really in about 1880 and continues until the end of "pacification" in about 1920. While some territories were taken without much warfare, others required a long military effort (even for the year 1915, Belgian records show as many as thirty "armed operations" against Africans in what was then the Belgian Congo and became Zaire in 1960); generally it will be true to say that about forty years were required to complete the colonial enclosure. This is worth remembering when we are told, as nowadays we sometimes are, that the establishment of the colonial system was a relatively peaceful and even benevolent affair. Three brief though painful extracts for this period will suffice. True enough, the enclosure of Africa was not always as crude and harsh as these suggest, and here and there it even brought relief to war-shattered lands; but since this book has borne frequent witness to the services of Europeans in Africa, it may be right to show at least a little of the other side of the medal.

A new political consciousness was growing up among Africans even during the years of subjection, and Charles Domingo, our next author, is no unworthy representative of that. The Pan-African idea was also coming forth at this time, and those who want to read about its origins should turn to Colin Legum's selection of relevant documents, *Pan-Africanism* (London and New York: 1962) as well as to other works of synthesis, notably V. B. Thompson, *Africa and Unity* (London: 1969), I. Geiss, *The Pan-African Movement* (London: 1974), and A. Ajala, *Pan-Africanism* (London: 1974).

During the next period, that of stagnation between about 1920 and 1945, the brutality of conquest paled, except in the Portuguese colonies and here and there elsewhere, to a dull uniformity of deprivation relieved now and then, though not often, by strenuous individual efforts at improvement. There are not many general books from this period that need be remembered except for a small category of thoughtful inquiries of which Norman Leys's *Kenya* (London: 1926), remains outstanding; but there is a vast documentation in the form of official reports and correspondence, much of which is now available to public inspection. At the same time there were other writers who had begun to devote their lives to scientific rediscovery. As a tribute to their work and that of their successors—often solitary, seldom recognized except by their colleagues, always demanding great physical and moral effort—I take particular pleasure in offering a fragment from my friend Theodore Monod's memoirs of Saharan travel.

Today we are still in the third period, that of struggles for liberation, which may be said to have opened in 1945, to have passed its first large milestone with the independence of Ghana in 1957, and to have begun to grapple with its second major phase, that of economic reconstruction, in the early sixties.

This period is already rich in books and papers of every kind. It is also, in a potent sense, the African present rather than the African past, for the dynamic trends set going by anti-colonial struggles are still in midstream of their development. Apart from the contents of state and other archives which gradually now become open to access, many of the leaders of these struggles set down their thoughts, and sometimes with a memorable clarity and breadth of vision. But they, too, are still part of the African present.

On the threshold of new approaches and enlightenments, however, there is room for a few indications; and so I close this anthology with three passages which point to the many-sided revaluation of the worth and validity of Africa's historical cultures and civilizations that remains in powerful progress.

K. SCHWABE

Colonial Conquest

The following is from an account of the German imperialist conquest of what Europeans then called South-West Africa, the Namibia of our own times.

In 1883-1885 the Bremen businessman Luderitz managed to obtain important land concessions—at first in the hinterland of Angra Pequena, later named Luderitz Bay—by means of treaties with various native chiefs. By 1884, the whole region between the Orange and the Cunene had become a German protectorate. . . .   [But the inhabitants objected, and this "protectorate" was soon threatened.]   Then, in the twelfth hour, Captain von Francois began the war in the course of which, through many victorious battles, he destroyed the power of Hendrik [Witboi], and an end to which was made at last by Major Leutwein, after fortunate but difficult battles, in 1894.

The overthrow of these powerful chiefs, whose names were known far beyond the boundaries of the colony . . . nonetheless did not avert the need for new warlike expeditions every year, so as to stifle the resistance of various tribes. In 1894-1895 the Hottentots of Khauas and Simon Copperschen had to be dealt with. The year 1896 saw heavy losses in the campaign against the rebellious Eastern Hereros, Ovambandjeru and once more the Khauas Hottentots. . . . Then came a period of apparent peace until the end of 1903 when serious troubles broke out in Amboland and on the Okavango as well as in the Bondelzwart region. And the Herero, who had long been systematically preparing their national uprising, used these troubles as a springboard. . . . [Massive operations were undertaken against the Herero, who were crushed without pity.] The

Herero people, who had brought such trouble to our protectorate, were driven into the waterless sands [of the Kalahari]
by a terrible though just fate. Thousands were killed and died
of thirst. . . .*

From Captain K. Schwabe, *Der Kreig in Deutsch-Sudwestafrika 1904-1906*
(Berlin: 1907). Translated by B. Davidson.

LEO FROBENIUS

Leopold's Congo

Leo Frobenius is best known as a pioneer writer on African
art, ethnography and history. Although not a liberal-minded man—
"Certainly," he wrote, "one must handle the Negro with a firm
hand"—he was disgusted by what he saw and experienced in the
Congo Free State of King Leopold of Belgium. Time has gratefully
erased much that happened then, yet the Congo Free State remains
an integral part of the history of a large part of Central Africa. It
was administered by a system that may be called colonialism at its
worst and most wasteful. Reporting in 1919, for example, the
Belgian Permanent Commission for the Protection of the Natives
came to the conclusion that the population of the country had
been "reduced by half" since the beginning of European occupa-

*For these appalling and even genocidal persecutions, see H.
Dreschler, *Sud-West Afrika unter Deutschen Kolonial-Herrschaft*,
Akademie Verlag (Berlin: 1966); and, in English translation, *Let Us Die
Fighting*, Zed Books (London: 1980), *passim*.

tion.* Here, from a copious Congo literature, is a passage from
Frobenius, who travelled there in 1904-1906, which suggests some
of the reasons why.

Everyone in the Congo State has accustomed himself to
exercise an illegal private police service, so that he becomes
independent. Later I will describe even worse events [than the
coercion and beating of Africans which he has just related],
such as when the missionaries of Bena Makima, although they
were living only two days from the government station, put the
chiefs of the Bakuba in chains, because these chiefs refused to
build for them; and such as when the Superior of Luluabourg
caused women who had voluntarily left the mission station to
be bound and brought back from the nearby government
station because these women were not "free." ...

The whole system rests upon a mean utilitarianism. While
the Company [that is, the Belgian concession company in the
area where Frobenius was] takes the severest measures against
any of its agents who may steal from it or falsify accounts or in
any way damage the company's commercial interests—while
the Company is absolutely merciless in these cases, yet it is
satisfied merely to dismiss those agents who are guilty of acts
of violence [against Africans, such as here described].... On
October 4, during our second stay at Kabeja, a sixth unhappy
Negro, the Kaloshi Watobelle, was captured. He too was a
Kapita [agent] who had failed to deliver his stipulated supply
of cotton. He must have been an excellent fellow, was a
Christian, and brought up at the mission of Luebo. He came in
the evening and was seized the next morning and held on the
ground. On one side stood a Kapita, on the other a European.

*Report of the Commission's third session, Leopoldville,
December 8-12, 1919, reproduced in *Bulletin* of Centre d'Etude des
Problemes Sociaux Indigenes (Elisabethville: Feb. 1953), p. 197).

Each held a whip. It sounded like a mill, flip-flap, flip-flap. And when one stick was broken, so another was quickly seized so that there should be no interruption in the rhythm. I counted 53 flip-flaps, or 106 blows. . . .

From L. Frobenius, *Im Schatten des Kongostaats* (Berlin: 1907), p. 95 and (for the last incident) p. 282. Translated by B. Davidson.

R. MEINERTZHAGEN

White Man's Country?

[Nairobi, Kenya, 1902] Apparently Charles Eliot, the High Commissioner, learned that Beatrice Webb is my aunt, so he asked me to dine with him this evening. My only clothes were a dirty old shirt and shorts. I explained my predicament and refused, but he insisted on my coming. He is not my idea of a High Commissioner, he looks more like a university don or a priest. He is a scholar, a philosopher, and a very able man with great vision. He amazed me with his views on the future of East Africa. He envisaged a thriving colony of thousands of Europeans with their families, the whole of the country from the Aberdares and Mount Kenya to the German border [i.e., of Tanganyika] divided up into farms; the whole of the Rift Valley cultivated or grazed, and the whole country of Lumbwa, Nandi to Elgon and almost to Baringo under white settlement. He intends to confine the natives to reserves and use them as cheap labour on farms. I suggested that the country belonged to Africans and that their interests must prevail over the interests of strangers. He would not have it; he kept on using the word "paramount" with reference to the claims of Europeans. I said that some day the African would be educated and armed; that would lead to a clash. Eliot thought that that day was so far distant as not to matter and that by that time the European element would be strong enough to look after themselves; but I am convinced that in the end the Africans will win and that Eliot's policy can lead only to trouble and disappointment.

From Colonel R. Meinertzhagen, *Kenya Diary, 1902-1906* (London: 1957). There appears to be evidence that Meinertzhagen doctored his diary in the long interval between writing and publishing it; but the substance of what he wrote reads genuinely.

CHARLES DOMINGO

The African Awakening

The roots of African nationalism lie in many fields, but one of them is certainly the Christian religion, especially in its African forms and communities. Probably born in Mozambique, Domingo became a missionary in Nyasaland (Malawi). His contribution to twentieth-century nationalism has been assessed in detail by George Shepperson and Thomas Price in the masterly book from which this striking citation is drawn.

[1911] Poor Resident, he thinks too much of his skin and not of his heart. What is the difference between a white man and a black man? Are we not of the same blood and all from Adam? This startles me much—is Europe still Christian or Heathen? . . . There is too much failure among all Europeans in Nyasaland. The three combined bodies, Missionaries, Government and Companies, or gainers of money—do form the same rule to look upon the native with mockery eyes. It sometimes startles us to see that the three combined bodies are from Europe, and along with them there is a title "CHRISTIANDOM." And to compare or make a comparison between the MASTER of the title and his servants it pushes any African away from believing the Master of the title. If we had power enough to communicate ourselves to Europe we would advise them not to call themselves "Christendom" but "Europeandom." . . .

From Charles Domingo, "To the Pastors and Evangelists," pamphlet, Seventh Day Baptist Historical Society, 1911, quoted in G. Shepperson and T. Price, *Independent African* (Edinburgh: 1958), p. 163.

THÉODORE MONOD

Rediscovering Africa

For long the director and guiding spirit of the Institut Français d'Afrique Noire at Dakar, Theodore Monod has been one of the eminent scholars that French civilization has given to the Continent. Pioneer of Saharan exploration, he traversed the daunting sands of the inner desert in days when motor transport was still a rarity. His brief and modest memoirs are a delight to read. They suggest by what process of resolute and painful discovery the cultural truths of Africa have been determined.

[1936] Tichitt [far out on the western fringe of the true Sahara] is very interesting. I should like to stop here so as to see more and see better. But the trail is long. Back to wandering again.

Now, by way of Walata, I approach Nema whence a last leap will take me to Timbuktu. . . .

More and more archeological discoveries: from the locality of Aghrejit alone I have more than a thousand prehistorical objects, among them some precious documents, for example, a splendid bone harpoon.

Excursion to Taokest . . . . A hard journey but fruitful: a bone boring tool.

I follow again the great cliffs of Tichitt towards the east. After Tennegue, traversing a gorge and seeing ahead some rocks which augur badly for an eye practised in the search for rock-drawings, I make sacrilegious vows to the gods that they should rub out any such drawings, or make it seem as though there had never been any. It's five in the evening, the night is drawing in, and the water-point is far.

A moment later I bump into a formidable site of Libyco-Berber engravings in excellent condition.   What to do? Impossible to lose such fine documents, impossible also to leave the work of copying them until tomorrow.

I halt the caravan and begin copying at 17 hours 30. And under what conditions . . . . At night; with a carbon lamp which suddenly decides to burn deplorably; and across a vertical face which I have to climb like a lizard on a wall, but a lizard with a drawing board at the end of its fingers instead of suction pads.

I finish the job towards midnight. . . .

From Théodore Monod, *Méharées, Explorations au Vrai Sahara* (Paris: 1947). Translated by B. Davidson.

VINIGI GROTTANELLI

Points of Arrival

Just as a few thoughtful writers have profoundly affected modern thought about the intellectual truths of "savage Africa," so have a few others changed the approach to African art. Dr. Vinigi Grottanelli is a distinguished Italian ethnographer.

Of European art—for example, of Gothic sculpture—no criticism would have been taken seriously if it had offered explanations based on banal generalities such as primitive faith, mysticism, collectivism; yet such crudities have been nonetheless accepted as true and profound when applied to Negro sculpture. . . .

African sculpture, like so-called primitive art in general, is not in itself "primitive" at all and nor were the men who created it. In considering it we are not confronted by primordial gropings, any more than by the spontaneous self-expressions of a suppositional (but nonexistent) "natural man."

On the contrary, we are looking at the outcome of ancient and most elaborate traditions. These are works not of exuberant youth, nor even less of inexpert childhood; they are the products of a conscious and thoughtful maturity, even of old age. They are not points of departure, but points of arrival. . . .

From V. L. Grottanelli, "Sul significato della Scultura Africana," Lugard Memorial Lecture, 1961, reprinted in *Africa*, Oct. 1961. Translated by B. Davidson.

ONWUKA DIKE

African History

Several Africans turned to the major task of writing African history in what I have termed the second and third periods of the first half of the century. One thinks especially of the Ghanaian, J. B. Danquah. But I have chosen to end this anthology with something from K. O. Dike, sometime chancellor of the University College of Ibadan, because his book on the politics of the Niger Delta was a pioneering and influential example of the way in which the rewriting of African history from a noncolonial standpoint began to free the world of destructive misconceptions.

The pivot of Delta social organization was the "House System" or "House Rule." This peculiar constitution is common to all the trading states and was the direct result of the trade with the Europeans. . . . The mixture of [African] peoples [in the Delta] often meant that African law and custom vanished and a new law and order was evolved based partly on African precedent and experience and partly on the lessons of the contact with Europe. In its full development the House became at once a cooperative trading unit and a local government institution. . . .

It was in the interest of every House Head to foster and increase the trade of his people: as trade cannot flourish under conditions of terror, the Heads must have used their absolute power with great discretion and restraint. . . . For the difference between the plantation slavery of the New World and the domestic slavery as practised in the Niger Delta lies in this: whereas in the former the slaves performed, on the whole, an indirect and impersonal service and were regarded as some form of capital goods, in the latter the wealth produced by a slave eventually set him free, for the master knew the slave intimately and the value of his work and rewarded him accordingly. It was this incentive, ever present in the House system, that made it in the nineteenth century an institution full of vitality, flexible, and in a large measure beneficial to all. . . .

From K. O. Dike, *Trade and Politics in the Niger Delta, 1830-1885* (Oxford: 1956).

Acknowledgments

I HAVE ESPECIALLY TO THANK PROFESSOR Philip Curtin, Professor J. O. Hunwick and Professor George Shepperson for generous help and advice, Professor E. H. Carr for permission to quote from him, and the London Library for its unfailing and often indispensable patience. Thanks for photographs are equally due to the American Research Centre in Egypt, Dr. A. D. H. Bivar, the Clarendon Press, Dr. Lyndon Harries, Mrs. F. Elwyn Jones, Professor J. Leclant, Professor R. Pankhurst, Sayed Hasan Thabit, and Mr. David Williams.

Acknowledgments are also due to the following for permission to quote copyright material:

Cambridge University Press for material from *Science and Civilization in China,* by J. Needham; the Carnegie Institution of Washington for material from *Documents Illustrative of the History of the Slave Trade to America,* edited by E. Donnan; E. H. Carr for material from his Trevelyan Lectures; the Clarendon Press, Oxford, for material from *Trade and Politics in the Niger Delta,* by K. O. Dike; *The East African Coast, Select Documents* by G. S. P. Freeman-Grenville; and from *Swahili Poetry,* translated by L. Harries; Constable & Co. Ltd. for material from *The Land of Zinj,* by C. H. Stigand; the Controller of H. M. Stationery Office for material from Plymouth Customs accounts (Crown-copyright); Federal Ministry of Education, Lagos, Nigeria, for material from *The Rise of the Sokoto Fulani*, by E. J. Arnett; *Lugard Lectures* (1955) by S. O. Biobaku, and *Sudanese Memoirs* by H. R. Palmer; Edinburgh University Press for material from *Independent African*, by Shepperson and Price; the editor of the *African Ecclesiastical Review* and the author for material from "Islam and Christianity in East Africa Before the Mid-nineteenth Century" by G. S. P. Freeman-Grenville; the editor of the *Ethiopian Observer* for material from the "Chronicle of Zara Yaqob"; the editor of the *Journal of African History* and the authors for material from "Ife and Its Archaeology" by F. Willett, "An Analysis of the Sources of Coins" by G. S. P. Freeman-Grenville, and "Maramuca" by D. P. Abraham; the editor of the *Journal* of the Historical Society of Nigeria and the author for material from "The Nok Culture in Prehistory" by B. A. B. Fagg; the editor of *Kush*, Khartoum, and the author for material from "The Decline and Fall of Meroe" by L. P. Kirwan; the editorial board of the *Bulletin* of the School of Oriental and African Studies and the authors for material from articles on dan Fodio and Muhammad Bello by M. Hiskett and A. D. H. Bivar; Chief J. V. Egharevba for material from his book *A Short History of Benin* (Ibadan University Press); the Government Printer, Pretoria, for material from *Records of South-eastern Africa* by G. M. Theal; the Hakluyt Society for material from *Europeans in West Africa* by J. W. Blake, *The Book of Duarte Barbosa*, translated by M. Longworth Dames, and *A Journal of the First Voyage of Vasco da Gama*, translated by E. G. Ravenstein; M. Hiskett for material from his translation of *Tazyin al-Waraqat*, by Abdullah Ibn Muhammad (Ibadan, 1963); J. O. Hunwich for material from his translation of al Maghili; the Institut Francais d'Afrique Noire, Dakar, for material from "Sundiata's Triumph," published in *Notes Africaines*; the International African Institute and the author for material from "Sul Significato della Scultura Africana" by V. L. Grottanelli, published in *Africa*; the Junta de Investigações do Ultramar, Lisbon, for material from *O Muata Kazembe* by A. C. P. Gamitto, translated as *King Kazembe* by I. Cunnison; Guy Le Prat for material from *Méharées: Explorations au Vrai Sahara* by T. Monod; Librairie Orientaliste Paul Geuthner for material from *Masalik al Absar fi Mamalik al Amsar*, translated by Gaudefroy-Démombynes; R. Mauny for material from his translation of *Esmeraldo de Situ Orbis*; Oliver & Boyd Ltd. and the author for material from *Kenya Diary* by Colonel R. Meinertzhagen; Penguin Books Ltd. and Penguin Books, Inc., Baltimore, Maryland, for material from *The Prehistory of Southern Africa* by J. D. Clark and from Herodotus: *The Histories*, translated by A. de Selincourt; the Loeb Library for other brief extracts from Greek classics; Presses Universitaires de France for material from M. Kati, *Tarikh al-Fettash*, translated by O. Houdas and M. Delafosse; Arthur Probsthain for material from *China's Discovery of Africa* by J. J. L. Duyvendak; Routledge & Kegan Paul Ltd. for material from Ibn Battuta, *Travels in Asia and Africa*, translated by H. A. R. Gibb, and *History of the Yorubas*, by S. Johnson; the Trustees of the British Museum for material from the account of Sir John Hawkins's voyage in Cotton MS, Otho E. viii, and the University of Chicago Press for material from *Ancient Records of Egypt*, by J. H. Breasted.

Index

GODLY SEED

American Evangelicals Confront Birth Control, 1873-1973

ALLAN CARLSON

Transaction Publishers
New Brunswick (U.S.A.) and London (U.K.)

Library of Congress Catalog Number: 2011018303
ISBN: 978-1-4128-4261-7
Printed in the United States of America

Library of Congress Cataloging-in-Publication Data

Carlson, Allan C.
  Godly seed : American evangelicals confront birth control, 1873–1973 / Allan Carlson.
    p. cm.
  ISBN 978-1-4128-4261-7
  1. Contraception—Religious aspects—Protestant churches.
  2. Birth control—United States—History. I. Title.
  HQ766.35.C37 2011
  261.8'36—dc23
                2011018303

Contents

For Betsy, again…

Acknowledgments

The idea for this investigation initially came from Howard Ahmanson, a philanthropist given to asking fresh questions about matters that have been conveniently forgotten, or deliberately buried. I deeply appreciate both his personal encouragement and the practical support received through Fieldstead & Company.

Others who have read all or part of this manuscript and offered most useful recommendations include Jeremy Beer, Bryce Christensen, D.G. Hart, James Kushiner, Mark Kalthoff, Bill Kauffman, Paul Mero, and Robert W. Patterson. I am also grateful for the special assistance provided by staff members of: the Billy Graham Center Archives at Wheaton College; the Medical Library and Archives at the University of Wisconsin-Madison; and the Library/Archives of the Wisconsin Historical Society.

Colleagues at The Howard Center for Family, Religion & Society—John Howard, Lisa Gibson, Larry Jacobs, and Don Feder—have provided their usual good help. Carol Griesbach and Lisa Youngblood have given valuable assistance with the word processing chores.

Finally, I note that a good marriage is one where each spouse opens new aspects of life to the other, so making their mate a better and wiser person and their marriage something greater than the sum of its parts. My wife Elizabeth, or Betsy, has taught me many things and has enriched my world in ways too numerous to count. To her, I am pleased to dedicate this volume.

Introduction:
The Christians
and Birth Control

...that he might have a godly seed.

—Malachi 2:15

For most contemporary Americans, contentious questions about birth control are considered a peculiar "Catholic" problem. With the use of contraceptives at some point being nearly universal among fertile adults (and quite common among teenagers, as well) and with birth control enjoying the blessing of state and federal governments as the alternative to both "unwanted" births and abortion, only a minority of especially devout Catholics seem to be left to puzzle occasionally over the issue. Even their interest is commonly understood to be a consequence of medieval thinking codified in Pope Paul VI's reactionary 1968 Encyclical, *Humanae Vitae*.

Mostly forgotten is the fact that, as recently as one hundred years ago, it was American Evangelical Protestants who waged the most aggressive and effective campaigns against the practice of birth control within the United States; Roman Catholics quietly applauded on the sidelines. It was Evangelicals who—starting in 1873—successfully built a web of federal and state laws that equated contraception with abortion, suppressed the spread of birth control information and devices, and even criminalized the use of contraceptives. And it was Evangelicals who attempted to jail early twentieth-century birth control crusaders such as Margaret Sanger. All the same, by 1973—the year the U.S. Supreme Court overturned the abortion laws of all fifty states—American Evangelical leaders had not only given a blessing to birth control; many would also welcome the Court's decision in *Roe*

1

v. *Wade* as a blow for religious liberty. This book traces the transformation of American Evangelical leadership from fervent foes to quiet friends of the birth control cause. It examines, in particular, the shift in motives for this change over time: from a sweeping culture war against all forms of vice; to a desperate effort to salvage dreams of Protestant world empire; to swelling anti-Catholicism; to fear of "population explosion," and surrender to a newly dominant culture.

The introduction focuses on three background questions to the broader investigation: What circumstances shaped teaching about contraception among the early Christians? Did the Protestant Reformers of the sixteenth century alter this teaching? And how should "American Evangelicals" be defined?

Sex and Civilization

Nearly two thousand years ago, what would become Western Christian Civilization began to take form in a time of growing sexual disorder. The moral and family disciplines of the old Roman Republic were fading, being replaced by the intoxications of empire. Slave concubinage flourished in these years. Divorce by mutual consent became easy and common. Adultery was fashionable and widespread.

In the swollen city of Rome, homosexuality emerged as an open practice. Indeed, there is some evidence that same-sex marriage might have occurred (even if never taken seriously by the law). As a poem attributed to the late second century put it: "The bearded Callistratus married the rugged Afer/ Under the same law by which a woman takes a husband./ Torches were carried before him, a bridal veil covered his face."[1]

There was also a disregard for infant life, with infanticide and abortion being regular practices. St. Ambrose wrote in the fourth century AD: "Women are in a hurry to wean their children; if they be rich, they scorn to suckle them; poor women expose their children; and if found, refuse to take them back; the rich, rather than see their fortune divided, use murderous juices to kill the fetus within the womb; men have not the affection of crows for their little ones."[2]

As early as 18 BC, Caesar Augustus—worried about the plummeting Roman birthrate—implemented the so-called "Augustan Laws," measures that punished adultery, penalized childlessness, and showered benefits on families with three or more children. These laws appear to have slowed the Empire's demoralization for about a century. Thereafter, the old trend lines returned.

Between 50 and 400 AD, and out of this same circumstance, the Fathers of the Christian Church—and in this case the usually unheralded Mothers of the Church as well—crafted a new sexual order. Procreative marriage served as its foundation. Importantly, they also built this new order in reaction to the Gnostic heresies which threatened the young church; and perhaps even human life itself.

The Gnostic idea rose independent of Christianity, but successfully invaded the new movement. The Gnostics drew together myths from Iran, Jewish magic and mysticism, Greek philosophy, and Chaldean mystical speculation. They also appealed to an exaggerated freedom from the law, in this case said to be proclaimed by Jesus and Paul. In this sense, they were *antinomians*; that is, they believed that the Gospel freed Christians from obedience to any law, be it scriptural, civil, or moral. The Gnostics claimed to have a special "gnosis," a "secret knowledge" denied to ordinary Christians. They appealed to unseen spirits. They denied nature. While they developed a mélange of moral and doctrinal ideas, most Gnostics shared two views: they rejected conventional marriage as a child-centered institution; and they scorned procreation.

This heresy posed a grave challenge to the early Christian movement. Indeed, the Epistles are full of warnings against Gnostic teachings. In *1 Timothy* 4, for example, Paul writes that "some will depart from the faith by giving heed to deceitful spirits and doctrines of demons....who forbid marriage." In *Jude* 4 we read that admission into the Christian community "has been secretly gained by...ungodly persons who pervert the grace of our God into licentiousness." *2 Peter* tells of false prophets corrupting the young church, "irrational animals, creatures of instinct,...reveling in their dissipation, carousing with you. They have eyes full of adultery, insatiable souls."[3]

Relative to sex, it appears that Gnosticism took two forms. One strand emphasized total sexual license. Claiming the freedom of the Gospel, these Gnostics indulged in adultery and ritualistic fornication. The Church Father Irenaeus pointed to those who "introduced promiscuous intercourse and marriages..., [saying] that God does not really care about these matters."[4] The Church Father Clement described abuse of the eucharist by the Gnostics in the church at Alexandria, Egypt:

> There are some who call Aphrodite Pandemos [physical love] a mystical communion....[T]hey have impiously called by the name of communion any common sexual intercourse.

3

This problem festered in the Egyptian church for at least two centuries. Indeed, Epiphanius, a future Bishop of Salamis, described in detail his involvement as a náive young man with a Gnostic group in Egypt that had infiltrated another local church; the year, about 335 AD. After a lavish meal of meat and wine, he said, the men of this group would exchange their wives and "indulge in promiscuous intercourse." This would be done, he noted, "not to beget children, but for mere pleasure." The group's rituals again included grotesque perversions of the holy eucharist, this time involving menstrual blood and aborted babies. In this episode, ninety members of the congregation were eventually excommunicated.[5]

Other Gnostics of the libertine persuasion taught that "marrying and bearing [children] are from Satan"; that sexual relations by "spiritual men," in and of themselves, would hasten the coming of the Pleroma, the Gnostic vision of "the fullness of the divine hierarchy of the eons"; and that the true believer should enjoy every possible sexual experience.

In marked contrast to this polymorphous romp, a second Gnostic strand totally rejected sexuality. Tatian led a faction called the Encratites, or "the self-controlled." According to Irenaeus, they "attacked marriage as corruption and fornication." He also complained that these Encratites rejected "the ancient work of God in forming mankind and implicitly blam[ed] Him – God – for making male and female for the generation of men."[6]

The so-called Gnostic Gospels drove these points home. In the *Gospel According to the Egyptians*, Salome asks: "How long shall men die?" Jesus is said to answer: "As long as you women bear children." From this, the ascetic Gnostics concluded that they could defeat death by ceasing procreation. They also celebrated androgyny, since a being without sexual identity could obviously not be procreative. The *Gospel of Thomas*, a favorite of modern feminist theologians, has Jesus saying: "Every woman who makes herself male enters the Kingdom of Heaven."

Considering these two Gnostic forms, historian John Noonan summarized: "The whole thrust of the antinomian [Gnostic] current was to devalue marriage [and] to deprive marital relations of any particular purpose."[7] Within the broad context of a Roman Civilization sliding into family breakdown and sexual anarchy, the young Christian church faced as well this infiltration of life-denying ideas into its own ranks. For Christian leaders, the question became: *Just what is marriage for?*

Answers came from several sources. Church leaders noted, for example, the fierce hatred shown by the Gnostics toward the Hebrew Scriptures. From Judaism, accordingly, the Christian could see children as a Divine blessing for their parents and for the community as a whole. As told in *Deuteronomy*:

> And because you harken to these ordinances, and keep and do them, the Lord your God will love you, bless you, and multiply you; he will also bless the fruit of your body....You shall be blessed above all peoples; there shall not be male or female barren among you....[8]

Genesis conveys promises from God to the patriarchs that their wives would be fruitful and that the Lord "will multiply your descendants as the stars of heaven and as the sand which is upon the seashore."[9] Throughout the centuries, the Jewish sages had declared that "One without children is considered as though dead." Another early source stated that "he who does not engage in procreation is as if he diminished the Divine image."[10]

A second Jewish inspiration may have been the small, ascetic Essene community, now known for compiling the Dead Sea Scrolls. According to the first-century historian Josephus, members of this order entered marriages "not for self-indulgence, but for the procreation of children."[11]

Still another source may have been Philo, a Jew trained in Greek philosophy, who expressed revulsion over pagan Roman pleasure-seeking. "Like a bad husbandman," he wrote, "[the homosexual] spends his labor night and day on soil from which no growth at all can be expected." The sexual act was for procreation, Philo insisted. Seeking a consistent sexual standard, he also opposed marriage to women known to be sterile.[12]

An additional source for early Christian leaders was apparently the Stoic ideal. Also repulsed by the sexual excesses of first- and second-century Rome, the Stoics—including philosophers such as Epictetus and Musonius Rufus—summoned reason to control human passions and behavior. Moderation in all things, including sexuality, was their goal. They also held that there was a natural law which gave purpose to human life and revealed acts unworthy of human beings. Sexual intercourse in marriage, the Stoics concluded, found its clear and natural purpose in the propagation of the human race. However, intercourse only for pleasure was suspect. As the first-century Stoic, Seneca, declared:

> All love of another's wife is shameful; so too, too much love of your own. A wise man ought to love his wife with judgment, not affection.... Nothing is fouler than to love a wife like an adulteress.... Let men show themselves to their wives not as lovers, but as husbands.[13]

Or as another Stoic text explained:

> ...we have intercourse not for pleasure, but for the maintenance of the species.[14]

According to John Noonan, Clement of Alexandria's influential work on the purposes of Christian marriage was simply "a paraphrase" of the Stoic, Musonius Rufus.[15]

And of course, these early Christian leaders also drew on the Gospels and the letters of Paul. The orthodox Gospel texts showed Jesus attending the wedding feast at Cana and performing there his first miracle, turning water into wine. Jesus also condemned adultery and divorce. In *1 Timothy* (2:15), Paul taught that "woman will be saved through bearing children." And in *Ephesians* 5, he equated the marital love of husband and wife to the bond between Christ and his Church:

> Wives, be subject to your husbands, as to the Lord. For the husband is the head of the wife as Christ is the head of the Church....Husbands, love your wives, as Christ loved the Church and gave himself up for her.... 'For this reason a man shall leave his father and mother and be joined to his wife, and the two shall become one.' This is a great mystery....[16]

All of these influences guided the early Church leaders to one conclusion: *the first purpose of marriage is procreation*. While also praising lifelong chastity, they refused to abandon the need for children. As Justin explained in the mid-second century: "We Christians either marry only to produce children, or, if we refuse to marry, are completely continent." Two centuries later, John Chrysostom taught that "there are two reasons why marriage was instituted, that we may live chastely and that we may become parents." Consistent with Greek and Roman ideals and recent Jewish practice, Christians also insisted on monogamy: one woman married to one man, for life.

In the year 400 AD, Augustine, Bishop of Hippo, wrote the book, *On the Good of Marriage*. He argued that God desired man's perpetuation through marriage. *Offspring*, he insisted, were an obvious "good" of marriage (the other two being *fidelity* and *sacramental union*). As Augustine elaborated:

> What food is to the health of man, intercourse is to the health of the human race, and each is not without its carnal delight which cannot be lust if, modified and restrained by temperance, it is brought to *a natural use* [i.e., procreation].

Augustine also insisted that the act of procreation included "the receiving of [children] lovingly, the nourishing of them humanely, the educating of them religiously."[17] Regarding contraception, he was equally clear: "Sexual intercourse even with a lawful wife is unlawful and shameful, if the offspring of children is prevented. This is what Onan, the son of Juda, did and on that account God put him to death."[18]

The Reformers on Procreation

The Protestants of the sixteenth century introduced no change on these matters. As demographic historian Flann Campbell has summarized:

> Even the coming of the Reformation and all it represented in the way of challenge to the dogmas of the medieval Catholic Church had no apparent influence on Christian doctrine concerning birth control. Protestant divines were as much in agreement on this point as they were in disagreement about others.[19]

The key figure in elaborating the Protestant family ethic was the former Augustinian monk and priest Martin Luther. In theological terms, however, Luther's opposition to contraception was actually amplified by his rejection of clerical celibacy.

Luther's critics have seen him as a failed celibate, a man unable to control his lusts. Luther blamed the doctrine of celibacy itself. For Luther, writing in his 1521 treatise on *The Estate of Marriage*, God's words in Genesis 1:28, "Be fruitful and multiply and fill the earth," represented more than a blessing; even more than a command; they were rather "a divine *ordinance* which it is not our prerogative to

7

hinder or ignore."[20] Addressing the celibate Teutonic Knights, the Reformer also emphasized Genesis 2:18: "It is not good that man should be alone; I will make him a helper who shall be with him." Setting himself squarely against the Papacy and the Church Councils here, Luther declared: "[w]hoever would be a true Christian must grant that this saying of God is true, and believe that God was not drunk when he spoke these words and instituted marriage."[21] Except among those rare persons—"not more than one in a thousand" Luther said at one point—who received true celibacy as a special gift from God, marriage and procreation were divinely ordained. As he wrote: "For it is *not* a matter of free choice or decision but a natural and necessary thing, that whatever is a man must have a woman and whatever is a woman must have a man."[22]

The Geneva-based reformer John Calvin put even greater emphasis on Genesis 1:28. He argued that these words represented the only command of God made before the Fall that was still active after God drove Adam and Eve out of Eden. This gave this phrase a unique power and importance. Calvin added that this "pure and lawful method of increase, which God ordained from the beginning, remains firm; this is that law of nature which common sense declares to be inviolable."[23]

While occasionally acknowledging in unenthusiastic fashion St. Paul's defense of the single life, the Reformers were far more comfortable with the social order described in Luther's *Exhortation to the Knights of the Teutonic Order*. "We were all created to do as our parents have done, to beget and rear children. This is a duty which God has laid upon us, commanded, and implanted in us, as is proved by our bodily members, our daily emotions, and the example of all mankind."[24] Marriage with the expectation of children, in this view, represented the natural, normal, and necessary form of worldly existence.

Marital fertility was also a spiritual expression. Luther saw procreation as the very essence of the human life in Eden before the fall. As he wrote in his commentary on *Genesis*:

> Truly in all nature there was no activity more excellent and more admirable than procreation. After the proclamation of the name of God it is the most important activity Adam and Eve in the State of innocence could carry on — as free from sin in doing this as they were in praising God.[25]

The fall of Adam and Eve into sin interrupted this pure, exuberant potential fertility. Even so, the German reformer praised each conception of a new child as an act of "wonderment ... wholly beyond our understanding," a miracle bearing the "lovely music of nature," a faint reminder of life before the fall:

> This living together of husband and wife — that they occupy the same home, that they take care of the household, that together they produce and bring up children — is a kind of faint image and a remnant, as it were, of that blessed living together [in Eden].

Elsewhere, Luther called procreation "a most outstanding gift" and "the greatest work of God."[26]

As his theology mandated, Luther sharply condemned the contraceptive mentality that was alive and well in his own time. He noted that this "inhuman attitude, which is worse than barbarous," was found chiefly among the well born, "the nobility and princes." Elsewhere, he linked contraception and abortion to selfishness:

> How great, therefore, the wickedness of [fallen] human nature is! How many girls there are who prevent conception and kill and expel tender fetuses, although procreation is the work of God! Indeed, some spouses who marry and live together ... have various ends in mind, but rarely children.[27]

Regarding the sin of Onan, involving the form of contraception now known as "withdrawal," Luther wrote:

> Onan must have been a most malicious and incorrigible scoundrel. This is a most disgraceful sin. It is far more atrocious than incest and adultery. We call it unchastity, yes, a Sodomitic sin. For Onan goes in to her, that is, he lies with her and copulates, and when it comes to the point of insemination, spills the semen, lest the woman conceive. *Surely at such a time the order of nature established by God in procreation should be followed.* Accordingly, it was a most disgraceful crime.[28]

On this matter, Luther was again joined by Calvin who, in the strongest possible terms, equated the sin of Onan with abortion:

> It is a horrible thing to pour out seed besides the intercourse of man and woman. Deliberately avoiding the intercourse, so that the seed drops on the ground, is doubly horrible. For this means that one quenches the hope of his family, and kills the son ... before he is born .... *When a woman in some way drives away the seed out the womb, through aids, then this is rightly seen as an unforgivable*

crime. Onan was guilty of a similar crime, by defiling the earth with his seed....[29]

Although a few dissenting clerical voices could be heard in England starting in the 1880s, Luther's and Calvin's sixteenth-century commentaries framed the accepted "Protestant" view of contraception into the early decades of the twentieth century.[30]

Defining "Evangelical"

The term, Evangelical, has had a variety of meanings. In its origins, the word was synonymous with Protestant, albeit embodying a positive witness to the Gospel rather than a negative "protest." This interchangeability of Evangelical and Protestant was found in the United States until about 1900 and is still common in Germany, France, and other parts of continental Europe.

In the United States and Great Britain, however, the label Evangelical has also become attached in a distinctive way to persons and institutions affected by the religious renewals or "Awakenings" that have periodically swept through these lands. The First Great Awakening, associated with figures such as Jonathan Edwards, George Whitefield, and the Tennent family, reached its peak in the 1730s and 1740s. America's Second Great Awakening, tied to names including Charles Grandison Finney, Lyman Beecher, and Lorenzo Dow, ran roughly from 1800 to 1840. Some observers of the great Revivals of Dwight Moody and Billy Sunday, which spanned from 1873 to 1917, thought that they were living in a Third Great Awakening.

In any case, the Evangelical spirit in this sense can be understood through certain commonalities:

- *The expectation of a personal conversion experience.* To be a Christian involves a wrenching process of being "born again." As understood from the time of Jonathan Edwards, this commonly starts with an overwhelming sense of one's sinfulness, followed by throwing oneself on God's mercy, followed next by an inpouring of the Spirit, or of grace, and completed by a deep sense of gratitude for being redeemed through Christ.[31] The "born again" Christian subsequently turns with enthusiasm to evangelization, seeking to bring others to Christ. The process has often been encouraged by "revivals" that feature sermons, hymn sings, prayer meetings, and altar calls, often lasting a week or more. The Revival Tent became a symbol of this style of Evangelicalism.
- *Disregard for denominational lines.* The conversion experience pays no attention to ecclesiastical structures. Evangelists have eschewed distinctions between Congregationalists, Episcopalians, Baptists,

Lutherans, Methodists, and so on: born-again Evangelicals might be found in all of them or in unaligned congregations. In consequence, Evangelicals have held little regard for church hierarchy. They have focused instead on building institutions that met specific needs: mission societies; tract societies; and the like. In the late twentieth century, this array of specialized organizations would be called "para-churches." The Evangelical "anti vice" societies, described in detail in Chapter 1, stand as solid late nineteenth-century examples of the same phenomenon.

- *The Centrality of the Bible.* The concept of *Sola Scriptura*, or Scripture alone as a guide to Christian belief, is shared by all Protestants. However, given their disdain for church hierarchies, Evangelicals have given the authority of the Bible still greater emphasis. Most Evangelicals have also affirmed the inerrancy of Scripture: that every word, phrase, and passage is literal truth, directly inspired by God.

Other common Evangelical traits should be mentioned. These include: *emotionalism*, which has been carried over from the conversion experience; *crucicentrism*, or stress on the sacrifice of Christ on the Cross; and—particularly among Americans—*a sense of living in a "chosen land" with "millennial purposes"* regarding the coming of the Kingdom of God.

The story which follows examines how American Evangelicals, so defined, moved from fierce opposition to quiet affirmation of the practice of birth control. Chapter 1 provides a novel interpretation of the career of "Purity Crusader" Anthony Comstock, who placed contraceptive information and devices prominently on his list of obscene materials. He emerges as the late nineteenth-century point man for a broad Evangelical defense of children and families. Chapter 2 explores the theology of Horace Bushnell, Josiah Strong, and other influential Americans who envisioned building a Righteous Protestant Empire, relying primarily on the high fertility of born-again believers. Crisis came when fertility among the Righteous fell sharply, leading to close attention to the question of birth control. Chapter 3 describes how birth control advocate Margaret Sanger skillfully exploited both old animosities and "new sciences" to shatter the millennia-old Christian consensus on birth control, beginning with the "mainline" Protestant churches. Chapter 4 shows how American Evangelicals of the mid-twentieth century, using peculiar Biblical exegesis, eventually followed the "mainline" into an acceptance of contraception. Chapter 5 examines the aftermath, as well as the actual demographics of American religious groups during this transition. Did the delay by Evangelicals in accepting birth control have consequences? Are these effects still evident today? The book closes by suggesting that the issue of birth control use by Evangelicals may be opening up again in the early decades of this, the twenty-first Christian century.

Notes

1. Quotation from: Anna Quindlen, "The Same People," *Newsweek*, June 9, 2008, 70.
2. From Carle Zimmerman, *Family and Civilization* (Wilmington, DE: ISI Books, 2008 [1947]), 249.
3. Similar warnings or admonitions are found in *1 Corinthians* (5:1–8; 6:12–13), *Romans* (6:1; 8:2), *Philippians* (3:18), *Galatians* (5:13), *2 Timothy* (3:6–7), *Ephesians* (5:5–7), and *Revelation* (2:14–15). Simon Magus, described in *Acts*, chapter 8, was most probably a Gnostic, evidenced by his use of magic.
4. Robert M. Grant, *Gnosticism: A Source Book of Heretical Writings from the Early Christian Period* (New York: Harper and Brothers, 1959), 47–48.
5. Giovanni Filorama, *A History of Gnosticism* (Oxford, England: Basil Blackwell, 1990), 183–84.
6. Grant, *Gnosticism*, 47.
7. John Noonan, *Contraception: A History of Its Treatment by the Catholic Theologians and Canonists* (Cambridge, MA: Harvard University Press, 1986 [1965]), 8.
8. *Deuteronomy* 7:12–14.
9. *Genesis* 22:17.
10. *Babylonian Talmum Nedarim* 64b and 63b. Cited in Lewis D. Solomon, *The Jewish Tradition, Sexuality and Procreation* (Lanham, MD: University Press of America, 2002), 89–91.
11. Josephus, *The Jewish War*, ed. and trans. H. St. John Thackery (Cambridge, MA: Harvard University Press, 1961), 2, 120, 160.
12. Philo, *The Special Laws* 3.36; quoted in Noonan, *Contraception*, 54.
13. Seneca, *Fragments*, ed. Friedrich G. Haase (Leipzig: Teubner, 1897), 84.
14. *The Nature of the Universe*, section 44; in Richard Harder, ed., *Ocellus Lucanus* (Berlin: Weidman, 1926).
15. Noonan, *Contraception*, 48.
16. *Ephesians* 5:22–23, 25, 31–32.
17. Augustine, *On Genesis According to the Letter* 9.7, CSEL 28: 276; in Noonan, *Contraception*.
18. In Flann Campbell, "Birth Control and the Christian Churches," *Population Studies* 14 (November 1960): 131.
19. Ibid.
20. Martin Luther, "The Estate of Marriage," in *Luther's Works, Vol. 45: The Christian in Society*, trans. W. A. Lambert (Philadelphia, PA: Muhlenburg Press, 1962), 18.
21. Martin Luther, "An Exhortation to the Knights of the Teutonic Order that They Lay Aside False Chastity and Assume the True Chastity of Wedlock [1523]" in *Luther's Works, Vol. 45*, 144.
22. Luther, "Estate of Marriage," 18, 21, 41. (Emphasis added.)

23. John Calvin, *Commentary on Genesis*, vol. I, part 4, trans. John King [1847], 5–6. http://www.idnet.org/pub/resources/text/ipb-e/epl-01/cvgnl-0.4txt

24. Luther, *Exhortation to the Knights of the Teutonic Order*, 155.

25. Martin Luther, *Luther's Works, Vol. 5: Lectures on Genesis, Chapters 1–5* (St. Louis, MO: Concordia, 1958), 117–18.

26. Ibid., 133.

27. Ibid., 118.

28. Ibid. (Emphasis added).

29. Calvin, *Commentary on Genesis*, vol. 2, part 16, 8–9, http://www.iclnet. org/pub/resources/text/ipb-e/epl-02/cvgn2-16.txt (Emphasis added).

30. Campbell, "Birth Control and the Churches," 132.

31. An early, yet remarkably detailed description of the conversion experience is Jonathan Edward's *Revivals, Containing a Faithful Narrative of the Surprising Work of God* (New York, Dunning and Spalding, 1832 [1736]).

1

Comstockery
and Contraception

The only effective laws suppressing birth control information and devices in American history were pure products of Evangelical Protestant fervor; nary a single Roman Catholic was involved. In key respects, these measures were actually the construct of one man: Anthony Comstock, a son of Connecticut, the last and—in a certain respect—the greatest of the Puritans. He won passage of a sweeping Federal measure that banned nationwide the import, sale, and distribution of contraceptive devices or information; another twenty-four state laws that effectively banned their possession and/or use: and judicial determinations that spread similar provisions to still another twenty-two states. Adopted mostly during the 1870s, none of these measures had been either repealed or significantly amended prior to his death in 1915; some residual aspects of the federal "Comstock Law" survive to this day.

Comstock's foes commonly spoke in fulminations. His "free love" contemporary D. M. Bennett called Comstock "a first-class Torquemada" who had shown "the same energy, the same cruelty, [and] the same intolerance" of "the envenomed persecutors of the past centuries." Bennett continued: "He has evinced far too much pleasure in bringing his fellow beings into the deepest sorrow and grief," and added: "It is seriously doubted whether the church has ever had a cruel zealot in its employ who has labored with more resolution and zest than this active agent of the Young Men's Christian Association."[1] Another "free love" advocate, Ezra Hervey Heywood, called Comstock "a religio-monomaniac" whom the U.S. Congress and "the lascivious fanaticism of the Young Men's Christian Association" had empowered to suppress free thought.[2]

More recently, literary historian Robert Bremner places Comstock as a featured exhibit in his supposed "national rogues' gallery

15

of reformers."[3] Biographers Heywood Broun and Margaret Leech, while not without a certain sympathy toward their subject, find Comstock to be "naïve beyond all other" late nineteenth-century reformers. Reflecting the worldview of a more sophisticated America, they are amused by: his effort to shut down Turkish belly-dancing and "hootchie-coochie" shows at the 1893 Chicago World's Fair; his attempted suppression of George Bernard Shaw's play on prostitution, *Mrs. Warren's Profession* (which led the British playwright to label "Comstockery...the world's standing joke at the expense of the United States"); his denunciation of art "which had been exhibited in the Saloons [sic] of Paris"; and his dismissal of French and Italian novels as "little better than histories of brothels and prostitutes in these lust-cursed nations."[4] Historian Paul Boyer finds Comstock to be "devoid of humor, lustful after publicity, and vastly ignorant."[5]

Even Comstock's political "descendants" in contemporary America, the socially conservative Religious Right, are either oblivious to or somewhat contemptuous of his legacy. This author's own rough survey of a dozen contemporary pro-family leaders found only one who had even heard of Anthony Comstock. Journalist Marvin Olasky, reputed architect of President George W. Bush's "compassionate conservatism," does briefly describe Comstock's work in his pro-life history of abortion in America. While the moral reformer supervised the arrest and conviction of over ninety abortionists in New York City during the 1870s and the successful suppression nationwide of advertising for the trade, Olasky is unimpressed, complaining that the Comstock laws "unwisely included contraceptive information and devices on its forbidden list."[6]

Who was Anthony Comstock?

The Flower of Puritanism

Biographers Broun and Leech are correct that Comstock was a man not really born for the late nineteenth century. Living out of time, "[h]e was the apotheosis, the fine flower of Puritanism." They elaborate:

> No other person connected with the cause of purity was so forthright, so colorful, so extravagant and fanatical. The square energetic figure, the passionate, whiskered face – here, at least, was a symbol, a caricature, a physical embodiment of the entire cause of purity and puritanism.[7]

Comstock was a product of Connecticut. During the 1840s, this state still held the reputation of being the most socially conservative and religiously orthodox corner of the land. Born March 7, 1844, in the village of New Canaan, Comstock claimed Puritan ancestry on both sides of his family, the first of whom had arrived in America in 1661. His father Thomas was a successful farmer, owning 160 acres and two saw-mills, with 30 employees. His mother—Polly Lockwood Comstock—was the real influence in his life. Bearing ten children (seven of whom survived to adulthood), she reared them in the stern Puritan faith most recently invigorated by the spiritual enthusiasms of the Second Great Awakening. While Polly Comstock died when Anthony was age ten, her Bible readings, morality tales, prayer life, and frequent church attendance profoundly shaped his character. Over a half-century later, Comstock would tell an interviewer that the "whole purpose of his life" had been to honor the memory of his mother.[8]

Young Comstock attended the district school near his farm and then enrolled in the New Academy run by the New Canaan Congregational Church. Here, he learned something of writing (he went on to author several popular books and numerous articles, although spelling would be a lifelong problem) and gained his frame of reference, his vocabulary, and his perception of duty. Commenting on his Church's 150th Anniversary, Comstock explained: "I carried into my daily life the lessons I learned here, and if I have accomplished anything in the cause of moral purity..., it is because I have...been true to the principles taught me here."[9] His faith was indeed strong. Common to him were the sentiments he recorded in his diary in spring 1863, then age nineteen: "One of the sweetest days of my life, so near to Jesus.... Not myself, not a whit, but all, all in Christ. His grace shed abroad in my heart. O to praise him with a pure heart in Spirit and Truth."[10]

Shortly thereafter, Comstock's older brother Samuel died from wounds received at Gettysburg, and Anthony felt duty-bound to enlist in his place in the Seventeenth Connecticut Regiment. He mostly saw occupation duty in a peaceful corner of Florida. Appalled by "the oaths of wicked men" heard in the barracks, he recruited a circle of about twenty-five young soldiers who took a contrary oath that "they would not swear, drink, nor chew tobacco" while they were in the army. Comstock became a sort of volunteer chaplain and recruited nearby clergymen to preach to his group. He attended four to nine such services *a week*. He also taught newly freed slaves how to read and spell[!]. Comstock's lack of compassion for public sinners showed as he poured his whiskey and rum rations on the ground before his drinking comrades-in-arms. His diary entries from this time reveal a young man struggling with his own temptations: "If I could but live without sin, I should be the happiest soul living: but Sin, that foe is ever lurking, stealing happiness from me." During the last few months of his enlistment, Comstock became an agent of the Christian Commission, a ministry to the military organized by the new and ambitious Young Men's Christian Association (YMCA).[11]

Down at the YMCA

The years immediately following the Civil War were in their own way harrowing and disturbing, nowhere more so than in New York. Memories of that city's antidraft riots of July 1863 were still vivid, when mobs roamed the streets, sacked homes, stores, and armories, and killed eighteen people. Only the dispatch of Federal troops and the deaths of four hundred rioters finally brought some order. City authorities faced the "dreadful revelations" that "a great, ignorant, irresponsible class" and "the fires of a social revolution" lay "just beneath their feet."[12]

More broadly, the late 1860s launched the reign of the Robber Barons within a web of rampant financial speculation; the emergence of female emancipation, personified in New York by the "wild" sisters Victoria Woodhull and Tennessee Claflin, who managed to combine stock speculation, socialism, spiritualism, and free love; widespread political corruption, seen in New York's Boss Tweed ring and Tammany Hall; political scandals such as the Credit Mobilier affair; justice for sale, via bribe-taking police and judges; and a veritable explosion in the number of New York saloons, gambling halls (two thousand and climbing by 1870), and houses of prostitution. As Margaret Leech has ably summarized: "Social behavior, notoriously lax in the years succeeding war, dissolved in the easy warmth of plentiful money. All that was vulgar in the Republic, all that was raw and crude, rose to the surface and floated there."[13]

At the religious level, evangelical Christians faced fresh challenges as well, notably the fundamental theological problems posed by Charles Darwin and by the new historicist critics of the Bible. All the same, the strong currents of the Second Great Awakening, launched from Yale Divinity School around 1800, continued to flow. The number of church edifices was 38,183 in 1850; by 1890, 142,521, an increase of 272 percent. Church membership and attendance figures also soared. Dwight L. Moody and Ira D. Sankey, fresh from unanticipated success in Great Britain, brought their Revival Crusade back to America in 1875; Moody explained: "I do not know of anything that America needs more today than men and women on fire with the fire of heaven." Millions responded.[14]

The YMCA "was in the vanguard of the 'evangelical empire' in an increasingly Christian America."[15] Across the country, religious societies or parachurches were mushrooming, all seeking to carry the Gospel from the churches into the streets. Among these Christian Industrial Clubs, Magdalen Homes, Purity Alliances, Reserve Midnight Missions, White Cross clubs, Salvation Armies, and temperance societies, the YMCA and its sister Young Women's Christian Association stood out as "prestigious organizations for directing the evangelistic fervor."[16] Launched in London in 1844, the first American YMCA organized in Boston in 1851; the New York branch came a year later.

The YMCA's core task was to save the young males pouring into the cities from the "traps of immorality" awaiting them. In 1866, the New York YMCA issued a report on that city "As a Field for Moral and Christian Effort Among Young Men." As of 1860, males aged 15–40 formed 46 percent of New York's population. "Many are utter strangers from the country and Europe," while employers no longer looked after "the social and moral interests of young men"; they "are consequently led to frequent saloons and like places, where they are exposed to the most contaminating influences." The YMCA report precisely counted 3,417 female prostitutes in the city (many disguised as "pretty waiter girls"), 653 billiard tables in the saloons, and bar rooms serving 600 barrels of beer a day. Turning to "Obscene Books and Papers," it continued:

> The traffic in these is most extensive. They are to be obtained at very many newspaper stands....[A]t one place, on a principal thoroughfare, there are openly exposed for sale two vile weekly newspapers, which can be purchased at ten cents a copy, and more than fifty kinds of licentious books, each one illustrated by one or two cuts... [T]he proprietor will [also] show [an interested buyer] a catalogue of a large number much more vulgar and atrocious, illustrated with the most obscene cuts.... The debasing influence of these publications on young men cannot be overestimated: they are the feeder of brothels.[17]

In response, the YMCA sent lobbyists to Albany in 1866, seeking a state law for "the suppression of obscene literature." Two years later, such a bill passed. However, convictions were few and by 1871 "the traffic was more open than ever."[18]

Into this situation stepped Anthony Comstock. His family farm in Connecticut had been lost in the war; and his father had remarried. Comstock moved to Tennessee and worked for a time as a construction superintendent at Lookout Mountain. Disliking the trade, in 1866 he joined the flow of war veterans into New York City. He took a job as a porter for Ammidon, Lane & Co., a dry goods establishment, earning $12 a week. Later, he became a clerk. In these early months, he spent many lonely evenings, fearing "for his soul, and for the souls of the young men he boarded with." He soon joined the YMCA, finding direction in its lectures and pamphlets. Two years later, he attended a lecture on obscene literature, and left very disturbed.[19]

Comstock's early arrests as a "volunteer detective" set a pattern for his later life. His first action took place in 1868, apparently after a friend of his had purchased a pornographic book, visited a brothel, and contracted a venereal disease. Comstock blamed the original book merchant, Charles Conroy. He tracked him down, made a citizen's arrest, and turned him over to the police.[20] Several years later, he launched a successful campaign against two saloons in his neighborhood that openly violated the Sunday closing law. Lending him legal and financial support were Mr. and Mrs. H. B. Spelman, prominent New Yorkers whose daughter would later marry a Rockefeller. Comstock wrote in his diary: "They both seem so earnest.... Give me a man who dares to do right and one ready at all times to discharge his duty to the community and to God."[21] Throughout his career, Comstock skillfully recruited such wealthy and influential backers.

In January 1871, Comstock married Margaret Hamilton, daughter of a Presbyterian elder whose business had failed. At age thirty-six, she was ten years his senior. "Maggie" nonetheless filled him with joy. "O so bright, so sweet," he confided in his diary. "O let me consecrate myself to the one who has bestowed all this upon me. Let my home, my all, be his.... It is so bright and sweet now to live."[22] In December, Maggie bore a daughter, Lillie; the baby died the following summer. "The Lord's will be done," Comstock wrote on the night of her death. They had no other natural children. However, Comstock and Maggie did soon after adopt a newborn found beside its dying mother in a Chinatown tenement. Named Adele, Comstock's chief biographers report (in strangely uncharitable words) that she "was never very bright. She grew into a straggling, subnormal child." (Shortly after Comstock's death, a judge placed Adele—now age forty-three—in an institution.)[23] During the first years of their marriage, the Comstocks lived in a house in Brooklyn. Later, joined by Maggie's invalid sister, the family moved to a New Jersey suburb.

In early 1872, Comstock sought to expand his volunteer work for the YMCA. He wrote a clumsy letter to YMCA Secretary Robert McBurney, describing his own take on the horrors of the trade in obscene books and materials in New York, and asking for the organization's help in suppressing this business. McBurney sent the letter back to Comstock, asking that it be rewritten. Meanwhile, the YMCA's new President—Morris K. Jesup—had seen the letter on McBurney's desk. Intrigued by Comstock's spirit, Jesup visited the young man in the store where he worked. A more thorough interview took place in Jesup's Madison Avenue mansion. Comstock's career as a Christian warrior against all forms of vice, including most especially contraception, would soon commence.[24]

Obscenity and Contraception

Historian Nicola Beisel correctly argues that Comstock's intellectual and political achievement "was to link abortion and contraception to the availability of obscene literature in city streets."[25] Countless observers have pointed to both aspects of this linkage—abortion equals contraception and both acts equal obscenity—as naïve, foolish, and the product of raw ignorance. In truth, Comstock's views on contraception were framed by his sense of the dangers facing children and by his own psychology of the human mind; and they enjoyed the full support of a new and progressive American medical leadership.

In Comstock's mind, all his work focused on the protection of the young. As he explained to his colleagues, children were the Devil's first target: "We have been assigned by the Great Commander to constantly face some of the most insidious and deadly forces of evil that Satan is persistently aligning against the integrity of the children of the present age."[26] In defending his "sting"-like detective practices before a hostile judge, Comstock declared that "my integrity is an essential element in the success of the defence of the twenty millions of children in this country from the moral 'cancer planters'...."[27] Writing for the *North American Review*, Comstock reiterated the number of children at risk: "upwards of twenty million of youth and children are in the plastic, or receptive state, open to every insidious teacher, and subject to every bad influence—a period of life when character is forming."[28]

Indeed, while using different language, Comstock would have agreed with contemporary theorists about the addictive nature of pornography, particularly when introduced to the young. As Comstock wrote in 1880: "The susceptible mind of the boy receives impressions that set on fire his whole nature. His imagination is perverted. A black stain is fixed indelibly upon it, and conscience, once a faithful monitor, is now seared and silenced."[29] Later, he elaborated:

> In the heart of every child there is *a chamber of imagery*, memory's storehouse, the commissary department in which is received, stored up and held in reserve every good or evil influence for future requisition....
>
> If you allow the devil to decorate the Chamber of Imagery in your heart with licentiousness and sensual things, you will find that he has practically thrown a noose about your neck and will forever exert himself to draw you away from the 'Lamb of God which taketh away sins of the world.'
>
> If you open the door to anything, the filth will all pour in and the degradation of youth will follow.[30]

Comstock reported how one obscene book, "in thirty six hours after it had been delivered in a sealed package from the mails to a boy to whom it had been sent, was found to have passed through thirteen different boys' hands," so doing "its work of destruction and defilement."[31] The suppression of this trade, he argued, must be thorough and complete.

It is important to note that the post-1865 surge in obscene materials was driven in large part by new technologies—notably photography and vulcanized rubber—which entrepreneurs in the sex trade quickly exploited. Were these items truly pornographic? Historian Richard C. Johnson says "yes": "the vast majority of the materials which [Comstock] found were…specifically and without question designed to take commercial advantage of prurience."[32] A more authoritative answer comes from James Petersen, a longtime editor of *Playboy* and author of that magazine's "history of the Sexual Revolution," entitled *A Century of Sex*. He writes: "Comstock never described the objects he suppressed, but some pictures survive. Even today these postcards have the power to arouse." Among others, Petersen describes "a series from San Juan" which shows a bemused nude woman in a straw hat aiming a stars-and-stripes dildo at her male partner.[33]

All the same, Comstock's linkages of obscenity to birth control and of birth control to abortion seem to modern minds unclear and disjointed. Broun and Leech note that "[i]n no cause did he show a more passionate zeal than in the fight against the purveyors of contraceptive remedies or devices."[34] And yet, there is little evidence that other leaders in the antiobscenity campaign shared the same animus, beyond a vague association between obscene books and improper devices. Comstock, in historian Janet Brodie's words, was clearly "hostile to abortion and the prevention of conception, and it was largely his focused energy that secured the criminalization of reproductive control" at both the Federal and state levels. She goes on to suggest that Comstock's own near-childlessness had a psychodynamic effect, creating "hostility toward women who could bear children but chose not to."[35] While this may have been a factor, simpler and more direct explanations also exist. What were Anthony Comstock's beliefs regarding contraception?

To begin with, Comstock had at least a rough sense of a natural law that encompassed human sexuality. In chiding a young female journalist for seeking a decriminalization of contraception, Comstock appealed to "Nature's law." He added:

> The prevention of conception would work the greatest demoralization. God has set certain natural barriers. If you turn loose the passions and break down the fear you bring…disaster…. It would debase sacred things, break down the health of women, and disseminate a greater curse than the plagues and diseases of Europe.[36]

Second, his own practical experience showed that dealers in obscene books and prints also commonly sold contraceptives and abortifacients. As he wrote about one of his early arrests for the YMCA, pornographic books "were publicly advertised and sold in connection with articles for producing abortion, prevention of conception, articles to aid seductions, and for indiscrete and immoral purposes."[37] Other early arrests involved a mix of printed items together with immoral "rubber goods" [this phrase encompassed masturbation aids and early condoms and diaphragms] and syringes for abortion.[38] Comstock and his allies also associated contraception with prostitution because such pleasure houses frequently sold birth control potions and devices on the side.[39]

Third, Comstock believed that the availability of contraceptives encouraged immoral behavior. In an early report to his backers, Comstock explained how obscene words and pictures were tied to birth control and promiscuity. Such literature, he said, was "cunningly calculated to inflame the passions and lead the victims from one step of vice to another, ending in utmost lust." With victims "polluted in thought and imagination,... the authors of their debasement [then] present a variety of implements by the aid of which they promise them the practice of licentiousness without its direful consequences."[40] Birth control allowed the despoilers of the innocents "to minister to the most degrading appetites" and "conceal the crime which may be contemplated or per chance already committed."[41]

Finally, Comstock linked abortion and contraception together for the common danger they posed to women's health. In this view, Comstock actually stood in solidarity with the cutting-edge medical authorities of his day.

During these years, the ancient practice of midwifery was giving way to the modern discipline of gynecology. A key figure in this transition was D. Humphreys Storer, MD, Professor of Midwifery at Harvard University. In 1855, he gave the Introductory Lecture to the new Medical Class at the University. Entitled "Two Frequent Causes of Uterine Disease," he pointed first to the growing practice among new brides of turning "to means, readily procurable, to destroy the life within her." Storer underscored "the probability of there being increased detriments and irretrievable harm" to the woman's own body. The second cause of an upswing in uterine disease, he reported, was "the means so extensively employed to prevent conception." While some doctors who rejected abortion accepted contraception, Storer insisted that interference of any sort with the sexual act would produce trouble: "If...the operations of nature are interrupted, different results must follow.... [N]umberless cases of induration, and finally of organic disease, must be the inevitable consequences."[42]

For unclear reasons, Harvard suppressed publication of the lecture for fifteen years. However, Storer's son, Horatio Robinson Storer, MD, kept the issue alive. He played a key role in guiding the American Medical Association (AMA) to a fresh condemnation of abortion, except to save a mother's life. In his prize-winning 1865 AMA essay, "The Criminality and Physical Evils of Forced Abortions," the younger Storer also concluded: "Intentionally to prevent the occurrence of pregnancy, otherwise than by total abstinence from coition, intentionally to bring it, when begun, to a premature close, are *alike disastrous to a woman's mental, moral, and physical well-being*."[43]

A year later, E. M. Buckingham, MD, writing in *The Cincinnati Lancet and Observer*, added his voice: "The evil results of the whole system of avoiding offspring in the married state are so palpable and so gross, that one can scarcely find language strong enough to denounce it in suitable manner." He cited the "catalogue of the female diseases" caused by these practices.[44]

These architects of modern gynecology received important support from two major works published in 1870. In *Conjugal Sins*, Augustus K. Gardner—Professor of Diseases of Females and Clinical Midwifery at New York Medical College—asserted that "[l]ocal congestions, nervous affections and debilities are the direct and indisputable results of *coitus imperfecti*...." Whenever contraceptives were used, "sexual congress is thus rendered but a species of self-abuse." Gardner concluded: "Inquiry of any gynecologist will convince the most skeptical that *the general employment of any means for the prevention of conception is fraught with injury to the female certainly*, if not to the other sex also."[45] In *The Preventive Obstacle, or Conjugal Onanism*, the French physician L. F. E. Bergeret used a lifetime of clinical work to conclude that "Genesiac frauds [contraception] may provoke in [the woman] diseases of the genital organ, from simple inflammation to the most serious degenerations." Regarding uterine cancer, for example, he reported that "[w]hen I review in my memory all the cases of cancers of the womb which have come under my observation, I *do not really recall one* which was not preceded by sexual frauds [another term for birth control]." Blurring distinctions still more, Bergeret declared that "[e]very fraud is an indirect infanticide; a germ lost and made unproductive."[46]

Despite his dismal reports, Bergeret refused to despair. He doubted that ancient morals had been any better than those of modern times. Indeed, "[m]orals have undoubtedly improved with time; but *there remain some ancient errors to reform*." He called on all physicians to proclaim "that man cannot with impunity transgress that great behest of nature, that imperative law presiding over the propagation of the human race...: '*Crescite et multiplicamini*' [be fruitful and multiply]."[47] In short, Comstock could see his own suppression of contraceptives as an act in line with the very best medical advice, for the protection of women's health, and as an expression of future hope.

What was Comstock's alternative to birth control for persons facing the "hard cases"? His answer was simple: "Can they not use *self*-control? Or must they sink to the level of the beasts?"[48] And in truth, this had been the orthodox Christian answer for about 1,800 years.

The Consummate Advocate

From the initiation of his legislation through its passage and implementation, Comstock provides a textbook example of successful policymaking by a nonlegislator; or better put, of highly effective lobbying. By comparison, today's socially conservative Religious Right has completely failed. Why did he succeed?

To begin with, Comstock was larger than life: a figure right out of the "dime novels" of his era that he deplored; a stirring champion of virtue against a terrible enemy. He was physically imposing, one biographer describing him as having "Atlas shoulders of enormous breadth and squareness," a "chest of prodigious girth surmounted by a bull-like neck," and short legs that "remind[ed] one somewhat of tree trunks." Throw in his signature mutton-chop whiskers, and you have a mythic physique.[49] Comstock employed colorful language in describing his foes and their work: "pathways of lust," "abortionists' pimps," "putrifying sores," "diabolical trash," and "jackals."[50] And he was a leader. "Even among the righteous, zealots are few," note Broun and Leech. "But Comstock's burning words kindled fires of righteous indignation."[51]

As a leader, Comstock also believed in personal action and responsibility. He was directly involved in almost every legal case brought under the Federal and New York State Comstock laws: from investigation through arrest to witness for the prosecution. His office blotter can be found in the Library of Congress. Numerous notations simply read: "No warrant. Arrested by Comstock in the act of violating the law."[52]

Two early actions on behalf of the YMCA show both his honesty and relentlessness. Using detective methods, Comstock had identified four New York publishers largely responsible for all of the obscene books to be found in the city. Titles included *The Adventures of a French Bedstead, Lord K's Rapes and Seductions*, and *Peeps Into the Boraglio*. Comstock personally arrested the four in a single day; before being caught, one malefactor had sent a note to another: "Get out of the way. Comstock is after you. Damn fool won't look at money."[53] In a letter to his chief Congressional patron, Clinton L. Merriam, Comstock reported the results:

> There was one year ago published in and about New York and vicinity one hundred and forty four different obscene books. I have seized the stereotype plates, steel and copper plate engravings, & c for one hundred and forty-two of these books. There were four publishers on the 2d of last March, today three are in their graves, and it is charged by their friends that I worried them to death. Be that as it may, I am sure the world is better without them.[54]

The same qualities could be seen in his arrest of Madame Restell, the purveyor of abortions to New York's rich and famous. Said to have accumulated a fortune of $1.5 million, the sixty-six-year-old woman lived in a prominent Fifth Avenue mansion. Comstock came to her home, posing as a man who had impregnated his lover. After Madame Restell sold him an abortion potion, he arrested her. She offered him $40,000 in cash to forget the matter, a huge sum for the time. He refused the bribe. Comstock's notes on the case tell the result: "[Restell] committed suicide by cutting her throat [the] morning of trial. A bloody ending to a bloody life."[55]

Comstock's success also came from his single-minded focus on protecting the young from vice. For example, he never entered into the antisocialist agitation of his time, something that would certainly have endeared him to his wealthy supporters. And while personally a nondrinker, Comstock had little to do with the Women's Christian Temperance Union (WCTU) and its crusade for prohibition. As one WCTU leader complained: "The trouble with Mr. Comstock is that he thinks no one has a right to work for social purity without first obtaining permission from him."[56]

Many twentieth-century accounts of Anthony Comstock cast his antiobscenity laws as strange flukes or accidents of the legislative process, adopted against the will of the people.[57] In truth, he should be seen as the point man for a powerful group of backers, Evangelicals all, who repeatedly encouraged his work.

Following on its 1866 report, and in response to Comstock's urging, the New York YMCA created a secret Committee for the Suppression of Vice in March 1872.[58] The key mover here was Morris K. Jesup, the young YMCA President who was also accumulating a fortune as a merchant, banker, and railroad financier. Jesup shared a background with Comstock. Born into a devout Congregationalist home in small town Connecticut, Jesup too had lost a parent when young. In later years, he became President of the New York State Chamber of Commerce, a key mover in preservation of the Adirondacks, and the founder and chief benefactor of the American Museum of Natural History. While others backing Comstock grew cold feet at some point, Jesup supported him without reservation for forty-three years. As Comstock noted in his diary: "Only one Man thinks as I do and that is Mr. Jessup [sic]. He is alive!"[59]

At first, Comstock served the Committee as a volunteer, while continuing to earn his living as a dry goods clerk. However, in early 1873 he left that work to become an employee of the YMCA. During its twenty-two months of operation, the Committee spent only $8,498.14. The results, though, were impressive. Now going public, the 1874 YMCA Report claimed the following seizures:

> 13,000 lbs. of bound books, containing from 150 to 300 pages each; 4,000 lbs. of the same books in process of manufacture; 199,500 pictures and photographs; 6,250 microscopic pictures; 625 negative, photographic plates; 350 engraved steel and copper plates; 501 engraved wood-cuts and electrotype plates; 14,200 lbs. stereotype plates, for printing 145 different books; 20 lithographic stones; 60,300 improper [rubber] articles; 700 lbs. of lead molds; three establishments for the manufacture of these were closed; 130,275 circulars, catalogues and songs; ...20,000 letters from various parts of the United States ordering goods, 6,000 names of dealers....[60]

Despite these imposing numbers, there was trouble within the Committee. Jesup grew discouraged over jealousies among its members. Some thought that Comstock had been too aggressive in several of his arrests. McBurney, the YMCA Secretary, was distraught over publicity surrounding Comstock's handling of the Woodhull–Claflin case (see p. 38). In the end, the committee agreed that "...the matters with which [Comstock] had to deal were too unpleasant to be touched by persons of sensitive feeling."[61] Defending a civilization was a task only for extraordinary men. The Committee resolved to spin this work off from the YMCA, creating an independent New York Society for the Suppression of Vice. The new entity received its Charter from the New York state legislature on May 16, 1873, and was operational by the following December.

This Society has gone down in American mythology as a den of fanatics. Yet, as historian Paul Boyer has put it, if the founders of the antivice society "were moral fanatics, ...they were at least highly successful ones."[62] Joining Jesup and McBurney as incorporators were the rising financier J. Pierpont Morgan and copper magnate William

E. Dodge. Samuel Colgate, head of his family's New Jersey soap business, became the first President of the New York Society, so serving until his death in 1898. Other early officers were textbook publisher Alfred S. Barnes (of later Barnes and Noble fame); Killean Van Rensselaer, representing one of New York's oldest and most prestigious families; and attorney William Beecher, son of the celebrated preacher Henry Ward Beecher. Subsequent donors to the Society included Andrew Carnegie, John Wanamaker, Mrs. Russell Sage, Louis C. Tiffany, and Joseph H. Choate.

In May 1878, Comstock spoke in Boston and enlisted equally prominent figures to create The New England Society for the Suppression of Vice (later renamed The Watch and Ward Society). Dr. Homer P. Sprague, principal of the Girls High and Normal School, became its President. Vice Presidents of the Society included the President of Amherst College, Rev. Julius Seelye; the President of Yale University, Rev. Noah Porter; the President of Brown University, Rev. E. G. Robinson; and the President of Dartmouth, Rev. S. C. Bartlett. The Society's contributors' list soon sported names such as Abbott, Beebe, Cabot, Coolidge, DeWolf, Eliot, Endicott, Fletcher, Forbes, James, Lodge, Lowell, Lyman, Peabody, Pickering, Tufts, and Wigglesworth: "almost a roll call of the [New England] Brahmin aristocracy."[63]

Beyond this extraordinary support from America's most prominent families, both "old" money and "new," there is another curiosity about the Antivice Societies: the all-male cast of leaders. Most social reform movements of the late nineteenth century were heavily dominated by women: consider the prohibition and antichild labor campaigns. Not in this case. Some historians have sought to explain this by casting Comstock's work as "a campaign to ensure the reproduction of the families and the social world of the upper and middle classes." Nicola Beisel argues that Comstock and company sought to keep "children and homes morally pure – a task predicated on, but not confined to, the labors of moral mothers."[64] Boyer suggests that these men were especially uneasy about their own offspring: "Would the temptations of wealth seduce their children from the stern morality by which they themselves had been reared?"[65] Stripped of neo-Marxist language regarding socioeconomic class, such interpretations are probably correct—and not terribly shocking: these *were* men attempting to protect their homes and children from corrupting influence.

Mr. Comstock Goes to Washington

The U.S. Government entered the antivice business through the Tariff Act of 1842, which empowered the Customs Office to seize and bring suit to destroy "obscene or immoral" prints and pictures. In 1857, Congress added obscene "images," including photographs and daguerreotypes, and "obscene articles" to the prohibited list. Reports of nasty materials being mailed to soldiers led Congress in 1865 to ban obscene publications from the U.S. mails. Comstock complained that only items "obscene on their face" were stopped by this measure. Amendments adopted in 1872 strengthened the law only slightly.[66]

In early 1873, few members of the still-extant YMCA Committee for the Suppression of Vice wanted to pursue the matter further. Comstock, though, insisted. He wanted the law extended to outlaw obscenity in newspapers and advertisements and—notably—to ban contraceptive devices and abortifacients. As he explained in a letter to Congressman Merriam:

> ...there are scores of men that are supporting themselves and families to-day by sending out these rubber goods, &c, through the mails that I cannot touch for want of law. There are men in Philadelphia, in Chicago, in Boston and other places who are doing this business, that I could easily detect and convict if the law was only sufficient.[67]

To an unusual degree, then, the law that emerged was Comstock's work. As Bremner puts it, "no one else had the wile and experience to devise such a cunning, wide-mouthed trap for evil-doers."[68] Historian Carol Flora Brooks reports that "[a]ll accounts agree" about the validity of Comstock's "claiming the bill was his own."[69]

Comstock's first task was to blend together his proposed measure with two other pending bills, one dealing with the possession of obscene items in the District of Columbia and the Federal territories and a second that would increase penalties under the existing act. Attorney Benjamin Vaughan Abbott, the brother of theologian and Christian journalist Lyman Abbott, performed this task. The result became what Comstock always called "my bill."

He traveled to Washington in January 1873, with his bill and a cabinet of horrors as evidence: a collection of recently seized obscene prints, postcards, books, and "rubber items" used to educate members of Congress on the nature and scope of this national emergency. As Comstock reports in a diary entry for February 3:

> About 11:30 went up to the Senate with my exhibits. [Journalist] A.H. Byington of Norwalk very kindly aided me by securing the Vice-President's room and inviting Senators out to see me. I spent an hour or two, talking and explaining the extent of the nefarious business and answering questions. [Senators] Buckingham, Pratt, Ames, Ramsey, Cole and numerous others were present. *All were very much excited, and declared themselves ready to give me any law I might ask for*, if it was only within the bounds of the Constitution. I also saw the Vice-President.[70]

As this extract suggests, Comstock worked the Washington system in extraordinary fashion. Connecticut Senator (and wartime Governor) William A. Buckingham was his chief Senate sponsor; Congressman Merriam of New York took that role in the House of Representatives. Astonishingly, U.S. Supreme Court Associate Justice William Strong personally helped Comstock to refine the language of his bill and served as a liaison with friendly Congressional elements.[71] Another powerful Senator, William Windom of Minnesota, used his position on The Committee on Appropriations to secure $3,425 for a special postal agent to enforce the pending law, on the promise of the Postmaster General that Comstock would be so appointed. Comstock had several meetings with James C. Blaine, the Speaker of the House. At a key point in the deliberations, Blaine received personal telegrams from Jesup and Dodge in New York, stressing their "personal interest" in Comstock's bill. Comstock's diary records Blaine promising that he would "put my bill through sure tonight." During these weeks, Comstock even attended a reception at the White House, where he met President Grant (the young New Yorker was unimpressed by the women of Washington, though, finding them "brazen – dressed extremely silly – enameled faces and powdered hair – low dresses – hair most ridiculous [sic] and altogether most extremely disgusting to every lover of pure, noble, modest woman").[72]

The key innovation in Comstock's bill were passages that banned the import and distribution through the mail of:

> Every obscene, lewd, or lascivious, and every filthy book, pamphlet, picture, paper, letter, writing, print or other publications of an indecent character, and *every article or thing designed, adapted, or intended for preventing conception or producing abortion*, or for any indecent or immoral use; and every article, instrument, substance, drug, medicine, or thing which is advertised or described in a manner calculated to *lead another to use or apply it for preventing*

conception or producing abortion, or for any indecent or immoral purpose. [Emphasis added.]

More broadly, Section One of the bill prohibited the distribution by any means of such materials in Washington, DC, and the Federal territories. Section Two prohibited the use of the U.S. mails for such distribution. The third section prohibited the importation of contraceptive devices and provided for their confiscation. Section Four created sanctions for officials who knowingly aided such trade. And the fifth section authorized writs for search and seizure.[73] As journalist Mary Alden Hopkins would later put it, the measure "covers – well, everything."[74]

Birth control advocate Mary Ware Dennett, in her sharply critical 1926 book on the Comstock laws, describes legislative action on the federal bill. "There was practically no discussion on the subject matter," she notes. "There were no speeches delivered, until after the bill was passed. The measure was granted unanimous consent action in the Senate, and was passed under a suspension of rules in the House. It slipped under the wire for the President's signature on the very last day of the session." And, she adds: "the control of conception was not once mentioned by any member on the floor of either House."[75] This account is essentially true. Comstock's bill was part of a flood of legislation that Congress considered in a push toward adjournment by March 1, and the bill's chief sponsors—particularly Congressman Merriam—ably manipulated the resulting, but all too common, confusion.

Several odd things did occur. On February 11, the Vice President referred Comstock's bill to the Committee on Post Offices and Post Roads. In committee, an amendment was adopted that would have granted an exception to the ban on selling contraceptives and abortifacients in the District of Columbia and territories, through "a prescription of a physician in good standing." The bill reported to the Senate on February 18 included this change. When one Senator asked for time to read the measure, Senator Buckingham agreed to put off consideration for a while. It appears that Comstock lobbied frantically to strike the exception. In any case, on February 20 the bill was called up again, with the physicians' provision gone. When Senator Conkling asked what changes had been made, Buckingham replied "that there is no material alteration in the section. It is rather to strengthen it than otherwise." When pressed, he noted that the "words in the thirteenth line are stricken out. I cannot give the details without looking at the bill." While at least one other Senator urged caution here, the missing words were not identified, and the Amendment to the Amendment was approved. A day later, "the bill was read the third time, and passed," with no actual vote recorded.[76]

On the House side, meanwhile, Rep. Merriam bided his time, much to Comstock's frustration. Finally, on the last day of the session, Merriam moved for a vote on the Senate bill, which did not have the physicians' exemption. Congressman Kerr tried to refer the bill back to the Committee on the Judiciary, arguing that "[i]ts provisions are extremely important, and they ought not to be passed in such hot haste." A curious exchange followed:

> MR. COX: Is debate in order?
> THE SPEAKER: It is not.
> MR. MERRIAM: I move to suspend the rules and pass the bill with my amendment.
> MR. KERR: Is my motion in order?
> THE SPEAKER: Not under that motion.
> The House divided; and there were – ayes 52, noes 79, no quorum voting
> MR. KERR demanded tellers.
> Tellers were ordered; and MR. KERR and MR. MERRIAM were appointed.
> The House again divided; and the tellers reported – ayes 100, noes 37.
> So (two-thirds voting in favor thereof) the rules were suspended, and the bill as amended was passed.[77]

President Grant signed the measure the same day.

It has been said that law-making, like sausage making, is a process best not closely observed. In any case, Comstock got his law. Referring to the ongoing Credit Mobilier bribery scandal, the *New York Times* declared that Congress could now be forgiven its improprieties, since it had "powerfully sustained the cause of morality.... Those wretches who are debauching the youth of the country and murdering women and unborn babes, will soon be in the strong grip of government."[78] Later that week, Comstock received his Commission as Special Agent of the U.S. Post Office, charged with enforcing his own law.

The "Mini-Comstocks"

In subsequent years, Comstock carried his advocacy to the states. In his home of New York, Comstock and his YMCA associates drafted a bill and he appeared in Albany in 1873 along with his cabinet of obscenities. The measure's chief innovation would be to ban the sale, gift, or exhibiting of contraceptives and abortifacients. Only one Assemblyman appears to have opposed the bill: "a Methodist exhorter" in the import business. Comstock privately charged that "obscene rubber goods were among the articles in which he traded," which the reformer threatened to reveal. Several assemblymen intervened to spare their colleague "disgrace and exposure." Opposition dissolved, and the bill passed.[79]

The push for a "mini-Comstock" law in Massachusetts coincided with the founding of the New England Society for the Suppression of Vice in 1878, noted earlier. Legal historian Thomas Dienes reports that like the Federal law, this measure "was sweeping in character and passed with maximum dispatch." Also prohibiting the sale, gift, or exhibiting of contraceptives, the bill was introduced in the Assembly on February 5 and approved on February 28. There is no extant evidence of either debate or dissent. The Senate approved the measure on March 20, and six days later the Governor signed it into law. Comstock's "free love" foe Ezra Heywood fulminated again: "No citizen of Massachusetts asked for the passage of the 'law'; it was *slyly worked through* by Comstock himself.... What do the Republican Party and Governor Talbot mean by importing this pious scamp from Brooklyn to 'regulate' morality in Massachusetts?"[80]

The push for a new law in Connecticut appears to have been sparked by still another speech by native son Anthony Comstock. The whole purpose of the measure was to add an anticontraceptive provision to the state's existing obscenity statute. The key provision reads:

> Every person who shall...*use* any drug, medicine, article or instrument whatsoever for the purpose of preventing conception, or causing unlawful abortion, shall be fined not less than fifty dollars nor more than one hundred dollars, or imprisoned not less than sixty days, nor more than one year or both.

Amazingly, the *New York Times* reported that no less a figure than Phineas T. Barnum, the celebrated showman, was responsible for moving Comstock's bill through the legislature. Recently the mayor of Bridgeport, Barnum now served in the Connecticut House, where he chaired The Committee on Temperance. The actual legislative history is sparse, but this was the Committee which did report out Comstock's bill. While somewhat at odds with the Congregationalism of his day, Barnum was "a religious and God-fearing" man, noted for his opposition to tobacco and alcohol and for an earlier campaign against prostitution. Sympathy for Comstock's work would have come naturally. Deemed by a House colleague to be "in the interest of the highest morality and against crimes of the worst sort," the measure passed without apparent opposition.[81]

By 1885, mini-Comstock laws which went beyond the Federal statute had emerged in about half the other states. Twelve of these—Colorado, Indiana, Iowa, Minnesota, Mississippi, Missouri, Montana, Nevada, New Jersey, Pennsylvania, Washington, and Wyoming—made illegal the verbal transmission of information on contraception and abortion. Eleven states deemed the possession of instructions for preventing conception a criminal offense. Four states—Colorado, Idaho, Iowa, and Oklahoma—legalized search and seizure for contraceptive information. Connecticut's law alone criminalized use. In another twenty-two states, existing obscenity laws were interpreted in light of the federal statute. By 1900, about 75 percent of antivice arrests nationwide occurred through these state laws.[82]

A Man of His Time

D. M. Bennett, twice jailed by Comstock for publishing obscene works, complained in 1878 that passage of the federal Comstock law took place in the closing hours of the Congressional session, "when the House was in the wildest state of confusion, [when] numbers of the members were under the influence of ardent spirits, [and when] some two hundred and sixty acts were hurried through without inquiry or consideration." The state Comstock laws, he continued, had passed "by a similar style of tactics," with little debate and considerable backroom political maneuvering.[83] All of this was, in a way, true. Yet, the fact remains that attempts to repeal "the Comstocks," or even amend them in a meaningful way, repeatedly failed. On his death in 1915, Comstock's legal empire was intact. Indeed, a significant weakening of the anticontraceptive clauses came only in the 1930s, and then only through court decisions. How can this durability be explained?

To begin with, Comstock's values and initiatives were wholly in line with the right-thinking and progressive currents of his age. Essentially, Comstock and his allies had learned how to repackage the moral values of the Seventeenth Century in the modern language of "Reform."

Among the progressive social and educational elites of his day, Comstock's work drew repeated praise. In 1898, Harvard Professor

Francis G. Peabody, famed for his course on social reform, favorably compared the antivice associations with the abolitionist crusade: both were typical of "the American way of social reform." In 1911, former Harvard President Charles William Eliot declared Boston's Watch and Ward Society to be a "thoroughly scientific charity." In his Presidential Address to the new American Social Hygiene Association three years later, Eliot urged that the organization "should always be ready to take part in the prosecution of men or women who make a profit out of obscene publications." In 1903, settlement house leader Robert A. Woods praised the antivice societies as "a sort of Moral Board of Health" which made a "profound contribution to the work of every uplifting agency." Other contemporaries saw Comstock standing shoulder to shoulder with Jane Addams and Jacob Riis as reformers battling the poverty, crime, and violence of the city.[84]

The antivice groups were particularly adept at framing their mission as "preventive social policy," then the rage among progressives. The Watch and Ward Society explained: "The old idea of 'charity'...has gradually given way to a larger conception...to prevent the moral diseases which lead to misery and crime." As the organization stated elsewhere:

> [W]hile others endeavor to remedy the effects of crime, we strive to remove the causes.... [E]very successful blow at immoral literature, the brothel, or the gambling hall goes far to remove the necessity for the hospital, the asylum, and the charity ward.[85]

The suppression of obscenity fit in neatly with other campaigns for poor relief, the protection of children, prison reforms, and labor laws to prevent the exploitation of women. Three months before Comstock's death, the *New Republic*—a fresh journalistic voice for the Progressive cause—ran an editorial largely praising the old reformer. It described the post-Civil War flow of obscene books into schools, adding: "[t]he idea of giving up your life to suppressing these dirty trades probably would not ever occur to you. Anthony Comstock *is the exceptional man* to whom this idea did occur and who acted on it." Only those who knew the magnitude of the problem fifty years before and "how difficult and risky this trade has been made nowadays, can realize the vast amount of good Mr. Comstock has accomplished."[86]

Progressive supporters for Comstock's work also included the feminists of his day. Figures such as Elizabeth Cady Stanton never publicly opposed the Comstock laws, largely because they themselves disapproved of contraception, seeing the practice as a threat to their vision of "voluntary motherhood."[87] Historian Nicola Beisel effectively refutes allegations that Comstock's "real aim was the control of women." She notes that neither his laws nor the rhetoric behind them ever reflected this goal.[88] In fact, Comstock carefully avoided any criticism of the women's suffrage movement. And some prominent feminist voices at least indirectly endorsed his campaign. For example, the first American woman to receive a medical degree, Elizabeth Blackwell, MD, shared Comstock's view about the effects of "vicious literature" on the young: "The *permanent and incalculable injury* which is done to the young mind by vicious reading, is proved by all that we know about the structure and methods of growth of the human mind."[89]

Moreover, Comstock enjoyed the quiet support of America's literary establishment. As Paul Boyer notes in *Purity in Print*, the great American publishing houses between 1865 and 1915 practiced a form of self-censorship, which sought elevating themes while condemning the "bad book." This censorship "was simply the sum total of countless small decisions by editors, publishers, booksellers,...critics, and—occasionally—vice societies, all based on a common conception of literary propriety." Authors and journalists joined in as well. The feminist writer Julia Ward Howe argued that literature "must bring pure and beautiful ideals to...the human mind" while avoiding "the brutal, the violent, [and] the excessive." Princeton English Professor Henry Van Dyke stated in 1905 that the only enduring literature "is that which recognizes the moral conflict as the supreme interest of life, and the message of Christianity as the only real promise of victory." Writing in 1913, Paul Elmer More, editor of the *Nation*, condemned writers who did not realize that readers "still require such old themes as *home* and *mothers* and *love's devotion*."

Even librarians worked relentlessly to keep "bad books" off their shelves. In 1908, American Library Association President Arthur Bostwick called for the suppression of books of an "immoral tendency." Facing a "menacing tide" of obscene literature, each librarian must declare: "This far shalt thou go and no further."[90]

Comstock also enjoyed uniform support from America's Christian churches. It is true, as Brooks notes, that American religious bodies took no formal part in passing or enforcing the Comstock laws between 1873 and 1900 and that leading theological journals rarely mentioned the birth control question during these years.[91] Yet, this was at least partly because evangelical "para-churches"—the YMCA and its spin-off antivice societies—were effectively attending to the question. Johnson is closer to the truth when noting that "Protestant and Catholic churches were united in their common concern over public immorality" in this era. Indeed, on the specific issue of contraceptives, Roman Catholics, conservative Evangelical Protestants, and even the emerging "Social Gospel" Protestants stood in effective harmony. "This broad front of religious concern could hardly be called narrowly sectarian."[92]

The "Free-Love" Liberals

Of equal importance, perhaps, Comstock faced no important opposition. His most vociferous foes tended to be in the small "free love" movement, a campaign essentially seeking the abolition of marriage laws. Such repeal, advocates held, would promote the "nobility of sexual love, individual health, social purity, and harmony."[93] Early on, Comstock tangled with Victoria Woodhull and Tennessee Claflin, bringing an indictment against their *Weekly* newspaper for publishing the details of an adultery charge leveled against the sainted preacher Henry Ward Beecher. The sisters denounced Comstock as "this illiterate puppy," relabeled the YMCA the "Young Mules' Concubine Association," and stated that "the new order of Protestant Jesuits, called the Y.M.C.A., is dubbed with the well-merited title of the American Inquisition." The two eventually left for England (where they did make good marriages!). Comstock also suppressed Ezra Heywood's 1876 volume, *Cupid's Yoke*, essentially a manifesto for "free love."

The reformer had a low opinion of these foes. As he wrote in his diary regarding the April 1873 trial of George Francis Train: "There were present the most disgusting set of Free-lovers. The women-part, thin-faced, cross, sour-looking, each wearing a look of 'Well, I am boss' and 'Oh, for a man.' The men, unworthy the name of men, licentious looking, sneakish, mean, contemptable [sic]...."[94]

On June 25, 1878, Heywood received a sentence of two years at hard labor and a $100 fine for mailing copies of *Cupid's Yoke*. In early August, Heywood's supporters held an "Indignation Meeting" in Faneuil Hall, Boston. Nearly six thousand persons attended. The presiding officer denounced Comstock as the lying employee of a "bigoted and aggressive religious sect." A letter from Theron C. Leland, read into the record, called Heywood's punishment "the work of the Christian church," adding: "The Church owns Comstock and he runs the United States Courts." A. L. Rawson said from the podium that the YMCA was "as sincere as were the managers and tools of the Inquisition of the Catholic Church, who believed that by roasting one man they evangelized many others." To roaring applause, he concluded:

> ...if there is an endless hell, where the devil reigns because he is the greatest sinner that ever lived – when Anthony goes to that place, his Satanic Majesty will arise, doff his hat, make his lowest bow, and say, "Mr. Comstock, you have beaten me; please take the chair."

The meeting endorsed by acclamation a resolution calling for Comstock's dismissal from government employment, citing his repeated attempts "to suppress free thought, free speech, and free press" and his "despicable and immoral methods." The meeting also launched the National Defense Association, to give legal support to those charged under the Comstock laws.[95] Comstock kept his job and the National Defense Association proved ineffective.

Another Comstock opponent was the National Liberal League, formed in 1870 to advance secularism. Its original causes included the repeal of Sunday closing laws and the abolishment of official religious holidays. Within a few years, though, the League routinely took on Comstock. In his book, *Frauds Exposed*, the reformer wrote: "It is not a strange thing, then, that of all the different religious or irreligious bodies...the only ones that shield and defend the smut dealers, and oppose the laws for their suppression and punishment, are the National Liberal League, its auxiliaries, and the Free Lovers."[96] Comstock's successful prosecution of Heywood actually split the League. A radical faction led by Bennett sought not only the dismissal of Comstock but also a repeal of his various laws. A conservative faction, led by Francis Abbott and the famed atheist Robert Ingersoll, opposed repeal. The radicals prevailed, Abbott and Ingersoll resigned from the organization, and the League circulated a petition to Congress, eventually gaining fifty thousand signatures demanding repeal. A House of Representatives panel rejected the petition, stating: "In the opinion of the committee, the post office was not established to carry instruments of vice or obscene writings, indecent pictures, or lewd books."[97] This was the last serious effort at repeal that Comstock would personally face.

An Exercise of Power

The reformer also knew how to accumulate power and to use it toward his ends. As Special Agent for the U.S. Post Office, Comstock refused for thirty-three years to take his appropriated salary. "Give me the Authority that such an office confers," he confided in his diary, "and the Salary and honors may go to the Winds." His paycheck actually came from the New York Society for the Suppression of Vice, giving him a certain independence in his public actions. As Postal Inspector, he held a document requiring all mail-carrying American railroads to give him free passage, on demand. During his first ten months in office alone, he traveled twenty-three thousand miles. Comstock had the power to "make searches for mailable matters transported in violation of law," to "open pouches and sacks to examine the mail therein," and to "seize all letters and bags, packets or parcels, containing letters which are being carried contrary to law."[98]

Comstock also served as Secretary and chief operating officer of the New York Society for the Suppression of Vice. Its legislative charter essentially made police departments within the state of New York subordinate to the Society:

> The police force of the city of New York, as well as of other places,... *shall*, as occasion may arise, aid this corporation, its members or agents, in the enforcement of all laws which now exist or which may hereafter be enacted for the suppression of the acts and offenses designated in Section 3 of this Act.

Moreover, agents of the Society duly recognized by the sheriff of any New York county "may...make arrests and bring before any court...offenders found violating...any law for the suppression of the trade in and circulation of obscene literature...and articles of indecent or immoral use." Remarkably, the same charter declared that "One half of the fines collected through the instrumentality of the Society, or its agent, for the violation of the laws in this act..., *shall accrue to its benefit*."[99] Virtue now had a financial incentive.

As Comstock's foes knew all too well, most Federal and state courts actually stood behind the antivice crusader. Comstock had his favorite judges: Federal district judge Charles L. Benedict of New York, "in whose court Comstock claimed to have never lost a case";[100] and Federal judge Daniel Clark of Boston who, in giving his charge to the jury in the Heywood case, stated in characteristic manner that the defendant's free love ideas would transform Massachusetts into a brothel.[101] In this case, as in many others dealing with obscenity, the judge refused to let the jury even see the offending items, deeming them "too obscene." Accordingly, the sole issue before the jury was whether the defendant had indeed mailed the item in question.

By mid-1915, Comstock had won a total of 3,873 arraignments, with 2,881 guilty pleas or convictions. His greatest successes came with obscenity arrests, which were successfully prosecuted in over nine of ten cases. His least success came with charges dealing with gambling, where juries tended to be more forgiving.[102]

The U.S. Supreme Court indirectly affirmed the constitutionality of the federal Comstock Act though an *arbiter* decision in *Ex Parte Jackson* (1877). The case actually involved the dispatch of lottery materials in the mails. In its decision, though, the Court cited Comstock's law as a positive example of Congress' authority to police the mails, so confirming its validity. The Supreme Court considered the Comstock law directly in the case, *Rosen v. United States* (1896). In sustaining the act, the Court adopted "the *Hicklin* standard," articulated by Britain's Chief Justice Cockburn in the case *Queen v. Hicklin* (1868): the test of obscenity is "whether the tendency of the matter charged as obscenity is to deprave and corrupt those whose minds are open to immoral influences, and into whose hands a publication of this sort might fall."[103] Indeed, it was with scant exaggeration that Assistant District Attorney William P. Fiero, in the trial of Mr. Bennett, could declare:

> Now, gentlemen, this case is not entitled "Anthony Comstock against D.M. Bennett"; this case is not entitled "The Society for the Suppression of Vice against D.M. Bennett".... It is *the United States* against D.M. Bennett, *and the United States is one great society for the suppression of vice.*[104]

The sexual morality of Evangelical Protestantism, including its opposition to birth control, had triumphed.

The Old Prophet

In 1892, on the twentieth anniversary of the founding of the YMCA Committee for the Suppression of Vice, Anthony Comstock's admirers feted him at Carnegie Hall. As a gift, they presented the culture warrior with an elegant dinner service of hand-painted China. According to the *New York Mail and Express*: "It was a testimonial of admiration for his splendid career and of respect for the intrepidity, sincerity and self-sacrifice of the man who twenty years ago set out almost single-handed to fight the battle for purity and cleanly lives." Five years later, a second celebration occurred at Carnegie Hall. "Crowds filled the edifice," while Jesup and his business friends presented Comstock with a gift of $5,000. As his biographers conclude, "he had seen his dream fulfilled – the dream of an ambitious Puritan, if ever there was one. He was recognized as the champion of purity…. Good folk were on his side, the Christian laymen, many of the clergy, mothers and fathers, school teachers – all right thinking people, in fact."[105]

Later, there would be rumors that he was about to fall from grace. The unfortunate suicide of a scatter-brained author under indictment, Ida Craddock, hurt his reputation. So did a raid in 1906 to seize pamphlets with nude sketches from the Art Students League, which made him a laughing-stock in sophisticated circles. Enemies whispered that he was about to loose his commission from the Post Office. Instead, Postmaster-General George B. Cortelyou publicly praised Comstock's "war upon impurity and obscenity," declaring that "[h]e has stood as a barrier between the youth of the land and a frightfully demoralized traffic, and I want him to know that… he has had and will continue to have the hearty support of this department." In 1913, the New York Society appeared to pressure him to cede day-to-day operations of the antivice campaign to a younger, more flexible man, John S. Sumner. Yet in early 1915, President Woodrow Wilson named Comstock to lead the American Delegation to the International Purity Conference, held that year in San Francisco [!]. As historian Paul Boyer concedes, of the four thousand delegates present, "there were probably not two persons who did not unreservedly share his point of view."[106]

Indeed, Anthony Comstock—the aging prophet and moral advocate—could bask in the sunlight of almost complete success in the realm of public policy. Regarding the suppression of contraception, historian (and later Federal judge) John T. Noonan notes that the Comstock laws, in penalizing the trade in birth control devices and information, "went further than any Pope or canonist."[107] According to historian James Reed, Comstock made it dangerous "to discuss contraception in print." Even medical books written prior to 1873 edited out discussions of birth control in subsequent editions. One volume simply left blank pages. Comstock's work also "exacerbated tensions in the [modern] companionate family" focused on the adult relationship, so reinforcing the preservation of the more traditional, procreative family form.[108] Mary Ware Dennett, a fierce critic of Comstock's work, correctly notes that under the federal and state Comstock laws, not even parents could lawfully advise their married children on how to space babies; nor could doctors lawfully study the control of conception, or advise their patients on the matter. Federal law, in particular, made no exceptions.[109] Comparing results to goals, then, Comstock's achievement was huge.

So, too, regarding abortion. Despite Marvin Olasky's fairly dismissive treatment of Comstock, the record shows that between 1873 and 1877, this reformer "probably prosecuted more abortionists…than any other person in the United States." After his five years of aggressive action, "abortion-related advertising declined precipitously throughout the nation." Indeed, historian James Mohr concludes that because of Comstock's work, "[a]bortion's period of commercial visibility, which had lasted since the 1840s, was over."[110] Another historian of the abortion issue, Leslie Reagan, concludes that abortion was off the agenda of organized religion until the late 1950s simply because, "for nearly a century, abortion was a crime and no social movement suggested otherwise."[111] Again, for Comstock, this was a large achievement.

Almost single-handedly, Comstock also shut down the American trade in hard-core pornography. Early on, Comstock had learned that "to attack a book or paper, and not carry through the prosecution to success in the courts, was to secure…a large ground of free advertising for the offensive material." On such matters, Comstock rarely lost. In 1888, he took 103 of these cases to trial, with 101 convictions; the next year, 127 cases and 125 convictions; in 1890, 156 cases and 155 convictions.[112] These came on top of earlier, more local successes. As noted before, the New York City "porn library" of 1872 numbered 144 books. By 1880, only two were still in print. The next year, the New York Society could report but twenty pounds of seized books, and a mere twenty-five improper pictures to be destroyed.[113] Up in Boston, the Watch and Ward Society reported in 1885 that the trade in obscene books had been "substantially suppressed." By 1899, the Society declared that "nothing further" was needed except for "constant watchfulness."[114]

Comstock could count other policy achievements, as well. By 1877, he had ended the corrupt black market lottery, or numbers game, in New York City.[115] In an era with little consumer protection, Comstock's successful campaign against medical quacks and the purveyors of patent medicines even drew the praise of his most vociferous opponents. Indeed, virtually all of the "contraceptives" and "abortifacients" on the open market in 1872 were, at best, ineffective; at worst, poisons. Comstock insisted that "such a mighty medium, power, and agency" as the newspapers "ought not to become the tool of the villain, the vampire, nor the ghoul, to rob the simple-minded, honest laborer; or oppress, curse, and destroy the sick and afflicted."[116] More than anyone else of his generation, he put teeth into such words.[117]

A Last Crusade

Anthony Comstock died at the right time: 1915, the last year of the old world order. The Great War in Europe was just turning into the senseless slaughterhouse that would bring vast political and moral revolutions. Even so, there had already been signs of a culture in flux: art such as Cubism which abandoned classical forms; the music of Igor Stravinsky and the choreography of Vaslav Nijinsky, combined in *The Firebird* (1912), which mocked Western ideals of beauty; and the emergence of "sexology" among writers such as England's Havelock Ellis.

Prior to 1915, these changes were more obvious in Europe than in America. Yet in retrospect, one can see an aging Comstock and his allies struggling to comprehend these new challenges. It was the Watch and Ward Society which explained in 1909 that: "As the twentieth century swings into its second decade, the tone of much of its clever fiction is depressing; it is unbelieving; it seems to be written in a spirit of revolt against the old ideals of chivalry and chastity."[118] Past foes such as "free lover" Ezra Heywood were actually chaste in comparison to those now emerging. Heywood and his wife, despite their rejection of marriage, were apparently faithful to one another throughout their lives and produced four children; and they actually opposed contraception as degrading. Broun and Leech note that "the advocates of birth control had always evoked Comstock's wrath. In his old age he saw these people growing more numerous, more brazen."[119]

This new threat was soon embodied in the person of Margaret Sanger. In symbolically rich manner, Comstock's last campaign was an attempt to put this woman in prison.

Historian Janet Brodie actually suggests that it was Comstock's very success in suppressing contraceptive information that had turned Sanger, a nurse, into a birth control advocate. Following the reputed death of a pregnant woman in her care, through a botched self-abortion, Sanger launched in 1913 a search in the Library of Congress, the New York Academy of Medicine, and the Boston Public Library for information on how to control reproduction. As she wrote in her autobiography, "At the end of six months I was convinced that there was no practical medical information on contraception available in America."[120] Brodie drives home the point: "the most dramatic legacy of the new social and legal policies of Comstockery was the void Margaret Sanger found where once there had been information."[121]

Sanger soon published a pamphlet, *Family Limitation*, which described the relative merits of various contraceptive techniques. Comstock went after her. Using a fake passport, she left her husband and children behind and fled the country through Canada. Sanger eventually arrived in England, where she became a protégée (and perhaps a lover) of Havelock Ellis. In January 1915, a secret agent of the Society for the Suppression of Vice approached her husband, William, who gave the agent the offending pamphlet. Arrest followed. Comstock tried to use the threat of prison to bring William Sanger to divulge his wife's location. He refused, and stood trial in September. In perhaps his last appearance as a court witness, Comstock testified against Sanger. The judge in the case told the jury that "[i]n my opinion, this book is contrary not only to the law of the state, but to the law of God." The jury found Sanger guilty. Despite his earlier protest that he was the father of "three lovely children," he chose to spend thirty days in jail rather than pay a $150 fine.[122]

According to some accounts, Comstock took a chill at the Sanger trial, which turned into pneumonia.[123] Others attribute the initial cold to his trip to California to attend the International Purity Conference.[124] Whatever the case, Anthony Comstock died quite suddenly on the evening of September 21, 1915. He was buried in Evergreen Cemetery, Brooklyn, beneath the epitaph, "In memory of a fearless witness," and words from *Hebrews* 12: "Lay aside every weight – looking unto Jesus – despising the shame."

Notes

1. D. M. Bennett, *Anthony Comstock: His Career of Cruelty and Crime* (New York: Liberal and Scientific Publishing House, 1878), 1009–11.

2. From: Heywood Broun and Margaret Leech, *Anthony Comstock: Roundsman of the Lord* (New York: The Literary Guild, 1921), 172.

3. Robert Bremner, "Editor's Introduction," in *Traps for the Young*, ed. Anthony Comstock (Cambridge, MA: The Belknap Press of Harvard University Press, 1967 [1883]), vii.

4. Broun and Leech, *Anthony Comstock*, 21, 228–29, 240–41.

5. Paul Boyer, *Purity in Print: The Vice-Society Movement and Book Censorship in America* (New York: Charles Scribner's Sons, 1968), 2.

6. Marvin Olasky, *Abortion Rites: A Social History of Abortion in America* (Washington, DC: Regnery, 1992), 191–92.

7. Broun and Leech, *Anthony Comstock*, 89, 189–90.

8.   In Broun and Leech, *Anthony Comstock*, 36. Also: Richard Christian Johnson, "Anthony Comstock: Reform, Vice and the American Way" (Doctoral diss., The University of Wisconsin, 1973), 17.
9.   From Johnson, "Anthony Comstock," 19.
10.   Broun and Leech, *Anthony Comstock*, 39.
11.   Ibid., 26, 33, 45–47; Janet Farrell Brodie, *Contraception and Abortion in Nineteenth Century America* (Ithaca, NY: Cornell University Press, 1994), 259.
12.   Boyer, *Purity in Print*, 4.
13.   Broun and Leech, *Anthony Comstock*, 75; also C. Thomas Dienes, *Law, Politics, and Birth Control* (Urbana: University of Illinois Press, 1972), 27–28.
14.   Dienes, *Law, Politics and Birth Control*, 30–31.
15.   Mark Noll et al., *Eerdman's Handbook to Christianity in America* (Grand Rapids, MI: William B. Eerdmans, 1983), 284.
16.   Dienes, *Law, Politics and Birth Control*, 31.
17.   *A Memorandum Respecting New-York as a Field for Moral and Christian Effort among Young Men; Its Present Neglected Position; and the Fitness of the New-York Young Men's Christian Association as a Principle Agent for Its Due Cultivation* (New York: Published By the Association, 1866), 3–6.
18.   Broun and Leech, *Anthony Comstock*, 81–82.
19.   Anna Louise Bates, *Weeder in the Garden of the Lord: Anthony Comstock's Life and Career* (Lanham, MD: University Press of America, 1995), 50–53.
20.   Bates, *Weeder in the Garden*, 53.
21.   Broun and Leech, *Anthony Comstock*, 69–73.
22.   Ibid., 64.
23.   Ibid., 67.
24.   Bates, *Weeder in the Garden*, 58–59.
25.   Nicola Beisel, *Imperiled Innocents: Anthony Comstock and Family Reproduction in Victorian America* (Princeton, NJ: Princeton University Press, 1997), 37.
26.   Quoted in Mary Alden Hopkins, "Birth Control and Public Morals," *Harper's Weekly* 60 (May 22, 1915): 490.
27.   Anthony Comstock, *Defense of Detective Methods. An Open Letter to Judge Jenkins of Milwaukee, Wis.* (New York: The Christian At Work, 1892), 3.
28.   Anthony Comstock, "Vampire Literature," *North American Review* 153 (August 1891): 164.
29.   From the New York Society for the Suppression of Vice, *Sixth Annual Report* (New York, 1880), 11; in Dienes, *Law, Politics and Birth Control*, 33.
30.   Quoted in Hopkins, "Birth Control and Public Morals," 490.
31.   Comstock, *Defence of Detective Methods*, 16.
32.   Johnson, "Anthony Comstock," 79.
33.   James P. Petersen, *The Century of Sex: Playboy's History of the Sexual Revolution* (New York: Grove Press, 1999), 13.
34.   Broun and Leech, *Anthony Comstock*, 148.
35.   Brodie, *Contraception and Abortion in Nineteenth Century America*, 262–63, 274.

36. Hopkins, "Birth Control and Public Morals," 490.

37. Ibid., 489.

38. Beisel, *Imperiled Innocents*, 45.

39. James Reed, *From Private Vice to Public Virtue: The Birth Control Movement and American Society since 1830* (New York: Basic Books, 1978), 39.

40. The New York Society for the Suppression of Vice, *Second Report* (1876); in Beisel, *Imperiled Innocents*, 40.

41. Ibid., 41.

42. D. Humphreys Storer, "Two Frequent Causes of Uterine Disease," *Journal of the Gynaecological Society of Boston* 6 (March 1872 [1855]): 195–203.

43. Horatio Robinson Storer, MD, "The Criminality and Physical Evils of Forced Abortions [Prize Essay to Which the American Medical Association Awarded the Gold Medal for MDCCCLXV]," *Transactions of the American Medical Association* 16 (1866): 741. (Emphasis added.)

44. E. M. Buckingham, "Criminal Abortion," *The Cincinnati Lancet and Observer* 10 (1867): 139–43.

45. Augustus K. Gardner, *Conjugal Sins against the Laws of Life and Health* (New York: J.S. Redfield, 1870), 230–31. (Emphasis added.)

46. L. F. E. Bergeret, MD, *The Preventive Obstacle, or Conjugal Onanism: The Dangers and Inconveniences to the Individual, to the Family, and to Society, of Frauds in the Accomplishment of the Generative Functions*, trans. P. DeMarmon, MD (New York: Turner and Mignard, 1870), 13, 43, 158. (Emphasis added.)

47. Ibid., 8, 165. (Emphasis added.)

48. In Hopkins, "Birth Control and Public Morals," 490.

49. In Bates, *Weeder in the Garden*, 56.

50. From Mary Ware Dennett, *Birth Control Laws: Shall We Keep Them, Change Them or Abolish Them* (New York: The Grafton Press, 1926), 37.

51. Broun and Leech, *Anthony Comstock*, 86.

52. Bremner, "Editor's Introduction," xvii.

53. Bates, *Weeder in the Garden*, 58–59; Broun and Leech, *Anthony Comstock*, 84.

54. Appendix to *The Congressional Globe, Third Session, Forty-Second Congress,* March 1, 1873, 168.

55. As related in Beisel, *Imperiled Innocents*, 46–47.

56. In Bremner, "Editor's Introduction," xxvii. Also: Johnson, "Anthony Comstock," 119, 125.

57. For example, see: Dennett, *Birth Control Laws*, 7.

58. L. L. Doggett, *Life of Robert R. McBurney* (New York: Association Press, 1917), 108.

59. Broun and Leech, *Anthony Comstock*, 152. Comstock never did learn how to spell his patron's name correctly.

60. *Twenty-First Annual Report of the Young Men's Christian Association of the City of New York, Presented January, 1874* (New York: Published by the Association, 1874), 15–16.

61. From William Adany Brown, the biographer of Morris K. Jesup; noted in Broun and Leech, *Anthony Comstock*, 153.

62. Boyer, *Purity in Print*, 5.

63. Ibid., 8; Carol Flora Brooks, "The Early History of the Anti-Contraceptive Laws in Massachusetts and Connecticut," *American Quarterly* 18 (Spring 1966): 6.

64. Beisel, *Imperiled Innocents*, 49, 57.

65. Boyer, *Purity in Print*, 8.

66. Hal D. Sears, *The Sex Radicals: Free Love in Victorian America* (Lawrence: The Regents Press of Kansas, 1977), 70.

67. *Congressional Globe, Third Session, Forty-Second Congress, Appendix,* March 1, 1873 (Washington, DC: Office of the Congressional Globe, 1873), 168.

68. Bremner, "Editor's Introduction," xiii.

69. Brooks, "Early History of the Anti-Contraceptive Laws," 5.

70. In Broun and Leech, *Anthony Comstock*, 131. (Emphasis added.)

71. Dienes, *Law, Politics and Birth Control*, 34.

72. From his diary, in Broun and Leech, *Anthony Comstock*, 134, 139.

73. Dienes, *Law, Politics and Birth Control*, 35–36.

74. Hopkins, "Birth Control and Public Morals," 490.

75. Dennett, *Birth Control Laws*, 21, 24.

76. *Congressional Globe. Third Session, Forty-Second Congress*, February 20, 1873, 1525.

77. *Congressional Globe. Third Session, Forty-Second Congress*, March 1, 1873, 2005.

78. *New York Times* March 8, 1873, 7, col. 2.

79. Broun and Leech, *Anthony Comstock*, 148; Dienes, *Law, Politics and Birth Control*, 44.

80. Dienes, *Law, Politics and Birth Control*, 44–45.

81. Brooks, "Early History of the Anti-Contraceptive Laws," 10–13; Neil Harris, *Humbug: The Art of P.T. Barnum* (Boston, MA: Little, Brown, 1973), 14–15.

82. Brodie, *Contraception and Abortion in Nineteenth Century America*, 256–58; Petersen, *Century of Sex*, 13.

83. Bennett, *Anthony Comstock*, 1017.

84. Boyer, *Purity in Print*, 13, 22, 24, 27–28; Johnson, "Anthony Comstock," 130.

85. Boyer, *Purity in Print*, 13–14, 25.

86. "Editorial," *The New Republic* 3 (June 19, 1915): 100–1.

87. Brodie, *Contraception and Abortion in Nineteenth-Century America*, 280.

88. Beisel, *Imperiled Innocents*, 39.

89. In Boyer, *Purity in Print*, 17. (Emphasis added.)

90. Ibid., 16–17, 20–21, 30–32.

91. Brooks, "Early History of the Anti-Contraceptive Laws," 20.

92. Johnson, "Anthony Comstock," 106.

93. Sears, *Sex Radicals*, 158.

94. Broun and Leech, *Anthony Comstock*, 112.

95. *Proceedings of the Indignation Meeting held in Faneuil Hall, Thursday Evening, August 1, 1878, To Protest Against the Injury Done to the Freedom of the Press by the Conviction and Imprisonment of Ezra H. Heywood* (Boston, MA: Benj. R. Tucker, 1878), 4, 6, 47–48, 53, 62.

96. Anthony Comstock, *Frauds Exposed, or How the People Are Deceived and Robbed, and Youth Corrupted* (New York: J. Howard Brown, 1880), 446.

97. In Beisel, *Imperiled Innocents*, 92–95; Brodie, *Contraception and Abortion in Nineteenth Century America*, 279.

98. Broun and Leech, *Anthony Comstock*, 136–37; Dennett, *Birth Control Laws*, 30.

99. Dennett, *Birth Control Laws*, 31–32.

100. Broun and Leech, *Anthony Comstock*, 87.

101. Beisel, *Imperiled Innocents*, 91.

102. Hopkins, "Birth Control and Public Morals," 489.

103. Sears, *Sex Radicals*, 71–72.

104. Quotation in Broun and Leech, *Anthony Comstock*, 89.

105. Ibid., 213–14.

106. Boyer, *Purity in Print*, 28; Broun and Leech, *Anthony Comstock*, 219–20, 258–59.

107. John T. Noonan, *Contraception: A History of Its Treatment by the Catholic Theologians and Canonists* (Cambridge, MA: The Belknap Press of Harvard University Press, 1986), 412.

108. Reed, *From Private Vice to Public Virtue*, 38–39.

109. Dennett, *Birth Control Laws*, 3–4, 7, 42.

110. James C. Mohr, *Abortion in America: The Origin and Evolution of National Policy, 1800–1900* (New York: Oxford University Press, 1978), 197–99.

111. Leslie J. Reagan, *When Abortion Was a Crime: Women, Medicine and Law in the United States, 1867–1973* (Berkeley: University of California Press, 1997), 6–7.

112. Comstock, "Vampire Literature," 161.

113. Broun and Leech, *Anthony Comstock*, 186–87.

114. Boyer, *Purity in Print*, 11.

115. Bremner, "Editor's Introduction," xviii.

116. Quotation in Broun and Leech, *Anthony Comstock*, 169.

117. See also: Broun and Leech, *Anthony Comstock*, 161; Johnson, "Anthony Comstock," 101–2.

118. In Boyer, *Purity in Print*, 42.

119. Broun and Leech, *Anthony Comstock*, 249.

120. Margaret Sanger, *My Fight for Birth Control* (Fairview Park, Elmsford, NY: Maxwell Reprint, 1931), 58.

121. Brodie, *Contraception and Abortion in Nineteenth-Century America*, 288.

122. Reported in Broun and Leech, *Anthony Comstock*, 249.

123. Reed, *From Private Vice to Public Virtue*, 97.

124. This is the view of Broun and Leech, *Anthony Comstock*, 258–59.

2

"Race Suicide" in the Righteous Republic

The year 1873 not only saw the advent of the federal Comstock law, an evangelical Protestant-inspired measure that effectively banned the advertising and distribution of contraceptives nationwide. It also marked the year of the first great international meeting of evangelical Protestants on American soil. The Evangelical Alliance convened in New York City that October; fifteen thousand enthusiastic delegates and attendees raised up the United States as God's vehicle to convert the world to the true Christian faith. Cleansed of the stain of slavery by Union victory in the Civil War, the United States seemed to Northern Protestant minds to be The Righteous Republic, chosen by God as the means for building His Kingdom on Earth.

And yet, over this contagious triumphalism and dreams of the End Times fell certain shadows. The implications of Darwinism for Christian confidence remained unclear, although a few prescient minds warned of an imminent crisis of belief. Historical criticism of the Bible still seemed largely confined to skeptics in France and Germany; however, copies of Renan's *Life of Jesus* and similar works were appearing at the New England seminaries.

Most immediately, the strategy offered up by leading American Evangelicals for global Christian victory had a glaring, if not fully understood, weakness. Their vision for achieving The Kingdom did not rest primarily on the conversion of Roman Catholics, Muslims, and heathens to the true Evangelical faith. Rather, evangelical Protestant strategists looked to biology for success, arguing that Protestant—and most specifically Anglo-Saxon Protestant—fecundity would bring on The Kingdom. For two hundred years, they reasoned, the Anglo-Saxons had spread their seed across the globe, displacing or assimilating other peoples in North America, Australia, New Zealand, and now Asia and Africa. This process, they believed, would accelerate over the next century, with New Englanders in the lead. The hidden problem, still not widely grasped in 1873, was that the fertility of New England Protestants had by then been falling for nearly a half century. Rather than prepared to populate the world, New England Protestants could barely replace themselves by the time of the 1873 Congress, and were actually losing ground to new, decidedly non-evangelical immigrants on their own soil.

As this reality sunk in over the following several decades, two responses emerged. At first, tumbling fertility among the evangelical Protestants reinforced calls among their leaders for bans on birth control. Later, the same concern for bringing on The Kingdom led other leading Evangelicals to see birth control as a necessary social policy tactic... particularly when aimed at certain groups.

Evangelical America, 1873

Nineteenth-century American Evangelicalism was a product of the First and Second Great Awakenings, events that featured simplified senses of piety and theology, a focus on sin and Christ's redeeming grace, a conversion experience requiring "drastic personal reorientation towards God," and a disregard for denominational lines. As D. G. Hart has argued, these events also tended to separate "the essence of Christianity from the external practices and observances of it," so shifting the focus of faith from the congregation to the individual. In addition, these revivals reinforced a growing identification of the American Union with the Kingdom of God.[1]

In 1873, memories of the Second Awakening (roughly 1800–1845) remained vivid, as did recollections of the Great Revival of 1857–1858, centered in cities and featuring noonday prayer meetings led by businessmen. Even before the Civil War, most American Protestants believed that the United States had a special mission to shape a perfect Christian and democratic order, which would usher in the Millennium and bring the return of Christ and Judgment Day. With the curse of slavery lifted in 1865, focus intensified on America's providential role. As one Presbyterian writer explained, the Yankee triumph confirmed that "we... as a nation, are identified with that Kingdom of God among men, which is righteousness, and peace and joy in the Holy Ghost." In 1870, Methodist Bishop Cyrus B. Foss declared that the "August Ruler of all the nations designed the United Sates of America as the great repository and evangelist of civil liberty and of pure religious faith. And these two are one." The same year Professor Samuel Harris remarked that the "sublime idea of the conversion of the world to Christ has become so common as to cease to awaken wonder."[2]

Adding to this sense of confidence was a largely intact and still orthodox educational edifice. The elementary and secondary schools continued to use textbooks such as *McGuffey's Readers*, rich in moral and generic Protestant content. The great eastern colleges—Yale, Princeton, Harvard, Brown, Amherst—remained evangelical in spirit, and governance. The Eastern seminaries continued under the sway of Scottish Common Sense Realism, which saw God's truth as "a single unified order" and the universe as governed by a rational system of laws. Resting on the inductive logic of Bacon, this school of thought held that the function of science was to discover those Divine laws. Only a few observers, such as Oliver Wendell Holmes, warned that the Bible could no longer stand up to scientific challenge and that the Christian educational edifice would soon face crisis.[3]

Piety toward the Christian family also grew between 1830 and 1870, adding to the optimism of the time. The Evangelical home solidified as a religious center, where Victorian values—personal morality, piety, and belief in Anglo-Saxon superiority—received further legitimation. Encouraged by evangelical writers, gender roles became more specialized. For men in the growing industrial sector, the breadwinner role cast the world of work as strenuous, unsavory, and ruthless. Business was a battle, the arena of commerce a jungle. The home emerged as a refuge, where the virtuous woman—the domestic priestess—would preside. This Christian wife, mother, and homemaker gave succor to her husband when home from the economic wars, and provided protection and religious and practical instruction to her children. The Christian home became a combination of domestic workplace, school, and church, a theme finding richest treatment in Catharine Beecher and Harriet Beecher Stowe's 1869 treatise, *The American Woman's Home*. Official Protestant views on marital sexuality continued to see birth control as degrading and immoral; religious leaders especially feared the demoralizing consequences of separating sexual pleasure from procreation.[4]

This American Protestant sense of world-historic opportunity linked to a confidence in key institutions took concrete form with the refounding of The Evangelical Alliance in 1866. Originally created in 1847 as the American branch of a London-based movement, the Alliance dissolved as the United States moved toward civil war. When that conflict ended, Protestants of various denominations were anxious to join in a more cooperative future. "Old School" Presbyterians gathered on May 23, 1865, in Pittsburgh. This assembly charged that Roman Catholicism and infidelity were "arch enemies of Truth" and "arch traitors to the civil and religious freedom throughout the world." It called for "more outward fellowship and more vigorous cooperation for the defense of Protestant Christianity." "New School" Presbyterians and the Synod of the Dutch Reformed Church concurred. Representatives from congregations, missionary and tract societies, YMCA's, and similar parachurch organizations gathered in Cleveland on September 27. The meeting's purpose was to "organize a National Society for Evangelization" modeled on the wartime Christian Commission and carrying "the Religion of Jesus, in all of its saving efficacy" to non-Christians. The presiding officer was Salmon P. Chase, Chief Justice of the United States Supreme Court; three hundred delegates took part. The assembly set in motion a process that revived The Evangelical Alliance the following year, with copper magnate and financier William E. Dodge Sr., as its President. Other leaders included John Jay, scion of New York's prominent Jay family (and Alliance President in 1884–1885), and R. R. McBurney, Secretary of the New York YMCA.[5]

In its "Doctrinal Basis," adopted in January 1867, the Evangelical Alliance insisted that it had "no intention or desire to give rise to a new denomination or sect; nor to effect an amalgamation of churches." Rather, the Alliance sought "simply to bring individual Christians into closer fellowship and cooperation." Also offering "no new creed," the statement affirmed the "Divine-human person and atoning work of our Lord and Saviour Jesus Christ, as *the only* and *sufficient* source of salvation" and reproduced other articles first drafted by the London-based Alliance in 1846, including: "the Divine inspiration, authority and sufficiency of the Holy Scriptures"; the "right and duty" of private Scriptural interpretation; the Trinity; the "utter depravity of human nature"; and justification by faith alone.[6]

The Alliance took on the task of organizing a great international conference, to convene in New York in 1870. European unpreparedness and the Franco-Prussian War pushed the event into 1873. The victory in that conflict of Protestant Prussia over Catholic France actually added to the sense of new possibilities for global evangelization. Held October 2–12, the Alliance conference featured one hundred speakers representing the elite of global evangelical Protestantism, five hundred formal delegates, and another fifteen thousand attendees.

Speech topics ranged from methods for protecting the Sabbath to the efficacy of revivals in renewing primitive Christianity to the challenge posed by Darwin. The primary theme, however, was "the conversion of the world to the American way" of political and religious life. As theologian Daniel Curry explained, "[t]he foreign delegates who have been among us have had an opportunity to learn something of the working of our system of Church life.... The best argument in favor of a free Church in a free state is in the demonstration of facts as presented in this country." He was confident that the American example would decide "pending contests about this subject... in the Old World." The New York Synod of the Presbyterian Church saw the fate of America and the world resting on the cooperative union seen in the Evangelical Alliance: "No such council was ever before assembled in the New World.... [I]t was one of the most remarkable religious events of the age."[7]

The year 1873 also saw the inauguration of another period of revivalism, patterned on the Second Great Awakening and sparked by Dwight Lyman Moody and his chorister Ira David Sankey. Born in Massachusetts in 1837, Moody arrived in Chicago nineteen years later. Successful in business and as a fundraiser, he joined the Christian Commission in 1861, founded the independent Illinois Street Church two years later, and became President of the Chicago YMCA in 1865. Six years later, a reconsecration experience "set him on fire with a 'passion for souls.'" On YMCA business in London in 1872, Moody filled in as a substitute preacher and four hundred persons responded to his altar call. The next year, he and Sankey launched their British crusade. By 1875, they had reached as many as four million hearers. Returning that year to America in triumph, they launched their first American crusade. As historian Sydney Ahlstrom summarizes, "[w]ith listeners in the millions, converts in the thousands, their hymns on every lip, their names a household word, Moody and Sankey rejuvenated the revival."[8]

Moody's theology was simple, commonly summarized as the "Three R's": "Ruin by sin, Redemption by Christ, and Regeneration by the Holy Ghost." His sermons avoided "hellfire," emphasized the love of God, and rarely touched on sociopolitical issues (the telling exceptions were emphasis on motherhood and domesticity, reflecting "the widespread evangelical conviction that stability in the home" was the key to solving most social problems).[9] Yet the organizers and participants in the Moody revivals felt they were part of a unique and important experience, with vast implications. For example, the leaders of the 1879 Cleveland Revival reported that "The United States is now in the midst of the throes of the *third* of the great Religious Awakenings that have become so memorable in its historic development." They described the powerful religious and political consequences of the First and Second Awakenings: the former ending in the American Revolution; the latter resolved in a "second baptism of blood... which burned away the fetters of the enslaved and set the bond people free." These "successive broodings of the Spirit of God upon the face of the becalmed waters of the Church" also generated a great tide of evangelical Bible and Tract Societies, the Sunday School movement, missionary associations, and most recently the YMCA, "whose homelike halls now dot the country." By the late 1870s, another "great throng of devout and self-sacrificing evangelists have gone abroad in the strength of the Lord, with their souls hungering for the saving of imperiled souls."[10] Although Moody retired in 1892, still another wave of evangelists—including Reuben Torrey, Samuel Porter Jones, Benjamin Fay Mills, and Billy Sunday—sustained the spirit of revivalism through 1917. In that peak year, Billy Sunday's New York Crusade alone brought 1.45 million attendees and 98,264 converts.[11]

Animating both the new movement toward evangelical Protestant cooperation and the new Revivalism were profound millennial expectations, a belief that the End Times and the Coming of the Kingdom were near. In the heady optimism of the decade after Appomattox, most Protestant theologians, writers, and leaders tended toward "post-Millennialism." Examining the world, they saw Satan in retreat, Roman Catholicism and Islam in decline, and new energy infusing the "true" evangelical faith. They believed that human actions and social and political reforms taken now would actually inaugurate the Millennium, establishing The Kingdom of God, to which Christ would then return. Relatively few American Protestants of the early 1870s held to the more pessimistic "pre-Millennialism," which saw little, if any hope for society until Christ came and established the Kingdom himself. Four decades would pass before pre-Millennialism—"a movement of the disinherited"—gained sway.[12]

Fertility and the Coming of the Kingdom

During the middle decades of the nineteenth century, New England's religious leaders set out to transform America into a truly Protestant, Christian land. The Abolitionist campaign might be seen as one aspect of this drive. As historian Robert Handy explains, another phase of this transformation involved use of the Christian family for extraordinary ends:

> As the denominations faced their country they saw no reason why their influence should not continue to grow and the numbers increase, and they set out to evangelize and Christianize every aspect of American life.[13]

Theologians reasoned that the reproductive family would become an agent of God, a tool of His mission, the vehicle for Christianizing the world.

The central figure here was Horace Bushnell. Called "*the* creative force in New England theology of the nineteenth century,"[14] Bushnell was a pastor and preacher who wrote theology from a parish setting. Born in 1802 and graduated from Yale in 1827, he was caught up in Yale's Revival of 1831. Bushnell abandoned plans to become a lawyer, turning instead to Divinity School, and eventually became pastor of North Church in Hartford. He focused in particular on the Christian education of children.

In this regard, his most important book was *Christian Nurture* (1861). Noting the modern penchant for individualism, he lamented that "we have well nigh lost... the idea of organic powers and relation." His purpose was "to restore, if possible, the conception of one of these organic forms, viz: the family." To that end, he emphasized words from the Old Testament book of Malachi: "That he might have a godly seed (2:15)." Bushnell elaborated: "We perceive, accordingly, that God is, from the first, looking for a godly seed; or, what is nowise different, inserting *such laws of population that piety, itself, shall finally over-populate the world*." Put simply, he held that while the conversion of heretics and pagans would play a role in bringing on The Kingdom, *family propagation* was at least equally important. God's "law of population" dictated that "by *this increase from within*, quite as much as by conversion from without," comes "the complete dominion promised."[15]

Through infant baptism and church membership, where "a believing parentage sanctifies the offspring," God framed "the order of the church economy" to bring "family propagation." Bushnell insisted that it was through "a kind of ante-natal and post-natal nurture combined" that successive new generations would learn Christian piety "and the world itself [be] over-populated and taken possession of by a truly sanctified stock. This I conceive to be the expectation of Christianity."

Signs of the process at work were evident in his time. Christians were pouring out "great tides of population, creating a great civilization, and great and powerful nations," while the Muslims were "falling away into a feeble, half-depopulated, always decaying state, that augurs final extinction at no distant period." A similar picture appeared if one compared "the populating forces of the Puritan stock" with "the inferior superstitions, half-Christian stock and nurture of the South American states." There were other signs of God's grace. Protestant American Christians enjoyed a stronger "tide of health." Wealth grew more rapidly "under the condition of Christian living." More talent could be found in "a Christian people." God gave these advantages to Christians so that "salvation will become an inbred life and populating force, mighty enough to overlive, and finally to completely people the world." The whole Gospel plan rested on a Church which has "within itself a stronger law of population, as well as a mighty power to win over and assimilate the nations." Christians "have more truth, beauty, weight of character to exalt their predominance." Most importantly, "*God is in them* by his all-informing, all-energizing Spirit, *to be Himself unfolded in their history*,"[16] and thereby "over-people... eternity itself."[17]

A more strident iteration of the same argument appeared a quarter century later from the pen of Josiah Strong, soon to become General Secretary of the Evangelical Alliance and lead that organization through its most activist phase. Who was he?

Strong was born on January 19, 1847, in Napierville, Illinois, to devout evangelical parents. He proudly reported that abolitionist John Brown had stayed in his home, telling tales of his work in "Bloody Kansas." In 1871, he graduated from Lyman Beecher's Lane Theological Seminary. Ordained a Congregationalist minister, he held pastorates in Cheyenne, Wyoming, and Sandusky and Cincinnati, Ohio, served as chaplain at Western Reserve College, and supervised the Home Mission Society of Ohio, Kentucky, West Virginia, and Western Pennsylvania.

Strong's first book, *Our Country*, had a powerful, "electric"[18] message which immediately catapulted him into the leadership of American Protestant thought. Blending Bushnell's biological eschatology with Lyman Beecher's Christian sociology, *Our Country* introduced other novel themes: a remarkably prescient understanding of Europe's political problems and troubled future; a remolding of Protestant anti-Catholicism into the Social Gospel; an unusual melding of Darwinism and Christianity; and the distillation of Bushnell's favored Christian people into the chosen Anglo-Saxon race.

Regarding the first of these themes, Strong showed a certain wisdom in his analysis of contemporary European and American affairs. While opposed to the "new" immigration into America, he exhibited real sympathy for the newcomers' motivations: the prospect of owning their own farms; the chance to start fresh in a land of plenty; abundant food and good schools in contrast to high taxes and social rigidity in the old countries; and the aggressive promotions of steamship companies. Strong also noted that militarism "lies like a vampire over Europe." Over the next twenty-five years, he predicted "Great Revolutions" there, adding: "they will not be peaceful." War was inevitable, he thought, and new nations would replace the Empires. He predicted the eventual triumph of democracy across the continent: "All the races of Europe will one day enjoy the civil liberty which now seems the peculiar birth right of the Anglo-Saxons."[19]

The problem of Catholicism, Strong maintained, was intertwined with the dark side of immigration. Most of the new arrivals were peasants "whose moral and religious training has been meagre or false." Three-quarters of Irish convicts, he reported, wound up in America. Following "continental ideas," the new immigrants sought to turn the Sabbath from a Holy day into a holiday. Most saloon-keepers were foreign born. "Romanism" was also subversive of American civic liberties. By investing the Pope with supreme sovereignty, Catholics subverted democracy. Romanists rejected the public schools, "another foundation stone of our free institutions." They plotted especially to lay claim to the American West, with the Jesuits out front. Strong quoted California pastor J. H. Warren: "The Roman Catholic power is fast becoming an overwhelming evil."[20] Strong's favored response, however, was a new evangelical mission to reform the cities, launch social welfare initiatives to forestall sin, and convert Catholic and Jewish populations to the true faith: in sum, the Social Gospel.[21]

Rather than denouncing Darwin and friends for subverting the faith, Strong praised their work and used it to build his case for American exceptionalism. He argued that America succeeded because it was a special kind of "mixed" race: "a new comingling of races" where "the largest injections of foreign blood are substantially the same elements that constituted the original Anglo-Saxon admixture." Strong referred here to the Social Darwinist Herbert Spencer, who wrote that "the eventual mixture of the allied varieties of the Aryan race...will produce a more powerful type of man than has hitherto existed, ...more plastic, more adaptable, more capable of undergoing the modifications need-ful to compete in social life." Darwin himself, Strong noted, claimed that "the wonderful progress of the United States" was the result of natural selection, "for the more energetic, restless, and courageous men from all parts of Europe have emigrated during the last ten or twelve generations to that great country." Darwin and Strong agreed with one Rev. Zincke that "all other series of events," including those creating "the culture of mind in Greece" and the Empire of Rome, "only appear *to have purpose and value* when viewed in connection with, or rather as subsidiary to, the great stream of Anglo-Saxon im-migration to the West."[22]

Indeed, Strong emphasized how the Anglo-Saxons had become "the great representative" and depository of two great blessings: "civil liberties" and "a pure spiritual community." In a unique way, the An-glo-Saxon was "divinely commissioned to be... his brother's keeper." Putting one people and numbers behind Bushnell's theory of salvation through procreation, Strong noted that the number of Anglo-Saxons had grown from 6 million in 1700 to 20.5 million by 1800 and to an estimated 120 million by 1890. Assuming that this group continued to grow by 6.89 percent per decade (as it had in the 1880s), he estimated that the Anglo population would be 1.111 billion by 1980. Of this number, 373 million would be Americans, giving them the natural leadership in their civilization and world. Strong praised the "money-making power" of the Anglo-Saxons as a sign of divine favoritism. The Anglo-Saxon also had a "genius for colonizing": "He excels all others in pushing his way into new countries." The Americans, in particular, exhibited an exemplary social mobility, which magnified the display and use of talent.

Strong concluded that "God, with infinite wisdom and skill, is training the Anglo-Saxon race for an hour sure to come in the world's future." There would be no more empty lands when this "final compe-tition of races" came. In a remarkable passage, the Protestant writer concluded:

> Then this race of unequaled energy, with all the majesty of numbers and the might of wealth behind it, the representative, let us hope, of the largest liberty, the purest Christianity, the highest civilization—

having developed peculiarly aggressive traits calculated to impress its institutions upon mankind—will spread itself over the earth. If I read not amiss, this powerful race will move down upon Mexico, down upon Central and South America, out upon the islands of the sea, over upon Africa and beyond.[23]

Strong had no illusions that this process would always be pretty. He did maintain that no "war of extermination is needful; the contest is *not* one of arms, but of vitality and civilization." Yet he also admitted that "the pioneer wave of our civilization carries with it more scum than salt." Alongside one missionary would be a hundred traders, miners, and adventurers "ready to debauch the native." However, Anglo-Saxon vitality and aggressiveness had a higher purpose: "...what Dr. Bushnell calls 'the out-populating power of the Christian stock,'" which formed "God's final and complete solution of the dark problem of heathenism among many inferior peoples." Mohammedans, Jews, Buddhists, and Brahmins were all in decay. Educated minds in Catholic nations increasingly abandoned the Roman faith. In short, God was training the Anglo-Saxon race in North America for its mission; at the same time, he was "preparing mankind to receive our impress." An "Anglo-Saxonized mankind" was inevitable as God's will. The only issue was when? Strong concluded:

> I believe it is fully in the hands of the Christians of the United States, during the next ten or fifteen years, to hasten or retard the coming of Christ's kingdom in the world by hundreds, and perhaps thousands of years. We of this generation and nation occupy the Gilbraltar of the ages which commands the world's future.

Unspoken, but clear, was one implication: everything—*Everything!*—depended on continued, high Anglo-Saxon fertility.[24]

Members of the Board of Directors at the Evangelical Alliance grew ecstatic over *Our Country*. They scrapped plans for their December 1886 conference in Washington, DC, redrafting the program in line with Strong's agenda. The Board's records note that "there exists, then, the crisis of peril, the sufficient resources, the providential organization, *the seemingly appointed man.*" On October 29, "sight unseen," they elected Josiah Strong as General Secretary. He took office on December 27. As Board President Samuel Dodge Jr., wrote to Strong: "nothing could be more delightful than the perfect unanimity and cordiality with which your nomination and election were made.

The whole thing from the beginning has been so strangely led and marked by Providence." Strong immediately launched new program strategies: the creation of grassroots branches through house-to-house visitation; and "a cascade of conferences" that "would be councils of war preparing for future campaigns." The time was ripe: "the Alliance is called of God to a sublime opportunity. To save our American civilization and thoroughly season it with the salt of Christianity *is to give a Christian civilization to the world*."[25]

Silent Peril

Indeed, by 1886, the naïve optimism of evangelical Protestant leaders twenty years earlier was giving way to a catalogue of worries: mass immigration; urbanization; Mormonism; "Romanism"; socialism; secularism. Evangelical America—"The American mission"—hung in the balance.[26] The Republic of God stood imperiled!

The less visible, but more fundamental, peril came from the silent spread of birth control among the Protestant faithful, beginning well before Anthony Comstock's anti-vice crusade. Reformation leaders such as Martin Luther and John Calvin had been adamant in their condemnation of birth control, casting it as a violation of nature and of the will of God. And for three centuries, Protestant theologians, pastors, and laymen taught and mostly lived in that spirit.[27] All the same, historian Herschel Yates Jr., argues that there were principles or values also inherent to Protestantism that left open the possibility of accepting the practice. Most fundamental was the judgment of Reformation leaders such as Luther and Calvin that Scripture did not cast marriage as a sacrament. Noting that pagans and heathens also engaged in marriage, the Reformers praised Christian marriage as the highest of human endeavors and a channel of common grace, yet refused to see it as conferring redemptive grace.[28]

A second vulnerability was the Reformed emphasis on the individual. According to Social Gospel advocate and Harvard professor Francis Peabody, the substitution of the individual for the family was fundamental to "the religious life and thought of Protestantism."[29] Another Protestant family advocate from the era, Samuel Dike, noted that the Reformation "was a protest against the claims of the church by an assertion of the individual.... The note of Protestantism is distinctly individualistic."[30] Over time, this orientation toward the individual allowed Protestants to lose sight of the family as "the germ cell" of society, with its own rights and claims.

The third weakness was the Protestant emphasis on companionship in marriage. While innate to understandings of Christian marriage since at least the time of Augustine, the mutual relationship of husband and wife was always linked, or even subordinate, to procreation. Over the course of the nineteenth century, though, Protestant writers tended to give more emphasis to the companionship ideal. Typical was George Weaver's *The Christian Household*, published in 1856: "The grand idea of companionship is unity, and that companionship is perfect just in the degree that unity is secured." Procreation and the nurture of children subtly gave way to a focus on the moral, physical, psychological, and intellectual development of the couple. In turn, this tended to legitimate sexual pleasure as an end in itself, making companionship "a significantly receptive value for conception control."[31]

Meanwhile, over the same decades, knowledge of birth control techniques steadily spread. During the 1830s, Charles Knowlton's *Fruits of Philosophy* appeared in America. Arguing that the control of births was essential to civilizational progress, he advocated douches containing spermicide. Appearing about the same time was Robert Dale Owen's *Moral Philosophy*, which favored male withdrawal.[32] Frederick Hollick published his *Marriage Guide* in 1850; its subtitle promised information on "The Production or Prevention of Offspring." By 1860, the book had appeared in *two hundred* editions. In his chapter "On the Prevention of Conception," Hollick noted "that everyone" was now familiar with the idea of birth control. While possibly "productive of great evil,... it is now impossible to prevent its dissemination." His duty, he felt, was to show "that safe and efficacious means can be employed" to prevent conception. He cited the technique of Onan, or withdrawal, but advised against it as "unsatisfactory and injurious." While vaginal sponges were unreliable, he praised certain types of "injections" able "to destroy the *power* of the semen." Solutions to this end included Alum, Sulphate of Zinc, Chloride of Zinc, and Sulphate of Iron. Hollick favored "a vegetable substance" that "destroys the Animalcules almost instantaneously" without damaging the female organs. He noted the effective use of condoms, yet criticized the way they distorted the sexual act. He concluded that "the most certain plan of avoiding conception" was "by practicing association only at those times when it cannot occur," later known as the rhythm method.[33] Edward Bliss Foote Sr. discussed birth control in his 1858 book, *Medical Common Sense*, which sold 250,000 copies. His *Words in Pearl for the Married*, appearing in 1870, described four methods of effective birth control: "membraneous envelopes" (condoms fashioned from fish bladders); "apex envelopes" (using vulcanized rubber); "womb veils" (diaphragms); and his own "electro-magnetic preventive machine."[34]

It appears that readers heeded such advice. Well before Josiah Strong's enthusiastic celebration of Anglo-Saxon Protestant fertility, there were contrary reports in the popular press of "dramatic" shifts in the American family. In early 1869, for example, *Harper's New Monthly Magazine* carried an article on "Changes in Population." The "most important" of these was "the increasing proportion of children of a foreign descent, compared with the relative decrease of those of strictly American origin." New York's 1865 census showed that nearly one-fourth of all the married couples in the state had no children at all; in three-fourths of such homes, "there was, on average, only a small fraction over one child to each family." In 1665, the old Massachusetts town of Billerica had counted 95 families with 1,043 children: "equal to a regiment." Two hundred years later, such large families had vanished. Schools were closing for want of children.

Part of the problem, the article explained, lay in a shift of public attitudes: "Once such fathers and mothers [of large families] were considered by the wise, the good, and the great as public benefactors; but now their conduct is not only questioned and censured, but by some they are regarded almost as human monsters." Other factors included later marriages, an outmigration of the young, the rise of industry, men's "eager struggle for rapid gains," and women's pursuit "of mere pleasure and fashion." Moreover, "the plain teachings of Scripture... are entirely ignored" while "the laws of life and health are set at defiance, and *worse expedients are resorted to*... than were ever countenanced by the doctrines of Malthus." Indeed, the article concluded, "here in the very heart of Christendom foeticide and infanticide are extensively practiced under the most aggravating circumstances."[35]

Also in 1869, sociologist Nathan Allen gave a paper at the meeting of the Western Social Science Association, in Chicago; Rev. Edward Beecher arranged for its immediate publication. Entitled "Population: Its Law of Increase," the paper warned that the native stock of New England would soon be as in France: a diminishing population. Comparing census returns from 1865 with those of 1765, there were now only half as many children, relative to the adult population, as before. This was happening to "the best stock that the world has ever seen, under what would be considered the best family training, the highest order of religious influence, and the purest religious instruction." Meanwhile, new immigrants, "with far less intelligence and a religion entirely different," proved to be "wonderfully prolific," bearing nearly three times as many children per family.

What were the causes? Allen offered a list much repeated over the next several decades. To begin with, he held that the hiring of servants to do domestic labor left New England women with inadequate exercise and weak bodies. Similarly, New England girls spent too much time in their school studies, leaving them frail with "overtaxed" nervous systems. Meanwhile, the female fashions of the day displaced internal organs and interfered with bodily functions. More plausibly, Allen noted that "the nourishment which nature designed cannot be found for the child." Barely half of American women now nursed their children: "Some will not do it; others cannot, having neither the organs nor the nourishment requisite for it."

Most of Allen's proposed solutions fell short of the real problem. He would have all girls thoroughly trained in household duties so they might "practice the lighter gymnastics of domestic labor." He would alter women's fashions to remove pressure on the chest or abdomen (although he thought the prospect of much improvement here "rather discouraging"). And he would alter diets, replacing fine flour bread with whole wheat while banning coffee and tea. The result, he reasoned, of "a well-developed body, good health, a sound constitution, [and] a practical knowledge of domestic duties" would be "an increase of healthy offspring."

However, Allen also acknowledged the deeper problem: "This change in the law of human increase and other evils have been brought about entirely by human agency—principally by violation of the great law of life and health." The only precedent for this was the experience of the Roman Empire, where "infanticide," an "aversion to marriage," and a "general reluctance to rear families" resulted in a "want of population." If New England civilization similarly destroyed or weakened "those two great relations—the matrimonial and parental—which lie at the foundation of all society," America's fate would be the same. "A longer career of prosperity and a nobler destiny should await our native people," he concluded. "Let these evils be exposed and discussed," so that social reform might follow.[36]

Alarm over the falling birthrate of "old stock" Americans eventually reached the religious press. In 1882, *The New Englander*, a Congregationalist journal, featured a long editorial on "The New

England Family." Why such a focus? The editors stressed that the New England family was "a historic family; it is the root and seminal principle of American civilization." And it was now in trouble. The "well ordered families" of the Puritans, after two hundred years of fecundity, were shriveling. Over half of Massachusetts adults were unmarried. The editors were particularly indignant about the decline in breastfeeding: "the failure to nurse offspring shows something radically wrong.... Evidently the divine office of maternity, woman's brightest crown, her grandest privilege, is here passing away." To Allen's list of causes for these woes, the editors added delayed marriages, higher living-standard expectations, urbanization, licentiousness, and adultery. However, unlike Allen, they quickly zeroed in on the core issue. Throughout New England, they reported with words borrowed from Samuel Dike, "the destruction of unborn life goes on as fast, or faster, than ever. Physicians... speak with great indignation of the wicked practices of some church members." However, "the 'arts of prevention' who are also being extensively employed are a far more dangerous foe." Methods of birth control long used in France "have become not only well understood here, but improved upon by Yankee skill and ingenuity." The editors warned that if such "violations of law" were tolerated in married life, they would soon spread to the unmarried. "The *very existence* of the family is imperiled, we believe, more by these practices than by all other agencies combined." The editors concluded that in New England there was now "a lack of that patriotism which leads one to endure pain and practice self-denial to people his land." The spirit of luxury corrupted both men and women. Finally, there was "too little of that high moral principle that prompts people to forget self and find their life in giving life and happiness to others."[37]

These concerns festered over the balance of the decade. Focusing on divorce, Noah Davis lamented its spread among native-born Americans. Divorce "invades the home, defiles its sanctities, lays open its privacy, dishonors its parentage, shames its childhood, and arrests the only pure revenues of human life." Numerous children, he noted, served as "a safeguard against divorce," hovering "like a guardian angel over the sanctity of conjugal love." However, in New England children were now "considered obstacles to the freedom of separation, and whenever that is the case, the malaria of divorce is fatal to maternity." The result was a surrender of "our country" to "the races of immigration... who are happily taught obedience to the laws of nature as a religious duty."[38]

In their book, *The Family: An Historical and Social Study*, Western Reserve College President Charles Franklin Thwing and his wife Carrie F. Butler Thwing combined the same fear of Catholic immigration with admiration for that churches doctrines on sexuality and family. "The Church of Rome," they wrote, "has since the Reformation been less timid than the Protestant in denouncing sexual sins both within and without the bonds of marriage." Protestants, they said, could also learn from Catholic doctrine about the need to surround marriage with religious sanctification. More broadly, the Thwings lamented how the focus of law steadily substituted the individual for the family, to the point where "[t]he family, as an institution of prime importance, has passed away." The commonwealth had so lost its "conservative" brake, for "the individual is radical, a progressive." Relative to fertility, they reported that the family was increasingly "dominated by the sociogenic or cultural forces and less and less by the so-called 'natural' or phylogenetic desires." Their policy responses included a call to end "the present drift of the population to the city," favoring "the calm, the conservatism, and the simplicity of the country" which "tends to develop the family."[39]

Writing in *The Methodist Review*, Richard Wheatley took issue with the Thwings argument that the family had ceased to exist as a meaningful social unit: "never have family considerations been more powerful in the commonwealth than at present." Yet, he agreed with them that Protestantism had failed in its treatment of marriage. In their "extreme reaction against the errors and superstitions of popery," the Reformers "erroneously defined marriage as a civil contract, and lodged it in the hands of the justices of the peace." This left marriage subject to the whims and perils of politics. While avoiding a discussion of birth control, deeming it "too delicate for handling in the pages of a religious review," Wheatley did note that "illegitimate births are rapidly increasing." Moreover, "loose notions of sexual morality, and the absence of clear ideas of the family obligations, unquestionably foster the shamefully criminal practice of pre-natal infanticide." Abortion, he continued, had already "reduced the descendants of the Puritans in some localities to an insignificant minority." In his "Yankee" corner of northeast Ohio, for example, "careful medical investigation" revealed that abortion "annually robs the family of one third of its legitimate increment."[40] This development soon gained a name: "race suicide," a term introduced by sociologist Edward A. Ross.[41]

Momentous Crisis

Such sentiments heightened interest in the Evangelical Alliance's Washington Conference, held in December 7–9, 1887. The "Call" for the conference, signed by "the elite of American Protestantism,"[42] reflected the crisis mentality and providential nationalism of the Alliance's new General Secretary, Josiah Strong. The closing years of the nineteenth century, it declared, "constitute a momentous crisis in the history of the nation." With the rise of cities, "severe" competition, an unemployed class, and mounting pauperism and crime, America was "beginning to approximate European conditions." The time had come to set things right. "Is not this the nation, and is not this the generation *providentially called* to make such application of the gospel to the life of the people as has never yet been made." The Protestant denominations had "fallen into harmful competition." They would now engage in "an intelligent and comprehensive cooperation" to transform the nation, and world.[43]

Birth control was not formally on the agenda. However, its direct and indirect effects were recurring concerns. In his opening address to the assembled 1,500 delegates, Alliance President William E. Dodge pointed to the immigrants "pouring into the country." They "are not absorbed and Americanized as before," he complained, and were "rapidly changing the character of our people." The immigration-fed "Roman Church" held "first allegiance to a foreign power" and so posed "a dangerous menace to the Republic." Dodge continued:

> The growing disregard of the proper use of the American Sunday, the loose opinions as to family ties, the increased licentiousness, the materialism of the age, the absorption in money making, the increased luxury and enervation in many classes, the dying out of religious influences in sparsely settled portions of the old states, all tend to show a change in the condition of our land....

In this time of peril and opportunity, duty was clear and "the call of God direct": "The Christian Church must be united in heart, must cooperate fully, must assume the aggressive [sic], and advance along the whole line." As citizens of a Christian nation, "[w]e need a revival not only of higher spirituality, but of the complete acceptance of the idea that each Christian man has real work to do for which he is re-

sponsible—*such a revival as the Crusades were, or the Reformation.*"
He hoped that this conference would be "the precursor and promise"
of this "new birth."[44]

Another notable address came from Rev. Samuel W. Dike, then
emerging as a leading and thoughtful Christian analyst of the family
in America. He defined the "simple, ideal family" as "one man and
one woman, united in wedlock, together with their children;" this
was "the true family of nature and Christian civilization." Threaten-
ing this natural family were a climbing divorce rate, ever more "illicit
unions" as substitutes for marriage, and "the declining fruitfulness
of the family...especially among people of the so-called native stock."
Regarding the latter, Dike reported that physicians estimated that
"legitimate children would be fifty percent more numerous but for
criminal deeds," presumably abortion and birth control. Accordingly,
only the "so-called dangerous classes multiply." He concluded that no
other "civilized people in the world" was taking "so great risks with the
family as we are in these United States." The family was "the germ" of
all other social and political institutions. It "perpetually" reproduced
and "continually reconstructed the constitution of society." In calling
for a more systematic sociology of the family, Dike was sure that statistics would show that "the immoralities of sex" had more to do with
crime and poverty "than even the monster evil of intemperance." The
lesson taught by the histories "of all the great Aryan peoples" was that
"religion is the source and soul of all social power, and the family is its
first great place of development, and remains its stronghold so long
as national vigor continues." To reverse America's imminent decline,
he urged cultivating "a greater intimacy" between Evangelicals and
teachers and scholars "in the great social sciences."[45]

Samuel Dike actually was the pivotal figure in the emergence of a
broad "pro-family" movement in the last two decades of the nineteenth
century, an often forgotten component of the Social Gospel campaign.
Serving as Secretary of The National Divorce Reform League, he gave
primary attention to divorce laws; the key project here was gaining
ratification of a constitutional amendment that would allow the federal
government to standardize—and presumably strengthen—marriage
and divorce law nationwide. Dike mostly avoided the racialism of
Josiah Strong and he regularly and richly wrote on broader themes.
Drawing on Bushnell, he saw the family as the first order of creation,
"a revelatory model of the Kingdom of God in the evangelization and
reform of the social order."[46] "The root of the family," Dike explained,

was "in nature or, in other words, in Natural Law and this is exactly where Jesus himself put it."[47] He emphasized the organic nature of marriage, where two became one creature, "something more than the sum of the two." In turn, this united "moral person" should be "treated politically as such, having duties and rights to be discovered and maintained and becoming the subject of rewards and penalties" in so far as it was "true or false to its own being."[48] Social reform should aim at public policies that encouraged the natural, organic, procreative family.[49]

The "left wing," so to speak, of this budding pro-family Social Gospel cause was the Purity Movement. With roots in the Episcopal Church, this Purity campaign focused on voluntary motherhood and an end to the "double standard" in sexual relations. Advocates condemned birth control, yet defended the right of women to control the frequency of sexual intercourse. They favored women's suffrage as a means to social reform. They sought to raise "age of consent" to eighteen. They also condemned the "social vice" of prostitution. Addressing the National Purity Congress of 1895, William T. Sabino warned that "vicious and immoral practices in a people surely and proportionally engender national decay." Rome "had conquered the world only to be conquered by her own licentiousness." The Turks had been done in by the Harem; France by its "vast proportion of illegitimate births"; and Hawaii by the Hula and the frequent exchange of wives. Today, he noted, the Anglo-Saxons ruled the world. The "chief secret" of their power lay in their historic "reverence for a pure family life." The Anglo-Saxon race would "continue to have that power and rule the world if it continues that pure life. Otherwise not."[50]

Purity advocates elevated procreation to the grandest of endeavors. As Col. J. L. Greene told the 1887 Evangelical Alliance conference: "The reproduction of human life, the gendering of a human soul to live and act...eternally—this is the highest moral act of which human beings are capable."[51] Purity campaigners launched The White Cross Movement, where young men would pledge to: treat all women with respect and protect them from wrong and degradation; reject "indecent language and coarse jests"; maintain "the law of Purity" as equally binding upon women *and* men; and fulfill the command "Keep Thyself Pure."[52] All the same, they held, marriage, purity, and moral procreation were at great risk in America. In the face of "Freeloveism," sophisticated cynicism, loose divorce laws, and plunging fertility, Rev. J. B. Welty summoned throughout the land "an earnest, aggressive, red-hot propaganda of Christian ideas and principles concerning marriage, divorce, the family, the home, and the duties of men and women pertaining thereto."[53]

The conflation of concern over falling Protestant fertility and family decay with the turn to social reform also colored the work of Walter Rauschenbusch, prophet-in-chief of the Social Gospel. He emphasized the Christian's procreative responsibility, so to extend the kingdoms of man and God. He quoted from the Psalms: "Happy is the man that hath his quiver full of [children]." Rauschenbusch added: "If a man and woman do marry, they do not yet constitute a true family. The little hand of a child, more than the blessings of a priest, consecrates the family." He contrasted monasticism, which effectively sterilized the best individuals, with "the wonderful fecundity of the Protestant parsonage in men of the highest ability and ideality." Rauschenbusch noted that France had long been seen as "a terrible example" of fertility decline. In America, though, "the older portions of our country are saved from the same situation only by the fertility of the immigrants." In explaining fertility decline, he favored economic arguments. In cities, high rents and high prices "made family life expensive, suppress[ing] child life." The factory system "emptied the home of its women folk." New theories of education sapped "the virtues of self-restraint and patience." Wealth brought on the "temptations of idleness" and alcoholism, so that "the restraints of sex passion are weakened." When a rich woman "has no children and does no useful work in the home, what ground is left for reverence?" Notably, he added: "The freedom of movement in American life and the growing knowledge of preventives makes sin easy and safe." What should be the response? "Unless the rest of society is christianized [sic], the christianized family cannot survive in it." Evangelization and social reforms must be combined to restore the Righteous Republic.[54]

In 1903, reports from both Harvard and Yale Universities bemoaned "the sad family condition" among their male alumni, where the average graduate did not even reproduce himself. A physician, George Engelman, responded in *The Popular Science Monthly* that the problem was *not* education. No other portion of the native-born American population reproduced itself either, he said. The family "conditions now existing among the American people are worse than those found in any other country," Engelman reported, adding: "They are those of a decadent race, those of Greece and Rome in the period of decline." In Massachusetts, as example, the old Puritan stock had a fertility rate of seventeen births per one thousand people; among "the foreigners [read "immigrants"]," the figure was fifty-three! Explaining these numbers, Engelman noted that venereal disease now affected 20–25 percent of American adults, with sterility a common result. The higher education of women was also correlated with fewer children born. And "the ever-increasing desire for the luxuries of life and the morbid craving for social dissipation and advancement" played a role, as well. However, "the most important factor" was [quoting Dr. John S. Billings]: "deliberate and voluntary avoidance, the prevention of child-bearing on the part of a steadily increasing number of married couples, who not only prefer to have but few children, but who 'know how to obtain their wish.'"[55]

The obverse side of concern about the falling fertility of the native-born was mounting alarm over the surging number of new immigrants, especially Roman Catholics. Writing in *Watson's Magazine*, Thomas E. Watson reported that "Roman Catholicism is sweeping all before it" in America. "Fourteen million of our people profess its creed.... While we Protestants are reaching out after Cuba, Jamaica and South America, Rome is conquering North America!" Free Methodist Bishop Walter Sellew declared that the "spirit of Protestantism is in decay," surrendering the nation to Rome. In a 1910 article entitled "Will Roman Catholicism Ever Conquer North America?" the author notes that "New York is now the strongest Catholic city in the world," while the "United States has become the fourth Catholic power, being surpassed only by France, Austria and Italy."[56] In 1910, once-Puritan Massachusetts counted only 450,000 Protestants, of all sorts, compared to 1,100,000 Roman Catholics. Article headlines also included "Faint Hope Over Church Statistics" and "Protestantism Falling Behind Through Unproductive Marriages." Writing in *The Hibbert Journal* in 1915, Dr. Meyrick Booth noted that "modern Protestantism is now (*in practice* if not in theory) virtually identified with a very extreme type of Malthusianism.... The cream of its human material is suffering gradual extinction."[57]

Dr. Booth was correct to note that while Protestant "practice" was increasingly "Malthusian," the Evangelical churches remained opposed to birth control "in theory." Through 1915, Protestant leaders and theologians continued to condemn contraception. Hoping to raise Protestant fertility, they affirmed their support for the Comstock laws, federal and state. Their social–political program looked for ways to protect and strengthen families, in quiet, desperate hope of raising the

(Protestant) birthrate. As Harvard's Francis Peabody wrote in his 1907 book *Jesus Christ and the Social Question*, attention to the family "is illustrated by the mass of new legislation which deals with questions of social welfare; by the new expansion of philosophy into problems of social structure; ...[and] by the new emphasis of Christian theology upon the organic life of the Church or of the world." In these ways, "the integrity of the family, as the most elementary group of social life, will be reverently guarded and stringently secured."[58]

The Alternative

However, there was an alternative. Anglo-Saxon ascendancy, so vital to American Protestant dreams of realizing the Kingdom of God, might be achieved another way. Oddly, the first prominent Protestant writer to see and articulate this alternative was Josiah Strong.

In his 1893 book, *The New Era, or The Coming Kingdom*, Strong gave his Christian Darwinism a very different spin. Drawing directly from the great naturalist, he now emphasized how Christians sheltered "the imbeciles," the maimed, and the sick. Accordingly, although Christian civilization was "on the whole the most powerful force for uplifting humanity," it also tended "directly toward the enfeeblement of the stock." Moreover, "civilization" tended as well "to reduce the fecundity of the more highly cultivated." As a result, the "semi-civilized" women of the Appalachian South might have twenty children each while "the old New England stock is dying out." These small New England families also afforded "a painful contrast to those of alien blood who are transforming New England into a New Ireland or a New France." These observations led him to formulate a new theorem of population: "It seems to be a general law of life from the lowest forms [e.g., bacteria] to the highest that as the scale of being rises fecundity decreases."[59]

All the same, Strong refused to abandon his Anglo-Saxon and American triumphalism. This people, he asserted, combined the highest religious development, the virtues of individualism and freedom, and the "profoundest genius" for organization and government. They superbly united spiritual, intellectual, and physical life. They carried the legacy of the Hebrews, the Greeks, and the Romans. Strong continued: "And now for the first time in the history of mankind these three great strands pass through the fingers of one pre-dominant race to be braided into *a single supreme civilization* in the new era, the perfection of which will be the Kingdom fully come." Although this race was scattered over the earth, "more than one half of its members are already found in the United States; and more and more will this land become the centre of its influence, the seat of its power." Indeed, "[h]e does most to Christianize the world and to hasten the coming of the Kingdom who does most to make thoroughly Christian the United States."[60]

How did Strong reconcile the apparent decline of America's Anglo-Saxon stock with his continued faith in the group's world-historic mission? First, he urged stringent new immigration controls that recognized "the importance to mankind and to the coming Kingdom of guarding against the deterioration of the Anglo-Saxon stock in the United States." And second, to escape "the gloomy conclusions" of Malthusian and Darwinian theories, "[e]levate the masses and the rate of increase of the [lower] race will be correspondingly reduced." Through a happy convergence of "Christian motive" and self-interest, "the better elements of society, the 'higher classes,' *must in self-defense level up the lower.*"[61]

By improving the life prospects and living standards of the poor, social reformers would *reduce* their fertility and possibly salvage the grand Anglo-Saxon project. In making this argument, Strong did not directly advocate that the poor use birth control. Indirectly, though, this is precisely what he wanted. If the true "law of population" meant that the most cultured persons would invariably find ways to reduce their fecundity, little would be gained by battling the spread and use of contraceptives. The key was to inspire the "lower classes" and the "inferior races" also to control their births. Stripped of its more egregious racialism, Strong's "revolution" in thought would find a growing number of hearers among early twentieth-century Protestants.[62]

Two other legacies of the bio-religious Righteous Republic should be noted. The turn by Strong and other Social Gospel theorists to family policy brought forward some arguably positive themes, such as improved urban housing for the poor ("each family shall have its own front door") and encouragement to suburban life (involving the "more natural conditions of rural life"). However, the same agenda also embraced "the modern science of child-saving" and "the placing out system," where city children would be taken from their parents and put in rural homes. Such strategies opened the way to an unprecedented level of state intervention into and control over families.[63]

Second, the "Catholic problem" facing Anglo-Saxon America loomed ever larger in the first two decades of the new century. One response was the turn by Strong and other Protestant leaders to demands for strict immigration controls, as laid out in the *New Era*. Another result was to open a crack between Protestant and Catholic leaders and theologians on the birth control question. The Christian consensus on the sinfulness of birth control (other than through abstinence) was subtly undermined by Strong's new "law of population." Margaret Sanger would soon discover how to widen that fissure into a virtual canyon, and so transform America.

Notes

1. Darryl G. Hart, *That Old-Time Religion in Modern America: Evangelical Protestanism in the Twentieth Century* (Chicago, IL: Ivan R. Dee, 2002), 57.
2. From: Phillip D. Jordan, *The Evangelical Alliance for the United States of America, 1847–1900* (New York and Toronto: The Edwin Mellen Press, 1982), 10, 15–18, 70; George M. Marsden, *Fundamentalism and American Culture: The Shaping of 20th Century Evangelicalism: 1870–1925* (New York/Oxford: Oxford University Press, 1980), 11–12, 17.
3. Marsden, *Fundamentalism and American Culture*, 14–18.
4. Betty A. DeBerg, *Ungodly Women: Gender and the First Wave of American Fundamentalism* (Minneapolis, MN: Fortress Press, 1990), 18–19, 24; Colleen McDannell, *The Christian Home in Victorian America, 1840–1900* (Bloomington, IN: Indiana University Press, 1986), xv, 29–51; Catharine Beecher and Harriet Beecher Stowe, *The American Woman's Home, or Principles of Domestic Science* (New York: J.B. Ford, 1869), Chapter 1; Henry Wilson Yates, Jr., "American Protestantism and Birth Control: An Examination of Shifts within a Major Religious Value Orientation" (doctoral diss., Harvard University, 1968), 134.
5. Jordan, *Evangelical Alliance*, 72–77.
6. In *Eighteenth Annual Report of the Evangelical Alliance of the United States of America* (New York: Evangelical Alliance for the United States, 1886), 25–26; in Pamphlet Collection, State Historical Society of Wisconsin, Number 01-8921.
7. Quotations from Jordan, *Evangelical Alliance*, 69, 97. Also: Marsden, *Fundamentalism and American Culture*, 12–13, 18.
8. Sydney A. Ahlstrom, *A Religious History of the American People* (New Haven, CT and London: Yale University Press, 1972), 743–46.
9. Marsden, *Fundamentalism and American Culture*, 37; also 32–35.
10. The Cleveland Tabernacle, *The Great Redemption; or, Gospel Light Under the Labors of Moody and Sankey, Containing the Sermons, Addresses, Prayer-Meeting Talks, Bible Readings and Prayers, From the Commencement of Their Labors Until Close of Revival Meetings Held at The Cleveland Tabernacle, During Oct. and Nov. 1879* (Chicago, IL: The Century Book and Paper, 1880), 9–11.
11. Ahlstrom, Religious History of the American People, 747–48.
12. Marsden, *Fundamentalism and American Culture*, 27–32.

13. Robert Handy, "The Protestant Quest for a Christian America," *Church History* 22 (1953): 12.

14. William A. Johnson, *Nature and the Supernatural in the Theology of Horace Bushnell* (Minneapolis, MN: Lund Press, 1963), 10. (Emphasis in original.)

15. Horace Bushnell, *Christian Nurture* [1861 ed.] (Grand Rapids, MI: Baker Book House, 1979), 91–92, 197–98. (Emphasis added.)

16. Ibid., 198, 201, 205, 209–11, 214–18. (Emphasis added.)

17. It should be noted, perhaps, that despite Bushnell's remarkable—some might say outlandish—claims, there is some evidence that the success of the early Christian Church actually lay in its progenitive qualities. While pagan Romans practiced abortion, infanticide, and contraception, allowed for easy divorce, and had a preponderance of males (due to infanticide), the new Christian movement strongly opposed abortion and infanticide, discouraged birth control and divorce, and had a high proportion of members who were women in their fertile years. Religious sociologist Rodney Stark concludes that "a nontrivial portion of Christian growth was due to superior fertility." Rodney Stark, *The Rise of Christianity: A Sociologist Reconsiders History* (Princeton, NJ: Princeton University Press, 1996), 122–26, 128.

18. Jordan, *Evangelical Alliance*, 163.

19. Josiah Strong, *Our Country*, ed. Jurgen Herbst (Cambridge, MA: The Belknap Press of Harvard University Press, 1963 [1886]), 42–49.

20. Ibid., 59–87.

21. Jordan, *Evangelical Alliance*, 158.

22. Strong, *Our Country*, 210–12.

23. Ibid., 213–14.

24. Ibid., 206–8, 212–18.

25. Jordan, *Evangelical Alliance*, 154–55, 157, 160. (Emphasis added.)

26. Ibid., 155.

27. Allan Carlson, "Children of the Reformation," *Touchstone: A Journal of Mere Christianity* 20 (May 2007): 20–25.

28. Yates, "American Protestants and Birth Control," 9.

29. Francis Greenwood Peabody, *Jesus Christ and the Social Question* (New York: The Macmillan Company, 1907), 132.

30. Quoted in Yates, "American Protestants and Birth Control," 198.

31. Ibid., 171; also 122, 126–28, 177–98.

32. See: Janice Ruth Wood, *The Struggle for Free Speech in the United States, 1872-1915. Edward Bliss Foote, Edward Bond Foote, and Anti-Comstock Operations* (New York and London: Routledge, 2008–2009), 19.

33. Frederick Hollick, MD, *The Marriage Guide or Natural History of Generation; A Private Instructor for Married Persons and Those About to Marry, Both Male and Female; In Everything Concerning the Physiology and Relations of the Sexual System and the Production or Prevention of Off Spring—Including all the New Discoveries, Never Before Given in the English Language* (New York: T.W. Strong, 1850), 332–40.

34. From Wood, *Struggle for Free Speech*, 18.

35. "Changes in Population," *Harper's New Weekly Magazine* 38 (February 1869): 386–92. (Emphasis added.)

36. Nathan Allen, *Population: Its Law of Increase* (Lowell, MA: Stone and Huse Book and Job Printers, 1870), 5–7, 11, 22–32.

37. "The New England Family," *The New Englander* 41 (March 1882): 137–59. (Emphasis added.)

38. Noah Davis, "Marriage and Divorce," *North American Review* 139 (July 1884): 33–35.

39. Charles Franklin Thwing and Carrie F. Butler Thwing, *The Family: An Historical and Social Study* (Boston, MA: Lee and Shepard Publishers, 1887), 103–4, 107, 110, 197–99, 214–15.

40. Richard Wheatley, "The Alleged Decay of the Family," *The Methodist Review* 47 (November 1887): 860–64, 867–68, 871–72, 878–79.

41. Edward A. Ross, "The Causes of Race Superiority," *Annals of the American Academy of Political and Social Science* 18 (July 1901): 67–89.

42. Jordan, *Evangelical Alliance*, 165.

43. "Call for the Washington Conference. To the Christian Public," in *National Perils and Opportunities. The Discussions of the General Christian Conference, held in Washington, DC, December 7, 8, and 9, 1887, Under the Auspices and Direction of The Evangelical Alliance of the United States* (New York: The Baker and Taylor, 1887), v–vi. (Emphasis added.)

44. W. E. Dodge, "Opening Address," in *National Perils and Opportunities*, 3–7. (Emphasis added.)

45. Rev. S. W. Dike, "Perils to the Family," in *National Perils and Opportunities*, 167, 170–73, 178–80.

46. Yates, "American Protestants and Birth Control," 144.

47. Samuel W. Dike, *The Theory of the Marriage Tie* [Publications of the National Divorce Reform League, Special Issues of 1893, no. 1] (Montpelier, VT: Watchman and State Journal Press, 1893), 7.

48. Samuel W. Dike, *The Family in the History of Christianity* [Publications of the National Divorce Reform League, Special Issues of 1893, no. 2] (Montpelier, VT: Watchman and State Journal Press, 1893), 20.

49. On Dike's worldview, see also: Samuel W. Dike, *Syllabus of a Course of Six Lectures on Sociology in the Study of Family Problems* (Boston, MA: C.H. Simonds and Co., 1893), 9–12.

50. William T. Sabine, "Social Vice and National Decay," in *The National Purity Congress, Its Papers, Addresses, Portraits. An Illustrated Record of the Papers and Addresses of The First National Purity Congress, Held Under the Auspices of the American Purity Alliance, in The Park Avenue Friends' Meeting House, Baltimore, October 14, 15 and 16, 1895*, ed. Aaron M. Powell (New York: The American Purity Alliance, 1896), 43, 46, 48–51, 53–54.

51. J. L. Greene, "The Social Vice," in *National Perils and Opportunities*, 184.

52. Aaron M. Powell, "The President's Opening Address," *The National Purity Congress*, 7.

53. J. B. Welty, "The Need of White Cross Work," in Powell, *The National Purity Congress*, 242. See also: DeBerg, *Ungodly Women*, 36–37.

54. Walter Rauschenbusch, *Christianizing the Social Order* (New York: The Macmillan Company, 1912), 134–36, 302; Walter Rauschenbusch, *Chris-*

tianity and the Social Crisis (New York: The Macmillan, 1914), 271–79; Yates, "American Protestants and Birth Control," 268, 270.

55.   George J. Engelmann, MD, "Education Not the Cause of Race Decline," *Popular Science Monthly* 63 (June 1903): 172–84.

56.   "Will Roman Catholicism Ever Conquer North America?" *Current Literature* 49 (November 1910): 525–26.

57.   "Protestantism Falling Behind Through Unproductive Marriages," *Current Opinion* 58 (January 1915): 40–41; "Faint Hope Over Church Statistics," *The Literary Digest* 44 (February 10, 1912): 272.

58.   Peabody, *Jesus Christ and the Social Question*, 133.

59.   Josiah Strong, *The New Era or The Coming Kingdom* (New York: The Baker and Taylor, 1893), 34–36.

60.   Ibid., 60–72, 80. (Emphasis added.)

61.   Ibid., 36. (Emphasis added.)

62.   In 1898, internal quarrels in the Evangelical Alliance forced Strong's resignation. He founded The League for Social Service, known after 1902 as the American Institute for Social Service, and played a key role in establishing The Federal Council of the Churches of Christ.

63.   See: Peabody, *Jesus Christ and The Social Question*, 166–68; Josiah Strong, *The Challenge of the City* (New York: Eaton & Mains, 1907), 131–33.

3

Margaret Sanger Divides the Christians

As Anthony Comstock was to the late nineteenth century, Margaret Sanger would be to the early twentieth. They were, in a curious way, ideological mirror images of each other. They shared the same prophetic style, the same absolute certainty, and the same relentless will, while standing at opposite ends of the birth control question.[1] Where Comstock built and successfully enforced a legal empire that equated contraception with obscenity, Sanger transformed birth control from a perverse act into—for many—a righteous practice. Where Comstock mobilized a united American Evangelical Empire behind his enterprise and also enjoyed the tacit support of Roman Catholics, Sanger used latent anti-Catholicism and a form of "soft" eugenics to swing the postmillennial Social Gospel Protestants behind her cause.

All the same, Sanger held Comstock in awe, attributing the whole range of federal and state laws affecting birth control to "his psychosexual hyper aesthesia" alone. She continued: "His fanaticism generated a terrific energy. Galvanized into incessant and frenzied activity by the intensity of his obsession, he discovered obscenity everywhere. He came to be a national pontiff of prurience. Congress quailed before his passion." She even paid the late culture warrior a backhanded compliment. "With the passing of that patriarch," she wrote, "any experienced observer must have noted the rapid decline of the Comstockian school." His successors proved to be "totally ignorant of what may be termed the classical tactics of suppression." Compared to the "fanatical zeal" and "inexhaustible" energy of Comstock, the guardians of Christian morality in America after 1915 were "like school boys playing with chemicals…. Instead of silencing an idea or a book, they merely dramatize it."[2] Her judgment here is accurate. For example, where Comstock would surely have used some law to shut down Sanger's *Birth Control Review*, his successor at the New

York Society for the Suppression of Vice—John S. Sumner—agreed in 1922 to contribute an article for the *Review*'s symposium on the issue of overpopulation.[3]

Growing up Anti-Catholic

The "radical" phase of Sanger's career in birth control coincided with the last three years of Comstock's life. She had been raised in Corning, New York, in a stridently socialist, feminist, and atheist home. Her father especially "deplored" the Roman Catholic Church. When he arranged for the famed atheist Robert G. Ingersoll to speak in their town, and when a largely Catholic crowd disrupted the event, her father announced that the speech would resume in the woods near their home. Accompanying him and Colonel Ingersoll in the walk to the new site, "I trudged along again, my small hand clasped in his, my head held just as high."[4] In 1913, she journeyed to Europe to study contraceptive techniques. The following year, she launched her publication *The Woman Rebel* under the revealing masthead, "No Gods, No Masters." That same year she also popularized the phrase, "birth control." Hounded by Comstock, she returned via Canada to Europe, becoming the protégé of England's prominent "sexologist" Havelock Ellis.

On July 5, 1915, she gave a remarkable speech at the Fabian Society Hall in London, laying out a radical agenda. She asserted that "the basis of feminism was a woman's right to be an unmarried mother." She dismissed labor union efforts at better wages, if untied to birth control: "No matter what the increase a strike will bring—one baby added to the family" would eliminate the gain. Sanger ridiculed reform efforts to support motherhood—"better baby funds, Little Mothers leagues, milk stations for babies, child nurseries for the children" and "mothers pensions"—as so many slaps in the face of women. Her object, she said, was to give working women "a class independence which says to the masters produce your own slaves—keep your religion, your ethics and your morality for yourselves...." She also threw in a little popular eugenics—the emerging "science" of controlled human reproduction—citing Friedrich Nietzsche's warning that the world was becoming peopled by a ludicrous species, "a gently grunting domestic animal called man."[5]

However, over the next few years, Sanger shifted tactics. In order to cultivate people of wealth and influence, she largely jettisoned her socialist proclivities. She recruited women of means such as Janet

Barrett Rubles, who "practically turned over her home in Turtle Bay Gardens" for "lunches, teas, and dinners in behalf of the cause."[6] Sanger now focused simply on making birth control available, combining social action, civil disobedience, and feminism with this conservative financial support. In 1917, she opened her first birth control clinic in Brooklyn. Arrested, tried, and convicted under New York's mini-Comstock law, she spent thirty days in the Queens County Penitentiary, becoming a celebrity in the process.[7]

Sanger also set out to recraft her case for birth control. Part of this meant perfecting her negative message. She showed a "special genius" in confronting her religious, scholarly, and political foes with the brutal realities to be found in some women's lives. As she remarked, "How academic, how anemically intellectual and how remote from throbbing, bleeding humanity all of these prejudiced arguments sound, when one has been brought face to face with the reality of suffering."[8] It also meant finding a positive vision of birth control that would break through traditionalist opposition. The Great War of 1914–1918 came to her aid. It shattered moral and religious certainties, allowing Sanger to offer instead a "new" morality attuned to the times. "[M]orality is nothing but the sum total, the net residuum, of social habits, the codification of customs," she wrote. "The only 'immoral' person, in any country, is he who fails to observe the current folkways." As a corollary, this meant that changes in actual behavior or "custom" would necessarily summon a new morality justifying that behavior.[9] Sanger added that when children would be "conceived in love and born into an atmosphere of happiness," then parenthood would become "a glorious privilege and the children will grow to resemble gods." Now avoiding praise of unwed mothers, Sanger instead argued that:

> We want mothers to be fit. We want them to conceive in joy and gladness. We want them to carry their babies during the whole nine months in a sound and healthy body and with a happy, joyous, hopeful mind.[10]

Again using the language of eugenics, Sanger asserted that through birth control, "Mothers will bring forth, in purity and joy, a race that is morally and spiritually free."[11]

Finally, Sanger needed an enemy; the Roman Catholic Church fit the bill perfectly. Sanger correctly perceived that pre-1914 fears of Roman Catholic expansion in America would swell into a mighty wave of anti-Catholicism after the war. At the extreme level, the Ku Klux Klan enjoyed explosive growth after 1918, with membership climbing briefly into the millions and with "Catholic hordes" among its foes. At the level of law, the new immigration act of 1924, as a Congressional Committee report put it, was an effort "to guarantee, as best we can at this late date, racial homogeneity in the United States"; by this, the law's architects implicitly meant White, Anglo-Saxon, and Protestant. Opposition to Catholicism also suited Sanger personally. As noted earlier, her father had tutored her on the presumed evils and dangers of Rome. Moreover, her study of and involvement in socialist activities before the war had taught her the value of a clearly identified foe when launching a social–political movement. Already marginalized in American life, Catholicism was the obvious choice. Finally, in her desire to gain a sacred canopy for birth control, she could easily play on four-century-old antipathies between Protestants and Catholics to bring the former to her side.[12]

As historian Herschel Yates Jr., has noted, Sanger's "battle with the Roman Catholic Church was an ideological one."[13] Among other necessary tasks, she rewrote the history of the Church. The early Christian community, she argued in *Woman and the New Race* (1920), was actually antinatalist, focused on celibacy and conversion. Only later would it use the "sex force for its own interest," to produce laymen who would sustain, financially and otherwise, a growing ecclesiastical order. While pagan Roman women had considerable freedom, she said, the Christian Church now "exhorted women to bear as many children as possible." Sanger added:

> If Christianity turned the clock of general progress back a thousand years, it turned back the clock two thousand years for women. Its greatest outrage upon her was to forbid her to control the function of motherhood under any circumstances, thus limiting her life's work to bringing forth and rearing children.

The Church, she said, also used "fear and shame" as "grim guardians against the gate of knowledge and constructive idealism"; it "has always known and feared the spiritual potentialities of woman's freedom"; and while long a fierce opponent of science, "only in sex matters has [the church] succeeded in keeping the bugaboo alive."[14] As another writer put it in an early issue of *The Birth Control Review*, "the [Catholic] church refuses to learn anything. It prefers myths to facts, tradition to experience, darkness to light."[15] This focus on Catholicism's reputed war on science and knowledge would later blossom into an appeal to Protestants to break ranks with Catholics, since the birth control movement was seeking what "any good Protestant" would want, only to be "prohibited from achieving this goal by an alien, half-Americanized Roman Catholicism."[16]

Clarifying the Catholic View

A contemporary clarification of the Roman Catholic position on birth control actually played into Sanger's hands, and set the stage for two decades of jousting between the female birth controller and her major, post-Comstock foe: Father John A. Ryan. Among American Protestants and Catholics alike, there was relatively little public discussion of contraception between passage of the federal Comstock law in 1873 and Comstock's death in 1915. His resolution of this issue and his suppression of the trade in contraceptives simply seems to have been supported by a broad consensus of American Christians, whatever private behaviors might have been. Sanger's activism opened a new debate. In 1915, Father Ryan—professor of social ethics at Catholic University of America and the champion of a "living family wage"—received an invitation to join the nascent Birth Control League. He responded:

> I regard the practice which your organization desires to promote as immoral, degrading, and stupid. The so-called contraceptive devices are intrinsically immoral because they involve the unnatural use, the perversion of a human faculty.... Such conduct is quite [as] immoral as self mutilation or the practice of solitary vice.

The letter subsequently appeared in an article for *Harper's Weekly*, where author Mary Alden Hopkins labeled it as the only extant evidence of contemporary American Catholic belief regarding birth control.[17] While Ryan tried to clarify matters in a letter to the editor, the episode clearly inspired him to write a more complete account of church teaching in light of new press attention in America to "birth control" and "contraception." Addressed to his fellow priests and appearing in *Ecclesiastical Review*, the essay "set forth the new emphases in American Catholic Policy on birth control," arguments that would stand unchanged for over five decades.[18] Indeed, historian Kathleen Tobin asserts that Ryan's essay and advocacy were the primary reasons "that the Catholic Church in America developed such a vocal stance against birth control."[19]

Ryan's article declared that there "is no possibility of a legitimate difference of opinion among Catholics" regarding contraception, while still acknowledging that many of the laity were "considerably tainted" by the practice. Why did the Church condemn "all positive methods of birth prevention"? Because "all these devices constitute the immoral perversion of a human faculty.... Actions which are in harmony with nature are good; those which are not in harmony with nature are bad." It was clear that the "generative faculty" had as its "essential end the procreation of offspring." When this faculty was so employed that the fulfillment of its purpose was impossible, "it is perverted, used unnaturally, and therefore sinfully." What harm was done? Ryan replied that the "moral order is violated; ...the sanctity of nature is outraged; the natural law of the human organism is transgressed." By degrading the wife to the level of a prostitute, birth control also led to a "loss of respect toward the conjugal partner, and loss of faith in the sacredness of the nuptial bed." What about poverty? Ryan's response was to urge improvement of the earning power of workers. Overpopulation? "What we know is that for the present there is no occasion to worry," provided that "the good things of life" are "reasonably and justly distributed."[20] As head of the Social Action Department of the National Catholic Conference, Ryan subsequently drafted a "Pastoral Letter" reiterating these arguments, which the American Bishops duly sent out in 1919 to priests and the laity.[21]

In late 1921, Sanger won a huge public relations victory over the Catholic Church in the so-called "Town Hall" incident. The occasion was a conference in New York City designed to launch formally the American Birth Control League (ABCL). Sponsors of the session included such notables as novelist Theodore Dreiser and English statesman Winston Churchill. Two days of organizational and medical meetings took place without incident. However, on Sunday evening a mass meeting was to be held in Town Hall, on West forty-third Street. The subject was "Birth Control: Is It Moral?" According to Sanger's account, when she and colleagues pulled up to the Town Hall's doors, they were blocked shut. A policeman told her "There ain't going to be no meeting. That's all I can say." With a confused crowd milling about, Sanger managed to slip inside, where she found the hall half-filled. She attempted to start the meeting, but was pulled from the stage by a policeman. A man strode to the platform, and asked a Sanger associate, "Who's in charge?"

"I am," Anne [Kennedy] had answered.

"This meeting must be closed."

"Why?"

"An indecent, immoral subject is to be discussed. It cannot be held."

"On what authority? Are you from the police?"

"No, I'm Monsignor Dineen, the Secretary of [Catholic] Archbishop [Patrick] Hayes."

"What right has he to interfere?"

"He has the right."[22]

With the crowd shouting "Defy them! Defy them!" and following the spontaneous singing of "My Country, Tis of Thee," the police arrested Sanger and two other speakers. According to some accounts, they insisted on walking to the precinct station, accompanied by hundreds of their followers. Anne Kennedy brought along the reporters, completing the political theater.

A subsequent investigation determined that the police had acted responsibly, without pressure from Archbishop Hayes. However, the story quickly gained momentum as a tale of Catholic oppression of free thought and free speech. Sanger's status also rose. Only a few days later, after the *New York Times* published the Archbishop's Christmas letter in which he denounced birth control ("Children troop down from Heaven because God wills it.... Heinous is the sin committed against the creative act of God...."), Sanger was invited to write a reply. Here, she sharpened the argument that she would employ for the next two decades:

> There is no objection to the Catholic Church inculcating its doctrines to its own people, but when it attempts to make these ideas legislative acts and enforce its opinions and code of morals upon the Protestant members of this country, then I do consider its attempt an interference with the principles of this democracy, and I have a right to protest.[23]

Elsewhere, she crowed about the incident: "The idea of Birth Control was advertised, dramatized, made the recipient of column upon column of publicity.... The clumsy and illegal tactics of our opponents made the whole country aware of what we were doing.... Thus our first national conference was crowned with triumph."[24]

In vain did Catholic advocates note that as of 1921 not a *single* Protestant denomination or group had endorsed birth control; all remained formally opposed to the practice. In vain did they point out that existing laws against contraceptives were the uniform product of nineteenth-century evangelical Protestant political influence. In vain did they compare current Catholic opposition to birth control with the recently successful Protestant suppression, through law, of alcoholic beverages.

Instead, Sanger had set the new terms of debate. As she wrote in her *Autobiography*, "Ever since the outburst of religious intolerance at Town Hall, it [has] been apparent that in the United States the Catholic hierarchy and officialdom were going to be the principle enemies of birth control."[25] She fixed the issue as one of Catholic attempts to muzzle and control Protestants. The "Town Hall" incident, she explained in *Birth Control Review*, "has shown up the sinister control of the Roman Catholic Church, which attempts—and to a great extent succeeds—to control all questions of public and private morality in these United States." Drawing in old Protestant complaints in a new way, Sanger declared that "All who resent this sinister Church Control of life and conduct...must now choose between Church Control and Birth Control." Neutrality was not a choice. "You must make a declaration of independence, of self-reliance, or submit to the dictatorship of the Roman Catholic hierarchy..., a dictatorship of celibates."[26]

In subsequent years, certain Catholic organizations would apply economic or political pressures to suppress birth control meetings. In 1922, the Knights of Columbus put such pressure on the Mayor of Boston to prevent a lecture by Sanger. Similar political episodes occurred in Albany (1923) and Syracuse (1924). In other cities, the Knights used the threat of economic boycotts on owners to close off meeting halls from birth control advocates. In Milwaukee, the pressure came from the Catholic Women's League.[27] In most cases, these tactics succeeded in their immediate, local purpose. Yet, unlike the nationwide suppression achieved by Anthony Comstock, such actions were now spotty and uncoordinated. Sanger delighted in reporting on them,[28] for they underscored her claims to speak for liberty in the face of "Romanist" machinations.

Whither the Protestants?

Another of Sanger's brilliant strategic techniques was simply to ignore Protestant writers, preachers, and churches that continued to denounce birth control. By demonizing the Catholic Church alone (although, on some occasions she also lashed out at Missouri Synod

Lutherans), by claiming to defend the Protestant conscience from Roman oppression, she left the impression that Protestants were on her side, in apparent hope that this would become a self-fulfilling prophecy. What actually was going on beneath the surface among Protestants during the 1920s?

Historian David Kennedy notes that debate over birth control did grow during that decade, particularly among the Episcopalians, the Presbyterians, the Methodists, the Northern Baptists, and other denominations which had formed the Federal Council of Churches of Christ (FCCC) in 1908. This debate became entwined with a broader struggle for power between theological liberals and conservatives, as the evangelical consensus of the nineteenth century unraveled.

Ultimately and oddly, given its frequent Roman pretensions, the church most vulnerable to doctrinal change proved to be the Episcopalians. That was not clear in 1908 when the Lambeth Conference—a gathering of Anglican Bishops from around the globe normally held every ten years—adopted a statement with strong echoes from Josiah Strong, condemning the effects of contraception on the providential mission of the Anglo-Saxons: "there is the *world-danger* that the great English-speaking people, diminished in number and weakened in moral force, should commit the crowning infamy of race-suicide, and so fail to fulfill that high destiny to which in the Providence of God they have been manifestly called." While labeling "self-restraint within marriage" a "man's right," the statement called for a prohibition of all "neo-Malthusian appliances," the prosecution of those who enabled "preventive methods," a tighter regulation of midwives (who might also perform abortions), and a national recognition of "the dignity of motherhood." In 1920, the next, war-delayed Lambeth Conference downplayed the Anglo-Saxon mission, yet still delivered "an emphatic warning against the use of unnatural means for the avoidance of conception." The primary purpose of Christian marriage was "the continuance of the race through the gift and heritage of children"; the bishops specifically condemned that teaching which "encouraged married people in the deliberate cultivation of sexual union as an end in itself."[29]

Meanwhile, among the premillennial Evangelicals moving toward what would be called fundamentalism, the first signs of engagement in the birth control debate emerged. As will be shown later, the postmillennial doctrine that man must first create the Kingdom of God to bring on Christ's return left its adherents vulnerable to eugenic arguments. For their part, premillennialists doubted men's capabilities here, distrusted all modern science, and especially objected to Darwinism. This stance is commonly misunderstood. The imposing figure of William Jennings Bryan provides clarity. While he apparently never offered a direct opinion on birth control, the great Evangelical did object to the use of Darwinist ideas to bolster political and economic conservatism. Shaken by the slaughter of the Great War, Bryan also linked German nationalism, militarism, and materialism to philosopher Friedrich Nietzsche, whom he considered the ultimate Darwinian. The Great Commoner complained that Nietzsche's philosophy "condemned democracy,... denounced Christianity,...denied the existence of God, overturned all standards of morality, eulogized war,...praised hatred...and endeavored to substitute the worship of the superman for the worship of Jehovah."[30] This led him to accept an offer in 1920 from the new World Christian Fundamentals Association to lead a "Layman's Movement" against evolution and modernism, with Nietzsche—not Darwin—as his prime target.

Other evangelical leaders on the path to fundamentalism also linked Darwin to Nietzsche and the latter to the quest to create a "New Man" through eugenics. Professor Howard W. Kellogg, speaking at the Bible Institute of Los Angeles in 1918, noted Nietzsche's dismissal of Christianity as a "slave-morality" and as "life's fiercest enemy" through actions such as care of the weak, which ran counter to natural selection. He added that Nietzsche reached toward the Superman through "a Eugenics Revision of our present marriage laws,...a united Europe and the annihilation of the Christian Church." The German nihilist had thrown off the mask of Evolution, revealing "a monster plotting world dominion, the wreck of civilization and the destruction of Christianity itself."[31] In rejecting the Nietzschean reformulation of Darwin, Bryan, Kellogg, and other fundamentalists also implicitly rejected the temptation of eugenics.[32]

As early as 1916, the Moody Bible Institute's *Christian Workers Magazine* began editorializing against birth control. Commenting on a sermon by A. C. Dixon, it denounced the Malthusian argument that the Great War had been caused by overpopulation, saying that "that theory is from the devil." It also favorably described a speaker "of the Federated Catholics Societies" who traced the birth control issue back to the "detestable act" of Onan and who blamed "socialist leaders, aided by the anarchists and other neo-Malthusian 'uplifters,'" for bringing on "the national agitation of this wickedness in the name of social betterment." The journal positively quoted the unnamed

Catholic: "If men would only read and believe the Bible, and obey God who revealed it they would find that they might in a holy and proper way multiply and replenish the earth." The editors added that food for children would also be plentiful, for "The Creator knew what He was doing when He made the earth and placed man upon it." If men simply let sin alone, "all would still be very good."[33]

Several months later, the journal again raised the issue, this time through commentary on a speech by Leonora Z. Meder, former Chicago commissioner of public welfare. She had rebuked the disciples of birth control, saying that this behavior created selfishness, led to prostitution, increased crime, endangered the lives of the innocent, and imperiled the nation. Meder also pointed to Illinois' insane asylums, where one could "see the appalling ruin to both mind and body brought on by this heinous practice." She blasted idle "society women" who urged contraception onto "the good, honest women in our factories and stores," and concluded:

> Birth control is immoral, because it is a perversion of a natural human faculty; degrading because it logically leads to childless marriages, which is hardly distinguishable from prostitution; stupid, because it does not attain its purpose of human welfare.[34]

Other commentaries followed. Published by the Bible Institute of Los Angeles, *The King's Business* quoted evangelist R. A. Torrey: "Be fruitful and multiply. This command has never been abrogated. One of the sins that threatens our national life today is the sin of disobedience to this command."[35] In 1920, the *Christian Workers Magazine* blasted childless marriages, arguing from the Bible that "the happiness of man and woman" was only a secondary purpose of marriage; its "prime purpose is to produce healthy children."[36] In *Our Hope*, the editors described a 1925 gathering of birth control movement leaders, where "the scheme of limiting births was endorsed by infidels, professional men, and preachers." Indeed, "[b]irth control was pictured as a veritable saviour of the race. One preacher mumbled about the coming of the Kingdom if birth control becomes legalized." The editors also denounced the idea that overpopulation was the cause of war, but chose "not to defile our pages with a more detailed description of the movement and its methods." All the same, "the whole scheme" was surely "another sign of the times."[37]

Leading fundamentalist preachers took on birth control. Rev. Mark Matthews of Seattle denounced the childless home as "a menace to good government." The "natural" home was one "filled with children. Nature demands that the home be crowned with child life." He blamed "misguided, superficial women" for the "wicked and malicious actions" of birth prevention. Slipping back into postmillennialist language, Matthews declared that "If the women were spending their time trying to establish homes, rear children and do their full duty, the world would witness the dawn of the millennium within an inconceivably short time." He concluded: "Regeneration, consecration and absolute righteousness on the part of husbands and wives of this country, will abolish *the crimes* of *murder* [abortion] *and prevention*."[38]

Others concurred. John Roach Straton of New York, sometimes labeled "The Protestant Pope" by journalists, turned pessimistic and sharply conservative after 1920, as he took on the fight against modernism. Writing that year, Straton argued that "we are witnessing the widest wave of immorality in the history of the human race." He denounced the Flappers, or the "New Women": "They wanted to be...men's casual and light hearted companions; not broad-hipped mothers of the race, but irresponsible playmates." He blasted birth control as "artificial interference with the sources of life" and labeled the Birth Control League of New York a "chamber of horrors."[39] Rev. J. C. Masse of North Carolina dismissed birth control as "legalized concubinage." The fundamentalist Presbyterian Clarence E. MacCartney firmly rejected the Social Gospel of the liberals and embraced the task of saving souls, not the world. He condemned birth control as a violation of natural morality, adding: "where men are interested in the New Birth,...they will have little time or taste to discuss Birth Control." MacCartney was particularly incensed by emerging clerical supporters of birth prevention:

> Should the recommendations of many Protestant ministers today be followed, it will come to this...[a]fter a second or third child has been brought into the home..., the Protestant minister will be summoned to strangle it, so that the firstborn will have a chance to go to college.[40]

Billy Sunday, the greatest evangelist of the era, was a fierce foe of birth control. Perhaps influenced by his own precarious childhood, Sunday idealized the home and the place of the mother within:

> [O]ur homes are on the level with women. Towns are on the level with homes. What women are our homes will be; and what the town

is the men will be.... The devil and women can damn the world, and Jesus and women can save this old world. It remains with woman-hood today to lift our social life to a higher plane.[41]

Sunday scorned those "married women who shrink from mater-nity...simply because they love ease, because they love fine garments and ability to flirt like a butterfly at some social function." In a sermon targeted at women, he noted darkly that "Crimes have been and are being committed; hands are stained with blood; and that very crime has made France the charnel house of the world." In America, he continued, "we of our boasted intelligence and wealth, we are fast ap-proaching the same doom." More positively, he remarked that "there is not an angel in heaven that would not be glad to come to earth and be honored with motherhood if God would grant her that privilege." Sunday called "the birth control faddists...the devil's mouthpiece." Women who used pessaries wore The Mark of Cain. A woman "so selfish" as to dislike having children "is, in fact, a criminal."[42]

While anti-Catholicism grew among liberal Protestants, the fun-damentalists tended to be remarkably praiseworthy of the Church of Rome. In denouncing divorce, Billy Sunday declared "I am a Catholic" on this question.[43] Moody Institute publications regularly praised Catholic sexual ethics.[44] And in 1929, John Roach Straton stood alongside Father William J. Duane, President of Fordham University, at a rally protesting a proposed New York law to legalize the giving of birth control information to married couples. Straton congratulated The Catholic Church for its opposition to both divorce and "race suicide."[45]

Eugenics and Protestant Hope

The high-tide of the "science of eugenics" came in 1930, precisely correlated with the first official Protestant approval of birth control. This was not a coincidence. As historian Kathleen Tobin explains, "the religious debate over birth control did not begin with the legalization of contraceptives, it began with eugenics."[46]

The process was actually complex. On the Protestant side, some of the Social Gospel clerics—notably the aging Josiah Strong—now avoided the hereditarian premises of eugenics. His 1907 volume *The Challenge of the City* actually emphasized the power of America's as-similative process: "A foreign heredity is overcome by an American environment."[47] On the eugenics side, meanwhile, many prominent advocates opposed or distrusted birth control. They feared that only the better educated and "more fit" would practice contraception, leaving the "unfit" to breed. Eugenicist Henry Fairchild Osborn called birth control "fundamentally unnatural" and concluded: "on eugenic as well as on evolutionary lines I am strongly opposed to many directions which the birth control movement is taking." Fellow eugenicist Charles Davenport thought the birth control movement might "do more harm than good." Ellsworth Huntington considered birth control a "two-edged sword," which could be "used most effectively to fight the enemy, but may also cut the man who wields it."[48]

The convergence of birth control, eugenics, and Christianity followed two tracks. On the first, Margaret Sanger—"an ardent, self-confessed eugenicist"—courted other would be race-improvers.[49] In the early 1920s, birth control remained contentious and was still broadly seen as vile and immoral. In contrast, eugenics stood as a popular and seemingly obvious new science aimed at the production of healthier, stronger, and more intelligent children. Few denounced it; even leading Catholics admired the eugenicists' elevation of marriage. So when Margaret Sanger spoke at The Second International Eugenics Conference, held at New York's American Museum of Natural History in 1921, she did so as the supplicant. Sanger enthusiastically embraced eugenics, arguing that "[t]he most urgent problem today is how to limit and discourage the overfertility of the mentally and physically defective." She emphasized how the legalization and distribution of contraceptives would assist this goal. Indeed, early issues of *The Birth Control Review* would feature on their masthead the phrase, "Birth Control: To Create a Race of Thoroughbreds." The conference also launched the American Eugenics Society (AES), which had 1,200 members by 1930. Sanger soon had an important ally in Leon F. Whitney, who served as AES Executive Secretary. An enthusiastic supporter of Sanger, he repeatedly pushed for formal linkages between his group and the American Birth Control League (ABCL), including a proposed merger of the AES journal *Eugenics* with the *Birth Control Review*. By 1928, the Society's legislative program included two provisions promoting birth control. Three years later, the AES could report frequent "close contacts" with the ABCL.[50]

On the second track, the eugenicists courted the Christians, also with notable success. Writing in *Applied Eugenics*, analyst Paul Popenoe called Christianity the "natural ally of the eugenist."[51]

Florence Brown Sherbon declared that "One of our eugenic apostles is the preacher." It was the "job of the preacher," she said, "to tune the soul of man to the new universe." The average, well-meaning citizen depended "on his pastor to put things together for him and iron out incongruities..., like harmonizing science and religion." As such, pastors would be of considerable help in spreading the eugenic gospel.[52] Toward that end, the AES recruited religious leaders to its Advisory Council. A prominent catch was Rev. Harry Emerson Fosdick, Baptist pastor of New York's prestigious Riverside Church (his most prominent parishioners were the Rockefellers, who later became decisive advocates for birth control). Also joining the Council was Episcopal Bishop William Lawrence and Father John Cooper, a professor of theology and social ethics at the Catholic University of America. In 1925, the AES created as well a Committee on Cooperation with Clergymen; it quickly became the largest and best funded of the Society's fourteen committees. Chaired by Rev. Henry Strong Huntington, the brother of Yale geographer and eugenicist Ellsworth Huntington, the Committee had twenty-nine members by 1927, including: Charles Clayton Morrison, the editor of *Christian Century*; Methodist Bishop Francis John McConnell; and Rev. S. Parkes Cadman. The latter two would serve as successive presidents of the FCCC during the late 1920s. Roman Catholics actually included John A. Ryan, the leading Catholic foe of birth control. When the *Christian Century* listed twenty-five "men of prophetic vision, of pulpit power" in 1925, seven were members of the AES Committee (and an eighth—Newell Dwight Hillis—was also a prominent eugenicist). About 80 percent of the AES' total budget supported this committee's work, including funds for a highly successful, biannual Eugenics Sermon contest.[53]

The eugenicists also expanded on the theology of Horace Bushnell, emphasizing his theme of "The Out-Populating Power of the Christian Stock." In their eugenics-oriented history, *The Builders of America*, Ellsworth Huntington and Leon Whitney drew a long quotation from *Christian Nurture*, describing how "[g]ood principles and habits, intellectual culture, domestic virtue, industry, order, law, faith—all these...make a race powerful" and how "[a]ny people that is physiologically advanced in culture...is sure to live down and finally to live out its inferior." Huntington and Whitney noted Bushnell's conclusion that Protestant Christianity would conquer the world through its high number of descendants. They continued:

> He does not scientifically demonstrate the 'out-populating power of
> the Christian stock'; that, to our great surprise, has been reserved
> for us.... We do not believe that this will happen in a few genera-
> tions or even a few centuries. It will doubtless take thousands and
> perhaps tens of thousands of years, yet that is the direction in which
> the world is headed. *That way lies the millennium* if ever there is
> to be any.[54]

Liberal Christians needed little convincing, though, for eugenics
played directly into the ideals of the Social Gospel, especially the
postmillennial goal of creating the Kingdom of God on earth through
human action and social reform. Eugenics allowed leading Protestants
to reconcile their fear of being displaced by Roman Catholics with
the optimism of the Social Gospel. Birth control would be their tool.
While few Protestants openly called for family limitation among Roman Catholics and other "inferior" peoples, this was their implicit goal.
Eugenics, meanwhile, gave them scientific, "progressive" cover.[55]

Christian eugenicists mobilized a battery of arguments. Some were
straight out of the "hard" eugenics playbook. Writing in *Methodist
Quarterly Review*, C. L. Dorris charged that "too many physically,
mentally, and morally defective" persons were entering society. Marriages needed to be planned for their "racial consequences." Drawing
from Havelock Ellis, Dorris concluded that since "the birth of a child
is a social act," the community can "demand that the citizen be worthy." Only when society "frowns alike on the large family of the poor
and the childless family of leisure" would civilization advance. Other
preachers focused on the Old Testament. They noted the attention
paid to genealogy by the Hebrews. "Eugenic matings" included Abraham and Sarah, Isaac and Rebekah, Jacob and Rachael, and Moses
with the daughter of the priest of Midian. Isaac became "the eugenic
son" of Abraham. Joseph, another exemplary "eugenic son," had to
struggle against his "mongrel" brothers, the products of polygamy.
These preachers also stressed the importance of the genealogy of Jesus,
found in two of the gospels. As one asked: "Can we, after beholding
that stream of life coming down from the eternal, enriched by the
struggles of all the noblest and purest lives of the past, can we destroy
that divine image,...or shall we transmit it, pure and undefiled, in all
its richness to the coming generations?"[56]

However, the more powerful Protestant appeals were to eugenics
as the true path to the Kingdom. Rev. William A. Matson, a Methodist pastor in Livingston, California, reported that "we have assumed

that if we could sufficiently advance education, sanitation, and social surroundings the Kingdom of God would come." It had not worked, for "that is like trying to strengthen the pillars of society by painting them." Only eugenics could strengthen the pillars themselves—human beings—and open the way to the millennium[57] A. G. Kellor, a lay Christian preacher and professor of sociology at Yale University, welcomed "the contraception of the present" as "the enlistment of science in the service of a higher standard of living" and praised "companionate marriage" as sensible. Add in the rational control of reproduction found in eugenics, and "It promises a kind of millennium."[58]

Bolder voices emerged. The family of Rev. Kenneth MacArthur, pastor of the Federated Church of Sterling, Massachusetts, actually won the "Fitter Family Contest—Average Family Class [four children]," held at the Eastern Sates Exposition in 1925 and sponsored by the AES. In a subsequent sermon, he noted that a generation of church leaders had rediscovered "the social ideal of the Kingdom of God on earth." These "open-minded idealists have dared to dream of a new social order, a world made up of Christ-like men and women." He continued: "This structure of the temple of God among men must be built of the best human material." The true City of God on earth would also exclude (using Biblical language) the "unbelieving,...the abominable and murderers, and whoremongers and sorcerers and idolaters." In brash manner, MacArthur declared:

> Now, eugenics offers a way, consistent with Christian principles, of freeing the race in a few generations of a large proportion of the feeble-minded, the criminal, the licentious, by seeing to it *by means of surgery or segregation*, that persons carrying these anti-social traits shall leave behind no tainted offspring.
>
> At the same time, the eugenicists encourage the production of intelligent, healthy, high-minded folk with capacity for ideals, for cooperative action, for purposeful striving toward worthy goals; in other words, *the very material from which to recruit the citizenry* of the commonwealth of Christ among men.

Both poverty and ignorance were the consequence of "low-grade human beings." He cited the "sad spectacle" of eugenically desirable, albeit childless school teachers wasting their lives in "trying to educate the offspring of morons." In contrast, eugenics aimed at producing "a super race" marked by intelligence, health, and good will. It also provided a synthesis of the Christian "Law of Love" with Darwin's

"Survival of the Fittest," binding "ministry to the feeble-minded" with a plan of action that would prevent them "from pouring their corrupt currents into the race stream."

Importantly, MacArthur also insisted that "eugenics can set the church people right on the whole question of *birth control*." Ecclesiastical bodies, he noted, still tended to see contraception as sinful. Yet, there "must be legalized control of the human race" before overpopulation led to war. He continued: "The church in its striving after a better world cannot afford ignorantly to condemn *this powerful weapon of birth regulation* which has thus far largely been an injury to the race *but which has great capacities for racial improvement*." Along these lines, he urged Christian philanthropists to subsidize Protestant ministers so they "could afford large families" [!], while introducing "birth control for less desirable stocks and segregation [in institutions] for the patently unfit." In this way, "without any massacre or anything contrary to the love of Christ, race progress may go on to an ideal society, until we all attain to the fullness of the stature of Christ."[59]

In his popular sermon, "The Refiner's Fire," Rev. Phillips Endecott Osgood of St. Mark's Episcopal Church in Minneapolis cast Jesus as the ultimate eugenicist, the "Refiner" of men: "He was superlatively concerned to better the qualities of human living" and he saw children as "the near edge of the future, the beginning of the ultimate." Osgood labeled "missions to the future" as "the most vital contribution to the coming of the Kingdom on earth." That goal was now imperiled, though, for "the least fit members of society breed fastest" while "the right types are less self-perpetuating." Appropriately, "[n]ow we are turning to preventive measures." Marriage and child-bearing should be reserved "for those who are wholesome and normal." The unfortunate victim of hereditary malady should deny himself parenthood and so "become a redemptive helper of the next generation." This meant that the Church would also "have to take its stand on the question of birth control." He added: "In our cooperation with the Refiner's work, we must accept heredity as our major factor.... It is for the Kingdom of God upon earth." Osgood concluded: "God will provide His Spirit to our children's children; why handicap its incarnation?...The Kingdom of God on Earth is not an end of growth, but the beginning of true destiny."[60]

Another sermon published in *Eugenics*, this time by Edwin Bishop, Pastor of Plymouth Congregational Church in Lansing, Michigan, also wove together the themes of evolution, birth control, eugenics, and the Kingdom of God. This pastor insisted that men and women were summoned to *assist* God in the task of transformation: "Shall we humans not realize what God is trying to do for us and how He suggests that we participate with Him in conscious evolution?" With "the highest motive imaginable, that of bringing in a present Kingdom of God," the church should recognize "the extreme desirability" of seeing individuals "well-born." Bishop praised the attention given to an early form of eugenics by Horace Bushnell, who showed "how we may undergird our future by a well-considered eugenic program, or ruin it by a careless dysgenic one." Bishop fretted that "the eugenically endowed are not producing enough children to make good their own losses to say nothing about gaining on the population." In his own congregation, largely descended from old Puritan stock, 152 completed families had 218 children, an average of only 1.3 ("the same percentage as for Vassar and Bryn Mawr graduates"). He concluded that "the program of Jesus for capacity self-fulfillment for the individual and for the race" could only be accomplished with "more knowledge and practice of simple eugenic laws." Bishop's "practical suggestions" included the "right" of a state "to insist on sterilization" of "those notoriously unfit to marry and reproduce." And, "[a]s a corollary, the knowledge of birth control should be widely and freely disseminated so that *among certain groups* in our civilization there may be *not more* but *fewer and better children.*"[61]

Perhaps these were only peculiar or extreme manifestations of early twentieth-century postmillennial theology? In fact, these prize-winning sermons were simply the ablest written and most open examples of a broad shift in liberal or mainline Christian thought. In her brilliant and disturbing recent book, *Conceiving Parenthood: American Protestantism and the Spirit of Reproduction*, historian Amy Laura Hall shows how "eugenics gained popular support in large part through the endorsement of mainstream and progressive Protestant spokespersons." More importantly, she uses a meticulous study of 150 images of families found in both the mainstream and Protestant media during the middle decades of the twentieth century to reveal how these churches injected a form of "soft" eugenics deep into American culture. Typical was a 1929 editorial in *Parents'* magazine on "The Meaning of Easter." Largely ignoring Christ's resurrection, the editors focus instead on a "new covenant" between parents and children, where Easter is transformed into a "faith" in the "future of the race" which was "marching forward on the feet of little children."

As Hall explains, "The very Protestant tradition that should have emphasized a sense of divine gratuity, human contingency, sufficient abundance, and the radical giftedness of all life came in twentieth-century America to epitomize justification by meticulously planned procreation." Moreover, this vision of controlled domesticity was "a means to do no less than 'save the world,'" by appealing to a vague, residual sense of building the Kingdom of God. She also shows convincingly that this vision—resting on a eugenic form of birth control that emphasized child-spacing and precise gender balance—dominated mainline Protestant expectations through the 1950s.[62]

Sanger's Preachers

The first signs of shifting Protestant views regarding birth control appeared—with some irony—in that parachurch which had launched the career of Anthony Comstock: the Young Men's Christian Association (YMCA). As early as 1910, certain YMCAs were offering classes on "responsible parenthood" for "the betterment of the race," which may have included instruction in the value of birth control.[63] The experience of The Great War accelerated "fundamental changes" in the American organization, with "religious liberalism" gaining ground within its ranks.[64] The key figure here was Sherwood Eddy, the British-born "National YMCA Secretary for India" from 1896 to 1911, whose ideas dominated the Association during the interwar period. As he explained in his autobiography, subtitled *The Reeducation of Sherwood Eddy*, "After the World War religion became for me a social experience.... Our task, then, was not only to win or change individuals, all-important as that was, but to Christianize the whole of life and all its relations, industrial, social, racial and international."[65] This was a clear conversion from pre- to post-millennialist thinking. Eddy's Christianizing of the whole of life included an enthusiastic embrace of "emancipated womanhood" (e.g., "Man has had his innings, it is now woman's turn") and praise for the companionate marriage, which might or might not involve children. Eddy also waxed enthusiastic over eugenicist and birth controller Havelock Ellis, whom he called "the greatest authority" in the world on subjects of love and marriage. Moreover, "we would suggest for all young women without exception before marriage, Margaret Sanger's *Happiness in Marriage*. Had this book alone been read, it would have saved many failures in marriage."[66]

Such attitudes spread within the organization. As an official in Hamilton, Ohio, reported: "Our local Y.M.C.A. is not sponsoring this work by official action but sex education including Birth Control for married persons, is accepted as a natural part of our program and that is sanction enough." He praised "any technique...that will release sex from slavery to the procreative function [and] that allows normal sex function without fear of unwanted pregnancy." Perhaps unaware of the origin of the Comstock laws, he also expressed personal interest in the "revision of legislation to make the dissemination of Birth Control knowledge legal."[67]

There were other early recruits among the Social Gospel Protestants. Sanger won the support of Harry Emerson Fosdick (also, as noted earlier, a prominent friend of the AES). As he wrote in his autobiography, "I was associated with the planned parenthood—birth control—cause early in Mrs. Margaret Sanger's campaign, and on a few occasions have had opportunities to serve it." Mankind had to be "educated out of its careless, casual, unthinking, unpurposed, merely animal propagation of children" for its "dearest hopes to be achieved." Fosdick also blasted the "powerful, obscurantist" force of the Catholic Church for standing in the way of human progress.[68] Other early backers and correspondents with Sanger included: the Rev. Howard Melish, a prominent Episcopalian in Brooklyn; the Rev. E. McNeill Poteat of the Southern Baptist Convention; the Rev. James Oesterling, superintendent of the Inner Mission Society of the Evangelical Lutheran Synod of Baltimore (who complained to Sanger about "colleagues who practice but do not preach birth control"); and the Unitarian leader, Rev. John Haynes Holmes (who said that Sanger combined "the power of a saint" with "the mind of a statesman," becoming "one of the great women of our time").[69]

A few articles indirectly favorable to birth control also appeared in the Christian press. A 1921 editorial in the *Christian Advocate*, a Methodist periodical, condemned Roman Catholic behavior in the "Town Hall" incident and praised the "earnest men and women" of the ABCL, "whose laudable zeal for the welfare of the race has led them to advocate the artificial limitation of births."[70] A similar anti-Catholicism linked to soft eugenics appeared in the Baptist journal, *The Watchman—Examiner*, in 1926. It argued that "the oldest, strongest, and most autocratic body" in the world, the Catholic hierarchy, actually compelled birth control. The Church's "choice young men" were trained as priests, called "Father," but "denied the joy of fatherhood." Similarly, the "choice young women," trained as nuns, "are forced into a life that denies motherhood." The editors concluded: "Behold a great body, that assumes to be the Church, stabbing birth control!"[71]

Later, individual endorsements appeared in a symposium on "The Churches and Birth Control," published during 1930 in *Birth Control Review*. Soft eugenic language was common. The Rev. Jay Ray Ewers, of Pittsburgh's East End Christian Church, asked "Why should the well-to-do be able to practice...Birth Control while the knowledge is forbidden to those who need it most?" The Rev. W. Nelson Winter of Baltimore's Calvary Evangelical Church declared that "The followers of that revolutionary Teacher [Jesus] have too long been numbered among the reactionary forces—they should, like their Master, be the first to vision a brighter future." The Rev. William W. Peck of Albany, New York's First Unitarian Church called it "the churches' duty to advocate the cause of better-born children" and to lift parenthood "into loftier human standards of deliberation and spiritual consummation." The Rev. Robert S. Miller, of Lancaster, Pennsylvania's Church of Our Father, defended the "two rights of childhood...the right of the child to be well born and the right not to be born at all." The Rev. E. G. Gallagher, of Waseca, Minnesota's First Congregational Church, declared that "[b]irth control has within it possibilities for happiness, more abundant life and untold blessings for this old world." And the Rev. L. Griswold Williams of Reading, Pennsylvania's Church of Our Father, saw "the Divine coming to its fruition in human self-awareness" where "the control and sublimation of the sex life becomes a religious duty," so that to practice birth control "is to cooperate with God."[72]

In a characteristic exaggeration, the editorial accompanying the Symposium celebrated "the increasing support *of all other* [i.e., non-Catholic] denominations" and concluded that "with the churches in the vanguard, the cause of Birth Control is assured."[73] In fact, as of Spring 1930, only one local American Christian group had formally embraced birth control (or two, if you count the Universalists). In April of that year, the New York East Conference of the Methodist Episcopal Church endorsed a report of its Social Service Committee, which declared:

> In the interests of morality and sound scientific knowledge we favor such changes of the law in the States of New York and Connecticut as will remove the existing restrictions upon the communication by physicians to their patients of important medical information on Birth Control.

A few months earlier, The Universalist General Convention, meeting in Boston, had approved a report calling birth control "one of the most important facts of modern life, giving to man the power *to control the future of the race*," making it "one of the most practicable means of race betterment." That was it. The vast array of Protestant denominations—including the bulk of the Methodists—actually remained officially opposed to contraception.[74]

Lambeth Breakthrough

This would begin to change over the following twelve months. Margaret Sanger's first true "breakthrough" on the religious front came with the Anglicans. She played a direct role here. Among her correspondents during the 1920s were several friendly Episcopalian bishops, together with Guy Emery Shipley, editor of the influential Anglican publication, *Churchman*. She encouraged them to push for change. More importantly, perhaps, after the American House of Bishops of the Protestant Episcopal Church again approved in 1925 a resolution condemning birth control, an opportunity appeared. As Sanger reports in her autobiography, "...some of the wives of these same bishops had come to me in New York and asked my help in educating their husbands. A group of three had taken it upon themselves to see that every bishop was thoroughly enlightened."[75] This she attempted.

That 1925 meeting of the House of Bishops also took one other relevant action, expressing support for stricter marriage licensing so as to prevent "the marriage of persons of low mentality and infected with communicable disease."[76] This form of soft eugenics may have reflected the influence of William R. Inge, The Dean of St. Paul's Cathedral in London, the leading Anglican intellectual of his generation, and a recent visitor to America. As early as 1917, he wrote an essay on "The Birth Rate" for *The Edinburgh Review*, where he declared it futile to try to suppress a practice that most people believed to be useful and innocent. In a 1922 essay for *Birth Control Review*, he dismissed talk of "race suicide" as absurd; the decline in the birth rate was "made necessary" by prior improvements in sanitation and medical sciences, which had brought down infant mortality and had increased life expectancy. Moreover, "[e]very unwanted baby, kept alive by humanitarian interference, drives another baby out of the world or prevents him from coming into it."[77] Considering the higher fecundity of Roman Catholics when compared to Protestants, he proclaimed that a "high birth-rate always indicates a *low state* of civilization," which he saw exemplified in Ireland, Italy, Poland, and other Catholic lands. "The Roman Church, he wrote, was "the last survivor of political autocracies." This made it suited to the "Mediterranean race" and its love of magic and pathos. However, Catholicism "has never suited the Nordics, who rejected it as soon as they developed a national life and self-consciousness of their own." Rooted in the valor, honor, truthfulness, and fair-dealing of the Goths, Protestantism became "the natural religion of the Teutons," "the nurse of a lusty child, modern civilization," and "the religion of...the civilization of experimental science."[78] In face of primitive Catholic fecundity and with "England now breeding from the slums,"[79] the eugenic case for birth control grew urgent. Inge traveled to America in early 1925, lecturing on behalf of the Galton Society and other eugenic groups.

Another influence affecting the Anglican Bishops was a speech to the 1921 Lay Church Conference by Lord Dawson of Penn, the physician to the British King. As a student in the 1880s he had embraced neo-Malthusianism, co-authoring a leaflet entitled *Few in the Family, Happiness at Home*. He used his 1921 address to lash out at the Lambeth Bishops. "The love envisaged by the Lambeth Conference is an invertebrate joyless thing," he stated, "not worth the having. Fortunately it is in contrast to the real thing as practiced by clergy and laity." Lord Dawson concluded: "Birth control is here to stay.... No denunciations will abolish it." A year later, a confident C. V. Drysdale could tell the Fifth International Neo-Malthusian and Birth Control Conference that organized opposition among the Anglicans to birth control was over.[80]

All the same, debate over birth control at Lambeth in August 1930 was heated. Opposition came in particular from (in Sanger's words) "colonial and missionary bishops from distant quarters of the Empire,"[81] a group which included a majority of the American delegates.[82] However, on a vote of 193 to 67, with 46 abstaining, the Anglican bishops approved Resolution 15:

> Where there is a clearly felt moral obligation to limit or avoid parenthood, the method must be decided on Christian principles. The primary and obvious method is complete abstinence from intercourse (as far as may be necessary) in a life of discipline and self control lived in the power of the Holy Spirit. Nevertheless, in those cases where there is such a clearly-felt moral obligation to limit or avoid parenthood, and where there is a morally sound reason for

avoiding complete abstinence, the Conference agrees that other methods may be used, provided that this is done in the light of the same Christian principles.

So ended the 1,800-year-old Christian consensus on birth control.

The Americans Follow...Or Not

The first American echo of Lambeth came from the FCCC in March 1931. As late as 1929, its Committee on Marriage and Home had published a pamphlet deploring "the obsession of the stage and present day literature with sex, the disturbed condition of the home, a disquieting increase in divorce, and a growing laxness in the relation of the sexes," negative developments "affected by a widespread and increasing knowledge of birth control."[83] However, there were contrary signs of a shift toward accepting birth control, in the soft eugenic context of "sexual hygiene." For example, in 1925 the Council's Committee on the Church and Social Service announced collaboration with the American Social Hygiene Association for parenthood training, where "systematic efforts [would] be made to inaugurate sex education and community prophylaxis under the guidance of field workers of the association."[84] And in 1929, the Committee on Marriage and Home issued a report on *Ideals of Love and Marriage*, which concluded that a mother "needs to be out of the home as well as in it" and that "mothers, in order to provide their offspring with maximum opportunities in a fluid society, *should have fewer children and 'mother' them less.*"[85]

The Committee on Marriage and the Home adopted its statement on birth control, by a vote of twenty-three to three. The document affirmed "the rightfulness of intercourse in itself without the purpose of children," or as restated a little later: "that sexual union between husbands and wives as an expression of mutual affection, without relation to procreation, is right." Largely based on this principle:

> A majority of the committee holds that the careful and restrained use of contraceptives by married people is valid and moral. They take this position because they believe that it is important to provide for the proper spacing of children, the control of the size of the family, and the protection of mothers and children; and because intercourse between the mates, when an expression of their spiritual union and affection, is right in itself.[86]

Margaret Sanger waxed ecstatic. On release of the FCCC statement, she proclaimed: "Today is the most significant one in the history of the birth control movement."[87] Meanwhile, she said, the Lambeth statement "was inevitably to lead the way toward the crystallization of a universal Protestant acceptance of the moral necessity of birth control."[88] For its part, the *Birth Control Review* called the Federal Council statement "epoch-making" and predicted that it would have "a profound effect on the various legislatures and on the mores of the country." Incorrectly but significantly, it added: "Let it be remembered that it is the Catholics, not the non-Catholics, who have drawn the religious issue, and forced us to pit numbers against numbers."[89]

In actual fact, though, Sanger's immediate victory was very incomplete (which she surely knew). To begin with, the new birth control report almost tore apart the FCCC. Following a wave of lay and clerical protests, the Northern Baptist Convention resolved that the FCCC "did not speak for the Baptist denomination in endorsing birth control" and cut its financial contribution to the Council. In the Presbyterian Church in the United States of America (PCUSA), a revolt spread at the presbytery level; when the church assembly met in late May, conservatives elected one of their own as Moderator and they nearly succeeded in pulling the PCUSA out of the Council. Down South, the General Assembly of the Presbyterian Church in the United States did vote 175 to 79 to withdraw from the FCCC, pointing to the birth control report as a sign of the futility of winning consensus on moral and political issues within "the Protestant Church." The report also generated a storm of protest among the Methodists. The Methodist Bishop of Atlanta announced that the FCCC Committee, in "sanctioning birth control under certain conditions did not represent the Methodist Episcopal Church South." Meeting in Atlanta in October 1931, the Sixth Ecumenical Methodist Conference received a report on "Marriage, Home and Family" drafted by Rev. J. C. Broomfield. It condemned "the new abandon with which we write and talk on…such subjects as the science of eugenics, the education of youth in matters of sex, birth control, the use of contraceptives, [and] companionate marriage." It was time for Methodists "to get back to The Book." At the 1936 General Conference of the Methodist Episcopal Church, delegates approved a resolution stating "that it is the major responsibility of Protestant Christianity to urge Christian people to recognize the importance of reproduction rather than on [sic] birth control." The Reformed Church—General Synod also threatened to leave the Federal Council, pointing to the "unnecessary pronounce-ment of 'Birth Control' and 'Usurpation of Authority' as revealed in the 'deliverance' upon a moral question such as Birth Control." And the United Lutheran Synod of New York resolved that the statement "expressed views distinctly opposed to the moral and spiritual teach-ings of the Lutheran Church"; it also came close to severing ties with the FCCC.[90]

Indeed, financial pressures on the Federal Council grew so acute that the group secretly asked Margaret Sanger to help raise emergency funds to cover the costs of lobbying those Protestant bodies opposed to birth control. She agreed. As Sanger wrote to a friend:

> I want to send $300.00 to the Committee on Marriage and the Home, attention of Dr. Worth M. Tippy.... This added to Mrs. Lawrence's contribution will make $500.00, with which they can start something. I don't want to give my check for various reasons so I am endorsing the enclosed check over to you...send it in as *your* contribution.

She added that she might be asking her correspondent to do this again, "because I am quite certain that the project of keeping the Com-mittee working on Birth Control will be more worthwhile than any other single thing that we can do."[91] Between 1931 and 1934, Sanger and her second husband secretly donated about $2,000 to the FCCC, a sizable sum for the time.

Even the post-Lambeth American Episcopalians proved wobbly. At the September 1931 General Convention of the Protestant Episcopal Church, and despite Sanger's lobbying efforts, delegates implicitly rejected birth control, approving a resolution stating that "there is no bond of unity so compelling, so rich and so joy-giving as that of chil-dren," affirming "the necessity of children in the home," and labeling "procreation" as the purpose of intercourse. Three years later, Sanger resolved to try again. She dispatched her lobbyists to the Episcopalian convention, and sent copies of her agonizing *Motherhood in Bondage* to every American bishop. On a close vote, the convention approved a resolution giving indirect support to birth control. Revealingly, though, it succeeded this time only by appealing to eugenics, endorsing "the efforts now being made to convey such information as is in *accord with the highest principles of eugenics*, and a more wholesome family life, wherein parenthood may be undertaken with due respect for the health of mothers and the welfare of their children."[92]

The most important reaction to the Lambeth statement was Pope Pius XI's *Casti Connubii*, released December 30, 1930.[93] The Pope saw the Catholic Church "standing erect in the midst of the moral ruin which surrounds her" and acknowledged the reasons given by married people for wanting to restrict family size. He responded:

> But no reason, however grave, may be put forward by which anything intrinsically against nature may become conformable to nature and morally good. Since, therefore, the conjugal act is destined primarily by nature for the begetting of children, those who in exercising it deliberately frustrate its natural power and purpose, sin against nature and commit a deed which is shameful and intrinsically vicious.

Notably, given the linkage between birth control and eugenics developing among some Protestants, Pius also used this encyclical to clarify the Church's teaching on the latter. Referring to coerced sterilizations, he replied: "Those who act in this way are at fault in losing sight of the fact that the family is more sacred than the state and that men are begotten not for the earth and for time, but for heaven and eternity." Accordingly, it was "wrong to brand men with the stigma of crime" for wanting to marry despite hereditary defects.[94] Father Ryan concluded from this that forced sterilization was "authoritatively declared to be intrinsically wrong," and he resigned from the AES clergy committee with a blistering public note, calling its proposals "abhorrent for religious, moral, and social reasons."[95]

In a far less official, but more pointed manner, the Catholic journal *Commonweal* blasted the FCCC statement "as the liquidation of historic Protestantism by its own trustees, the voluntary bankruptcy of the Reformation." Its editors acknowledged that this document had come from the theologically liberal side of the Protestant camp; and that many in the churches involved were still opposed to birth control (including "the great Lutheran Church"). However, as the editors continued in prescient fashion: "it is likely that the struggle of the orthodox will be futile; that at best they will only be able to maintain a failing rear-guard action as they retreat to dig themselves in for their last battle." Indeed, liberal Protestantism had now become in practice "pagan humanitarianism, it is the creed of social science, built on the shifting and unstable experiments...of materialistic science." These churches had in practice surrendered "a supremely important moral problem into the hands of a clique of birth control advocates." The editors concluded by predicting that

...legalized contraception would be a long step on the road toward state clinics for abortion, for compulsory sterilization of those declared unfit by fanatical eugenists, and the ultimate destruction of human liberty at the hands of an absolute pagan state.[96]

In fact, opposition to birth control within the mainline Protestant churches did fade away by the end of the 1930s, partly for the reasons predicted by the editors at *Commonweal* and partly because of a 1936 decision by a U.S. Appeals Court. Ruling in the case *United States v. One Package of Japanese Pessaries*, the justices now interpreted the federal Comstock law to allow "conscientious and competent physicians" to provide birth control information and devices "for the purpose of saving life or promoting the well-being of their patients."[97] The great evangelical project of defending marriage and procreation through law, recently bolstered by Catholic activism, largely came to an end. Going forward, birth control would be primarily a moral issue, not a legal one.

Indeed, Margaret Sanger had achieved her goals. As Kathleen Tobin notes, "Sanger ignored critics who said she would achieve success more quickly if she stopped antagonizing Catholics and in doing so she accelerated much of the non-Catholic support of her movement." Her embrace of eugenics was also tactically brilliant, attracting Protestant clerics looking to racial improvement as a way of building the Kingdom of God on earth. At key points, such as the American Episcopalian turn in 1934, the eugenic argument proved decisive.[98]

Where were the fundamentalists during the 1930s? In many respects, they were outsiders looking in, suspicious of Roman Catholic motives and appalled by the behavior of their postmillennial Protestant brethren. Prior denunciations of birth control were allowed to stand, with little new said. To the degree it grappled with family issues, the Southern Baptist Convention focused on denouncing divorce. Other fundamentalist writers called for a return to the Bible, leaving out the specifics.[99]

A remarkable exception to all of these generalities was an editorial on "Birth Control," appearing during 1931 in the *Moody Bible Institute Monthly*. It opened with enthusiastic praise for Pius XI: "We trust we shall not be accused of going over to Roman Catholicism if we speak approvingly of the late Encyclical of The Pope." Indeed, "we wish all the great denominational bodies of Protestantism would be as positive and bold." The editors also pointed approvingly to a recent speech in

New York by the Catholic journalist "Gilbert Chesterton," where he had labeled the "new morality a 'filthy thing' which 'avoids birth and abandons control.'" As the Encyclical taught, the laws of marriage "are made of God, not man" and "children should be received with joy and gratitude from the hand of God." The Moody editors concluded:

> We cannot in this brief editorial go into all aspects of this grave subject, or even touch upon them, but we can warn our readers who have been redeemed by the precious blood of Christ and whose bodies are therefore the temples of the Holy Ghost, to see to it that they glorify God in their bodies which are His (I Cor. 6:20). "Whither therefore ye eat, or drink, or whatsoever ye do, do all to the glory of God" (I Cor. 10:3), is a principle to guide such in the contracting of marriage and afterwards in bearing its responsibilities as well as enjoying its blessings.[100]

This clear, Bible-based rejection of birth control among the fundamentalists would face new challenges after World War II.

Notes

1. As historian Tom Davis notes, Margaret Sanger "shared more than a few traits of biblical prophet." In: Tom Davis, *Sacred Work: Planned Parenthood and Its Clergy Alliances* (New Brunswick, NJ: Rutgers University Press, 2005), 44.
2. Margaret Sanger, "The War against Birth Control," *The American Mercury* 2 (June 1924): 232–33.
3. See: John S. Sumner, "Replies," *The Birth Control Review* 6 (January 1922): 10–11.
4. Margaret Sanger, *An Autobiography* (New York: Dover, 1971 [1938]), 20–21.
5. "Fabian Hall Speech, July 5, 1915," in *The Selected Papers of Margaret Sanger, Volume I: The Woman Rebel, 1900–1928*, ed. Esther Katz (Urbana and Chicago: University of Illinois Press, 2003), 142–49.
6. Henry Wilson Yates, Jr., "American Protestants and Birth Control: An Examination of Shifts Within a Major Religious Value Orientation" (doctoral diss., Harvard University, 1968): 297.
7. Davis, *Sacred Work*, 17, 29.
8. Margaret Sanger, *Motherhood in Bondage* (Columbus: Ohio State University Press, 2000 [1928]), xlvii; Davis, *Sacred Work*, 36–37.
9. Sanger, "The War against Birth Control," 231.
10. Margaret Sanger, "The Case for Birth Control," in *Handbook on Birth Control*, ed. Julia Johnsen (New York: H.W. Wilson, 1926), 135, 137.
11. Margaret Sanger, *Woman and the New Race* (New York: Brentano's, 1920), 185.
12. Kathleen A. Tobin, *The American Religious Debate over Birth Control, 1907–1937* (Jefferson, NC and London: McFarland, 2001), 80, 92–94. I need acknowledge my special debt in this chapter to Professor Tobin's work.

13. Yates, "American Protestantism and Birth Control," 303.

14. Sanger, *Woman and the New Race*, 170–79; also David M. Kennedy, *Birth Control in America: The Career of Margaret Sanger* (New Haven: Yale University Press, 1970), 141–42.

15. John Haynes Holmes, "The Church and Birth Control," *The Birth Control Review* 6 (November 1922): 228.

16. Yates, "American Protestantism and Birth Control," 331.

17. Mary Alden Hopkins, "The Catholic Church and Birth Control," *Harper's Weekly* (August 7, 1915): 144; from Tobin, *American Religious Debate over Birth Control*, 67–68.

18. Davis, *Sacred Work*, 31–32.

19. Tobin, *American Religious Debate over Birth Control*, 70.

20. John A. Ryan, "Family Limitation," *The Ecclesiastical Review* 4 (June 1916): 684–96.

21. Davis, *Sacred Work*, 32.

22. From: Sanger, *Autobiography*, 302–4.

23. From: Tobin, *American Religious Debate over Birth Control*, 77–83.

24. Sanger, "War against Birth Control," 284.

25. Sanger, *Autobiography*, 411.

26. "Church Control?" *Birth Control Review* 5 (December 1921): 3.

27. David Kennedy, *Birth Control in America: The Career of Margaret Sanger* (New Haven: Yale University Press, 1970), 149.

28. See: Sanger, *Autobiography*, 411; Sanger, "War against Birth Control," 234–35.

29. Kennedy, *Birth Control in America*, 162–65; Tobin, *American Religious Debate over Birth Control*, 54–55.

30. Lawrence W. Levine, *Defending the Faith: William Jennings Bryan: The Last Decade, 1915–1925* (New York: Oxford University Press, 1965), 260–63.

31. Howard W. Kellogg, "'Kultur-Applied Evolution," *The King's Business* 10 (February 1919): 110–15.

32. Christine Rosen, *Preaching Eugenics: Religious Leaders and the American Eugenics Movement* (Oxford: Oxford University Press, 2004), 17.

33. "Birth Control," *The Christian Workers Magazine* 17 (November 1916): 175–76.

34. "Birth Control, Unnatural and Immoral," *The Christian Workers Magazine* 17 (March 1917): 531.

35. "Be Fruitful and Multiply," *The King's Business* 10 (May 1919): 443.

36. "Childless Marriages," *The Christian Workers Magazine* 20 (January 1920): 360–61.

37. "The Agitation for Birth Control," *Our Hope* 31 (June 1925): 745–46.

38. Mark A. Matthews, "Childlessness The Nation's Curse," *Moody Bible Institute Monthly* 30 (November 1929): 110–11. (Emphasis added.)

39. C. Allyn Russell, *Voices of American Fundamentalism: Seven Historical Studies* (Philadelphia, PA: Westminster Press, 1976), 56–64.

40. Ibid., 117, 202, 269.

41. In Robert F. Martin, *Hero of the Heartland: Billy Sunday and the Transformation of American Society, 1862–1935* (Bloomington, IN: Indiana University Press, 2002), 85.

42. Billy Sunday, "A Plain Talk to Women," in *Billy Sunday Speaks*, ed. Karen Gullen (New York: Chelsea House, 1970), 109–13. Also: Roger A. Bruns, *Preacher: Billy Sunday and Big-Time American Evangelism* (New York: W.W. Norton, 1992), 145; William G. McLaughlin, Jr., *Billy Sunday Was His Real Name* (Chicago, IL: University of Chicago Press, 1955), 132–33.
43. Sunday, "Plain Talk to Women," 111.
44. See: "Birth Control," *The Christian Workers Magazine* 17 (November 1916): 175–76.
45. Russell, *Voices of American Fundamentalism*, 62, 64.
46. Tobin, *American Religious Debate over Birth Control*, 46.
47. Josiah Strong, *The Challenge of the City* (New York: Young People's Missionary Movement, 1907), 142.
48. Rosen, *Preaching Eugenics*, 155.
49. On Margaret Sanger's views regarding eugenics, see: Edwin Black, *War against the Weak: Eugenics and America's Campaign to Create a Master Race* (New York: Thunder's Mouth Press, 2004): 125–44.
50. Rosen, *Preaching Eugenics*, 155–57.
51. Ibid., 127.
52. Florence Brown Sherbon, "The Preacher's Part," *Eugenics* 1 (December 1928): 3–5.
53. Rosen, *Preaching Eugenics*, 115–33.
54. Ellsworth Huntington and Leon F. Whitney, *The Builders of America* (New York: William Morrow, 1927), 203–4. (Emphasis added.)
55. See Tobin, *American Religious Debate over Birth Control*, 28–29.
56. See: George Hunter Donaldson, "Eugenics: A Lay Sermon," *The Methodist Review* 112 (January 1929): 59–66; Rosen, *Preaching Eugenics*, 122–24; Amy Laura Hall, *Conceiving Parenthood: American Protestantism and the Spirit of Reproduction* (Grand Rapids, MI: William B. Eerdmans, 2008), 266–68.
57. William A. Matson, "A Chosen Seed for a Chosen People," *Eugenics* 2 (August 1929): 3.
58. A. G. Kellor, "Birth Control: An Editorial," *Outlook and Independent* 154 (April 16, 1930): 619, 637.
59. Kenneth C. MacArthur, "Eugenics and the Church," *Eugenics* 1 (December 1928): 6–9. (Emphasis added.)
60. Phillips E. Osgood, "The Refiner's Fire," *Eugenics* 1 (December 1928): 10–15.
61. Edwin W. Bishop, "Eugenics and the Church," *Eugenics* 2 (August 1929): 14–19. (Emphasis added.)
62. Hall, *Conceiving Parenthood*, 9–10, 63–65, 82, 219, 389–406.
63. "The Chief End of Man," *Current Literature* (May 1910): 528–31; from Tobin, *American Religious Debate over Birth Control*, 19.
64. Jun Xing, *Baptized in the Fire of Revolution: The American Social Gospel and the YMCA in China: 1919–1937* (Bethlehem, PA: Lehigh University Press, 1996), 52.
65. Quotation in Xing, *Baptized in the Fire of Revolution*, 52.
66. Sherwood Eddy, "The Problems of Marriage," in *Twenty-Four Views of Marriage: From the Presbyterian General Assembly's Commission on Marriage,*

Divorce and Remarriage, ed. Clarence A. Spaulding (New York: Macmillan Company, 1930), 151–55; this was an extract from Eddy's 1928 booklet, *Sex and Youth.*

67. J. J. Ray, "Sane Sex Education in Two Y.M.C.A.'s: It must include Birth Control," *Birth Control Review* 14 (September 1930): 251–52.

68. Harry Emerson Fosdick, *The Living of These Days: An Autobiography* (New York: Harper & Brothers, 1956), 284.

69. Davis, *Sacred Work*, 37–38.

70. "Editorial," *The Christian Advocate* 96 (December 1, 1921): 1515.

71. "Editorial," *The Watchman-Examiner* 14 (December 16, 1926): 1577.

72. "The Roll Call: Twenty Opinions," *Birth Control Review* 14 (May 1930): 132–48.

73. "The Churches and Birth Control: A Symposium," *Birth Control Review* 14 (May 1930): 131. (Emphasis added.)

74. Ibid., 149–50. The General Conference of American Rabbis, meeting in Detroit in June 1929, had also endorsed "the control of parenthood" as one way to cope with "social problems."

75. Sanger, *Autobiography*, 410; also Kennedy, *Birth Control in America*, 169.

76. In Tobin, *American Religious Debate over Birth Control*, 99.

77. W. R. Inge, "Sex and Reproduction," *The Birth Control Review* 6 (January 1922): 4–5.

78. William R. Inge, "Catholic Church and Anglo-Saxon Mind," *The Atlantic Monthly* 131 (April 1923): 440–49. (Emphasis added.)

79. Paraphrased in R. le Clerc Phillips, "Cracks in the Upper Crust," *The Independent* 116 (May 19, 1926): 633.

80. Peter Fryer, *The Birth Controllers* (London: Secker and Warburg, 1965), 243–45.

81. Sanger, *My Fight for Birth Control*, 337.

82. Kennedy, *Birth Control in America*, 165–66.

83. Quoted in Tobin, *American Religious Debate over Birth Control*, 140.

84. Ibid., 104.

85. Reported in Kennedy, *Birth Control in America*, 138–39. (Emphasis added.)

86. Federal Council of Churches of Christ in America, *Moral Aspects of Birth Control. Some Recent Pronouncements of Religious Bodies* (New York: Federal Council of Churches, 1936), 3–5.

87. Tobin, *American Religious Debate over Birth Control*, 164.

88. Sanger, *My Fight for Birth Control*, 337.

89. "Editorial," *Birth Control Review* 15 (April 1931): 99.

90. Kennedy, *Birth Control in America*, 155–58; Tobin, *American Religious Debate over Birth Control*, 170.

91. Letter, Margaret Sanger to Frances Brooks Ackermann, July 1, 1931; in Esther Katz, ed., *The Selected Papers of Margaret Sanger. Volume 2: Birth Control Comes of Age, 1928–1939* (Urbana: University of Illinois Press, 2006), 100.

92. Kennedy, *Birth Control in America*, 166–68. (Emphasis added.)

93. On Roman Catholic public teaching regarding birth control between 1876 and 1930, see: John T. Noonan, Jr., *Contraception: A History of Its Treatment*

by the Catholic Theologians and Canonists (Cambridge, MA: The Belknap Press of Harvard University Press, 1986), 414–32.

94. *Casti Connubii: Encyclical Letter of Pope Pius XI on Christian Marriage* at http://www.vatican.va/holy_father/pius_xi/encyclicals/documents/hf_p_xi_enc_31121930_casti-connubii_en.html (accessed July 30, 2009).

95. Rosen, *Preaching Eugenics*, 160–63; also John A. Ryan, "The Moral Teaching of the Encyclical," *The Ecclesiastical Review* 84 (March 1931): 265, 268–70.

96. "The Birth Control Revolution," *The Commonweal* 13 (April 1, 1931): 589–91.

97. *U.S. v. One Package*, 86 F. 2nd 737 (1936), 5–6.

98. Tobin, *American Religious Debate over Birth Control*, 211.

99. Ibid., 173–75, 190–91.

100. "Birth Control," *Moody Bible Institute Monthly* 31 (March 1931): 336.

4

Birth Control in the Age of Billy Graham

Conservative Protestantism seemed to be battered and beaten in the 1930s, a once-dominant religious and cultural movement humiliated at the Scopes "Monkey Trial" of 1925 and ill-suited for survival in twentieth-century America. Yet, to the surprise of virtually all observers, conservatives regrouped during that decade and actually turned some of the new tools of modernity to their advantage. By the 1940s and 1950s, conservative Protestantism would exhibit even greater strength and again exert itself in public life, while jettisoning the pejorative term "fundamentalist" and claiming exclusive use of the "evangelical" label. Meanwhile, in wake of the 1936 *One Package* court decision, the birth control movement swung in a markedly conservative direction, to which it held until the early 1960s. When the "population explosion" scare brought the issue of contraception back into public debate during the late 1950s, most leading conservative Protestants still opposed the practice. However, by 1968, the primary journal of the "New" Evangelicals—*Christianity Today*—not only embraced birth control as permissible, but also as a positive good. More surprisingly, Evangelical leaders called as well that year for a liberalization of the nation's antiabortion laws.

From Fundamentalism to Evangelicalism

Historian George Marsden has argued that, "on the surface at least," the evangelical vision of a Christian America was still intact as late as 1918, shared by conservative and liberal Protestants alike. While optimistic postmillennialism had largely disappeared among religious conservatives, "dispensational premillennialism"—emphasizing the apostasy of Christendom, the fulfillment of Biblical prophecies in modern times, and an imminent secret rapture of the saints linked to the Second Coming of Christ—filled the void. Most conservative

Protestants remained within the established denominations, battling liberal influences with hope of success.[1]

Over the next seven years, though, the situation changed rapidly. The World Christian Fundamentals Association, organized in 1919, gave an organizational focus to Fundamentalism, the new label for those adhering to what the General Assembly of the Northern Presbyterian Church called the five "essential and necessary" fundamental doctrines, including biblical inerrancy. Urged on by respected biblical scholars such as J. Gresham Machen (author of *Christianity and Liberalism* in 1923), these conservative Protestants launched an aggressive campaign to drive theological liberalism out of the churches. As matters turned out, they were themselves routed, particularly within the Northern Baptist and Presbyterian denominations. Press accounts of the 1925 Scopes Trial distorted the issues involved, leaving the image of "organized knowledge… [in] open conflict with organized ignorance." The death of William Jennings Bryan within a week of the trial's close symbolized, for many observers, the collapse of Fundamentalism as a serious national presence, a "spent force" in historian D. G. Hart's words. Indeed, when Reinhold Niebuhr contributed an article on born-again Protestantism to the *Encyclopedia of the Social Sciences* in 1937, he wrote about it entirely in the past tense.[2]

In practice, the fundamentalists actually had shifted to the strategy of separation. They tended to work outside the historic American denominations, and substantial numbers did retreat from the culture to lick their wounds. Yet, as historian Douglas A. Sweeney explains, "many others got back up and reinvested in the culture; repairing their ministries and reaching out to others." While driven out of mainline church leadership roles, these fundamentalists actually "survived, and even thrived, within America's heartland."[3] Most surprising, perhaps, was the strength of premillennial thinking that had been growing since the turn of the century, especially after The Great War. As a bewildered Martin Marty has put it, "Not for almost a century, since Dwight L. Moody, had [American Protestants] turned for an interpretation of history to a pre-millenialist."[4] Curiously, even within the mainline Protestant churches, the 1930s witnessed a broad retreat from postmillennial optimism. The translation of Swiss theologian Karl Barth's *Epistle to the Romans* into English sparked a rejection of the Social Gospel, in favor of a "neo-Orthodox" focus on God's act of redemption through Christ, as revealed on the Cross.[5]

Consequently, Fundamentalism continued to play to its strong suit: building fresh institutions independent of the denominations to propagate the old faith, a religious subculture "that would preserve stability and virtue, if not within the nation, at least among the faithful." Bible institutes, colleges, prophecy conferences, magazines, book publishers, and summer Bible camps created an alternative world. The fundamentalists proved particularly adept at exploiting the emerging medium of radio. Their hostility toward the constraints of church structure served them well here, as did "an entrepreneurial streak" which employed "any and all means for new converts."[6] One early religious broadcaster was Paul Rader, who launched the "National Radio Chapel" out of Chicago's WHT in 1925, soon supplemented by the "Shepherd Hour" and "The Request Hour." Donald Grey Barnhouse of Philadelphia's Tenth Presbyterian Church started "The Bible Study Hour" in 1928. In California, a former orange grower-turned evangelist, Charles F. Fuller, launched the "Old Fashioned Revival Hour" in 1937 on the Mutual Broadcasting System. Music by the Goose Creek Gospel Quartet complemented his wife's reading of excerpts from listeners' letters and his own "folksy," sentimental manner. Summoning up images of a rural, small-town, Christian America, the show had an amazing twenty million listeners each week. Evangelical mission groups—notably the Sudan Interior Mission and the China Inland Mission—also showed new energy during the 1930s. The latter alone sent out 629 missionaries between 1930 and 1936. Within a religious community with little apparent coherence, these missions "were the glue holding the movement together."[7]

Despite this apparent success, though, Fundamentalism in the 1930s lacked a "public face." It remained a disjointed subculture far removed from the mainstream of American political and intellectual life. In the first of several initiatives to move "beyond the constraints of polemical fundamentalism,"[8] Rev. Will Houghton of Chicago's Moody Bible Institute convened a small group of prominent pastors, mission board executives, and college presidents to explore formation of a National Association of Evangelicals (NAE). Neatly positioned theologically between the mainline Federal Council of Churches and Carl McIntire's separatist American Council of Christian Churches, the NAE would "affirm doctrinal fundamentals" but "with a more sophisticated hermeneutic."[9] It opened its membership to conservatives in the mainline, those outside the established denominations, the surging array of independent congregations, and "parachurches" gathering under the "New" Evangelical banner. Meeting at St. Louis' Hotel Coronado in 1942, 150 delegates elected Rev. J. Elwin Wright of the New England Fellowship as NAE Executive Secretary and Rev. Harold John Ockenga of Boston's historic Park Street Congregational Church as President. The next year, the organization adopted a full constitution and a seven-point statement of faith and opened an Office of Public Affairs in Washington, DC. In 1944, it created the National Religious Broadcasters and in 1945 founded its humanitarian arm, World Relief. The NAE inherited a vision of a Christian America, supporting in 1946 the Christian Amendment Movement, what Marty has called the "last stand for vision of [Christian] empire," which would have added to the U.S. Constitution language recognizing "the authority and law of Jesus Christ, Saviour and Ruler of nations."[10] However, the NAE's most notable achievement was linguistic: claiming the "Evangelical" label recently applied to all Protestants for their distinct born-again, literalist formulation.

To promote intellectual activity, radio host Charles Fuller joined with Pastor Okenga in 1947 to create The Fuller Theological Seminary in California, with the goal of turning it into the "Cal Tech of the evangelical world." Founding faculty members were Everett Harrison in Bible, Carl F. H. Henry in Theology, Harold Lindsell in History and Missions, and Wilbur Smith in Apologetics. According to historian Douglas Sweeney, "[f]or many years, they were the deans of neo-evangelical thought." Faculty members at Gordon Divinity School and other seminaries created the Evangelical Theological Society in 1949.[11]

The New Evangelicalism turned out to hold a special appeal for American teenagers and young adults. Hart explains this as a result of the movement's "message of deciding for Christ" coinciding with that stage in life where the young are seeking an identity independent of their parents. Several Evangelical youth ministries joined together in 1945 to form Youth for Christ, an organization that learned quickly how to combine gospel music, comedy, and conversion testimonials into an Evangelical "good show." The first full-time employee of Youth for Christ was a young, suburban Chicago preacher named Billy Graham.[12]

Graham quickly became the public face of the New Evangelicalism and the most important religious figure in America for, arguably, the next three decades. Born into a conventional North Carolina, fundamentalist home, Graham attended Florida Bible College before enrolling at Wheaton College outside of Chicago, just as that school was shifting from an aggressive Fundamentalism to the more open New Evangelicalism. Graham first attracted regional attention at Youth for Christ's 1945 "Victory Rally" in Chicago's Orchestra Hall, where he opened the event with the simple, yet stirring preaching style that would become his trademark. Graham laced his sermons with premillennialist declarations, such as "I sincerely believe...that we are living in the latter days" and "I sincerely believe that the coming of the Lord draweth nigh." Occasionally, he was more specific, predicting in 1950, for example, that "we may have another year.... maybe two years" before "the judgment hand of God" would fall. Named President of the fundamentalist Northwest College at the age of twenty-nine, Graham gained national fame through his September 1949 Crusade in Los Angeles. With "all the features of a Youth for Christ rally," this event in the "Canvas Cathedral" had already recorded some notable celebrity conversions when newspaper magnate William Randolph Hearst sent a telegram to all his editors and reporters: "Puff Graham!" Billy Graham so vaulted into the pages of *Time*, *Life*, and *Look* magazines as the youthful evangelist suited to a new, postwar, suburban America. By 1959, even mainline Protestants and many Catholic Bishops had endorsed his work.[13]

While claiming to be "completely neutral" in politics, Graham was relentless in his denunciations of Communism as a fake religion "that is inspired, directed, and motivated by the Devil himself who has declared war on Almighty God." He praised, indirectly, Senator Joe McCarthy and members of the House Un-American Activities Committee as "men who, in the face of public denouncement and ridicule, go loyally on in their work of exposing the pinks, the lavenders, and the reds who have sought refuge beneath the wings of the American eagle." And, like Dwight Moody before him, Graham confidently assumed that Christianity and economic individualism were but two sides of the same coin. One of his earliest film projects, for example, was "Oiltown, U.S.A." Focusing on Houston, Texas, the movie was advertised as "the story of the free enterprise of America – the story of the development and use of God-given natural resources by men who have built a great new empire."[14] At a decisive moment, Graham would also enter the debate over birth control.

In addition, Billy Graham conceived the bi-weekly publication that would "set the agenda" and serve as "the magazine of record" for New Evangelical leaders during the second half of the twentieth century: *Christianity Today*.[15] As he would later relate, "I was awakened one night at about 2 A.M. I went to my desk and wrote out ideas about a magazine similar to the [mainline] *Christian Century*, one that would give theological respectability to evangelicals." With the financial help of his father-in-law L. Nelson Bell, a former missionary doctor in China, Graham recruited Fuller Seminary professor Carl F. H. Henry as editor and produced the first issue of *Christianity Today* in October 1956. As the inaugural editorial explained: "Neglected, slighted, misrepresented – evangelical Christianity needs a clear voice to speak with conviction and love, and to state its true position and its relevance to the world crisis." Sun Oil Chairman J. Howard Pew and other wealthy Christian businessmen rallied to the cause, providing funds to mail free subscriptions of *Christianity Today* to nearly two hundred thousand Protestant ministers, a policy continued until 1967.[16]

When the New Evangelicals would enter the birth control debate, two background matters stood out. First, despite premillennial theological roots, mid-twentieth century Evangelicalism became closely identified with the American Way of Life exemplified by burgeoning suburbia and (as in the late nineteenth century) with a certain fusion of religion and politics. Most Evangelicals supported the proposed Christian Amendment to the Constitution. They favored (as did their mainline counterparts) adding "under God" to the Pledge of Allegiance (1954) and placing "In God We Trust" on the dollar bill and all coinage. Prospects for the Protestant Empire actually seemed to brighten again, albeit through a series of compromises with modern life. Martin Marty is probably correct in seeing the remarkable popularity of Billy Graham as demonstrating "how theologically inclusive and ethically disengaged the [religious] revival of the 1950s had become."[17] Importantly (as will be explained shortly), this "American Way" also included by the 1950s a tamed and seemingly conservative "family planning" movement. Second, in their reliance on parachurches and in their continued distrust of any institutional authority, the New Evangelicals—in Marsden's words—"emphasized all the more the Protestant principle of the exclusive and infallible authority of Scripture."[18] Indeed, it would be through a new and different reading of Scripture that key Evangelical leaders would find a way to join with their mainline foes to end 450 years of Protestant opposition to birth control.

Planned Parenthood, Population Explosion, and the Churches

Following the *One Package* court decision, which allowed physicians to provide birth control information and devices to their patients, and the endorsement of contraception by the American Medical Association, the birth control movement faced a new opportunity. Most leaders felt that the time was right for "an assault by statesmanship" to place birth control within federal and state health programs. There was a growing consensus that this meant jettisoning all vestiges of feminism and neo-Malthusianism from the movement's agenda. Among the dissenters, predictably, was Margaret Sanger.

All the same, the various factions did come together to create the Birth Control Council of America in 1937, to plan for a single, strong national organization. The Council brought in Kenneth D. Rose of the John Price fundraising firm, who recommended crafting a new image for the movement through two changes: replacing the phrase "birth control" with "family planning" in every possible way; and adopting "male leadership." Why the latter? Rose explained that it "is clear we face the fact that most pivotal groups upon which advancement of birth control is dependent are controlled by men, such as Federal and State legislatures, hospital boards, public health boards, etc." Sanger finally did agree to a merger, and in 1939 the American Birth Control League and her Clinical Reference Bureau combined into the Birth Control Federation of America, with Rose as interim director. She fought hard to retain the "birth control" label, yet Rose engineered a membership referendum on the matter. In January 1942, the organization was renamed the Planned Parenthood Federation of America (PPFA).[19]

The change was well-timed. As Planned Parenthood's own literature admits, "popular wisdom" during the 1940s held that a low birth rate between the wars had weakened the country: "'Pro-natalists' stepped up their rhetoric after the war was on, insisting that it was women's duty to give up their jobs for men, go home and raise families." Adjusting to this climate, the organization argued that Planned Parenthood "did *not* mean smaller families but, rather, *planned* families—and therefore healthier children." Again in the PPFA's own words, the 1950s were also "a throwback to Victorian times" where women "were expected to be happy at home, with...the requisite three toddlers lapping up their boundless attention." Planned Parenthood clinics commonly focused in their literature on marital counseling, infertility treatments, and child-spacing. As one advertisement for the Seattle-King County clinic explained, "You are invited to ATTEND OUR CHILD SPACING CLINIC," with a drawing of parents and three children dancing around a logo: "The happy family – we planned it that way." The patient load of PPFA clinics did climb from 46,000 in 1949 to 117,000 in 1959, with a "careful emphasis on keeping husbands happy and babies healthy."[20]

Among certain elites, however, the 1950s spawned a very different worry: a global "population explosion." It is true that relatively simple improvements in public health, such as advances in famine control and the use of DDT to control malaria, had dramatic results in the late 1940s, with death rates tumbling around the globe. By the early 1950s, annual global population growth through this "death control" reached the "alarming" figure of fifty million. Using his own funds, John D. Rockefeller III created in 1952 The Population Council, designed to coordinate response to the new crisis. The same year, Margaret Sanger guided the formation of the International Planned Parenthood Federation.[21]

Progress was slow, at first, and the "pro-natalism" of the postwar era peaked in 1957, when the American Total Fertility Rate reached 3.75 children per woman. A major achievement for the population alarmists came during 1959, in a report from The President's Committee to Study the United States Military Assistance Program, chaired by General William Draper. The "Draper Report" recommended, for the first time, that financial and technical support for "family planning" programs should be part of American development aid programs, if recipient governments so requested. The Report maintained that population control would mean "decreasing opportunities for communist political and economic domination" in emerging countries. Referring to the new population crisis; it added "that development efforts in many areas of the world are being offset by increasingly rapid population growth."[22] After meeting with Roman Catholic Bishops, President Dwight Eisenhower rejected the Draper recommendation, saying that he could not "imagine anything more emphatically a subject that is not a proper political or governmental activity or function or responsibility."[23] Yet, the tide was running in favor of the alarmists. Within a few years, Eisenhower—now out of office—would join fellow former President Harry Truman as Honorary Co-Chairman of a fundraising drive by PPFA to combat "the population explosion."

In decisive manner, the turn of the birth control movement toward a seeming "pro-family" stance during the 1940s and 1950s combined with the emergence of the "population explosion" crisis to enable, and perhaps even push, American Protestant churches into a fairly complete embrace of the ideology of birth control. Building on precedents from the 1930s, the process grew among the mainline and confessional churches in the mid- and late-1950s. The New Evangelicals would adopt an almost identical approach a decade later.

Leading Protestant theologians paved the way. In his Gifford Lectures, for example, Reinhold Niebuhr defended the "duality" of sex "for both the assertion of the self and the flight from the self." While procreation was the primary purpose of bisexuality, he said it was wrong to turn this "natural fact" into a universally valid "law of reason." Karl Barth reported "a moral and theological consensus on the need for responsible parenthood," with choice of method to be "made in faith and with a free conscience, in a joint and deliberate decision by husband and wife." Paul Tillich elevated the status of the libido: "unperverted life strives…for union with that which is separated from it." Otto Piper insisted that God's words in Genesis, "increase and multiply," were not a command but rather a blessing. Jacques Ellul argued that marriage had "deeper" needs than the creation of children: "Consequently, procreation is neither the purpose nor the essential of marriage…. [M]arriage is fully sufficient without children."[24]

The phrase, "Responsible Parenthood," became popular among the Protestants. In 1954, the Augustana Evangelical Lutheran Church in America approved a statement with that title, affirming all birth control methods within marriage. "None of the methods for controlling the number and spacing of the births of children has any special moral merit or demerit," this church body reasoned. "It is the spirit in which the means is used…which defines its 'rightness' or 'wrongness.'" More broadly, these Swedish–American Lutherans insisted that "an unrestrained production of children without realistic regard to God-given responsibilities…may be as sinful and selfish an indulgence of the lusts of the flesh as is the complete avoidance of parenthood." Two years later, The General Conference of the Methodist Church declared that "planned parenthood, practiced in Christian conscience, may fulfill rather than violate the will of God."[25] The 1958 Anglican Lambeth Conference called "responsible parenthood" a "right and important factor in Christian family life" that "should be the result of positive choice before God." It added: "The *means* of family planning are in large measure matters of clinical and ascetic choice…. Christians have every right to use the gifts of science for proper ends."[26]

Even the conservative Lutheran Church-Missouri Synod—in the early 1930s still Sanger's "Public Enemy #Two" among the American denominations—informally embraced "planned parenthood" in

1959. The key figure here was Alfred Martin Rehwinkel, Professor of Christian Ethics and Church History at Concordia Seminary. His book *Planned Parenthood and Birth Control in the Light of Christian Ethics* contained arguments both familiar and peculiar. Among the latter, he offered a certain praise for the Lutheran mothers of sixty years earlier, whose robust fertility was appropriate for a largely rural church, where life "was more simple and the community more stable." Rehwinkel continued: "But today all this has changed." Housing design and "everything else in society" conspired against the large family. "Today babies must be born in hospitals," adding to their cost. Meanwhile, life in the city "has apparently reduced the native vitality and reproductive ability of the modern woman, so that she is no longer physically or psychologically capable of bearing, nursing, and rearing families as large as her grandmother...."[27]

On more conventional ground, Rehwinkel reported that he could find "nowhere" in Scripture "a clear and definite statement on...which a positive law or rule making the use of contraceptives in marriage a sinful procedure could be established." More directly, he argued that birth control "is not sinful in its very nature, nor can birth control as such be declared as a sinful violation of God's creation order." Rehwinkel did assert that these arguments did not apply to abortion, which was fundamentally different. Nor was intentional childlessness by an otherwise "physically and mentally fit" Christian couple defensible. Nor would "race suicide" result, he said, pointing to the contemporary rise of the birth rate and the strong "desire for motherhood" among normal women. This meant (in seeming contradiction of earlier statements) "that they are bound to have children and many of them." In the end, Rehwinkel referred curious Christians seeking to "exercise their liberty to use contraceptives" to clinics "staffed with a professional personnel" who were "ready to serve with expert advice and aid." He concluded: "In most cases they will be listed in the telephone directory under 'Planned Parenthood Association.'"[28] Margaret Sanger had won another victory.

Indeed, the appearance of Rehwinkel's book in 1959 might be a sign of what Martin Marty calls a "dramatic cultural shift," which he dates between 1957 and 1960. The apparent postwar religious revival found most visibly among the mainline and confessional Christian churches had grown "self-defeating and produced a surfeit." The central, private quest for normal family life in the new suburbs gave way to engagement on the more public issues of civil rights, the atomic threat, unrest in the "third world," women's claims for equality, and the spread of Communism in Latin America and Southeast Asia. Professional theologians such as Harvey Cox, Marty suggests, would soon articulate the shift, offering an "updated version of postmillenial thought," one short on Scriptural symbols but one talking again about summoning the Kingdom of God through human action.[29]

Relative to birth control, this process might be more clearly seen in "The Mansfield Report," also drafted (like the Draper Report) in 1959 by an international study group organized by The World Council of Churches and the International Missionary Council, and meeting at Mansfield College, Oxford, England. Formally entitled "Responsible Parenthood and the Population Problem," the report tied birth control to both a broad "crisis" in the family and to Third World aspirations. The involvement of the Missionary Council was significant, for it was missionaries in the decolonizing nations who directly mediated the application of Christian faith to their peoples and who seemed most agitated by the "population explosion."

The Report opened by arguing that the "larger crisis of our time is reflected in families throughout the whole wide earth." Indeed, "[the family], too, is in crisis," caused by the emancipation of women and a welcome decline in "masculine-dominated social structures." From these pressures, "age old patterns of family relations are disintegrating on every side." The Report concluded: "Out of the ruins of the old must be built the new." Moreover, the world "confronts a doubling of the present number of people before the end of the century," a "population explosion" whose "repercussions...are vast and grave."

The study group acknowledged that the Christian Church had, from its origins, seen itself as "the Family of families." However, too often in the area of family relations the Church had "clung to tradition without taking into account new knowledge." "Responsible parenthood" built on "new knowledge and open" to the wider claims of the world must be part of the solution to the contemporary crisis, in both its familial and population aspects. Accordingly, "[t]rue marriage and parenthood are seen to be part of the realm of Christian liberty." This meant, in turn, "considerable latitude of choice, when the motives are right, in regard to mutually acceptable and non-injurious means to avert or defer conception."[30]

The Report deemed marriage "a divine institution," a "covenanted relationship within which man and woman receive the grace, security and joy promised by God to those who are faithful to it." The purposes of marriage were companionship and parenthood, "with sexual union as the ordained servant of both." God's gift of dominion in Genesis 1:28 was to be guided by knowledge, "a liberating gift of God." The knowledge of how sex works "gives to a couple the power, and therefore the responsibility, to lift the begetting of children out of the realm of biological accident." It also "enables husband and wife to decide…whether any one act of intercourse shall be for the enrichment and expression of their personal relationship only, or for the begetting of a child also." Put another way, the two purposes of the sexual act were "separable" and, in a way, procreation became subordinate to companionship. Regarding contraceptive method, "there appears to be no moral distinction between the means now known or practiced." All the same, this logic did not extend to abortion, "involving as it does the destruction of human life." Nor did the unmarried have the Christian liberty to utilize birth control.[31]

The Mansfield Report reflected policies also found in the American Baptist Church, the Methodist Church, the Protestant Episcopal Church, the United Church of Christ, the United Lutheran Church, and the United Presbyterian Church. Only the Eastern Orthodox churches within the WCC structure dissented.[32] It thus stands as perhaps the definitive mainline Protestant statement on the birth control question prior to the "sexual revolution" of the late 1960s. Evangelical leaders would draft their own consensus statement on birth control nine years after the Mansfield Report. While trying to distinguish themselves from the mainline Protestants as well as from Roman Catholics, the Evangelical embrace of birth control would actually employ no new arguments and—surprisingly—would be in some ways more sweeping, including an implicit acceptance of abortion as a form of birth control.

Birth Control in Christianity Today

From its origin in 1956 until late 1959, the New Evangelical "magazine of record," *Christianity Today*, avoided or ignored the birth control question. It was finally drawn in by controversy over the Draper Report. The "news" article on this subject stands, in retrospect, as one of three key turning points in elite Evangelical opinion. Ostensibly, it gives an account of a Thanksgiving statement by the U.S. Catholic Bishops which opposed any public assistance for promoting artificial birth control. Along with President Eisenhower, Democratic Senator,

Presidential aspirant, and Roman Catholic John F. Kennedy agreed that such a policy would be a "mistake." Yet, the article continued: "Among evangelicals, the hullabaloo perhaps served to crystallize some convictions," turning them "anew to the Bible for a re-examination of views on the legitimacy of sex severed from its procreative function." Registering opposition to birth control was Herbert E. McKeel, current President of the NAE, who was "firmly against any form of birth control. God has never revoked his great command to be 'fruitful and multiply.'" Seeming almost to channel Anthony Comstock, Wheaton College Professor Merrill C. Tenney argued that birth regulation must be a personal matter of "prayerful agreement and self-control rather than promiscuous use of chemical or mechanical aid."

More striking, though, were the Evangelical leaders now speaking in favor of birth control. P. Kenneth Geiser, MD, of the Christian Medical Society said that "[s]ome use of contraceptives is necessary. I do not see that they are harmful or unscriptural." From Fuller Theological Seminary, Professor Edward Carnell argued that "the question of contraceptives is simply one expedient within the creative possibilities of love." Most forcefully, NAE co-founder Harold J. Ockenga opined that birth control was needed to control the "population explosion," adding: "I don't think there's anything wrong with birth control per se."

Shifting into an editorial mode, *Christianity Today* concluded that the Bible did not discuss birth control, since "avoidance of parenthood was unheard of in biblical times." Through a not necessarily obvious leap of logic, this meant that the position of Evangelicals "is one of the liberty of a good conscience before God." However, showing some equivocation, the magazine did note the irony that this controversy had flared up just as Christians prepared to celebrate the birth of Jesus, so that "*God's sovereignty over the human reproductive process*, exhibited nowhere more strikingly than in the incarnation, fell into the background....."[33]

Further evidence of shifting opinions on contraception among Evangelical leaders, in light of the perceived "population explosion," came the same month in an interview by the *New York Times* with Billy Graham. The article reported that "The Rev. Dr. Billy Graham believes there is nothing morally wrong in the practice of birth control," although he felt that population control aid to countries requesting it should be provided by private agencies, not by outside governments. Graham emphasized that birth control was an important answer to the "terrifying and tragic" problem of overpopulation, that there was nothing in Scripture that barred its responsible use, and that the majority of Americans used contraception in any case, "whether they be Protestants or Roman Catholics."[34]

During the next year, however, most commentary on birth control in *Christianity Today* reflected continued opposition. A February 1960 editorial acknowledged that "[e]xploding world populations pose new problems," but that "much of the prattle stressing birth control as the main solution is more wordy than wise." Indeed, birth control offered at best "a quantitative solution" to humankind's moral and spiritual problems, and frequently led churchmen to "sheer relativism." While taking a slap at Roman Catholic "pretensions" in arguing "that birth control is moral by natural law but immoral by artificial means," the editorial ended on a somewhat ambiguous, yet still critical note:

> Many churchmen are uneasy because attempts to justify birth control by appeal to population explosions come dangerously near to making the end justify the means. So responsible parenthood, not exploding population, gets more and more emphasis. But just which parents are responsible for whose children?[35]

A review in the same issue by E. P. Schulze slammed the Rehwinkel volume on *Planned Parenthood and Birth Control in the Light of Christian Ethics.* After noting Rehwinkel's endorsement of birth control and his scorn for continence, Schulze replied that "[t]he command, 'Be fruitful and multiply,' has not yet been repealed, and children are still 'an heritage of the Lord!'" Citing several Old Testament precedents, he argued that Christians should "let the omniscient Father of us all determine the size of our families. He does it with infinite wisdom, and often permits us fewer children than we wish." The reviewer predicted that the "outstanding influence" of this book would be "to foster a sexual life divorced from its basic purpose and responsibilities."[36]

A subsequent review of a volume inspired by the Mansfield Report, Richard Fagley's *The Population Explosion and Christian Responsibility*, drew similar scorn. Reviewer Sherwood T. Wirt blasted the mainline Protestant churches advocating Planned Parenthood, "not for its own sake but as a deterrent to keep the hordes of the future from being born." The reviewer accused Fagley of distorting Scripture, as when the latter argued that 1 Timothy 2:15 "did not mean that faithful women would be saved through childbearing, but that they would come 'safely through childbirth.'" Wirt asked:

> Will barrenness produce godliness in America? ... Is a thinned-out population morally and spiritually superior to other kinds? Is this the divine path to peace and the abundant life?

He answered: "The truth is that God has ways of confounding the statisticians."[37]

For the next four-and-a-half years, the birth control issue vanished again from the pages of *Christianity Today*.[38] All the same, there were internal signs at the magazine that the issue was very much on the minds of its editors, especially Carl F. H. Henry and Harold Lindsell. Within the archival collection for *Christianity Today*, housed at The Billy Graham Center at Wheaton College, there are relatively few "subject" files from the early 1960s. Prominent exceptions are two thick files, marked "Population Information-General," which provide insight into what the *CT* editors were reading as they considered new views of birth control and abortion.

The materials collected bore two primary themes. The first was the catastrophe of the "population explosion." Items from 1962 included a strongly Malthusian commentary on the "Pitfalls of Progress" appearing in a January issue of the *Nation* and a news release from the Population Reference Bureau, "Birth Rate, Down; Baby Count, Up." The latter warned that the decline in the U.S. birth rate after 1957 was deceptive. Given the number of American women about to enter their prime child-bearing years, "the number of babies will go up, a way [sic] up." A "Population Doubling Table," possibly hand-drawn by Carl Henry, showed particularly scary numbers for The Congo, Turkey, India, Indonesia, Mexico, and Brazil. Another article, "The Birth-Control Explosion" from the Canadian magazine *Maclean's*, reported: "Now, at last, attitudes are changing toward the only thing anybody, anywhere can do about the population explosion."[39]

In November 1965, Henry forwarded a fundraising letter from a now more aggressive Planned Parenthood to Lindsell. Signed by John Gunther, the letter noted how "Pressures of population have become a national and world threat." On the domestic side, "Welfare rolls are rising steeply within our own urban centers; there is chronic nagging poverty within entire regions of Appalachia." "We cannot wait," Gunther declared, "we must expand our services to burdened families in this country." Attached was an article from the *New York Herald Tribune*, arguing that increases in food production had been "wiped out by rapid population growth." It quoted United Nations official B. R. Sen that the 1965–1975 period would be one "when the Malthusian correctives (war, pestilence, famine) will inexorably come into play" unless "dedicated endeavor" emerged, including "widespread rethinking of the attitude to population control." Another article forwarded from Henry to Lindsell was "The Problem of People," appearing in *Harvard Today*. It highlighted projections of soaring human numbers in Hong Kong, Latin America ("by the year 2000 there will be twice as many people in Latin America as in the United States and Canada"), Egypt, and "the Puerto Rican section of Harlem." A January 1965 news release from the Population Reference Bureau cited—in classic Malthusian fashion— "The Crucial Link" between "Poverty and High Fertility." This meant "that in the United States today poverty tends to be self-perpetuating."[40]

The one discordant note was an article, "East Bloc Frets over Birth Rate," appearing in the *New York Times*. Focused on fertility decline in Eastern Europe, it attributed low birth rates to housing shortages, the "large-scale employment of women," high divorce rates, and legal and illegal abortions. One official reported three abortions for every live birth in Hungary, what he called "an institutional killing of the nation." A Czechoslovak writer "charged his country's young people with a 'biological rejection' of their society." Hungarian author Gyula Fekete lamented: "The new hedonistic religion is everything for the present, nothing for the future. For 15 years our plays, novels and editorials rated participation in production work higher than motherhood – we emancipated childless women, but not mothers." Carl Henry's memo attached to the article noted that "not all populations are expanding," and he might have seen in this report portents of a future American life once the full contraceptive mentality had broken through. Instead, Henry seemed—like most others at the time—increasingly mesmerized by the "population explosion." As another commentary in this file put it: "It is clear that only an evangelistic advance of a proportion we have never imagined can save the Church from being buried, not by the Russians, but by a numerical landslide of our own kinfolk…. This peril is present and real." In an odd way, evangelism was blurring into birth control.[41]

The second theme found in these collected materials is the mounting support for a liberalization of birth control teachings found within the Roman Catholic Church. For example, a 1961 issue of *Population Bulletin* examined "New Trends in Roman Catholic Opinion." It noted that Pope Pius XII, in 1951, had agreed that certain people "can be relieved of this positive obligation" to procreate, for legitimate "medical, eugenic, economic and social reasons." It featured Professor of Theology John O'Brien of Notre Dame University, who argued that "the time has come for citizens of all faiths to unite in an effort to remove this divisive and nettlesome issue [of birth control] from the political and social life of our nation." The issue also carried an essay by John Rock, one of the researchers responsible for the birth control pill—and a Roman Catholic. Relative to public policy, he urged that *all restrictions* on birth control methods, "written or unwritten," should be lifted, so that "the communicant of any faith will be able to choose a method in accord with the dictates of his own conscience." The Associate Editor of *Catholic World*, Fr. Louis McKennan, hoped that the "population explosion" would lead Catholics to "sentiments more noble and more realistic than: there's enough food for everybody, so what are we getting excited about?"[42]

Another special issue of the same journal appears in the files: "The Vatican and the Population Crisis," from 1965. Noting that at "the highest levels" of Catholic leadership, there is "growing awareness of the population crisis and of related moral issues," editor Robert Cook anticipated that the Catholic Church would soon abandon its opposition to at least some forms of "artificial" birth control. In 1964, he said, Pope Paul VI had himself acknowledged that the Church "could not continue to bypass the surpassingly important question of population control." Cardinal Suenens, Archbishop of Malines-Brussels, exhorted his fellow bishops: "I beg you, my brothers: let us avoid a new Galileo case. One is enough for the Church." And Father George H. Dunne, SJ, an official at Georgetown University, acknowledged "the immediate problem of population" and his own hope "that the oral contraceptive, or 'the pill'…, would become a morally acceptable method of bringing population growth under reasonable control."[43]

Joint attention to the "population explosion" and debate within the Roman Catholic Church finally brought *Christianity Today* back to the birth control question in 1965. The magazine reported in January of that year that the Archbishop of St. Paul, Minnesota, had stopped the showing of a four-part television series on birth control, planned by the National Council of Catholic Men. This was part of an effort by Church authorities to minimize debate on the question until the

Vatican had clarified its position.[44] An April article pointed to mounting pressures within the Catholic Church for change. Twenty leading lay Catholics in England had declared the absolute prohibition of contraceptives "strangely unintegrated" in light of Rome's acceptance of the "safe period" and teaching on the "unitive" purpose of sexual intercourse. Another Archbishop had predicted that the Church would lose vast numbers of members unless it changed policy. And the Pope had summoned his Birth Control Commission to a special meeting in Rome, seeking advice on the progestin–estrogen pill. "There seems little doubt," the article concluded, "that public sentiment, religious and otherwise, is shifting increasingly toward acceptance of birth control."[45] While *Christianity Today* gave no notice to the U.S. Supreme Court's *Griswold* decision that year, overturning Connecticut's "Comstock" law, it did note a legislative effort in Massachusetts to repeal a similar measure. While Cardinal Archbishop Richard Cushing of Boston offered no opposition, it was blocked by Representative Lawrence P. Smith, a Catholic, "a Democrat and the father of fifteen children." Meanwhile, the U.S. Congress debated whether to charter Federal agencies to distribute contraceptives, at home and abroad. And the Vatican's Birth Control Commission remained "rather hopelessly split."[46] Two weeks later, under the title "Birth Control Bombshell," the magazine highlighted a "remarkable declaration by 37 American Catholic scholars," which called traditional Church arguments against birth control "unconvincing" and labeled contraceptive use not intrinsically immoral. Meanwhile, a perplexed Paul VI lamented in Rome: "We cannot remain silent. But to speak out is a real problem. The Church has not ever over the centuries had to face anything like these problems."[47]

The Evangelical Alternative

This was the context of events which saw *Christianity Today* publish its own "bombshell," the second turning point in New Evangelical opinion: "How to Decide the Birth Control Question," appearing in the March 4, 1966 issue. The author was John Warwick Montgomery, an evangelical Lutheran who taught church history at Trinity Evangelical Divinity School. His purpose was to lay out the case for a distinctive New Evangelical acceptance of birth control. To do so, he accentuated contrasts with both Catholic teaching and an amalgam he called "Secularists and Liberal Protestants." Regarding the former, he emphasized the "strange inconsistency" where Rome held up celibacy as the clerical ideal, while seeming "to do all within its power to encourage child bearing on the part of the married." Montgomery called the application of "natural law" thinking by Catholics to birth control "especially bizarre," for it held that man can appropriately control "natural" phenomena like animal populations and vegetation, "but cannot without sin control his own numbers *in the face of severe population pressures.*" He favorably quoted Harvard physician John Rock's condemnation of the Vatican-approved rhythm method as "unnatural," without noting Rock's role as co-inventor and major promoter of the birth control pill.[48]

Turning to his amalgamation of "Secularists and Liberal Protestants," Montgomery traced its origins to "the courtly love tradition" of the medieval era and "the romantic movement" of the nineteenth century. It "sees the union of man and women not as a means to an end but as an end in itself." When blended with "a thinly disguised contemporary humanism," the result was a sexual ethic—"the so-called new morality"—that cast "the love relation" alone as "the fulfillment of human aspirations and the manifestation of God-as-Agape"; notably, one not limited to marriage. Among such people, "the ethics of birth control becomes situational and ad hoc," while "the overpopulation issue engulfs birth-control thinking."[49]

Both of these formulations were somewhat argumentative straw men, particularly the latter, in light of documents such as the Mansfield Report. In any case, Montgomery argued that both Roman Catholics and the Liberal Protestant Secularists had "fallen into a more acute form of the same error." He labeled this the "naturalistic fallacy," the notion that the descriptive (that which is) automatically gives rise to the normative (that which ought to be). In contrast, Montgomery said, the Evangelical relied on Scripture. It was here that he introduced his novel argument: Ephesians 5 trumps Genesis 1–2 as the focal point of Scriptural teaching on marriage and procreation:

> The center is not to be found in the first two chapters of Genesis, so often cited in isolation, but in Ephesians 5:22-32, which quotes Genesis in the context of the New Covenant in Christ. Understood in the light of New Testament fulfillment, marriage cannot be regarded simply as a means ('Be fruitful and multiply and replenish the earth') or unqualifiedly as an end ('They shall be one flesh'). Rather, it is to be seen as an analogy – indeed, as the best human analogy – of the relationship between Christ and his Church.[50]

Relative to birth control, this meant that the Evangelical could avoid "the Hegelian-like dialectic extremes of the Roman and liberal Protestant views." Because Christ's bond to the church was a complete love relationship, "one must not view marriage simply as a procreative function." This meant that where "birth control can contribute to 'subduing the earth' in order to achieve a better human relationship, it is not to be condemned." He did acknowledge that "the marital union is properly fulfilled in natural birth" and he underscored that the use of birth control devices by the unmarried "is not to be tolerated," since this would violate "the high analogy of Christ and Church." All the same, Evangelicals could responsibly choose to use birth control "in light of their own physical, emotional, financial, and spiritual situation, and in light of the population picture in their area of the world." In this way, "the Christian stands free from the shackles of legalism [Roman Catholics] and from the chaos of libertarianism [Liberal Protestants]."[51]

Evangelical leaders were clearly delighted with this article; it would be frequently cited as the authoritative New Evangelical commentary on the birth control question.[52] Indeed, when *Christianity Today* published its editorial on Pope Paul VI's *Humanae Vitae* in 1968, it referenced the Montgomery article as providing the clear Evangelical alternative.[53]

Leading up to that editorial were two years of regular commentary on the Catholic birth control crisis, with a growing sense of quiet satisfaction over Rome's struggles. One article, "Thirteenth Century Thinking in Boston," complained of opposition to a repeal of the Massachusetts "Comstock" law by a state representative from Roxbury, "where the percentage of chain-pregnancy, child-a-year married couples is higher than in any comparable place in the nation."[54] Another piece had the boldness to conclude that, under the Catholic rubric of "Probabilism," "Roman Catholics can now freely and legitimately use the birth-control pill without any sin at all, nor need they confess its use in the confessional."[55] Still other articles focused on Roman authorities "limping behind on birth control" while dissenting voices calling for change grew in number and volume.[56]

Humanae Vitae, issued by Paul VI in late July 1968, startled virtually everyone, including the editors of *Christianity Today*. An editorial in the August 16 issue said that the Pope "deserves to be admired for the courage of the encyclical," which was clearly not just another accommodation to secular whims. Yet, "[t]he evangelical can but wish that the pontiff had reserved his valor for an authentically biblical commitment." The encyclical's "Achilles heel" was that "it is alien to biblical revelation," with the editors adding: "The Bible says clearly that marriage alone sanctifies sexual intercourse. But it does not teach – as the Pope does – that intercourse is justifiable only if conception may result." They rejected the traditional interpretation of the Sin of Onan (Genesis 38:8–10). Since there was "ample evidence" that birth control had existed in biblical times and since Scripture "does not speak directly to the issue," Evangelicals "tend to conclude" that methods which prevent conception—"as distinguished from those that abort a fertilized egg"—could be "good or bad, depending upon the motives." That this summation of the common Evangelical position was of quite recent origin was not noted.[57]

An extensive article in the same issue focused on the "groundswell of dissent" spawned by *Humanae Vitae* and "the crisis it seemed to be precipitating among the half billion members claimed by the Roman Catholic Church." *Schadenfreude*, delight in another's misfortune, was again the theme. The encyclical "was a statement of pathos, almost of apology" and it probably had "no counterpoint in papal history." As "a major sign of defiance," the article pointed to a statement by over a hundred American Catholic theologians rejecting the Pope's logic. "Never before in modern times has there been such open resistance to a papal edict." Among the "Outsider's Reactions" reported was a statement by Billy Graham: "In general I would disagree with it [*Humanae Vitae*].... I believe in planned parenthood." The article added: "Graham spoke of seeing the effects of the 'population explosion' in his worldwide travels."[58]

In a remarkable editorial the next month, the editors of *Christianity Today* basically gloated over the rising tide of dissent within the Catholic Church. Still more brashly, they compared the promulgation of *Humane Vitae* to an act of Communist repression: "confronted with the same type of problem that the U.S.S.R. faced among the freedom-seeking people of Czechoslovakia – erosion of authority – Pope Paul VI chose to halt the threat to his ecclesiastical structure by the means that the totalitarian inevitably must use: a show of power." While admitting that some Catholic dissent "stems from humanistic, secularistic presuppositions," the editorial scrupulously avoided any mention of nearly 450 years of Protestant opposition to birth control. Rather:

> What are Protestants to make of the current crisis in Catholic authority? Those whose theological roots rest deep in the biblical

theology of the Reformation recognize the present challenge to the papal authority that elevates church tradition over biblical teaching as a possible step toward Christian freedom and truth. They join with dissenting Catholics in their opposition to a position on birth control that exhibits a non-scriptural misunderstanding of the role of sex in marriage.

It is clear that the editors saw here an opportunity, hoping the crisis would guide Catholics everywhere "to a complete rejection of the false doctrine of Papal infallibility...."[59] Still another Editorial on *Humanae Vitae* called it "the most crucial test of papal authority and supremacy in centuries," noting with implicit hope that the Catholic Church "may be on the verge of collapse."[60]

The *Affirmation*

Importantly, running concurrent with Catholicism's civil war over *Humanae Vitae* was a special consultation on "The Control of Human Reproduction," jointly sponsored by *Christianity Today* and the Christian Medical Society and involving a Who's Who of New Evangelical leaders (only Graham was not present). The concept of the conference appears to have been jointly conceived by Walter O. Spitzer, General Director of the Christian Medical Society, and Carl Henry, during 1967. Tellingly, just as with the Mansfield Report, it was "the medical missionaries whose thoughtful inquiries from many lands" served as "the principal stimulus" to the project.[61] Spitzer selected the medical doctors and researchers who participated; Henry chose the theologians and sociologists. Spitzer reported that "scores of foundations" turned down his requests for funding of the conference "because they were afraid of the controversial nature of the proceedings."[62] Harold Lindsell, Henry's successor as Editor of *Christianity Today* in mid-1968, eventually covered the project's deficit with specially enhanced "honoraria" for papers published in the magazine, money sent not to the authors but instead to the Society.[63] These consultation papers were completed by June 20, 1968, about a month before the release of *Humanae Vitae*. Yet, the consultation itself convened in New Hampshire in late August, about a month after Pope Paul VI's encyclical. The Symposium's "Affirmation," which Lindsell played the "key role" in drafting, was clearly conceived as an Evangelical reaction to *Humanae Vitae*. Lindsell and Harold Ockenga co-chaired the August session. The Honorary Chairman was Tom Clark, retired Associate Justice of the United States Supreme Court.[64]

Four of the Symposium's papers would be published in the November 8, 1968 issue of *Christianity Today*. They partially illuminate the surprising statements to be found in the "Affirmation." Bruce Waltke of the Dallas Theological Seminary tackled the question of contraception and abortion in the Old Testament. While Assyrians of the 1450–1250 BC era had treated the fetus as a person and had so prohibited abortion, he said, "[t]he Old Testament…never reckons the fetus as equivalent to a life." Indeed, according to Waltke, "God does not regard the fetus as a soul, no matter how far gestation has progressed." Regarding the sin of Onan, the author rejected the argument of "Roman Catholic exegetes" that God punished him for practicing birth control (with no mention that Luther and Calvin also held to this view); rather, "the context clearly indicates that Onan's sin lay in his selfish unwillingness to honor his levirate duty." Following further exegesis, Waltke concluded "that the Old Testament prohibits infanticide, sterilization, and continence as means of avoiding pregnancy, but it does not prohibit contraception." It was also ambivalent toward abortion. Moreover, he turned the divine injunction in Genesis 1:28 upside-down, concluding that to "subdue" the earth "may apply to cases of overpopulation" where "God enjoins man to use his technological achievements to maintain a balance for the good life."[65]

"The Relation of the Soul to the Fetus" came from Paul Jewett, Professor of Systematic Theology at Fuller Seminary. He boldly stated that while the mother's "humanity cannot be doubted," the humanity of the fetus "cannot be demonstrated." In fact:

> Scripture offers no direct teaching on the question of the participation of the fetus in the divine image. The narrative of man's creation presents as full grown the one made in the image and likeness of God. Since the creation narrative speaks of God's 'breathing into man's nostrils the breath of life,' it might seem plausible to argue that the soul informs the fetus when the first breath is drawn, that is, at birth.

Jewett conceded that there was a Scriptural problem with Psalm 139:13–15 ("For thou didst form my inward parts. Thou didst cover me in my mother's womb…. My frame was not hidden from thee, when I was made in secret…."), and acknowledged that "the psalmist did not think of his humanity as uniquely tied to the moment of birth." So the fetus should be seen as "a potential person" or perhaps a "primordial person." This meant "that the Christian answer to the control of human reproduction" should focus on "the prevention of conception," with abortion as "a last recourse."[66]

Robert Meye of the Northern Baptist Theological Seminary examined "The New Testament and Birth Control." He acknowledged that "primitive" Christians had held to Judaism's "reservations" about birth control and "disavowal" of abortion; yet "this does not at all mean...that such practices are contradictory to the heart of the New Testament faith and practice." Meye rejected the arguments of Augustine: "Neither the Old Testament nor the New speaks of procreation as the end of the sexual union." The true end was "one flesh," with the sexual relationship itself—not the bearing of children—"assigned a redemptive significance." Regarding birth control, New Testament passages "on balance...seem to leave the door open for its responsible use." Regarding abortion, he insisted that the New Testament said nothing. Hence, on these matters, "[t]he Christian is not bound by a legal code; he is free to walk in the spirit through the world and to take the measure of all possible practices...." The one restraint was care that one not offend a Christian brother. The time was past when the use of contraceptives might so offend; "not so with abortion." All the same, "there are those within the Christian community who can see no final offense in abortion when entered into responsibly by a woman in consultation with her physician."[67]

A Medical Doctor from Canada, M. O. Vincent, presented "A Christian View of Contraception." While there was "no specific text in Scripture" to settle the matter, he argued, "the overall scriptural view of the nature of God, man, marriage, and sexual intercourse leads to the conclusion that we have a right to control conception." God's words that humans "be fruitful and multiply" were given "more as a blessing than a commandment," Vincent insisted. Woman was created as a companion to man, not as a breeder. Paul "implies frequent sexual relations as the norm in marriage, without any mention of procreation." And the Song of Solomon cast sex as "a sensuous delight." Relative to current social questions, Vincent saw contraception as "the means of preventing the birth of unwanted children." The "population explosion" meant that the "[o]ver-production of children may be as sinful as selfish avoidance of parenthood." And, since some couples "do not like children," they had "a right to marital companionship without children." While Vincent opposed the rhythm method of conception prevention, he favored sterilization. In sum: "Contraception in Christian marriage not only is permitted, but has a very significant value."[68]

136

Other Symposium papers also reflected a surprising affinity for abortion. John Scanzoni, a Wheaton graduate who had gone on to teach sociology at Indiana University, rejected the argument that abortion was the "killing of a human being." Indeed, he agreed with earlier writers that abortion was "a very effective birth control method." In support, he referred primarily to Garrett Hardin, a strident non-Christian who also favored a fairly aggressive program of euthanasia. Hardin had asserted that the "early stages of an individual fetus have had very little human effort invested in them; they are of very little worth. The DNA of a zygote is not a human being." Citing the example of war, Scanzoni argued that "there are times when it is permissible to snuff out human life. The same then would apply to the fetus." Abortion could also alleviate "the conditions which spawn the cycle of poverty," because "infinitely more important" than the right to life was "the right of the child to be a wanted child." In short, "in the case of abortion, if the couple is convinced the fetus is not human or if certain conditions warrant its termination, it then becomes legitimate (where legal) as a method of fertility control." Put another way, "I am persuaded that the decision to abort or to sterilize is a matter of Christian liberty."[69]

Professor of Human Genetics at the University of Minnesota V. Elving Anderson also embraced Garrett Hardin's argument that "the DNA in a zygote is only a promise of things to come." As Anderson summarized: "it is more accurate to say that the zygote is potentially human than that it is fully human." In order to restrict conception for genetic reasons, couples could morally choose between contraceptives, sterilization, and abortion. In the end, he agreed with Scanzoni: "Responsible decisions concerning the use of conception control, sterilization, and abortion require the freedom implied in Christian liberty."[70]

John Warwick Montgomery, writing on "The Christian View of the Fetus," found himself in a new and difficult situation. Two years earlier, he had built the case for Evangelical acceptance of birth control. Now, he labored to salvage the humanity of the unborn. Montgomery argued that conception was the time when soul and body unite: "...the pressure of modern embryological knowledge has pushed creationist theologians more and more to the view that the soul is supplied by God when conception itself occurs." He found this affirmed in the New Testament[71] and warned of the grave consequences of any other choice: "To argue otherwise is to become caught inextricably in a maze which would deny true humanity to those who, through organic defect, are incapable of carrying out certain rational activities." In this regard, he pointed to human experimentation in the Third Reich. And yet, Montgomery also acknowledged that some Evangelical theologians—notably Bruce Waltke and Kenneth Kantzer—had "definite reservations as to the genuine humanity of the fetus." Moreover, while declaring that "Abortion is in fact homicide," he added: "it must be clearly seen that Christians have no business 'legislating morality' in such a way that their non-Christian neighbors are forced to adhere to laws which create impossible stresses for them." The clear inference, even for Montgomery, was that abortion should be legal and available on demand, with no stated limits.[72]

Meanwhile, Lloyd A. Kalland, Professor of the Philosophy of Religion at Gordon Divinity School, took on the task of deconstructing the strong pro-natalism of Martin Luther and John Calvin. Nine years earlier, in a commentary on the Mansfield Report, Anglican author Richard Fagley had launched a similar project, but concluded in the end: "For all practical purposes, the ethos of Wittenburg and Geneva and Cantebury was as strongly pro-fertility as that of Rome."[73] Kalland took a different approach. He simply ignored Luther's numerous affirmations of fertility and denunciations of birth control and abortion, focusing instead on Luther's desacramentalizing of marriage. He incorrectly stated that, for Luther, "Love is the very essence of marriage." Kalland was also simply wrong in asserting that "[n]owhere does Calvin treat in a definitive way the control of human reproduction." And he was doubly wrong in concluding that:

> The point of importance with Luther and Calvin is that both emphasized the love relationship in marriage and their attitudes against a scholastic mentality were so decisive that both refused to be bound where the Scriptures were not explicit and thereby kept the channels open for further study on subjects such as the control of human reproduction.[74]

Carl Henry, for his part, drove the final nails into Anthony Comstock's coffin. "[E]ros has come alive again," he argued. Not since Paul had written his letters to the wayward Corinthians had Christian reflections on sex been so urgently needed. How could Evangelicals gain a hearing for "sound biblical perspectives" in 1968 America?:

> Not, surely, by the repetition of clichés or by an uncritical reasserting of Victorian traditions in the name of the Gospel and the Law of God. Needless defense of Victorian attitudes may provide

unmerited sympathy for the 'new morality' because, as Jesus warned the Pharisees, tradition too can make the Word of God void.

By taking a critical stance toward past and existing church pronouncements and by "testing its own mood as well as the contemporary mood by the scriptural standard," Evangelicalism "may be able to exhibit its cutting edge at the frontiers of ethical discussion."[75]

As noted earlier, this Symposium of twenty-five Evangelical leaders also drafted a consensus statement, "A Protestant Affirmation on the Control of Human Reproduction." In the sweep of American Evangelical history, it stands as a remarkable document. The Affirmation did contain some inherited Christian standards regarding sexual behavior. It said that sexual intercourse "is the gift of God and shall be expressed and experienced only through the marriage relationship." And it acknowledged that coitus "was intended by God to include the purposes of companionship and fulfillment, as well as procreation," a statement which even strict Catholics would affirm. However, reflecting the content of the papers presented, the innovations in Evangelical thought were more striking:

- "The Bible does not expressly prohibit either contraception or abortion...";
- "The prevention of conception is not in itself forbidden or sinful providing the reasons for it are in harmony with the total revelation of God for the individual life.";
- "The method of preventing pregnancy is not so much a religious as a scientific and medical question to be determined in consultation with the physician";
- "...there may be times when a Christian may allow himself (or herself) to be sterilized for compelling reasons which appear to be the lesser of two evils";
- "...about the necessity and permissibility for [abortion] under certain circumstances we are in accord";
- "...the prescriptions of the legal code should not be permitted to usurp the authority of the Christian conscience as informed by Scripture";
- "Changes in state laws on therapeutic abortion that will permit honesty in the application of established criteria and the principles supported in this statement should be encouraged.";
- "Much human suffering can be alleviated by preventing the birth of children where there is a predictable high risk of genetic disease or abnormality.";

- And, "[t]his Symposium acknowledges the need for Christians' involvement in programs of population control at home and abroad."[76]

At the Evangelical leadership level, at least, Margaret Sanger's victory was complete.

In a letter to Walter Spitzer a few weeks later, Harold Lindsell remarked: "I have concluded that the Affirmation is a good piece of work." Yet, he wondered how readers might react after it appeared in *Christianity Today*: "Maybe by that time you'll have to run for cover!"[77] In a subsequent letter to Carl Henry after the issue had appeared, Lindsell wrote: "Concerning the issue on birth control and abortion I'm happy to say that apart from the usual crank letters the thoughtful responses on the subject have been quite interesting."[78]

Three of those letters did appear in the magazine's December 20 issue. A reader from Missouri complained: "I was shocked at the permissive attitude toward abortion expressed in" the Affirmation. A woman from Oregon asked: "Why was the question of God determining and limiting the number of children in a given family of believers not mentioned even once in the articles on contraception and abortion?" And Rev. M. P. Krikorian of Philadelphia seemed to resurrect the voice of Anthony Comstock, when stating:

> I consider such plebian, flesh-featured, and sex-oriented subjects are wholly alien to a periodical supposedly dedicated to evangelical emphasis and to the exaltation of the Word of God and testimony of Jesus Christ. Such articles serve no fundamental purpose *no matter by whom they are authored.*[79]

Curiously, there is some indirect evidence that this *Christianity Today* project may have run into a hostile reception at a high level. In August 1969, the magazine ran a short, unsigned review of *Birth Control and the Christian*, the book carrying the Affirmation and papers from the Symposium. It made absolutely no mention of the Affirmation's support for birth control, sterilization, and liberalized abortion laws. Rather, the piece cited only the Affirmation's view of coitus as a gift from God "that includes the purposes of companionship and fulfillment besides procreation" and—strangely—a "sideline" discussion of "why increased knowledge of contraception is likely to increase the demand for abortion."[80] To call this a misrepresentation of the book is a serious understatement. Indeed, the review basically inverted the volume's main themes. Perhaps a board member or a key donor had not been pleased, and the editors intentionally dulled the New Evangelicals' "cutting edge."

The Giftedness of Life

On the issue of birth control, Evangelical leaders had sought to position themselves in the middle, avoiding the supposed extreme legalism of the Roman Catholics and the supposed extreme libertarianism of the secularizing mainline Protestants. However, when compared to the Mansfield Report of the World Council of Churches, the Evangelical *Affirmation* "out-libertined" the mainline. Where the former forthrightly condemned abortion, the latter essentially urged its legalization. Where the former frowned on sterilization, the latter embraced it. Where the former laid great emphasis on the covenantal nature of marriage, the latter seemed mesmerized by "the freedom of the Gospel." How might this be explained?

To begin with, the Evangelicals' latent anti-Catholicism seems to have got the better of them. Rome's conundrums over birth control and the controversy over *Humanae Vitae* seemed during the 1960s to be splendid opportunities to undermine an old foe: papal authority. Opposition to birth control—common to *all* Protestants for over four centuries—was recast as an act of repression, equivalent to the Communist suppression of Eastern Europe. Evangelicals lost both their memory and their focus. When the Metropolitan Nikodim of the Russian Orthodox Church also declared in 1969 that all forms of birth control were "undesirable because they are linked with sin and dull the conscience," *Christianity Today*'s response was again remarkably short-sighted: "The Soviet Union has repeatedly opposed family planning efforts in the United Nations."[81] When the Catholic Bishops issued a pastoral letter paying "tribute" to the "parents of large families," the magazine responded with an editorial frown.[82] The New Evangelicals did not yet realize that the real enemy that they faced was a new one (or, better put, a very old one in new guise): the sexual anarchy of the Gnostics.

Indeed, the Evangelical Symposium on Human Reproduction itself gave evidence that its participants did not recognize the nature and ambition of this foe. As noted, retired U.S. Supreme Court Associate Justice Tom Clark participated in the event, even presenting a paper on "The Law as It Governs Decisions Today." He pointed to the *Griswold* case which struck down Connecticut's "Comstock" law, and also noted that some legal commentators thought it as "authoritative for striking down restrictive abortion statutes." Clark, though, thought that the court system was the wrong place to settle the abortion question. Its complexities "could be better solved in the legislative arena" and "I rather doubt that the courts will interfere in the process." Alas, the *Roe* v. *Wade* decision doing just that would come in less than five years.[83] For his part, John Warwick Montgomery tried to establish a New Evangelical compromise on the issue of reproductive control: birth control acceptable; abortion a sin. As he explained in another book from the time: "...the Bible does not remove responsible birth control from the decision of the married couple" while "from the biblical standpoint, abortion is homicide." On the latter point, he added: "It is a sign of increasing paganism that we callously permit the killing of unborn children – genuine people who cannot defend themselves."[84] And yet, even at an Evangelical Symposium packed with his friends and admirers, the acceptance of birth control led inexorably to a quasi-acceptance of abortion. Perhaps, Anthony Comstock had not been completely wrong, after all: perhaps the two were bound together.

Third, this episode exposed the limitations of Evangelical Biblical exegesis. Using strained arguments, the new exegetes simply turned upside down long settled understandings of Genesis 1:28, Genesis 38:8–10, Exodus 21:22–25, Psalm 51:5, Malachi 2:15 and 4:5–6, Luke 1:41and 44, I Timothy 2:15, and various passages in I and II Corinthians. John Warwick Montgomery, for example, tried to defend the equality of mother and fetus in Exodus 21 from the new exegesis. Yet, Bruce Waltke, speaking for the "cutting edge," responded harshly: "He perverts truth.... [M]easured by the weight of scholarly opinion Montgomery's view has little support."[85] Looking back, the reader gains the sense that Scripture was being twisted to meet the dual crises of the moment—"eros has come alive again" and "the population explosion"—and also to justify new behaviors found among laity and clergy alike.

What could have been the alternative? There were possibilities other than a return to the Comstock regime. First, Evangelicals could have resisted the mounting hysteria about the "population explosion" through a faith in God's Providence, much like Pope Paul VI finally did in 1968 or as Eastern Orthodox leaders did throughout this period. For indeed, in the words of Sherwood T. Wirt, God did provide: He "had ways of confounding the statisticians." The Green

Revolution in agriculture of the 1970s and 1980s would sweep away all the claims and warnings of the alarmists. Food and resources proved to be abundant.

And second, borrowing words from Amy Laura Hall, the New Evangelicals could "have emphasized a sense of divine grace, human contingency, sufficient abundance, and the radical giftedness of all life."[86] Instead of this Christian Humanism focused on the sacredness of the human person, most Evangelical leaders cast their lot in the late 1960s with the sexual modernists, the agenda of Margaret Sanger, and—unwittingly—the old Gnosticism in new disguise.

Notes

1. George M. Marsden, "From Fundamentalism to Evangelicalism: A Historical Analysis," in *The Evangelicals: What They Believe*, ed. David F. Wells and John D. Woodbridge (Nashville and New York: Abingdon Press, 1975), 124–25.

2. Ibid., 126; D. G. Hart, *That Old-Time Religion in Modern America: Evangelical Protestantism* (Chicago, IL: Ivan Dee, 2002), 55, 57.

3. Douglas A. Sweeney, *The American Evangelical Story: A History of the Movement* (Grand Rapids, MI: Baker Academic, 2005), 170.

4. Martin E. Marty, *Protestantism in the United States: Righteous Empire* (New York: Charles Scribner's Sons, 1986), 248.

5. Larry Witham, *A City Upon a Hill: How Sermons Changed the Course of American History* (New York: Harper One, 2007), 240–41.

6. Hart, *That Old-Time Religion in Modern America*, 57, 59.

7. Ibid., 59–65.

8. Mark A. Noll, *The Old Religion in the New World: The History of North American Christianity* (Grand Rapids, MI: William B. Eerdmans, 2002), 153.

9. Ibid.

10. Marty E. Marty, *Righteous Empire: The Protestant Experience in America* (New York: Dial Press, 1970), 249.

11. Sweeney, *American Evangelical Story*, 172–75; more broadly, see George M. Marsden, *Reforming Fundamentalism: Fuller Seminary and the New Evangelicalism* (Grand Rapids, MI: Eerdmans, 1987).

12. Hart, *That Old-Time Religion in Modern America*, 78–79.

13. Marty, *Protestantism in the United States*, 248–49; Witham, *City Upon a Hill*, 241; Hart, *That Old-Time Religion in Modern America*, 79–81; Mark Noll, *A History of Christianity in the United States and Canada* (Grand Rapids, MI: William B. Eerdman, 1992), 509–11. On the broad emergence of Neo-Evangelicalism, see also: Joel Carpenter, *Revive Us Again: The Reawakening of American Fundamentalism* (New York: Oxford University Press, 1997).

14. William G. McLoughlin, Jr., *Billy Graham: Revivalist in a Secular Age* (New York: The Ronald Press Company, 1960), 94–105, 108–21; Witham, *City Upon a Hill*, 242–44.

15. Hart, *That Old-Time Religion in Modern America*, 130, 150–51.

16. Sweeney, *American Evangelical Story*, 175–76; Martin E. Marty, *Pilgrims in Their Own Land: 500 Years of Religion in America* (Boston, MA: Little, Brown, 1984), 411–13; Hart, *That Old-Time Religion in Modern America*, 129–30.

17. Marty, *Protestantism in the United States*, 249.

18. Marsden, "From Fundamentalism to Evangelicalism," 136.

19. James Reed, *From Private Vice to Public Virtue: The Birth Control Movement and American Society since 1830* (New York: Basic Books, 1978), 264–65; David M. Kennedy, *Birth Control in America: The Career of Margaret Sanger* (New Haven, CT: Yale University Press, 1970), 256–57.

20. [No Author], *A Tradition of Choice: Planned Parenthood at 75* (New York: Planned Parenthood Federation of America, 1991), 34, 44, 47.

21. Reed, *From Private Vice to Public Virtue*, 281–88; *Tradition of Choice*, 44.

22. President's Committee to Study the United States Military Assistance Program, *Composite Report of the President's Committee to Study the United States Military Assistance Program. August 17, 1959* (Washington, DC: U.S. Government Printing Office, 1959), 94–98. Also: Donald T. Critchlow, *Intended Consequences: Birth Control, Abortion, and the Federal Government in Modern America* (New York and Oxford: Oxford University Press, 1999), 41–45.

23. Reed, *From Private Vice to Public Virtue*, 304.

24. From a summary in: Richard M. Fagley, *The Population Explosion and Christian Responsibility* (New York: Oxford University Press, 1960), 198–200.

25. Fagley, *Population Explosion and Christian Responsibility*, 203–4.

26. Ibid., 233.

27. Alfred Martin Rehwinkel, *Planned Parenthood and Birth Control in the Light of Christian Ethics* (St. Louis, MO: Concordia Publishing House, 1959), 3–5.

28. Ibid., 88–93, 103.

29. Marty, *Protestantism in the United States*, 251.

30. "Responsible Parenthood and the Population Problem," appendix to Fagley, *Population Explosion and Christian Responsibility*, 226–29.

31. "Responsible Parenthood and the Population Problem," 229–33.

32. The Eastern Orthodox participant at the Mansfield conference, for example, argued that his Church "holds that parents have not the right to prevent the creative process of matrimonial intercourse; also, that God entrusted to them this responsibility for childbearing, with full confidence that His Providence would take care of material and other needs.

33. "Evangelicals Face up to Birth Control Issue," *Christianity Today* 4 (December 21, 1959): 31–32. (Emphasis added.)

34. George Dugan, "Graham Sees Hope in Birth Control," *New York Times* (December 13, 1959).

35. "Exploding Populations and Birth Control," *Christianity Today* 4 (February 1, 1960): 22–23.

36. E. P. Schulze, "Limitation of Offspring," *Christianity Today* 4 (February 1, 1960): 40–41.

37. Sherwood T. Wirt, "Birth Control," *Christianity Today* 4 (March 28, 1960): 32.

38. The sole exception was a brief news article on a U.S. Supreme Court decision striking down a challenge to Connecticut's "Comstock Law," using technical arguments. See: "Supreme Court Sidesteps Birth Control Issue," *Christianity Today* 5 (July 3, 1961): 25.

39. Collection 8: Christianity Today International, Archives of the Billy Graham Center [hereafter CTI-BGC], Box 24, File 32 ("Correspondence: Editor. Population Information. General, 1923-1964").

40. Letter, John Gunther to "Friend," November 18, 1965, with attachment, Darius S. Jhabvala, "FAO: Births Cancel Food Output Gains," *New York Herald Tribune* (October 8, 1965); Note, [Carl Henry] to Harold [Lindsell], n.d., and attached article, Roger Revelle, "The Problem of People," *Harvard Today* (Autumn 1965): 2–9; "Poverty and High Fertility: the Crucial Link," News Release from The Population Reference Bureau, Inc., January 25, 1965; all in CTI-BGC, Box 24, File 31 ("Correspondence. Editor. Population Information-General, 1965-67").

41. Memo, Carl F. H. Henry to Harold [Lindsell], n.d., with attached article, "East Bloc Frets Over Birth Rate," *The New York Times* (October 23, 1965); Typescript Commentary, [1965-?] page one missing, 2–3; both in CTI-BGC, Box 24, File 31.

42. "New Trends in Roman Catholic Opinion," *Population Bulletin* 17 (November 1961): 129–30, 133, 138, 148; in CTI-BGC, Box 24, File 32.

43. "The Vatican and the Population Crisis," *Population Bulletin* 21 (February 1965): 1, 9, 13; in CTI-BGC, Box 24, File 32.

44. "Moratorium on Debate," *Christianity Today* 9 (January 29, 1965): 49.

45. "The Papal Word and the Disputed Pill," *Christianity Today* 9 (April 23, 1963): 45.

46. "Birth Control and Public Policy," *Christianity Today* 10 (October 8, 1965): 55.

47. "Birth Control Bombshell," *Christianity Today* 10 (October 22, 1965): 39–40.

48. John Warwick Montgomery, "How to Decide the Birth-Control Question," *Christianity Today* 10 (March 10, 1966): 8–9. (Emphasis added.)

49. Ibid., 9.

50. Ibid., 10.

51. Ibid.

52. See: Bruce K. Waltke, "The Old Testament and Birth Control," *Christianity Today* 13, November 8, 1968, 6; Walter O. Spitzer and Carlyle L. Saylor, eds., *Birth Control and the Christian* (Wheaton, IL: Tyndale House, 1969), Appendix 5, 575–84.

53. "Pope Faces Birth Control Crisis," *Christianity Today* 12 (August 16, 1968): 41.

54. "Thirteenth Century Thinking in Boston," *Christianity Today* 10 (May 27, 1966): 31–32.

55. "Rome and the Pill," *Christianity Today* 10 (June 24, 1966): 30–31.

56. "Birth Control Pangs," *Christianity Today* 12 (January 5, 1968): 16; "Miscellany," *Christianity Today* 12 (October 13, 1967); Fred Pearson, "Pox on the Pill," *Christianity Today* 12 (March 29, 1968): 6.

57. "The Vatican on Birth Control," *Christianity Today* 12 (August 16, 1968): 28–29.
58. "Pope Faces Birth Control Crisis," *Christianity Today* 12 (August 16, 1968): 41–42.
59. "Widening Crack in the Wall of Catholicism," *Christianity Today* 12 (September 27, 1968): 38. Other *Christianity Today* articles in the late summer/mid fall on these questions included: "Birth Control Fallout," *Christianity Today* 12 (August 30, 1968): 43–44; "Contraception and Damnation," *Christianity Today* 13 (October 11, 1968): 34–36.
60. "The Real Issue," *Christianity Today* 13 (October 25, 1968): 28–29.
61. Spitzer and Saylor, *Birth Control and the Christian*, v.
62. Letter, Walter O. Spitzer to Harold Lindsell, October 21, 1968, 1; in CTI-BGC, Box 17, File 93: "Correspondence, Author's File."
63. Letter, Walter O. Spitzer to Harold Lindsell, October 15, 1968, 1; Letter, Harold Lindsell to Walter O. Spitzer, October 17, 1968, 1; in CTI-BGC, Box 17, File 93.
64. Spitzer and Saylor, *Birth Control and the Christian*, xi–xx.
65. Bruce K. Waltke, "The Old Testament and Birth Control," *Christianity Today* 13 (November 8, 1968): 3–6.
66. Paul K. Jewett, "The Relation of the Soul to the Fetus," *Christianity Today* 13 (November 8, 1968): 6–9.
67. Robert P. Meye, "The New Testament and Birth Control," *Christianity Today* 13 (November 8, 1968): 10–13.
68. M. O. Vincent, "A Christian View of Contraception," *Christianity Today* 13 (November 8, 1968): 14–15.
69. John Scanzoni, "A Sociological Perspective on Abortion and Sterilization," in *Birth Control and the Christian*, ed. Spitzer and Saylor (Wheaton, IL: Tyndale House, 1969), 316–25.
70. V. Elving Anderson, "Genetics, Society and the Family," in *Birth Control and the Christian*, ed. Spitzer and Saylor (Wheaton, IL: Tyndale House, 1969), 345–52.
71. References included Luke 18:15, Luke 1:41 and 44, I Peter 2:2, II Timothy 3:15, and Psalm 51:5.
72. John Warwick Montgomery, "The Christian View of the Fetus," in *Birth Control and the Christian*, ed. Spitzer and Saylor (Wheaton, IL: Tyndale House, 1969), 76–87.
73. Fagley, *Population Explosion and Christian Responsibility*, 190.
74. Lloyd A. Kalland, "Views and Positions of the Christian Church – An Historical Review," in *Birth Control and the Christian*, ed. Spitzer and Saylor (Wheaton, IL: Tyndale House, 1969), 441–43.
75. Carl F. H. Henry, "Foreword," in *Birth Control and the Christian*, ed. Spitzer and Saylor (Wheaton, IL: Tyndale House, 1969), vii–viii.
76. "A Protestant Affirmation on the Control of Human Reproduction," *Christianity Today* 13 (November 8, 1968): 18–19. An earlier news report on the Symposium is found in "Evangelical Scholars Endorse Birth Control," *Christianity Today* 12 (September 27, 1968): 33–34. The Affirmation also appears in Spitzer and Saylor, *Birth Control and the Christian*, xiii–xxxi.
77. Letter, Harold Lindsell to Walter O. Spitzer, September 19, 1968, 1; in CTI-BGC, Box 17, File 93.

78. Harold Lindsell to Carl F. H. Henry, November 27, 1968, 1; in CTI-BGC, Box 19, File 20 ("Correspondence: Editor – Henry, Carl F., May 1967–Nov. 1975").

79. "Controlling Birth," *Christianity Today* 13 (December 20, 1968): 18–19. (Emphasis added.)

80. "On Human Reproduction," *Christianity Today* 13 (August 22, 1969): 27–28.

81. "Contraception Again," *Christianity Today* 13 (January 17, 1969): 43.

82. Richard Ostling, "U.S. Bishops Speak, Ambiguity Lingers," *Christianity Today* 13 (December 6, 1968): 39–40.

83. Tom C. Clark, "The Law as it Governs Decisions Today," in *Birth Control and the Christian*, ed. Spitzer and Saylor (Wheaton, IL: Tyndale House, 1969), 361–63.

84. John Warwick Montgomery, *How Do We Know There Is a God? And Other Questions Inappropriate to Polite Society* (Minneapolis, MN: Dimension Books, 1973), 70–72.

85. The exchange is found in two letters to the editor: "Reproduction Restudied," *Christianity Today* 13 (December 6, 1968): 13; "Transmitting Life," *Christianity Today* 13 (January 3, 1969): 14.

86. Amy Laura Hall, *Conceiving Parenthood: American Protestantism and the Spirit of Reproduction* (Grand Rapids, MI: William B. Eerdmans, 2008), 9–10.

5

Return of the Gnostics

The United States Supreme Court's 1965 ruling in *Griswold* v. *Connecticut* stands in ever bolder relief as a profound break in American and Western history. True, a quiet revolution in American behavior had begun during the war years, 1917–1918, as the old moral order was deeply shaken and contraceptive use spread widely, partly through government distribution to sailors and soldiers. Over the next several decades, Margaret Sanger and the Birth Control League of America also won reform of many of the state "mini-Comstock" laws, usually allowing doctors to give birth control advice and to provide the necessary devices to patients. Relative to contraceptives, the Federal Comstock law fell through a Federal Appeals Court decision in 1936.

However, the strict Connecticut law—criminalizing even the use of contraceptives—still stood into the 1960s. And while not rigorously enforced, it continued to have some effect. A recent investigation found that use of the birth control pill in 1965 was significantly (about 25 percent) lower in those states banning the sale of contraceptives, when compared to the nation as a whole.[1]

Importantly, when overturning the Connecticut measure, the U.S. Supreme Court moved far beyond normal legal reasoning. Instead, it claimed to discover for the first time "penumbras" around and "emanations" emerging from the Bill of Rights, *legal spirits* which created "zones of privacy" hitherto undetected by Federal judges. [Tellingly, such strange logic and language would have been quite familiar to a First or Second Century Gnostic.] Cynically, given what would soon follow, the Court appealed to "the sacred precincts of marital bedrooms," to "the notions of privacy surrounding the marriage relationship," and to this bond's "sacred" nature to justify its decision.[2]

In truth, *Griswold* can be read in retrospect as a fundamental challenge to Western Civilization's unwritten Sexual Constitution. As same-sex marriage advocate Evan Wolfson has correctly stated, "The Court recognized [in *Griswold*] the right *not* to procreate in marriage."[3]

Only six years later, in the case *Eisenstadt* v. *Baird*, the Supreme Court appealed to the very same "penumbras" and "emanations" from the Bill of Rights, to the same "right of privacy," in order to declare marriage largely empty of meaning:

> It is true that in *Griswold* the right of privacy in question inhered in the marital relationship. Yet the marital couple is *not* an independent entity with a mind and heart of its own, but an association of *two individuals* each with a separate intellectual and emotional makeup. If the right of privacy means anything, it is the right of the individual, married or single, to be free from unwarranted governmental intrusion into matters so fundamentally affecting a person as the decision whether to bear or beget a child.[4]

With this decision, the Constitution's spirits now denied both the substance of publicly sanctioned marriage and its grounding in the natural law. A year later, 1973, the same curious logic led the Supreme Court to sweep away the abortion laws of all fifty states, creating in their place a new "right to abortion."[5] [Again, the Court's action in *Roe* v. *Wade* would surely have pleased the baby-loathing Gnostics.] In 1992, the Court appealed to "the right to define one's own concept of existence, of meaning, of the universe, and of the mystery of human life" in its reaffirmation of abortion rights.[6] [Actually, such language is very close to the definition of the gauzy Gnostic ideal.] And in 2003, the Supreme Court in *Lawrence* v. *Texas* summoned the same "penumbras" and "emanations" of the Bill of Rights to find a right to uninhibited sexual expression, in this case a right to sodomy.[7] [Yet again, at least one branch of the Gnostics would have been delighted.] These legal changes were nothing less than a codification of sexual revolution, meaning destruction of the informal Sexual Constitution that had framed American life for over 450 years, and Western Civilization for an additional 1,500 years. The sexual anarchy—just as the language—of the Gnostics had decisively returned.

An Awakening

As described in Chapter 4, Evangelicals at first joined the "value revolution" that swept through America, starting precisely in the year 1965.[8] The *Griswold* decision, which finished off the last remnant of the Comstock regime, attracted at most a friendly yawn,[9] for it was fully in line with developing elite Evangelical opinion. When the Supreme Court issued its opinion in *Roe* v. *Wade* eight years later, many leading Evangelicals actually welcomed its appearance. Indeed, while the logic of its argument was different, the legal consequences of *Roe* were entirely in line with the "Affirmation on the Control of Human Reproduction" published in *Christianity Today* in 1968. Most notably, *Roe* freed the individual conscience regarding sexuality from the "prescriptions of the legal code" so frowned upon in the "Affirmation." W. A. Criswell, former President of the Southern Baptist Convention and Pastor of Dallas' mammoth First Baptist Church, was clearly delighted by the decision:

> I have always felt that it was only after a child was born and had life separate from its mother that it became an individual person, and it has always, therefore, seemed to me that what is best for the mother and the future should be allowed.

W. Barry Garrett, chief of the Washington Bureau of The Baptist Press, was still more effusive: "Religious liberty, human equality, and justice are advanced by the Supreme Court abortion decision." And Howard Moody, pastor of New York's Judson Memorial Church, praised the decision for its religious effect: "The Supreme Court may have saved the ecumenical movement, avoiding an all-out conflict between Catholics and Protestants on abortion."[10]

Unexpectedly, forceful Evangelical dissent came only from one source: *Christianity Today*. This remarkable turn by the magazine built, in part, on the legacy of John Warwick Montgomery's original 1966 "compromise" on sexuality: contraception acceptable; abortion to be opposed. More important, though, was the influence of another man, Assistant Editor Harold O. J. Brown. Who was he?

Born in 1933, Brown was raised as a Roman Catholic, including attendance at a Jesuit high school. He won a scholarship to Harvard University. While an undergraduate, as he later reported to Carl Henry: "I was converted to evangelical Christianity from Romanism ... through reading Luther's works, and to a certain extent making his spiritual pilgrimage after him." Brown called himself "a firm Nicene and Chalcedonian Christian .... far more interested in finding and promoting witness to the Gospel in all Protestant denominations, rather than in advancing the cause of a single one."[11]

Brown also reported "that I am rather heavily indebted to Francis Schaeffer for some of my own development."[12] An American-born Presbyterian minister, Schaeffer and his family had moved to

Switzerland in 1948, where he attempted to evangelize the young and to combat theological liberalism on the continent. He and his wife Edith established a Community, *L'Abri* ("the shelter" in French), in the Swiss Alps near Lausaunne, which attracted youthful Evangelical pilgrims from North America and Europe. Among them was Harold Brown. In his writing and teaching, Schaeffer emphasized the distinctive nature of the Christian worldview, and how the Bible provided truths regarding philosophy, the culture, the arts, and the sciences. He also drew a vivid contrast between Christian humanism rooted in Scriptural truth and the distorted, even "evil" humanism of secular culture.[13] Referring to Schaeffer, Brown wrote: "... I have been rather impressed by his emphasis on the need to stress over and over again that what we are speaking is not merely 'religious' truth, but actually 'true' truth."[14]

Brown had gone on to earn BD, Th.M., and Th.D. degrees at Harvard Divinity School, and to hold assistant minister positions at Boston's Park Street Church (home to Harold J. Ockenga) and Second Congregational Church in North Beverly, Massachusetts. During the early 1960s, he several times submitted articles for publication to *Christianity Today*. Most were turned down, with internal editorial evaluations ranging from the dismissive ("He has a point but it is a small one") to the nasty ("this man does not even glimpse from afar the meaning of baptism in what he calls the historic Reformed faith"; "not to publish" the essay would be "a kindness to the author.").[15] Nonetheless, he remained—in one editor's words—a "persistent beggar" and in late 1965, Carl Henry tried to recruit Brown as an Assistant Editor of the magazine. However, the young scholar had already been offered the post of Theological Secretary of The International Fellowship of Evangelical Students, based in Switzerland, and he turned down Henry's invitation.[16] Four years later, however, Harold Lindsell renewed the offer to Brown, and he joined the editorial team in 1970.

Notably, Harold O. J. Brown drafted the key *Christianity Today* editorial responding to the *Roe* v. *Wade* decision. Not only did it repudiate the Court's action and logic, it also implicitly rejected the abortion-related provisions of the magazine's 1968 "Affirmation." Brown's early exposure to Catholic natural law theology and his vivid sense of the deep divide between the Christian and the Modernist worldviews—derived from Schaeffer—both shine through. So does a keen awareness of who—or what—was the real enemy here.

Underscoring the revolutionary aspect of *Roe*, the Editorial argued that the Court "has clearly decided for paganism, and against Christianity." In explaining this point, Brown indirectly jettisoned still another portion of the "Affirmation," this time regarding the position of the early church:

> The Court notes that 'ancient religion' did not ban abortion ...; by 'ancient religion,' it clearly means paganism, since Judaism and Christianity did ban abortion .... [T]he High Court unambiguously prefers ... the common paganism of the pre-Christian Roman Empire.

The Editorial asserted that the *Roe* decision "runs counter not merely to the moral teachings of Christianity through the ages but also to the moral sense of the American people." The Court had "rejected the almost universal consensus of Christian moral teachers through the centuries on abortion." In addition, its appeal to "the right to privacy" was "without empirical or logical justification." Underscoring its antihuman implications, the argument in *Roe* could actually "be used with like — in some cases with greater — force to justify infanticide for unwanted or undesirable infants." In sum, the Editorial warned that antilife paganism had awakened and that "Christians should accommodate themselves to the thought that the American state no longer supports, in any meaningful sense, the laws of God"[17]

In related editorial comments, also probably crafted by Brown, *Christianity Today* rejected the argument of some Evangelicals that the *Roe* decision advanced religious liberty: "The fact that minority religious groups (e.g., Roman Catholics, Mormons) oppose abortion does not make easy abortion a triumph for 'religious liberty.' To say so is not analysis but sophistry."[18] Regarding the claim by Howard Moody and others that the Court's action had restored ecumenical prospects by "avoiding an all-out conflict between Catholics and Protestants," the magazine turned the argument around, in prescient fashion: "Moody may be right in a sense: the ruling may promote cooperation to fight abortion."[19]

In all this, though, there was no mention of birth control. Over the balance of the decade, Brown and other Evangelicals more fully developed the position articulated by John Warwick Montgomery in the 1960s: birth control acceptable (although not often discussed); abortion, a sinful crime. Regarding the latter, for example, Brown emphasized in a 1976 article for *The Moody Monthly* how legalized abortion was contributing to a demographic disaster for America, not the "population explosion" of recent emphasis, but depopulation: "Births in America have already dropped below the replacement rate .... We are headed toward a society of middle-aged and elderly people, with a dwindling supply of children and young adults." (The same point could have been made regarding birth control, but was not.) Brown labored as well to restore a correct reading of Christian history regarding abortion, stating that "Biblical Christians from the earliest days have considered abortion — widely tolerated in the pagan Roman Empire — to be a grievous crime." (Left un-noted was the similar treatment shown by early Christians toward contraception.) This was also the view of the early Reformers "such as John Calvin," the article continued, and of contemporary Protestant theologians, both "neo-orthodox" figures such as Karl Barth, Emil Brunner, and Helmut Thielicke and "American evangelicals such as Billy Graham, Harold Lindsell, and Francis Schaeffer." Brown offered special praise for the film-strip, *Abortion is Killing*, prepared by the Reformed Presbyterian Church—Evangelical Synod, and physician C. Everett Koop's book, *The Right to Live/The Right to Die*.[20]

Koop, in fact, was emerging as another prominent anti-abortion Evangelical, who also said little about birth control. In 1977, he joined with Francis Schaeffer to author a book and produce a film series, *Whatever Happened to the Human Race?* It sought "to rouse evangelicals to the abortion issue." In addition, Koop collaborated with Brown to create the Christian Action Council, an Evangelical parachurch that focused on founding local crisis pregnancy centers. Part of the project was to rescue Biblical interpretation from the "cutting edge" exegetes of the late 1960s. For example, Koop rejected the argument that Exodus 21 did not regard the fetus as fully human: "Francis Schaeffer checked the exegesis of these verses with five Hebrew scholars and was convinced that ... in no way does [God] mean to downgrade the worth of the unborn child." Moreover, the "story of the incarnation leaves no room for doubt.... He — the Lord — was a very tiny Baby.... He certainly was a Person." Koop concluded: "We evangelicals have already lost too much by being indecisive on these issues."[21]

Harold O. J. Brown, Francis Schaeffer, and C. Everett Koop successfully called Evangelical leaders back from their flirtation with abortion. These three men made opposition to abortion a defining characteristic of late twentieth-century Evangelicalism. As Christian Smith would note in his 1998 book, *American Evangelicalism: Embattled and Thriving*, "the vast majority of evangelicals oppose both abortion and gay rights."[22] At the same time, though, contraception or birth control was rarely—if ever—discussed. The implication was quiet approval. In short, following a delay of several decades, Evangelicals had followed the Protestant mainline in this accommodation to the new sexual order.

Demographic Consequences?

All the same, were there any measurable consequences to this delay in the acceptance of birth control? Did the fact that most Evangelicals continued to oppose birth control until the late 1960s, while the mainline Protestants had begun to accept the practice four decades earlier, have any effects? The answer appears to be "yes."

The analyst must first disentangle the general relationship between religion and fertility. Dean Hoge and David Roozen, in their *Understanding Church Growth and Decline: 1950–1978*, broadly concluded that "persons with stronger church commitment tended to desire larger families" and that "the birthrate in the United States has matched trends in traditional religious commitment for at least a half century." Put another way, "[w]hatever causes births to rise or fall somehow causes church participation to rise or fall." Yet, they were unsure of the causation.[23] Dennison Nash—examining the "Religious Revival" associated with the 1950s—also traced the growth in church membership to the presence of children: he calculated a correlation coefficient of .74 between church membership and the number of families with children under eighteen: "an extremely high value."[24] Working with Peter Berger and examining in depth three Congregational churches near Hartford, Connecticut, Nash sought to explain how their membership rolls had doubled between 1940 and 1960. He concluded: "… it was the prospect or presence of children which wholly or partly occasioned the act of joining by their parents." This commitment to the perceived needs of children demonstrated "the strength of the ethic of child-centered familism" found in the suburbs of that era. In short, "the direction in which 'the little child shall lead them' may be into further commitment to the 'O.K. World' which is the psychological environment which suburbanites have created."[25]

From a still broader perspective, Kevin McQuillan has noted that the only world religions where rules seem to have a measurable effect on fertility are those "of the book": Judaism, Christianity, and Islam. Even in these cases, though, religious beliefs have demographic consequences only when three criteria are met: (1) "the religion in question must articulate behavioral norms that have linkages to fertility outcomes," such as rules regarding contraception and gender roles; (2) the group "must possess the means to communicate its teachings to its members and enforce compliance"; and (3) members need to "feel a strong sense of attachment to the religious community." Examples that he provides include pre-1950 Quebec, where Roman Catholic strictures on contraception were widely followed. A 1971 survey, for instance, found that only 19 percent of Quebecois women born between 1906 and 1910 had ever practiced contraception. The subsequent "Quiet Revolution" in Quebec, involving among other developments a sharp fall in average family size, also showed that a religion's influence on fertility could "crumble quickly."[26]

One of the most striking developments on the American religious landscape during the twentieth century was the "decline of the mainline" denominations (the Methodists, Presbyterians, Episcopalians, Congregationalists, and liberal Lutherans). Between 1900 and 1975, the mainline's share of the Protestant population fell from 60 percent to 40 percent, while the market share claimed by "conservative" denominations (Southern Baptist, Assemblies of God, Pentecostal and holiness churches) rose conversely from 40 to 60 percent.[27] Controversy ensued over how to explain this shift. Some sociologists of religion, such as Roger Finke and Rodney Stark, simply concluded that nothing was new: "Since at least 1776 the upstart sects have grown as the mainline American denominations have declined." This "sect-church" process was basically a constant in American history: "the decline of the Protestant mainline is a long, steady trend," making it "pointless to search the 1960s for the causes of a phenomenon that was far along by the War of 1812."[28] Attracting greater attention, though, were the arguments of National Council of Churches official Dean Kelley. In his book *Why the Conservative Churches Are Growing*, Kelley asserted that the dynamic behind mainline decline was adult conversion. People were leaving the mainline and joining the conservative churches because the latter offered *strict* expectations that the former had abandoned. Growing conservative churches "... are not 'reasonable,' they are not 'tolerant,' they are not ecumenical, they are not 'relevant.' Quite the contrary!" He added: "Strong [religious] organizations are strict ... the stricter the stronger."[29]

However, both explanations seemed to have missed the real dynamic: namely, differential fertility. In 1966, a team of researchers reported that, when Protestant women were divided into "liberal," "intermediate," and "fundamentalistic" groups, the latter proved to be the most fertile, after controlling for education, income, occupation, and community size.[30] More recently, using data from the General Social Survey of 1974–1998, sociologists Michael Hout, Andrew Greeley, and Melissa Wilde have shown that "a combination of higher birth rates and earlier childbearing among conservative women" accounts for "over three-quarters of the observed change in Protestant denominational affiliations for cohorts born between 1900 and 1970." Specifically, among Protestant women born between 1900 and 1915, those religiously "conservative" bore an average of 3.1 children; women affiliated with "mainline" churches bore an average of 2.1: the former figure was 47 percent higher. For women born between 1915 and 1935—the mothers of the mid-century "Baby Boom"—the gap narrowed. "Mainline" women saw their average family size climb sharply from 2.1 to 3.1; for conservative women, the increase was less, from 3.1 to 3.3: the "conservative" advantage—while still present—had fallen to only 7 percent. For "mainline" women born between 1935 and 1951, fertility fell sharply, reaching 1.85 for those born in 1951. *However, among "conservative" women born those same years, fertility remained high for another five to six years*, but then fell as well, reaching 1.95 for those born in 1951. If the year of a mother's birth is translated into "Total Fertility Rate," the sharp fall in "mainline" fertility began in 1958/59; among "conservative" Protestants, in 1965/66.[31]

Explaining these results, the researchers noted that "[w]omen and clergy from mainline Protestant denominations were prominent in the movements to promote family planning and repeal bans on birth control devices in the United States; conservative Protestants and Catholics opposed these actions." This implied that "mainline Protestant women adopted birth control ... sooner than other Protestant women did." Accordingly, "[t]here are more conservatives today because their parents had larger families than did Episcopalian, Presbyterian, Methodist, Lutheran, and Congregationalist parents."[32] Put another way, "the so-called decline of the mainline may ultimately be attributable to its earlier approval of contraception."[33]

Hout and colleagues have also argued that measures of belief regarding abortion and sexual liberalism strongly converged among Protestants born after 1960: "the gap between the people who are still in conservative denominations and those who have switched to the mainline is shrinking, not growing." This suggested, in turn, "that the trends underlying mainline decline may be nearing their end." With the acceptance of birth control by "mainline" and "conservative" Protestants alike, "the demographic momentum is spent."[34] This conclusion has dovetailed with arguments by Christian Smith, among others, that American Evangelicals are more egalitarian on gender issues and more liberal on social issues other than abortion and gay rights—such as pre-marital cohabitation and divorce—than generally recognized.[35]

Evangelical Exceptionalism?

Other research, however, has suggested that an Evangelical fertility advantage remains. Writing in *Population and Development Review*, for example, demographers Ron Lesthaeghe and Lisa Neidert use data from 2000 to 2004 to test whether the United States fits into the model of the Second Demographic Transition. The latter term involves the new moral order found most notably in post-1965 Europe, characterized by "secular and anti-authoritarian sentiments," gender egalitarianism, "self-actualization," and individualism. Relative to fertility, it is "a matter of postponing or eschewing parenthood altogether because of more pressing competing goals such as prolonging education, achieving more stable income positions, increased consumerism associated with self-expression orientations, ... realizing a more fulfilled partnership, [and] keeping an open future."

Compared then to Europe and Canada, did the USA stand outside the Second Demographic Transition? Was there an American exceptionalism? Lesthaeghe and Neidert answered, in part, "No." When they examined data for the northern Atlantic Coast, the Pacific Coast, the Great Lakes states, and parts of the West (Arizona, New Mexico, and Colorado), the "post-family" values of the Second Transition dominated and fertility was "lower and later." On the other hand, part of the answer was:

> Yes, there is an 'American exceptionalism' among a non-negligible section of the population. That sector is mainly located in the Midwest, the Plains, and the South. It is on average much more rural than metropolitan, less well-educated, [and] adheres more to Evangelical Christianity or Mormonism...."[36]

Mobilizing fertility data from 1998 to 2002 compiled by the Reproductive Health Information Source of The U.S. Center for Disease Control, geographer Lisa Jordan of The University of Colorado has reported even more striking results. Using the religious categories of Protestant-Mainline, Protestant-Evangelical, Catholic, Jewish, Muslim, Eastern Orthodox, Mormon, and Utopian, she found that "Mainline" Protestant, Jewish, and "Non-Hispanic Catholic" adherence had no positive effect on fertility. However:

> Everywhere in the U.S., there appears to be significant and positive relationship between Evangelicalism and fertility. In some areas, such as West Virginia, Virginia, Nevada, and Oregon, the coefficient is twice as high as other parts of the country. A ten percent increase in Protestant Evangelical adherence [within a given county] is associated with a 0.6 to 1.4 percent increase in the general fertility rate.

Mormon and Utopian [e.g., the Hutterites] affiliations also showed positive effects, while the presence of family planning clinics in any county proved "insignificant."[37]

These results are illuminating. The failure of Non-Hispanic Catholicism to have a positive effect on fertility (indeed, in a majority of states, the correlation was negative) underscores McQuillan's point that pro-natalist doctrine is not sufficient; it must be reinforced by some method of forceful compliance. The finding that the presence—or absence—of birth control clinics in a given county has no effect on fertility suggests as well that "worldview," or ideology, on the question of birth control continues to trump material factors. And the consistent, nationwide positive correlation between "Protestant-Evangelical" and fertility implies that Evangelicalism still holds to a distinctive pro-natalism, despite the tacit acceptance of birth control since the early 1970s.

And yet, something more may be stirring. One of the most striking developments in the American Evangelical subculture over the last twenty years has been the "Quiverfull" movement. Solid numbers are sparse, since this phenomenon is even more anarchic than the standard Evangelical ministry. Still, it is safe to conclude that thousands of Evangelical young adults have renounced the use of birth control—even the rhythm or natural family planning method—and have placed decisions regarding family size back "in the hands of God." For them, children remain as "an heritage from the Lord" and "happy is the man who has a full quiver of them."[38]

If Anthony Comstock and his Evangelical supporters might somehow be brought forward in time to 2011 America, their reaction could be easily predicted. They would, no doubt, be appalled by the dominant sexual ethics of this, the Age of Hustler, Norplant, and Viagra. Legal-ized abortion, ever more refined methods of contraception, ubiquitous pornography, the broad commercialization of sex, the celebration of nonprocreative sexuality, fourteen-year-olds on birth control, same-sex marriage: all would confirm their worst fears. In his own mind, Comstock would find fully justified his linkage of obscene pictures and objects to abortion and birth control. He would find equally justified his equation of birth control with abortion. All these things were of one package. When one had come, so had the others.

As noted before, Comstock and company were not complicated men. Yet they did understand the core legacy of Christian sexual ethics, to the defense of which they dedicated their lives. And they also understood the enemy: sexual anarchy, once found among the Roman pagans and the Gnostics, taking on new forms and clever arguments in the Modern era. In the Quiverfull movement, however, they might find some solace ... and hope that the Evangelical witness to the unity of Christian faith and family might continue—at least in minority fashion—onto the uncertain terrain of the twenty-first Christian century.

Notes

1. Martha J. Bailey, "Momma's Got the Pill: How Anthony Comstock and *Griswold* v. *Connecticut* Shaped U.S. Childbearing," *Economic Review* 100 (March 2010): 98–129.
2. *Griswold* v. *Connecticut*, 381 U.S. 479 (1965).
3. Evan Wolfson, *Why Marriage Matters: America, Equality, and Gay People's Right to Marry* (New York: Simon and Schuster, 2004), 79.
4. *Eisenstadt* v. *Baird*, 405 U.S. 438 (1972). (Emphasis added.)
5. *Roe* v. *Wade*, 410 U.S. 113 (1973).
6. *Planned Parenthood of Southeastern Pa.* v. *Casey*, 505 U.S. 833 (1992).
7. *Lawrence* v. *Texas*, 539 U.S. 558 (2003).
8. Religious sociologists Dean Hoge and David Roozen, examining this rapid change in Christian values toward marriage and sexuality, conclude that "virtually all the attitude change came after 1965." See: "National Contextual Factors Influencing Church Trends," in Dean R. Hoge and David A. Roozen, eds., *Understanding Church Growth and Decline: 1950–1978* (New York: The Pilgrim Press, 1979), 107.
9. The decision is not noted during 1965 in either *Christianity Today* or *Moody Monthly*.
10. Comments from "Abortion Decision: A Death Blow?" *Christianity Today* 17 (February 16, 1973); "What Price Abortion?" *Christianity Today* 17 (March 2, 1973): 39.
11. Letter, Harold O. J. Brown to Carl F. H. Henry, November 14, 1960, 1; in CTI-BGC, Box 17, Folder 23 ("Correspondence: Author's File – Brown, Harold O., Nov. 1960–May 1968.").

12. Letter, Harold O. J. Brown to Carl F. H. Henry, January 10, 1967, 1; in CTI-BGC, Box 17, Folder 23.
13. On Schaeffer's place in American Evangelical history, see: D. G. Hart, *That Old-Time Religion in Modern America: Evangelical Protestantism in the Twentieth Century* (Chicago, IL: Ivan R. Dee, 2002), 134–40.
14. Letter, Harold O. J. Brown to Carl F. H. Henry, January 10, 1967, 1; CTI-BGC, Box 17, File 23.
15. "Evaluation[s] of Manuscripts," received October 29, 1964 and November 24, 1964; Letter, James Daane to Harold O. J. Brown, November 3, 1964, 1-2; in CTI-BGC, Box 17, File 23.
16. Letters, Carl F. H. Henry to Harold O. J. Brown, October 25, 1965, 1; and November 17, 1965, 1; in CTI-BGC, Box 17, File 23.
17. "Abortion and the Court," *Christianity Today* 17 (February 16 1973): 32–33.
18. "What Price Abortion?" 39.
19. "Abortion Decision: A Death Blow?"
20. Harold O. J. Brown, "The American Way of Death," *Moody Monthly* 77 (December 1976): 32–35.
21. C. Everett Koop as told to Dick Bohrer, "Deception on Demand," *Moody Monthly* 80 (May 1980): 24–29; Dick Bohrer, "Abortion's Incredible History (and Where the Evangelical Fits)," *Moody Monthly* 80 (May 1980): 30–32.
22. Christian Smith, *American Evangelicalism: Embattled and Thriving* (Chicago, IL and London: University of Chicago Press, 1998), 199–201.
23. Hoge and Roozen, *Understanding Church Growth and Decline*, 117, 322.
24. Dennison Nash, "A Little Child Shall Lead Them: A Statistical Test of an Hypothesis That Children Were the Source of the American 'Religious Revival,'" *Journal for the Scientific Study of Religion* 7 (Fall 1968): 238–39.
25. Dennison Nash and Peter Berger, "The Child, the Family and the 'Religious Revival' in Suburbia," *Journal for the Scientific Study of Religion* 2 (Fall 1962): 85–93.
26. Kevin McQuillan, "When Does Religion Influence Fertility?" *Population and Development Review* 30 (March 2004): 25–56.
27. The definition of "conservative" churches usually involves measuring attachment to criteria such as "Biblical literalism" and the necessity of a "born again" conversion experience. See: Tom W. Smith, "Classifying Protestant Denominations," *Review of Religious Research* 31 (March 1990): 1–5.
28. Roger Finke and Rodney Stark, *The Churching of America, 1776–1990: Winners and Losers in Our Religious Economy* (New Brunswick, NJ: Rutgers University Press, 1992), 237–49.
29. Dean M. Kelley, *Why the Conservative Churches are Growing* (New York: Harper and Row, 1972), 25–26, 95.
30. Pascal K. Whelpton, Arthur A. Campbell, and John Patterson, *Fertility and Family Planning in the United States* (Princeton, NJ: Princeton University Press, 1966).
31. Michael Hout, Andrew Greeley, and Melissa Wilde, "The Demographic Imperative in Religious Change in the United States," *American Journal of Sociology* 107 (September 2001): 468–500.

32. Hout, Greeley and Wilde, "The Demographic Imperative in Religious Change in the United States," 471, 497.
33. Michael Hout, Andrew Greeley, and Melissa Wilde, "Birth Dearth: Demographics of Mainline Decline," *Christian Century* (October 25, 2005): 26.
34. Hout, Greeley, and Wilde, "The Demographic Imperative in Religious Change in the United States," 498.
35. Christian Smith, *Christian America? What Evangelicals Really Want* (Berkeley: University of California Press, 2000); Smith, *American Evangelicalism,* 199-201.
36. Ron Lesthaeghe and Lisa Neidert, "The Second Demographic Transition in the United States: Exception or Textbook Example?" *Population and Development Review* 32 (December 2006): 669–98. (Emphasis added.)
37. Lisa Jordan, "Religion and Fertility in the United States: A Geographic Analysis," Department of Geography, University of Colorado, [2005]. (Emphasis added.)
38. For a somewhat hysterical, yet still useful, feminist "expose" of this phenomenon, see: Kathryn Joyce, *Quiverfull: Inside the Christian Patriarchy Movement* (New York: Beacon Press, 2009). Books giving a positive defense of the Quiverfull life include: Rich and Jan Hess, *A Full Quiver: Family Planning and the Lordship of Christ* (Brentwood, TN: Wolgemuth R. Hyatt, 1990); Samuel A. Owen, Jr., *Letting God Plan Your Family* (Wheaton, IL: Crossway Books, 1990); Nancy Campbell, *Be Fruitful and Multiply* (San Antonio, TX: Vision Forum, 2003); Craig Houghton, *Family UNPlanning: A Guide for Christian Couples Seeking God's Truth on Having Children* (Longwood, FL: Xulon Press, 2007).

Index